THE SOUL IN
EVERYDAY LIFE

THE SOUL
IN EVERYDAY
LIFE

DANIEL CHAPELLE

STATE UNIVERSITY OF NEW YORK PRESS

cover photograph by Jonathan Manheim
Arches and Shadows—Fort Point, San Francisco
1973

© Jonathan Manheim

Published by
STATE UNIVERSITY OF NEW YORK PRESS
ALBANY

© 2003 State University of New York

For information, address
State University of New York Press,
90 State Street, Suite 700, Albany, NY 12207

Production, Laurie Searl
Marketing, Anne M. Valentine

Library of Congress Cataloging in Publication Data

Chapelle, Daniel, 1951–
    The soul in everyday life / Daniel Chapelle.
        p. cm.
    Includes bibliographical references and index.
    ISBN 0-7914-5863-6 (alk. paper) — ISBN 0-7914-5864-4 (pbk. : alk. paper)
    1. Psychoanalysis and philosophy 2. Soul—Psychological aspects. 3. Values—Psychological aspects. I. Title.

BF175.4.P45C48 2003
150.19'5—dc21
                                                                                    2003050527

10 9 8 7 6 5 4 3 2 1

The belief in the existence of a universal, uniform human mind is a rationalist prejudice. —BRUNO SNELL

What sort of thing the soul *is* would be a long tale to tell, and it would no doubt require some kind of divine being to tell the whole story. But what it *resembles*, that is something a human being can perhaps try to tell in fewer words. —SOCRATES

Some souls one will never discover, unless one invents them first. —ZARATHUSTRA

I wish I could find a good book to live in. —MELANIE

CONTENTS

PREFACE

Years ago, during a conversation I was having with a well known psychoanalyst, the topic of Oedipus came up. This was of course unremarkable enough in itself, since Freud had long ago made Oedipus central to psychoanalysis. But the conversation took a remarkable turn.

The issue under discussion called for a closer look at the Sophocles tragedy itself, at the text and its imagery. Yet my interlocutor confessed he was not familiar enough with the play for this. He had read it in high school or college, but subsequently he had never reread it—not during all the years of training and practice in psychoanalysis, nor during the subsequent years of teaching and writing about it. One could become a psychoanalyst, so it appeared, without ever reading *Oedipus* at all. Here was a situation fraught with irony: one hundred years of psychoanalysis, with an entire profession making a living off of Sophocles, and the author does not even have to be extended the courtesy of having his play read as part of the core curriculum.

The point is not, of course—and this cannot be said quickly enough—that a psychoanalyst automatically would be less qualified if he had not studied *Oedipus*. Conversely, it would be equally preposterous to suggest that knowing the play forward and backward would, by itself, make anyone a better psychoanalyst. And yet something significant is at hand when psychoanalysts can leave Oedipus behind in the literature department without ever looking back.

It is often said that psychoanalysis is more invention than discovery, that it was made up between an imaginative physician and his accommodating first patient. The physician's ideas were largely speculation based on his own dreams, while the patient's contributions were a mixture of questionable memories and private imaginings. So it was, and so it had to be, for the active ingredient in all attempts to treat the soul in the lives of individuals has always been, and will always be, an active imagination. Without active imagination there could have been no psychoanalysis and there can be no future for psychological treatment. It may even be said that all such treatment is, before anything else, about restoring activity to an imagination that has become inactive.

There is something profoundly self-defeating in the belief that one can know anything at all about the realm of soul with any certainty. Whenever a sense of knowledge is achieved in this field, the imagination that is essential to it tends to become inactive. One arrives at a conclusion, a view, an opinion, or a theory and becomes what the French call *un arriviste*, someone who has arrived, someone who has made it and who can rest on his laurels. Oedipus himself, at one time, lived the life of such a self-satisfied *arriviste*, until the seemingly unbelievable facts of his life caught up with him. Just when he thought he had made it, just when he thought he had things figured out, everything came crashing down. Whatever he thought he knew lost its validity, and what he was about to figure out would blow him away.

Whoever deals in ideas about soul needs to keep the sense of established knowledge to a minimum and to keep the imagination active. Leaving the story of Oedipus unread, presumably because Freud has dealt with him for us all, as it were once and for all, is not the best way to go. To read *Oedipus* or not to read *Oedipus*—that in itself *is not* the question. But to understand the difference between psychological theory as established knowledge and psychological theory as active imagination—that *is* the question.

This book is an exercise in active imagination about ideas concerning soul. It does not offer a body of knowledge that the reader is asked to accept more or less passively, as if it were firmly established fact. Rather, it insists on making the reader active by persistently prodding him or her to turn new corners. This requires a certain amount of sustained imaginative agility. By the same token—and this is the reader's reward for such efforts—it restores to old ideas grown rigid a sense of renewed vigor and to habits of thought turned stiff a sense of renewed nimbleness. There are rewarding vistas to be encountered as well.

To begin, there is the traditional but nebulous idea of soul itself. A culture that, like ours, owes much of its energy and success to rational and scientific ways of thinking is bound to have difficulties with concepts that are impossible to define. The idea of soul is a case in point. It cannot be defined in the same way that modern technical, scientific, rational, or logical terms can be defined. Yet that does not mean the word "soul" does not refer to anything. It means that it involves matters, subtle matters, that have to be imagined before anything can be said about them. Soul has to be imagined *so that* we can speak about it.

Unless we are willing to lose the sense of what "soul" can mean, we may perhaps try to keep the idea alive. For ideas, just like animal species, can be at risk for extinction as a result of historical developments. We may prevent the extinction of the vitality in the idea of soul by attending to it with thoughtful preservation efforts. Doing precisely that is this book's objective.

For now, let us simply say that "soul" means that intangible and elusive but real something that gives to all events a sense that they matter, that they have significance, that they have their own importance. It is what transforms the conditions of an experience into the experience itself, what makes the sum total of a situation more than simply the addition of its parts. "Soul" is what gives us about all things and events a sense that they have value.

With the notion of value we are at the heart of this book's concern. These days, one hears much talk about "values"—"traditional values," "lost values," "family values," or "the need to restore a sense of value." Yet as contemporary philosophers point out, it is difficult to speak about value in ways that avoid the twin errors of absolutism and arbitrary relativism. Either our claims about why something matters tend to become rigid and absolute, because they are built on prejudices we do not examine, or we tend to fall into the other extreme of saying that there are no absolute or even firm values at all. In the first case we are at risk of becoming dogmatists. In the second case we are at risk of believing that only power relationships count for anything. The one extreme is illustrated by fanatical religious fundamentalism, the other by self-pitying nihilism or rank sociopathy. These extreme cases are easy enough to recognize. The many subtle forms of absolutism and arbitrary relativism that permeate everyday life are not. Yet difficult though talk about value may be, it is a topic we must address, because the life of the soul is about nothing if not about value.

Theories about soul play a role in the discussion of value at two levels. Most manifestly, those theories are invented in order to help guard established social values. In that capacity, they are about social hygiene, of which mental hygiene or mental health is an aspect. But more importantly, soul is itself the original and autonomous source of all sense of value. Attending to the sense of value in everyday life at this deeper level is about recognizing the soul's imaginative and creative activity. The first function of psychological theory, insofar as it is handmaiden of the social paradigm, is about the practicalities of managing everyday life. The second, and in the end the more important one, is about seeing how all that seems ordinary in everyday life is truly extraordinary and miraculous.

This issue matters, because no human being wants to be only mentally balanced and socially adjusted. Every human being also wants to live a life that is filled with a keen sense of the value of living. This aesthetic sense, this sense for the extraordinary and miraculous in everyday life, is no added luxury for the well educated or the fortunate. Nor is it a reward bestowed on those who live wisely and well. It is a sense that every life demands and needs. As has been said, man does not live by bread alone.

Treatment of the soul in this deeper sense is about more than mental and social hygiene. It is about encouraging a life to develop not only intellectually, behaviorally, socially, and emotionally but also imaginatively and aesthetically. The life of the soul in this deeper sense that this book addresses is everyone's business, not just the business of specialists we call "psychologists," "psychiatrists," "psychoanalysts," or "psychotherapists," of whatever kind. But it is not enough to write self-help books or to popularize complex psychological theories, whether through education and the mass media or through easy step programs. Something else is needed.

What is needed is that we return the treatment of the soul to the arena of everyday life—up from the analyst's couch, out of the therapist's office and into the street, the workplace, the conversations we have with ourselves, with our fellow human beings, and ultimately with the world at large and with the universe itself. For ideas about the life of the soul are neither the property nor the restricted province of specialists. They are everyone's concern. Nor is their relevance confined to a narrow activity called "psychological treatment." They are everyone's daily business. They are the plots of the stories we tell ourselves about our lives and about what it is like to be human. These stories matter, because we inhabit them—*by enacting them*. They are the contemporary myths we live by.

These modern myths about what it means to be human which we call "psychological theories" are not only descriptive. They are also prescriptive. They tell us how to live. They are the coin and currency with which we calculate and designate the value of every event and of every life. Because of that, few decisions we face are more fateful than those about the theory of soul we accept. To paraphrase an old rule of thumb: Tell me about the theory of soul to which you subscribe and I will tell you who you are. And, as a matter of practical advice: Beware of any soul treatment you enter, because you will end up living the dramatic images that define its governing theory and, hence, its implied values. We have had a hundred years of Oedipal theory to prove the point. Once you enter a treatment course based on it, you put yourself through the wringer of classical Greek tragedy, whether that particular genre of story applies to your life or not.

No human life can ever be satisfied with a prefabricated theory of soul, no matter how well thought out or useful it is. In the matter of soul, everyone eventually has to come up with his or her own theory. This does not mean that well tested theory can be ignored at will, any more than the law of gravity can be dismissed. It means that every human being must find a way to articulate a sustainable vision of how the soul is to be imagined. That personal vision and theory of soul has to be grounded in the actual life one finds oneself living—in the circumstances to which one was born, in the way things are, in the here and now of life as is. But, and this is what matters here, those concrete circumstances add up to more than the factual substance of one's life. They also provide a subtle subtext of figurative images and metaphors that speak about soul. For as all theory of soul has always insisted, and will always continue to insist, inherent in every literal fact of life is also a more imaginative dimension.

This book emphasizes active imagination, because cultivating a sense for soul in everyday life has more to do with the *act* of seeing and with a *way* of seeing than with anything seen. What we end up finding in our life when we look for soul in it is determined by *how* we look. A century of psychotherapies derived from psychoanalysis has argued that what we see around us is largely a reflection of the life of the soul inside us. Ideas about soul have become increasingly narrowly determined by the small space occupied by the individual's body. Soul matter has become increasingly equated with processes taking place inside that space: brain activity, chemical balances, mental processes, learning, memory, neurotransmitters, neurolinguistic programming, biologically based impulses, genes and DNA, and all the rest.

Freud said that all finding of new experiences is a matter of refinding old ones, that new experiences are renewed editions of internal processes whose original blueprints are stored inside our mind. But what we find all around us is, in the first place, the stuff of the imagination itself—not the imagination as an internal mental faculty of the individual but the creative imagination that shapes the universe and that animates history. By making mythology the central ingredient of his theory, Freud implied as much. For as his reliance on the mythic imagination implicitly suggested in spite of his claim that anatomy is destiny—and as others before and after him have explicitly stated—the greater part of the soul is outside the body.

This too is vision first and fact only secondarily, just as psychoanalysis was and is invention before discovery. It suggests that the activity of theorizing about soul has to reach beyond a focus on the body and beyond the focus on the individual and the interaction of individuals. Only the world of the imagination itself, the *mundus imaginalis*, provides the range and depth of vision that can do justice to the life of the soul, which is about more than mental processes and the communal life of individuals. The approach to psychological theorizing underlying this book, an approach that is grounded in what James Hillman has termed "archetypal psychology," suggests that "psychological space" is delineated neither by the boundaries of the individual's body nor by the social community of a large body of individuals—nor even by a local or global ecosystem—but by this *mundus imaginalis*. If a world of autonomous, creative imagination is where we find ourselves living, then active imagination has to be the password required for exploring it and inhabiting it.

ACKNOWLEDGMENTS

I would like to thank Jane Bunker, senior editor at the State University of New York Press, for showing interest in a project that defies academic convention in its mannerisms and its arguments. I also would like to thank the staff at the State University of New York Press for transforming a manuscript into a book. Professor Leston Havens of Harvard University's Medical School, Department of Psychiatry, cannot be thanked enough for his generosity in reviewing earlier drafts. Professor Robert Kugelmann of the Institute of Philosophic Studies at the University of Dallas has my gratitude for his detailed critical comments. Last, but really first, I wish to thank Jane Lillis, who helped see the manuscript through, from conception to birth.

FINDING WAYS TO TALK
ABOUT THE SOUL

A CENTURY AGO, in 1901, Freud published a book entitled *The Psychopathology of Everyday Life*. It is the book that gave the world the notion of the Freudian slip. In it, Freud showed that unconsciousness is everywhere in Everyman's life, not just in psychiatric hospitals or clinics. Together with *The Interpretation of Dreams* it did more than Freud's other writings to make his name a household word. Today, a hundred years later, psychotherapy is available to everyone who wants it. We now know more than ever about what makes Everyman tick, and yet we seem to know less than before about Everyman's *psyche* or soul, or about what might even be meant by such a notion, if anything at all. The Freudian slip has become an accepted fact of life. The *psyche* or soul, however, even though it too appears throughout Freud's writings, has been slipping away from everyday consciousness. In a curiously self-defeating twist in the history of psychology, the very notion of *psyche* or soul, which should, after all, define the field that names itself after it, appears to be sliding back into oblivion.

Now that we are once again entering a new century—and this time also a new millennium—we need to bring along not only our knowledge about the psychopathology of everyday life but also a few fundamental principles about the soul in everyday life. This explains the title of the present book.

One would think that because psychology is named after *psyche*, it would somehow have to be about soul—in the same way that physics is about nature (*physis*), biology about life (*bios*), theology about God (*theos*), and cosmology about the universe (*cosmos*). Physicists regard nature as real, and biologists regard life as real, just as theologians regard God as real, and cosmologists regard the universe as real. Psychologists, however, stick out like a sore thumb. Generally, they do not seem to regard the soul as real. It probably would embarrass many of them if they were suspected of doing so. This may be part of the reason why they are silent about the soul. Soul has become a notion that is not even mentioned in psychology.

That silence has to do with a bullish modern pride about psychology having become a science. It serves to mask that psychologists have, to a significant degree, failed to do justice to their self-appointed charge. For as we have it today, psychology is not about soul. It is about other things, like mind and mental functions such as intelligence and memory. It is about behavior, emotion, and thinking; about development and learning; or about personality and the inner self. It is about consciousness and the unconscious; about the brain and its chemistry; about nature versus nurture; about normality and abnormality; about genes and DNA. None of these is the same as soul, even though soul is involved in all of them. All avoid and ignore the notion of soul itself. Just as air assumes the shape of any container in which it exists but is nonetheless not the container itself, so too is soul not the same as mind or any of the other areas with which psychology concerns itself and in which soul is present. Soul needs to have something said about itself. Otherwise life becomes devoid of a sense of soul, and that is not a good thing. A life without sense of soul is incomplete. It can never be fully satisfying.

It remains up to psychology to speak on behalf of the soul. This discipline that names itself after *psyche* has to find the right *logos* for its subject matter— the right words, the right ways of talking and thinking about it. That this is obvious is no reason for not saying it. That it goes against much of accepted academic psychology, clinical psychology, and popular psychology is no reason to avoid it. That it would be impossible—because "soul" is such an elusive term—is simply not true.

What is true is that, as Socrates said at the beginning of the West's philosophical history, it is impossible to say exactly what soul is. All we can do is say what it might be like, what it appears to resemble. We can know nothing about what soul is in any absolute and definitive terms. All we can know are the analogies, the metaphors, the figures of speech, the images we use to let us imagine what it might be like. This limitation offers a solution to an artificial problem before the problem can even be posed. If all we can say about soul is what it resembles, then the challenge of proving that there does exist an objectifiable and definable thing we may call "soul" becomes, surprisingly, irrelevant. What matters is not whether an objectifiable and definable thing called "soul" does or does not exist, but that the human condition involves certain laws and truths that may be described with the aid of that elusive term. That term has served humanity well, until it gradually came into disrepute and disuse with the spread of overly proud rationalism and its even prouder offspring, modern science and technology.

Just because soul is, in the first place, an image, a metaphor, a figure of speech, or an analogy does not mean it is "only" that, or that nothing real corresponds to it. It means that the idea of soul refers to a reality that has to be imagined before anything can be known about it. It refers to a reality that has to be imagined *so that* something can be known about it. Soul has image and imagination as its core substance, its essence, its active ingredient. That is what Jung meant when he said that soul is image, and image soul. Just because the soul is elusive does not mean it is unreal.

In a culture like ours, which is steeped in modern scientific ways and technologies, it is easier to think about mind and about definable mental processes than about soul, which is anything but readily definable. Just how strongly that modern mind-set exerts its influence, and how the notion of soul can become sacrificed in the process, is illustrated by what happened when Freud's writings were translated from their original German into English.

Freud's education was well rounded. It covered both the natural sciences and the humanities. In addition to being trained in medicine and scientific research in neurology, he was also well versed in the world's greatest literature. His own prose eventually would win him the Goethe prize in German literature. He had a lifelong interest in ancient cultures and a deep love for their art. His office, especially his desk, was crowded with statuettes of figures from ancient mythologies. Given his lifelong interest in the humanities it was only natural that he should write about *Seele*—"soul." Had he wanted to write about "mind" (*Geist*), he could have done so. But he did not. Instead, he opted for *Seele*.

The English word "soul" is so obviously the most natural and correct way of translating *Seele* that there is no acceptable excuse for doing otherwise. And yet the English translators and editors consistently substituted the more scientific-sounding "mind." When Freud writes about *die Wissenschaft vom Seelenleben* ("the science of the life of the soul"), this becomes, in translation, "the science of mental life." Freud's original German here encompasses both reason (*Wissenschaft*) and the largely irrational side of life that always escapes the grasp of reason and even definition (*Seelenleben*). The same dual focus appears in the choice of the term *psychoanalysis* itself. This too encompasses both reason (analysis) and something that eludes reason (*psyche*). By translating *Seele* into "mind," the translator simply hacks off the elusive irrational member, leaving only the more clinically objectifiable one. This is a case of the translator putting Freud and psychoanalysis into a Procrustean bed. For just as in the myth of Procrustes, in which a person who is forced to lie in a too-small bed has his limbs cut off to make him fit, so Freud and psychoanalysis are cut down to the size of concepts that are too small to house them. Few amputations in modern history have had a more profound impact than that administered by Freud's English translators. A similar mishandling occurs when Freud, in German, reminds his readers that "the German word for the Greek *psyche* is *Seele*."The translator has him say that "'*Psyche*' is a Greek word which may be translated 'mind.'" Not so, Mr. Translator. That *psyche* would mean "mind" is patently wrong. The one ancient Greek word that eventually comes closest to what we today mean by "mind" is *noos*, or *nous*.This notion, by the way, is one that only gradually comes into being, over multiple centuries of Greek cultural development, instead of being ready-made from the start. That late Greek, near equivalent of our modern "mind" eventually was imagined as the "pilot of the soul," which means it is not the soul itself.

This mistranslation has implications for what we mean by, and for what we can expect from, psychoanalysis and the psychotherapies that are derived from it. When Freud describes psychoanalysis as a form of treatment that affects *das Seelische des Menschen* ("man's soul"), the English translator has it that it acts "upon the mind." This is perhaps what, in keeping with Freud's "soul"-less English translations, much of later British and American psychology has become. It is not the same thing as a form of treatment that was meant to focus on *das Seelische des Menschen*.

Bruno Bettelheim's powerful little book, *Freud and Man's Soul*, goes a long way toward rescuing Freud from his English translators. He speculates that the reason for distorting Freud's references to *Seele* and *psyche* is a desire to insist on making psychoanalysis a medical specialty with a respectable scientific standing. He also suggests that Freud, who never once attempts to define the term *Seele*, chooses this term exactly because of its inability to be definitively defined.

This ambiguity in terminology reflects an ambiguity that is not merely a secondary and, to some perhaps, an annoying aspect of soul. It reflects the soul's very nature.That soul is inherently ambiguous becomes apparent in many ways. A case in point is in the way the Greek word *psyche* originally was imagined. As it appears in Homer's *Iliad* and *Odyssey* a man's *psyche* was imagined as an elusive something that is essential for life, and in whose absence life could not continue.Yet in spite of its necessary presence, that same *psyche* was not identified with any of the definable faculties or functions of life. Thus "mind" or *noos/ nous*, precisely because it is such a faculty or function, is not soul or *psyche*. More broadly, *whatever psychology defines and objectifies as its object of study, and whatever it points at in this manner, is not soul*. And yet this difficulty in defining and objecti- fying soul does not mean that there is a flaw in the concept itself. Rather, it sug- gests an essential aspect of the reality to which it seeks to allude. It also suggests something essential about the way in which we must talk about the soul if we wish to do it justice.

This book addresses twelve fundamental principles concerning the soul in everyday life.These fundamentals are the active ingredients in a psychology that is more truly about soul than much of modern psychology about identifiable and objectifiable processes can ever hope to be. Each principle takes up one chapter.As is to be expected, the chapters overlap.The twelve items are divided into two parts. Chapters 1 through 6 (Part 1) belong together and address the goal that unifies them. Chapters 7 through 12 (Part 2) belong together and address the method for achieving the goal spelled out in Part 1. The twelve issues at stake are as follows.

Chapter 1 emphasizes that the soul is irreducible. It cannot be defined, described, explained, understood, or judged in terms other than its own. Terms governing other fields do not apply to it and must not be imposed on it. The soul is truly sovereign. Its laws are cast in its own code, which is that of the imagination. But this is not the imagination as a mental faculty of the individual. It is the impersonal and collective imagination that shapes the universe at every moment and that animates all the facts and events of history. The laws in the life of the soul may be thought of as archetypal motifs, mythic themes, or universal symbols. They may be spoken of as patterns of consciousness, timeless human truths, or universal human experiences. They may be presented and preserved in the form of works of art, literary monuments, history-shaping ideas, religious notions, recurring figures of the collective imagination, or poetic images that are engraved in human consciousness. Yet no matter what the concrete language or medium in which they are cast, the laws of the soul have one thing in common as their essence. That common essence in the soul's laws is summarized in Augustine's words: "Nobody passes judgment on it; nobody judges well without it." That means the life of the soul cannot be understood and judged without a sense of that active essence in these laws, yet it alone is enough to say all that can and all that needs to be said about the soul. It determines the soul's own governing fundamentals—its bottom-line values, valuables, and models of valuation. True psychological evaluation is about more than clinical diagnosis. It is about beginning to sense what determines these values, these valuables, and these models of valuation that constitute the life of the soul at any given moment and in any given matter.

Chapter 2 emphasizes that the laws of the soul are recognizable in everyday life, where they exert their power in shaping the lives of individuals. They are readily recognizable in unchanging behaviors and experiences that seem to eternally and compulsively repeat themselves in individual lives. Freud recognized in these recurring patterns an essential and determining feature in the unconscious life of the individual, one that also makes it more or less transparent. Viewed more broadly than individual psychopathology, this "eternal return" of unchanging behaviors and experiences gains a much greater philosophical significance. That philosophical significance is spelled out in Nietzsche's central idea of the eternal return of all things. According to this most radical of notions in the history of Western thought, everyday life is to be imagined in light of a principle of eternal repetition. It is to be viewed not as an affair that takes place in linear time but as one that is based on timelessness and repetition. A view based on eternal return makes of every seemingly fleeting moment a timeless event in its own right. In Freud's view, the observable facts of compulsive repetition are what makes psychoanalytic treatment possible in the first place, for in psychoanalysis and in psychotherapies that are derived from it, eternal return is an actual experience. It appears there in the form of transference, in which the patient relives old and fixed experiences by compulsively reenacting them in the relation with the treater. In Nietzsche, the thought of the eternal return of all things is the active ingredient in a philosophy that seeks to reconcile man with the fact of impermanence, of which individual vulnerability and suffering are personal reminders. Freud and Nietzsche both view "eternal return" as a way to become reconciled with personal destiny.

Chapter 3 suggests that the soul sees beyond the duality of good and evil. It sees splendor where an all-too-human perspective recognizes only a mixture of pleasure and pain or good and evil. One Holocaust per history or one terrible experience per individual life can seem enough to condemn the whole lot in human eyes. The soul, however, knows no prejudice except that which affirms existence—all of it. It allows human beings to look beyond good and evil, beyond pleasure and pain. It lets them look into a dimension where true splendor becomes visible—as the extraordinary and the miraculous that exists in every ordinary life. Straining to look precisely this far stands a group of commentators on the human condition that includes, among others, Heraclitus, the ancient philosopher; Nietzsche, the first postmodern psychologist and philosopher; Augustine, the early Christian thinker; Job, the personification of piety, who loses his legendary patience with his God; and Zarathustra, Nietzsche's spokesperson, who teaches the life-affirming philosophy of eternal return. In their footsteps walks Everyman, himself unlegendary and ordinary, yet nonetheless capable of achieving in his everyday life the same life affirming vision and judgment that is identified in Heraclitus, aimed at in Nietzsche, promised in Augustine, realized in Job, and taught in Zarathustra.

Chapter 4 proposes that while daily life takes place in history, the soul factor in it reaches beyond what seems only historical. Soul gives us one foot in time and one foot in timelessness. Hence the paradox that psychology must address matters that are bound to the here and now of daily concerns but that it also must look beyond linear time for their larger significance. What starts as fascination with the historical uniqueness of the events of individual lives becomes fascination with what also is universal and timeless in them. This is how every human being becomes equal to all of humanity, and how unique and fleeting events become a revolving door through which we step into the dimension of timeless or mythic events. One ancient formula that helps us step from historical, linear time into the timelessness of mythic events is *Festina lente*—"Make haste slowly." It is a paradoxical formula for moving forward precisely *while* and *by* standing still. Modern depth psychology, like the life of soul itself, has one foot in history and one beyond the realm of linear time. It serves as a practical application of this ancient formula for moving forward by standing still and by going nowhere but deeper into whatever matter is at hand.

Chapter 5 follows from this as a natural further implication. Because the events of a life have their greatest significance in a dimension that lies beyond their strict historicity, that significance cannot be adequately described as history or in the terms of history. It is as Aristotle said: history is not and cannot be as universal and timeless as poetic images can be. And as Nietzsche's Zarathustra puts it, the facts of the soul are facts "one will never discover, unless one invents them first." This makes poetic imagination the true psychological coin and currency. It also explains the long tradition, in the psychology of unconsciousness, of equating the facts of life with the fictions from myth. But not just any fiction will do. For a psychological fiction to be true to the life of the soul, it must not only be believable. It must also offer the blueprint of a world that is inhabitable and the promise of a life in it that can be affirmed. It must be able to serve as what a popular song called "a good book to live in." A life becomes whole by developing a sense for the fictions it enacts. Those fictions are not only its true home and habitat but also its destiny.

Chapter 6 explores an idea implied in a remark by Oscar Wilde, who said that "There was no fog in London until the impressionists started to paint it." Psychology's theories have a similar effect, and so psychology's patients eventually end up suffering from the textbooks of their treaters. The implication is clear: Beware of the views about human nature and the human condition to which you subscribe, because you will end up living the plots or the myths in their theories. The story or Er, as Socrates told it in Plato's *Republic*, makes the same point, that the life and the facts of the soul are grounded in poetic imagination. But so is the folly of Don Quixote, whose taste for fiction brings him no end of suffering. A windmill may seem a giant, as it does to Don Quixote, but it also is a windmill. The art of choosing or creating viable images that may be inhabited, and that can live up to their promise, is personified by Claude Monet, the impressionist painter whose paintings added more fog to London's cityscape than England's industrial pollution. His life and work, especially his constantly further developing garden in Giverny and his paintings of it, serve as a paradigm for a life that is lived poetically and well. What Monet was able to do with his Giverny garden is something Everyman can do with his corner of the universe. Good citizenship, we can now argue against Plato, takes more than reason, as he insisted for all Western philosophy to come, and as most of Western thought has continued to insist after him. It also takes poetic sensibility and, above all, active imagination.

These first six chapters, then, are about the goal of finding a way to talk about soul that is consistent with everyday life and that is grounded in the imagination. The remaining chapters address the question of a method for making such a way of speaking about soul possible. The leading paradigm for this method is the ancient tradition of alchemy, where the central idea is one of magical realism.

Chapter 7 proposes that magical realism is not only a unique literary genre but also a general fact of everyday life. As a literary genre, magical realism tells stories in which the account of plausible events is interrupted by flashes of magic that defy the laws of nature and reason. The genius of the genre, and what makes it succeed as deeply satisfying storytelling, is the sense of veracity that accompanies these flashes of magical reality. They insert themselves into everyday history before one's disbelieving yet nonetheless believing eyes. The blatant lies that are being told in magical realism are considered acceptable because, paradoxically, they tell unquestionable truths about what it means to be human. To understand what magical realism means, in this respect, one must contrast it to its opposite. This we may call, after Aristotle, "common sense." Common sense is personified by Jocasta, Oedipus's mother, and eventually his bride. Their tragedy is less about parricide and incest than about rejecting magical realism in favor of common sense—and about then having to face the consequences of that proud reliance on reason. The psychology of unconsciousness and the life of the soul to which it alludes are nothing if not magical realism. They follow the laws of alchemy, not those of nature. Like alchemy, they often defy common sense by producing fantastic lies that are more true than some of the truths of reason.

Chapter 8 elaborates on a remark made by Joseph Campbell, the popular teacher of myth, who said: "Follow your bliss, and you will come to bliss." His recommendation is the treatment of choice for what Thoreau forever diagnosed as the "quiet desperation" that marks many human lives. The call to bliss is no simple or easy matter and by no means always an exclusively pleasurable one. It is a challenge and a mixed blessing. It comes in many shapes. Some of these are ordinary, others extraordinary. Each case serves as a case of Immaculate Conception in everyday life. It is an experience of being chosen for something larger than oneself, without having a choice about being so chosen, and without feeling in the least prepared or even basically suitable for this chosen lot. Because man is always, as Nietzsche put it, "the as yet undetermined animal," his life and the life of soul that animates him can never be preconceived, nor can his soul be determined once and for all, and then cast in a mold that would be universal and uniform. As Bruno Snell has stated the issue, "The belief in the existence of a universal, uniform human mind is a rationalist prejudice." The call to bliss is about the familiar sense of oneself being disrupted by an encounter with something that is other, and in many ways larger, than that usual sense of oneself. It is about that familiar sense of oneself being ravished by this larger and other something, and about becoming willingly subservient to it. In myth, the call to bliss is imagined as young girl Persephone being abducted by Hades in order to be made queen of his Underworld of Souls. In philosophical terms, it is about a Nietzschean transformation and revaluation of inherited values for the sake of an individual affirmation of existence and of one's place in the universe.

Chapter 9 shows how getting to the soul substance in any matter is done by "sticking to the images" in it, as Jung's student, James Hillman, insists. The images inherent in any given matter are the facts of the matter as they present themselves but now taken figuratively instead of literally. Viewed this way, facts become metaphors—metaphors that speak about soul. The rule of sticking to the images in all matters serves to value the soul's imaginative and creative activity on its own terms. That, in turn, serves Nietzsche's agenda of finding a way to affirm existence *as is*, rather than judging it in comparison to a standard of value lying outside it. Sticking to the images in a situation also changes the usual locus of the psychological significance it has. Psychological significance stops being something that is located inside the individual, as inner feelings or thoughts, and it becomes that inside which the individual is contained and that by which he or she is sustained. Soul stops being content and becomes container. Such an inversion of the locus of psychological significance—me inside it rather than it inside me—requires what Hillman calls "psychological faith," which is faith in the image. Psychological faith in the image is analogous to Abraham's legendary faith when his God tells him to sacrifice his son Isaac. Both cases require a willingness to sacrifice what one holds dearest, including, first of all, one's most dearly held ego positions, in compliance with the demands of an autonomous, irrational, and often pitiless greater power.

Chapter 10 suggests that even though the methods of modern scientific psychology yield findings that are fascinating and results that are useful, they do not always satisfy the soul. Whenever science answers one question, it raises new ones. That is, of course, its nature. It is forever underway, on a journey without end. This works well for the natural sciences, but it does not always work for psychology. When psychology emulates modern scientific methods, it risks failing to satisfy the soul, for the needs of the soul often elude the methods of scientific inquiry. The soul wants more than to be endlessly but restlessly fascinated and more than ideas that are useful without being satisfying. It wants to be able to feel and to say, as Augustine put it, "it is enough and it is good." In order to reach that point of being fully satisfied, the soul seeks what the ancient mystic philosopher Plotinus called *amplexis*, by which he meant a sense for the embrace between the unique historical facts of any given matter and a timeless dimension about it that gives it significance beyond its strictly literal context. Therapeutic psychology has a long-standing interest in what makes for "good enough" child care and patient care. It regards such "good enough" care as the prerequisite for the very experience of "good" itself—and, by extension, for a satisfying life. If therapeutic psychology is to fully satisfy the soul, then its own ideas about "good enough" care must themselves be fully satisfying, not only, as they now often are, fascinating and useful.

Chapter 11 addresses the crucial difference between the word "archetype" as noun and the word "archetypal" as adjective. The notion of archetype usually is associated with Jung, who reintroduced it to Western consciousness after an absence of centuries, during which it had come to be regarded as ancient history. While we should thank Jung for reanimating this important notion, we also have popularized "Jungian psychology" to thank for a major misunderstanding concerning archetypes. That misunderstanding consists in regarding archetypes as thing-like or objectifiable entities. It is based on confusing metaphors with metaphysics, analogies with absolute truths. Archetypes should not be thought of as such thing-like, objectifiable entities. We must see and say not that archetypes are things, but that things are "archetypal." To say that the life of the soul is archetypal refers more to a way of seeing than to things designated by the noun "archetype" that can or cannot be seen or proven to exist. The adjective "archetypal" is more real than the noun "archetype." In order to develop a sense of soul in everyday life, we need not so much a "psychology of archetypes" (Jung), but rather "archetypal psychology" (Hillman). The idea that something can derive its reality precisely from its inability to be objectified, defined, and named in a noun is itself an essential fact of the human condition. This fact is expressed in many ways, such as in the biblical tradition according to which the ground of all Being is designated by the unpronounceable, unspeakable, and undefinable tetragrammaton, "YHWH." Since it is said that man is made in the image of his God, it is no surprise that man's very essence, his soul, is itself undefinable as well.

Chapter 12 is about a threesome—life, death, and life's own double—in particular, about the great paradox that threesome presents. The paradox is hinted at in the seemingly mad proposition that "A life is judged by the suicide it commits." This modern form of the paradox begins to make sense when death stops being viewed in the first place as a physiological fact at the end of life and when it is seen, instead, as a lifelong psychic fact during it. Viewed that way, death delineates a life throughout its entire duration and serves as its animating feature. It becomes then, indeed, what gives life to life, confirming the idea that it is the lifelong suicide in every life that is the true and built-in standard for its appraisal. Freud wrote along these lines about the paradox that it is Death (Thanatos) that defines and shapes life—throughout its entire duration and requiring every minute of it to complete its task. A true psychology of death and dying is about developing a sense for what defines a life throughout its life, not about the last physiological fact at the end of it. Such a psychology requires an imaginative sense for the figure of the subtle and immaterial double that accompanies every life. This double may be imagined in many ways. One version is the Greek mythic figure of Hades, who coexists with everyday life as its subtle twin, its purely psychic essence.

As the above summaries suggest, the twelve chapters that follow touch on many and, at times, perhaps, seemingly unrelated, matters. Yet they have one recurring theme in common: value. For the life of the soul is first and last about value. This primacy of value in the life of the soul is dealt with here in the spirit of the four thinkers who together constitute the four generational dynasty presiding over twentieth-century depth psychology. They are, in order of historical appearance, Nietzsche, Freud, Jung, and Jung's most inspired student, Hillman.

Like the chronology of their lives, which overlaps between Nietzsche and Freud, Freud and Jung, and Jung and Hillman, their thought overlaps to a degree. In the bulk of that thought, however, and just as in the bulk of their active years, they work without overlap. Yet the one unwavering constant in all four is the idea that soul is in the first place about value—about values, valuables, and processes of valuation, and about the revaluation of what often is devalued.

First, not only in order of historical appearance but also in rank, is Nietzsche. With a self-confidence that has few equals in history, and that is less remarkable for its lack of modesty than for its uncanny accuracy, he declared himself "a psychologist without equal." Freud would eventually second that opinion. Nietzsche's estimation of psychology itself was that it is "the queen of sciences." He thought that it must always be at the center of all philosophy— which he considered a form of psychological autobiography with ambitions to legislate existence for everyone. Many of the concepts that would later appear in Freud's psychoanalysis, as well as in other areas of thought, are already spelled out in Nietzsche. In his assessment that it would take up to a century, and more, to appreciate the full significance of his ideas, he was again his own most lucid commentator. Today, more than a century after he fell silent in 1889, due to syphilis-induced insanity that would end his life in 1900, it still has to become widely appreciated that he changed the course of Western thought, and that the movement of that change still has all its momentum. The man who declared that the God of Christianity is dead, meaning that the ideas emanating from that religion were dying, is himself anything but dead. The spirit of his thought may well be shaping the new century and the new millennium for us who are underway into them, even though the man himself is no longer among us.

Nietzsche's philosophizing and psychologizing are about value, and about nothing but value. He called man "the esteemer," because in every one of his acts, thoughts, and feelings, he sits in judgment of existence. And always the one question is: Shall it be thumbs up or thumbs down? The central target of Nietzsche's writings is the life-negating pathos and morality that he identified as being at the heart of Christianity. That negative evaluation of existence is, in his view, given away by Christianity's desperate craving for a better world—after the present one, instead of the present one, to make up for the present one— and compared to which the present one must look all too shabby. In place of this life-negating pathos and morality, Nietzsche wanted to posit a life-affirming pathos and morality. And so the defining goal of his philosophical ambition became the revaluation of all values and of all value judgments that have been handed down by the history of Western philosophy.

This revaluation of values would change man. It would transform him from a creature that devalues existence, and that wants nothing more than to live in another world, into a creature that says Yes to all of existence just as it is. Such a new human creature wants nothing more than what is given, because what is given it considers good and enough. All Nietzsche's writings are focused on this revaluation, and all the major identifiable themes in them converge on it. At every step he proceeds by translating the philosophical notions he encounters in his path into the psychology of valuation that underlies them.

Heidegger, in his monumental study of Nietzsche's thought, wrote that it brings about a new turn in the history of philosophy, by making an altogether new beginning for it. This is precisely what Nietzsche himself had claimed. That new beginning, said Heidegger, again in accordance with Nietzsche's own assessment, is centered around value. But it is not only about a shift in focus or in the content of thought, one that proceeds without affecting the process of thinking itself. It is, instead, and before anything else, about a shift in the very process of thinking about value. As Heidegger put it, with Nietzsche, the activity of thinking Being becomes for the first time thinking Being as value, and with that all philosophical reflection begins to be value thinking.

For Nietzsche the process of value thinking is the central activity in the life of the soul and the central concern of all philosophy. Philosophizing itself, in his view, is not at all about seeking truth, as had been assumed and proclaimed to be the goal of all Western philosophy since Plato. It is about the human act of valuation that determines the value of existence—and that creates truths as evidence to support its judgment. Such a view of philosophy makes it necessary for philosophers and scientists to become psychologists of value before anything else. But, so Nietzsche lamented, the type of psychologists of value he had in mind had not yet been born and could not even be conceived of in his day. That is why he claimed he had to become the first of its kind.

Freud's invention of psychoanalysis, at the end of Nietzsche's life, provides proof for those who need it that the life of soul is about values and about processes of valuation. Those values and processes of valuation are hidden beneath the surface of ordinary concerns, and they can be quite different from those concerns. That much is obvious, and widely accepted by now, after one hundred years of psychotherapy. What is less obvious, and still widely resisted even after a century, is that speaking about this hidden dimension where the soul manages its values and valuation processes requires a different language than that of everyday life. It requires the development of a new language or, rather, the rediscovery of an old but forgotten one. This language that would speak about soul, about its values and value processes, is one that speaks in fantastic images, images that are borrowed from the extravagant stories we call "myths." It speaks about extraordinary events that are happening to figures from legend. The most fantastic thing of all, however, is that this is precisely what underlies the events of Everyman's own daily life, the ordinary ones just as much as the extraordinary ones. As Freud would make us rediscover, the facts of myth are made into truths, into lived realities, by being reenacted in daily life. This explains the endless procession of mythic figures that parades through the offices of psychological treaters everywhere and that forms the backbone of their theories. Oedipus, Eros, Narcissus, Thanathos, Ananke, and the others—this small band of figures from psychoanalytic theory is only the advance patrol of an endless parade. Today, these figures may no longer come dressed up in ancient Greek garb, but they are no less mythic for all their newfangled and often scientific-looking getup.

It is to Freud's everlasting and often underappreciated credit that he gave us access to the fantastic realm of the unconscious imaginative soul by adopting a way of speaking about it that provides a vocabulary suitable to the subject matter. That subject matter he recognized to be, like myth itself, multiple in its forms and values—polymorphously polyvalent. In the process of seeking a language that would be true to the soul, he took the personal risk of being viewed not as a serious thinker but as a fantast—Vienna's resident fool, the quack to its respected medical establishment. In this sense, Freud is not unlike the legendary Nietzschean madman who stepped into the town square to announce the most preposterous thing ever heard anywhere—that the immortal Christian God of all inherited moral values, feelings, and thoughts was dead and waiting to be replaced by the life-affirming spirit of a new kind of human being. Perhaps it is precisely because of Freud's equally daring and often preposterous-sounding declarations that he too became, and remains, a legendary figure.

Freud started out on his professional career with strictly scientific research in neurology. Then he moved on to pseudo-physiological speculations and hypotheses about the foundations of consciousness. From there he moved to a mixture of paradigms from biology and mythology, as well as from other fields, in order to create what became clinical psychoanalysis as it is most widely known. Finally, in his later years, he freed himself for uninhibited anthropological speculations that were meant to serve as new myths for modern men and women to live by. At that late and liberating point in his thinking and in his personal life, he gave a great sigh of relief that he could finally abandon the mind-set, the paradigms, and the habits of a physician scientist. This allowed him to take up, once again, in full freedom of expression, his lifelong love, the love of the great and timeless images that have shaped, and that continue to shape, the history and development of human consciousness itself. The fact that his writings eventually won him the Goethe prize in German literature should perhaps have been a hint for psychologists to come about what it means, and what it takes, to think Being psychologically.

The areas where Nietzsche and Freud overlap are easily identifiable, and they are frequently dealt with in Nietzsche–Freud commentaries and scholarship. It is possible to demonstrate that many of the ideas that make up psychoanalysis can already be found in Nietzsche's writings—and not just in vague outline only, but in specific details. It is also well established that Freud was keenly aware of how Nietzsche anticipated him in many ways and on many topics that eventually were incorporated into psychoanalysis. Freud even decided to stop reading Nietzsche altogether, out of an express concern that reading more would take the wind out of his own sails and would leave him no new territory to discover. There also is the unanswerable question of how much Freud picked up about Nietzsche's thought through cultural osmosis, simply by living in an intellectual climate where talk about Nietzschean ideas was increasingly in the air.

Nietzsche went on to exist in Freud's writings as the great silence Freud kept about him. As every psychoanalyst knows, it is those loud silences that form the most powerful presence. Freud, in developing psychoanalysis, relied heavily on metaphors from biology, mythology, archaeology, and even geology. In a well known statement, he compared the work and the objective of psychoanalysis—to make conscious what is unconscious—to a kind of reclamation of land from the sea, likening it to the way in which much of Holland was won from the sea. Yet over and above all the paradigms from biology, mythology, archaeology, geology, and the other fields from which Freud borrowed, psychoanalysis is an act of revaluation. It is a work of revaluation that examines Everyman's daily life as an unconscious moral economy of the soul's values and valuation processes. And here Freud is most directly in line with Nietzsche.

That Jung's psychology involves the revaluation of familiar and accepted values is implied in his choice of alchemy as the central paradigm for his theories of soul. Just as alchemy is about transforming ordinary matter into gold, so too is Jung's psychology about transforming issues from daily life into material that becomes substantially enriched in significance. Through a process of active imagination, events from everyday life are revisioned and become matters whose psychic value can only be cast in universal symbols and archetypal images. In taking up alchemy as his leading paradigm, Jung realizes the spirit of a Nietzschean revaluation of value. For as Nietzsche said: the alchemist is "the most worthwhile kind of man that exists. I mean the man who out of something slight and despicable makes something valuable, even gold itself. This man alone enriches, other men only give change." It is especially the last statement that counts most. It contrasts the formation of truly new and enriching ideas with what often seems an interminable exchange of flat notions and token ideas that add no new value to anything but that merely circulate set values with a fixed and well-worn significance.

It is perhaps this distinction, between alchemist and money changer, that makes the most important difference between Freud and Jung, over and above all explicitly stated differences in theory. Freudian and derived psychology easily can become an interminable process of adding endless explications to the facts of life without adding any sense of increased value to them. Psychological insight, so highly prized in such psychology, often can make life more interesting, but not necessarily richer. One can regularly see the opposite—an impoverishment and a drying up of the flow of emotions, thoughts, ideas, creativity, and spontaneity. Instead of displaying more life, there is sometimes more fear of life—more overly cautious and obsessive scrutiny of it, more analysis of it for the sake of analysis itself and for analysis only. Instead of a greater sense for the depth of riches that are everywhere in daily life, there can be an increasingly widening and lasting separation from it, by one of the most unbridgeable gaps there is—the permanent psychoanalytic second of guardedness that views every scrap of life with an iatrogenic reaction of suspicion. Often a life may end up wearing new and even fashionable labels after such psychology is done with it, but sometimes it does so without showing any added bounce or grace in the wearer of those labels. It is not for nothing that Paul Ricoeur, the French philosopher, called psychoanalysis a "hermeneutic of suspicion"—a commentary with vast, and vastly demoralizing, implications.

In contrast, the man or woman who is exposed to a kind of psychology that is more truly alchemical in nature, as Jung's tends to be, may have a better chance of becoming animated by truly inspiring images, ideas, thoughts, energies, feelings, and creative spontaneity. Jung therefore places his psychology squarely on a trajectory that is Nietzschean in spirit and ambition, in spite of his many misreadings of Nietzsche. His introduction of the notion of archetypal patterns of significance to our vocabulary is a case in point of adding value to everyday life. Because of that surplus in value that all things hold, due to their participation in archetypal motifs, Jung sought a larger container than Freud's individual unconscious to house humanity's psychic belongings. Hence, his expanded notion of unconsciousness in the direction of what became the "collective unconscious." That notion itself has been added to psychology's vocabulary as one of its most valuable concepts.

With Hillman, the fourth in line in the four generational dynasty of modern depth psychology, value is again explicitly identified as the first and last concern, just as it was in Nietzsche. In *Archetypal Psychology: A Brief Account*, Hillman explains why he speaks of "archetypal psychology." He puts it this way: "The word 'archetypal' . . . rather than pointing at something . . . points *to* something, and this is *value*. . . . By archetypal psychology we mean a psychology of value." Again: "By emphasizing the valuative function of the adjective 'archetypal,' . . . [archetypal psychology] restores to images their primordial place as that which gives psychic value to the world." But, so he is quick to emphasize, calling something "archetypal" "refers to a move one makes rather than to a thing that is." A psychology based on images it considers "archetypal" matters therefore less for the body of knowledge it can claim about the facts of existence than for the activity of revealing the archetypal side of all things. The psychic values with which archetypal psychology is concerned are not automatically given as such. Just as in alchemy, they must be won through the work of active imagination. They are less about something seen than about a way of seeing. They are about a way of seeing first, and about something seen as a consequence of that way of seeing.

Elsewhere, in a book on *Nietzsche and Psychoanalysis*, I have argued that Nietzsche's revaluation of values, for the sake of a life-affirming pathos based on eternal return, is realized in archetypal psychology. I have argued that archetypal psychology puts Nietzsche into practice—even though it did not set out with that in mind, and even though it is not generally realized that it does so. What follows is a continuation of that proposition, and a further attempt to draw familiar psychological theory and practice into that alchemical process.

The present book places itself squarely in that four generational tradition that includes Nietzsche, Freud, Jung, and Hillman. In the spirit of that tradition, it views psychic value as that which always comes first and last, and everywhere in between. To the extent that the book may perhaps succeed somewhat in its intention, it is offered as an exercise in thinking Being in everyday life as value, and it is meant as a contribution to the work of archetypal psychology. While much of what is suggested in what follows has been written in the work of Hillman, I would like to think that the book at hand contains a measure of original contributions as well. As Hillman himself has commented on my work linking Nietzsche's thought of eternal return with the psychoanalysis of repetition and with archetypal psychology, it provides an added basis for archetypal psychology. That also means it provides an added way of articulating archetypal psychology's relevance and, thus, its own inherent value.

While the book has a strong sense of the tradition in which it belongs, it has, like archetypal psychology itself, an equally strong conviction that certain traditional boundaries must be ignored if justice is to be done to the task at hand. These boundaries include, among others, those that too artificially separate academic departments and disciplines from each other. The life of soul and the imagination that animates it cannot be confined to the department of psychology or psychiatry. They require a multidisciplinary approach. To paraphrase: Soul is too important a business to leave in the hands of psychologists and psychiatrists. It belongs everywhere in everyday life, because it is Everyman's birthright, and because it is the one thing that calls him to task at every moment of every day, throughout all his works and days.

The scholarship that sustains this book is hidden behind the woodwork, rather than being put on display. That is because, as the Preface indicates, the book is meant in the first place as an exercise in active imagination about ideas concerning soul, not as a claim to knowledge about matters of soul that the reader is asked to accept, more or less passively, and as though it were firmly established fact. The reader who wishes to find his or her bearings in the intellectual history and scholarly terrain that form the background and basis for what follows is offered a lengthy, detailed Appendix with guideposts for the subject matters dealt with in each chapter.

PART I

THE GOAL

ONE

THE SOUL'S OWN
FUNDAMENTALISM

LANGUAGE IS FATEFUL.

Now and then history produces a new word or phrase that so well expresses an important truth about what it means to be human that we accept it as a law governing existence. Coinages of this kind become tokens of popular wisdom, not only in their original language and time but also in others. We seize these gifts from language, because they are precious finds. Like gems worn on the human body, they accentuate the natural features of the human condition.

We should be grateful for such expressions. They do us the service of saying clearly and in just a word or two what might otherwise take thousands of mumbled words to say much more incoherently. As a figure of speech, an inspired phrase of this kind conjures up a mental picture. Because a picture paints a thousand words, a well chosen figure of speech is a form of shorthand writing. Every metaphor is a mini-myth that tells a long story.

In addition to saying something important about what it means to be human, such original coinages often redefine who we are, for they can change who we think we are. Not only do they say something about the way things are with our human nature and with the human condition, they also contribute to shaping how human nature and the human condition are on the way of becoming. For who we are, what we are, or what it is like to be us is not cast in stone from time immemorial and for all eternity. It is, as Nietzsche said, forever in the process of becoming. Man is always, as he put it, "the as yet undetermined animal."

One such phrase that illustrates these matters is the expression "bittersweet love." It was coined some two and a half millennia ago by the Greek lyric

19

poetess Sappho. It captures the simultaneous but contradictory feelings of sweetness and bitterness in the longing for a loved one who is absent. Nobody who comes across the phrase is ever puzzled about what it means. It speaks so clearly to anyone who has ever longed for the presence of a beloved person that nobody needs to know the context in which the expression originated or the identity of the person who coined it in order to understand it. The figure was crystal clear from the start. It has stood the test of time as a perfectly defined law governing the life of the soul.

Today, the idea that love is bittersweet may seem trite, like a worn-out platitude or a coin that has become dull from age and use. This is especially so when its figurative nature is no longer fully appreciated. Yet that is precisely a sign of its genius. All metaphors, especially successful ones, risk this fate. When the make-believe of a figure of speech becomes accepted as common law and popular wisdom, it becomes less and less make-believe and more and more literal belief. What starts as poetic fiction that initially is greeted with what Coleridge called "willing suspension of disbelief" eventually is viewed as though it were a literal fact. This is how a metaphor becomes a metaphysics, how philosophy is born from poetics.

The genius of the early Greek lyric genre that Sappho's poetry represents, and of which "bittersweet love" is one of the crowning jewels, lies in shifting the focus from the external factors that affect the life of man to the internal and personal feelings he has about it. Whatever interest in love existed before Sappho's time—and there is no reason to think there was less interest in it then than there is now—was mostly focused on what was believed to be its external and divine causation through the machinations of Eros, god of love. The image of "bittersweet love" shifts this focus away from the external factor and toward the inner life of the person. It makes of love a human, a personal, a private and, above all, an interior experience. In this respect, "bittersweet love" is more than a play of words whose purpose is poetic entertainment. It stands for the kind of revolution in human self-consciousness that only takes place a handful of times in all of history. Its impact is comparable to that of Copernicus, when he proposed that the earth circles around the sun, rather than the other way around, or to that of Darwin, when he suggested the idea of the biological evolution of species rather than their individual divine creation. What "bittersweet love" and early Greek lyric poetry do is nothing less than introduce the idea of an inner province in the human realm, of a world inside man that could be explored. Modern self psychology was conceived, two thousand years before the word "psychology" came into being.

Sappho does not question the belief in the divine causation of love, even though she begins to abandon the Homeric mode of consciousness and of accounting for the facts of life. No longer is being human only a matter of serving as puppets in a two-dimensional shadow play of gods. It acquires a third dimension, that of psychological depth. Sappho redefines what it means to be human and becomes the Columbus of the inner world.

The choice of "bittersweet," an image involving taste, is no accident. It has implications for all later history. Taste is situated at the dividing line between everything that exists outside of man and everything that exists inside. Like the mouth, where it is located, taste is about the transition and interaction between external and internal. With her phrase "bittersweet," Sappho is perhaps the first Westerner to make that precise location of the boundary between external and internal the explicit focus of so much later reflection and commentary. She is among the first to speak on behalf of what we now matter-of-factly consider the personal inwardness of the soul.

The history of Western ideas about the inner life of the individual is long and complex. Yet when all is said and done, it has one central theme—the processes taking place at the boundary between what is outside of man and what is inside. From ancient Sappho through modern Freud and beyond, psychology has been about the exchanges between what is inner and what is outer. Ever since the beginning, this exchange, as it has been imagined throughout two and a half millennia of psychology, has involved the longing for an absent object. That absent object and the absence itself come in an endless variety of forms. This has preoccupied an equally endless variety of psychological and philosophical schools of thought about them. A host of such notions about significant absences springs to mind as soon as one casts even a glancing look at the history of ideas. Characteristically it involves an object that has somehow been lost—or that is perhaps forgotten, repressed, remembered, withdrawn, negated, abandoned, split off, destroyed, rejected, or altogether nonexistent. The absence may have to do with ideas about the impermanence of all things or about nothingness, nihilism, penis envy, castration anxiety, fear of death, meaninglessness, the death of all gods, or despair over the insufficiency of all human discourse. It may be about a void left behind by a golden age long past, by a sense of paradise lost, or by an idealized morality no longer to be found anywhere. It may involve longing for historical figures long dead, for fantasy figures displaced by reality, or for mythic figures replaced by science or gods now existing as *deus absconditus,* perhaps even dying at the hands of philosophy. These are just a few of the absences that come to mind.

It would, of course, be wrong to suggest that Sappho single-handedly set all this history of ideas and experiences involving absence and longing in motion. And yet her image of "bittersweet love" provided Western man with a new and revolutionary root metaphor about the human condition. It is a root metaphor that does not go away, because it bears the mark of genius. That genius lies in the way it captures something essential about the human condition, and in the way it captivates man's imagination about himself. Before other comparable ideas, and often better than many that came after it, the image of "bittersweet love" identified something essential about an important human experience. That something essential in what we tell ourselves it means to be human involves eternal longing, eternal exchanges between an outer world and an inner world, and a heart that is always filled with the taste of a human condition that is eternally bittersweet.

Such, then, can be the significance of an inspired new word or turn of phrase. For man is, as Emerson said, the eternal analogist. He is always trying to make sense of himself and of his existence in this, the only world he knows, by means of metaphors. As Socrates put it nearly two and a half millennia before Emerson, what manner of thing the soul *is* would take a long tale to tell, and it surely would require superhuman knowledge to tell the whole story, but what it is *like*, that is something we humans can perhaps risk to talk about with some degree of confidence.

But not every figure of speech about what it means to be human becomes accepted wisdom and common law. Not every one of man's self definitions is like a new suit he can put on at will, as it were off the rack. Near the opposite pole of the almost inevitable popularity of Sappho's "bittersweet love" is the notion of "injudicability," a word that does not exist in English, even though perhaps it should. While injudicability does not appear in dictionaries, the word "injudicable" does. Injudicability therefore would stand in the same relation to injudicable as the word "unaccountability," which does exist, stands to "unaccountable." It is therefore not unreasonable to propose "injudicability" as a viable word. The Oxford English Dictionary and Webster's Dictionary report the use of "injudicable" in the eighteenth century, further suggesting that it is "little used" and "rare" by the early nineteenth century, and altogether "obsolete" by the early twentieth century. The meaning of "injudicable" can be guessed by its parts—the negative "in" and the root "judic-," as in "judicial," "judiciary," "judicious," and, hence, "judge" and "judgment." Both the Oxford English Dictionary and Webster's Dictionary define "injudicable" as "not cognizable by a judge." Something is "injudicable" when it is incapable of being judged. What puts it beyond the reach of judgment is precisely its "injudicability." It is injudicable because it cannot be judged by any standard other than itself. Its injudicability points to the essential quality of the thing that defines its very nature and that makes it a standard to itself, preventing any other standard from being applied to it. Injudicability, in short, is a negative that defines a positive. A circle is a circle, not because it is a polygon with an infinite number of sides, but because it is circular. No amount of commentary about an infinite number of triangles with one shared apex and arranged as a polygon can ever say what a circle is. Only a circle itself possesses the property of circularity that makes it a circle. It takes a circle to judge a circle. Without circularity, no circle can be judged a circle. On the other hand, circularity itself is enough to judge all possible circles.

If "injudicability," unlike Sappho's "bittersweet love," does not roll off the tongue and stick in the imagination, that is no accident. It does not lend itself to casual uses or conversations, and it alludes to things other than those of daily practical concern. Only in special contexts can the notion be naturally at home, and then only with a whole discussion to go with it. Yet like "bittersweet love," the metaphor of "injudicability" suggests an important truth about what it means to be human. Talking about it makes sense, and is very much to the point, in the context of certain Platonist and Neoplatonist matters—not only in Plato and the Platonists or in the later Plotinus and the Neoplatonists but also in Augustine and all that he appropriated from Plotinus, and in the Neoplatonism of the Renaissance, in the Germanic offshoots of Platonism, and, finally, in the depth psychology of Nietzsche, Freud, and Jung, which is our own contemporary ground to work. The notion of "injudicability" is especially relevant in discussions of the unchanging and universal patterns that shape human experiences and that make them unchanging and universal. These are the patterns that, ever since Plato, have been discussed in philosophical contexts as absolute Forms or Ideas, and that in psychological contexts gave impetus to the notion of timeless and universal "archetypes." If everyone knows what love is—or grief, loneliness, work, joy, war, or poverty—then that is because they are timeless, because they are the same for everyone, everywhere. They are, quite literally, "archetypal," meaning "archaic" and "typical"—eternal and universal. If there were such a thing as an atomism of the soul—a question that can neither be affirmed nor negated—and if such atomism were understood as a theory about indivisible building blocks that constitute human experience, and beyond which experience cannot be further analyzed because they cannot be further divided, then archetypal patterns of experience would be those building blocks of the soul. Love, grief, loneliness, work, joy, war, and poverty are exactly that— indivisible or not further analyzable. Everyone knows what they are. They need not and cannot be reduced to anything else that is smaller than them and that would explain them any better. To reduce them to other processes and things says something about those other processes and things but not about the archetypal experience patterns themselves.

Because these archetypal experience patterns are truly autonomous, due to their indivisibility and irreducibility, they often are personified as living creatures with a will of their own. These personifications assume endless shapes. They most commonly appear in such familiar forms as mythological figures of antiquity, as legendary creatures from the world's imagination, or as allegorical figures portrayed in statues and paintings. As personifications of universal and timeless aspects of human life, they portray units of experience that are wholly self-contained, self-sufficient, and self-explanatory. Whether one lived twenty-five centuries ago as an ancient Athenian amid temples and images of gods or today as a modern Parisian in a city whose boulevards are lined with statues of Liberty, Equality, or Justice makes no difference. The personification of archetypal patterns in life happens everywhere, all the time. Freud and the psychology of unconsciousness have suggested that Oedipus is everywhere—as is

Narcissus, Eros, Thanatos, Ananke, and all the rest. Today they come in modern garb, but while their costumes change, the mythic plots these figures personify do not.

"Injudicability" is precisely that quality about archetypal patterns of experience that makes it impossible to understand or judge them in any other terms than their own. Archetypal configurations are what they are, and how they are, because archetypal is exactly what, and how, they are. By the same token, they themselves serve as the terms and the laws that must be understood but whose understanding is all that is needed in order to understand the life of the soul. Love cannot be explained in terms other than its own, yet love itself serves to explain a good deal of what goes on in human history. Augustine, in *De Libero Arbitrio* (*On Free Choice of the Will*), sums up what is at stake in this "injudicable" essence of things archetypal, in his characteristically succinct fashion: "Nobody passes judgment on it, nobody judges well without it" (*Nullus de illa iudicat, nullus sine illa iudicat bene*). As he puts it even more succinctly, our minds make judgments "not about it but through it" (*non de ipsa, sed per ipsam*).

While the term *injudicability* does not appear in everyday language, it is, nonetheless, a term whose own essence—whose own intrinsic "injudicability"—has a place in the lives of ordinary men and women. Common formulaic expressions of popular wisdom such as "That's the way things are," "That's life," or "That's what you get for doing such and such" are, each in its own way, about injudicability. These particular examples are obviously trite, but the larger issue that is at stake is anything but trite. Such expressions matter, because they suggest a natural human inclination, even if it often appears in petty forms, to look for final, irreducible principles governing the universe that every human life is. But more is at stake than merely being able to provide explanations for, or commentaries on, the psychological realities of everyday life. The more important issue is that catching a glimpse of injudicability can sometimes amount to a moment of discovery about a rock-bottom verity concerning creation itself. When the injudicability in a given matter is momentarily sensed, if ever so fleetingly, it can reflect a glimpse of miraculous splendor in the face of otherwise seemingly mundane affairs.

Developing the ability to recognize glimpses of injudicability in one's everyday life and history takes many years. Often it requires a whole lifetime, and, for many, even that is not enough. In prolonged contemplative exercises, such as psychoanalysis or other reflective and meditative disciplines, the discovery of injudicability is frequently the unspoken goal. When it is reached, it may be suddenly found as a priceless gift, a sudden clearing in the middle of a forest. If and when it is achieved—an achievement that is under no circumstances guaranteed, and that cannot be brought about by force or clever trickery—it can have the impact of a revelation. So it can sometimes happen that after years and years of living one sometimes, eventually, finally—and, typically, only infrequently, and, at best, fleetingly, but with a sudden clarity of vision that is equal to a revelation—sees that one's life is the way it is for no other reason than that this is the way it is. This seemingly most superficial yet deepest and most momentous of discoveries turns out to be, in the end, the most difficult one to make. Many a life ends without that discovery being made even once. Like a lightning bolt, the idea strikes that, perhaps for the first time ever, the interminable search for explanations of life can be abandoned, and that life can finally, at least briefly, be taken on its own and already built in terms.

If catching glimpses of injudicability is possible it is because, again according to Augustine and other Platonists and Neoplatonists before and after him, the soul is not only capable of knowledge but also of wisdom. Knowledge is about understanding the ever-changing events of history. Wisdom is about seeing patterns in creation that are timeless and immutable. Knowledge is about facts as bits of history, wisdom about bits of eternity that govern historical facts by giving them their shape. The way to shift from knowledge to wisdom is to stop viewing all things only historically, and literally, and to regard them also as images whose significance, even though squarely situated in the here and now of the moment at hand, extends also beyond the historicity of the moment. It extends into the timeless dimension that attaches to all time-bound events. Shifting from literal thinking about facts to image thinking that sees deeper than historicity is done by viewing historical events as figurative expressions of immutable eternal laws. It is a way of identifying the injudicability in one's personal history through a figurative reading of the events of one's life. Every experience, every situation, every action, every thought or feeling stops being viewed strictly situationally, as caused by the unique historical circumstances at hand. Instead, it is isolated from the flow of history, held still, and regarded as though it were itself a fixed pattern in the universe, with a law of its own. Everything can come to be seen as necessary in this fashion—necessary according to the archetypal law that governs it. Nothing is judged any longer according to terms other than its own. Therefore, nothing is negatively judged and devalued for being as it is. Nothing is compared to, and measured by, a norm that is external to it. All things stand redeemed as they are in this manner, for nothing has to be changed first before it can be redeemed. The world itself, as it has been and is, and is likely to continue to be, stands judged good enough. If my personal life and circumstance are turning out as they are, here and now, then that is as it should be.

The focus of attention shifts away from explanations that are based on historical and causal factors. My life story is no longer about the choices I made but about how I was made, and continue to be made, in those choices. It is no longer about the economic, social, familial, political, cultural, biological, physiological, and situational conditions that are or are not in my control. It is, instead, about the autonomous and imaginative ways in which all these factors fall together to make a psychological plot, a myth. And it is this plot, this myth, that is the destiny governing the life of the soul that animates me. I have to respond to this mythic fact of my life in its terms, not mine. That means I may have to abandon the primacy of my sometimes inflated ego and of any preconceived ego morality I might like to impose on everything. Every event or situation thereby stops being a call to action that is aimed at change. It becomes instead an opportunity for contemplation, sometimes even for worship. With luck, it may even become the setting for a personal mini-revelation. For the flow of the day's history can be briefly interrupted in this fashion by a brief devotional turn and bow toward the soul's own Mecca. Every life can make room for a quick reminder of Allah's splendor in this manner. Such a contemplative shift in attention, which goes against the constant press of history to move forever forward in restless activity, is a way of catching a glimpse of the divine mind or of the "world soul," the *anima mundi*, that governs the universe.

This is neither blaspheming lay theology nor religious counseling for the irreligious. It is a way of looking at the events of daily life in a way that tries to do justice to the soul substance that animates them. For as a centuries'-old tradition has it, the soul is that aspect of everyday life where all things historical and unique touch upon motifs that are eternal. It is that depth of significance in all events where the prosaic world of the ever changing becomes identical to themes that are immutable. It is what makes it possible to recognize in the utterly profane the incarnation and eternal reincarnation of the sacred. It is where all things human look like so many images of the divine. "Every day is a god," is how Emerson put this. And the day's divinity, in this Emersonian view, does not lie outside of it, at some unbridgeable distance. Nor does it hide behind it, as some sort of stage director. It is the day itself, with everything in it. Nothing about the day's inherent divinity is hidden, for it is visible in the injudicability of its events. Ordinary events become the living text with which archetypal themes inscribe themselves into individual histories. They become ways in which timeless and immutable principles of creation are put into effect in the lives of its creatures. Ordinary events thereby become the soul's own scripture.

A devoted interest in the life of the soul, an interest that searches for archetypal presences in everyday existence—and not only for the personal psychopathology of everyday life, or for ways to manage it—can then be conceived as exegesis of the soul's own scripture. The first rule of such an exegesis dictates that any reading and commentary must begin by sticking to the images of the text. That means every event must be viewed as a precise formulation of a divine thought, as sacred word spoken in the idiom of profane happenings. No carelessness in transcription or translation is to be tolerated, and not one iota is to be removed from the text. This means that a kind of fundamentalism of the soul is needed. For one thing, no reductionism of any kind is allowed. Nothing is to be explained by introducing terms that do not belong to it and to which it is compared and thus reduced. Every event, every situation, every thing has its explanation embedded in it. Each experience is therefore regarded as self-explanatory and self-justifying. It is allowed and encouraged to speak for itself about its injudicability.

Injudicability matters, because man is not only the analogist, as Socrates and Emerson said. He also is the esteemer, as Nietzsche added. He is constantly judging the value of existence. Daily life is not only about enacting perceptions based on images that are largely unconscious and that serve as metaphors to make existence intelligible. It also is about the value judgments concerning existence that are implied in those images and metaphors. The most fundamental value judgment in every life is one that either affirms or negates existence itself. It looks at the world on any given day of the week and says, "It is good," or "It is not good." This is a judgment every human being makes, and must make, all the time—at every moment of each day, throughout all the days of life, in every thought, feeling, and act. It makes everyone a moral philosopher, and it makes of each individual history a lifelong exercise in moral philosophizing with blood, sweat, and tears, with all one has of passion, experience, and knowledge, with all one acquires of education, wealth, or status, with all one ever does in every role one plays.

This inescapable call to judge the value of existence drives the history of ideas and of the world's great myths, and ordinary individuals reiterate these ideas and myths by endlessly reenacting them in their daily affairs. Unsuspecting men and women live lives whose events repeat the value judgments rendered in those ideas and myths. Unbeknownst to themselves, they use their own voices to express again and again the thoughts and sentiments of great men and women from history who are long dead, and of men and women, even gods, from legendary history. The accents and the idioms of these voices are contemporary, and shaped by changing circumstances, but the fundamental theme of an eternally ongoing human debate about the value of existence is the same. This makes for a perpetual conversation that man has with his fellow men and with himself, a conversation that is endlessly recast in new editions, and that begins anew all day long and all life long. Ordinary life in contemporary history is the stage for an endless procession of moral philosophers who are continually reincarnated. Daily existence is therefore not only filled with the voices of a private coterie of figures from one's personal psychosocial history. Every day, and all day long, we also meet again and again with the likes of Abraham, Paul, and Augustine, or with every Greek thinker from Anaximander and Heraclitus to Plato and Aristotle, or with every founder of every religion from East to West. The procession is as endless as the supply of figures that animate the history of human consciousness. And that is, in any case, why these figures matter. They are us, ordinary men and women, but magnified—magnificent magnifications of Everyman the esteemer judging the value of existence according to his many moods. Man the eternal analogist is therefore indeed also a perpetual judge at every moment of his life. He must continually complete creation by assigning to it a value. Through the very act of completing existence by assigning to it a value, man also completes himself. He becomes who he is and assigns value to his own life. The life of Everyman the esteemer is given its value in and by his own perpetual, inevitable, and built-in judgment.

Now archetypal images themselves are about nothing if not about value. They are, as it were, the world's own units of value. But unlike money tokens, invented by human culture for a commercial economy, archetypal images are neither man-made nor uniform and interchangeable. They are fully autonomous as well as multiform and unique, just as the spontaneous creative imagination that animates the world is autonomous and polymorphous, and just as each manifestation of life is unique. Nowhere is the value function of archetypal images more clearly suggested than in the ancient Greek myth of Hades, the god of the intangible underworld. He personifies the ruling principle that governs the world of intangibles underlying every identifiable form of life. Hades is the brother of Zeus, who governs the affairs of the upperworld. He is called "Lord of Souls." His underworld realm is the final destination of all souls, a realm where they go when they separate themselves from the bodies they animate in life. He is the purely psychic perspective to which we shift when we extricate the soul factor in daily life from its identification with the literal facts of it.

The souls that exist in Hades exist there as silent and intangible images that look like insubstantial doubles of the historical persons to which they belong in life. They are the exact replicas of the literal persons as we know them in life, but minus the physicality of the body. They are the plots of actual historical lives, but minus the literal mindedness about the factual behavior in those lives. As Ovid said, these soul images that are the stuff of Hades are bloodless, bone-less, and bodiless. They are pure form, pure image. They are the shape that gives shape to things and events but that has to be separated from their material, fac-tual, or literal conditions and manifestations. Hades is no realm of underlying causality. The reality he personifies is purely psychic and fully autonomous. He is not about biology, physiology, neurology, chemistry, or DNA—even though he is present in them as well. Nor is the psychic matter over which he presides the stuff of historical development, education, conditioning, sociology, dynam-ics, systemics, social construction or politics of power—even though they too have their own Hades factor built in. He is about autonomous images that breathe the life into life, and without which it cannot exist or continue. Hades, in brief, is the reality of the silent and hidden fictions that become the facts of life when they are historically embodied. He is insubstantial in essence, yet his essence is incarnate in life. He is the immaterial psychic matter that makes life matter to us at every moment.

If, as suggested earlier, a metaphor is a mini-myth, then the converse also is true, and a myth, such as the myth of Hades, is a mega-metaphor. A myth is a metaphor drawn out and magnified to the size and scope of a self-fulfilling and self-explanatory dramatic reality in the life of man. Reading the myth of Hades must therefore be done metaphorically and dramatically. It requires an eye for analogies between things that generally have nothing in common and a sense for dramatic events behind the impenetrable surfaces of hard facts.

The story of Hades suggests that all the facts of life have their ultimate basis in images. These images may well be silent and intangible, but they nonetheless form the animating essence of existence. Hades makes it possible to think about a soul factor in life as something that has its own reality in spite of being intangible. He makes it unnecessary to believe in, or to be able to prove, the existence of an objectifiable and definable entity called a "soul" that, like everything else under the sun, must obey the laws of physics if it is to be considered real. For the soul factor over which Hades presides is of a different order of rank than the usual facts of daily life. It exists as a fact of life according to the purely psychic perspective and prejudice of Hades. This is imagined in Homer's *Iliad* and *Odyssey* as the *psyche* playing no identifiable role and serving no observable function at all in the lives of men and women, even though it is necessary for life, and even though life ends when the *psyche* leaves the body. Hades personifies that mind-set in every human life whose interest is in the immaterial significance of all events, and without which life is unsustainable.

Transitioning to the mind-set of Hades requires a shift from the usual ways of thinking about the events of life to an imaginative way of rethinking them. The myth of Hades says that entering the underworld involves crossing the waters that separate it from the upperworld. This requires the help of Charon, the boatman who demands a token before he agrees to carry anybody across. That giving of a token is no empty gesture. It is about the need for a protocol to facilitate the move from concrete thinking about the facts of life to a more imaginative way of rethinking them. It is about shifting from biological models about the instinctual life of physical needs to less literally physical and biological models about the imaginative life of the soul. The token which Charon demands is a transitional object that has a dual significance. It is both concrete thing and image. Stationed at the boundary between upperworld and underworld, Charon is the factor that allows traffic between these two worlds and categories of reality. He is a master of dual significance who makes imaginative thinking about literal events possible. He personifies the active ingredient in metaphor itself, for there is no swifter way to move from one category of events to another than by the transport that metaphor provides. It is no accident that the Greek word *metaphora* means "to move." A Greek household moving company is a *metaphora* company and is likely to have the word *metaphora* painted on its moving vans. It is Charon who moves the world's psychic furniture around.

Hades personifies a prejudice about the sense of value in every life, and in everyday life. That prejudice is an unconditional positive valuation or affirmation of all imaginable forms of life, and therefore of existence itself. Hades also is called Pluto. That name alludes to riches, plenty, wealth. But his wealth is not about a mountain of gold or a portfolio of blue chip stocks. Nor is it about private collections of personal trophies obtained for great achievements, or about legacies of riches left behind for those who come after. The riches in the realm of Hades are the endlessly varied images of soul that fill his realm. His wealth lies in his prejudice that insists on eternalizing every event, and that makes every incident a universal and timeless law onto itself. It is what Emerson and Nietzsche called "genius," the life-affirming spirit that turns even the most fleeting and personal moment into an eternal law, not out of resentment over the passage of time and the temporality of all things, nor out of inflated self-importance, but out of a spirit of sheer affirmation. Such is the prejudice of Hades, a prejudice that considers no event and no thing complete until it eternalizes itself, until the question of its inherent value is placed under a sign that blesses everything for being thus and such, and not otherwise.

A mode of thinking or a psychological theory and treatment approach built on the Hades principle of affirmation does not use scientific methods of proof in order to affirm its truths. It does not use experimental studies with multiple large samples, no repeatable demonstrations with great numbers of data and with outside verification. It does what Emerson and Nietzsche saw as the mark of genius, and what the old, bold spirit of early psychoanalysis did, and what all true depth psychology still does: it generalizes from single cases. This is not poor science about the facts of life but pure affirmation of their value from the soul's point of view.

Because Hades affirms everything, he offers a perspective that looks beyond the all-too-human dichotomy of good and evil. He personifies life's insistence on self-affirmation. Through him, everyday life asserts itself independent of the ruling morality and value systems of good health or good citizenship, independent of the ideal life of which the ego dreams in its daydreams. Hades judges existence not from a position and perspective outside of it or after it but from within it.

Hades is no improver of mankind, and a Hades perspective does not look at life to change it for the better. This is not for lack of sympathy for the challenges of living. On the contrary. It is about insisting that precisely in the very way that any given life has been and is it has been and is already good enough. Nothing must be resented for not having been different. Hades does not join those brands of psychology that rush to modify existence behaviorally, to improve it morally, to explain and redo it rationally, or to treat it correctively. He is not as automatically intent as are habitual improvers of mankind on rearranging existence as it has been and is—by manipulating it systemically, reeducating it patronizingly, developing it emotionally, rehabilitating it socially, correcting it cognitively, brightening it affectively, or reengineering it structurally. Hades does none of this. He opposes change and does not allow it. Everything that is given over to Hades remains the same, unchanged. He takes life as is. Starting from that precise position, and from none other, he values all of existence, the whole kit and caboodle. To accomplish this task, he insists that nothing is touched, moved, or altered, that everything is first of all allowed to be and to remain as it is found. His job begins by being the world's archetypal holding environment that lets life be. Hades is life's triumph over human resentment about living.

By insisting on eternalizing everything as it is, Hades does away with the very category of time and becomes the personified dimension of timelessness. In his eyes, history stops being history only, and it becomes equal to eternity. This makes for the important point that Hades and the perspective he person-ifies do not belong in time, not even "after the facts." His is not a reality that comes after the events of life. He is not about another form of life, and not about a new quality of life that comes after proper treatment—after the proper behavioral change, the corrective moral improvement, or the empathic thera-peutic intervention. Because Hades thinks in terms that are timeless from the beginning, from his first take on everything, he does not come at the end of anything, even at the end of life or after death. Nor is he about life in retrospect or in hindsight. Hades is what remains, and what in fact comes into being, when all is said and done. He is what belongs beyond everything that can be said from any historical perspective.

The very dimension of linear time, this great metaphysical invention of Judeo-Christianity that does nothing less than invent history itself, dissolves into a dimension that is beyond time and beyond the very category of time. Here all points of departure and all points of view come together in an intan-gible yet real and shared dimension—their unfathomable depth of significance. For precisely that, so the myth says, is the first thing that has to be said about the underworld of Hades: that it is without limit to its depth.

This depth of soul or of psychic significance that Hades represents exists as a virtual eternity inherent in every fleeting moment. It is a dimension in every-day life where the multiplicity of historical beings and the timeless unity of Being become one. What unifies all historical beings here is the eternal Yes of the affirmation of existence that Hades personifies. Heraclitus was perhaps speaking first of all about Hades when he said that in the eyes of the gods all things are beautiful, and that it is man who considers some things beautiful and others ugly. Hades is the principal keeper of life's value and valuables.

Nietzsche raised one of philosophy's biggest and most famous questions ever. He asked his reader this: How well disposed would you have to become toward your life—and how would you manage to become so well disposed to your life—to wish for nothing more fervently than the opportunity to live it over and over again, eternally and without any changes in it? You would have to come to an affirmative value judgment about existence, as it has been and is, to wish that this thought could be true. *It is the Hades perspective and prejudice about the value of all life that makes the thought of the eternal return of all things not only imaginable and tolerable but also desirable—and potentially true.* It is Hades who insists on making all forms of life, every scrap of it, archetypal—precisely by viewing them as he does. It is Hades who places in front of every man or woman the challenge of affirming existence as a whole, and his or her existence in specific. It is through the Hades perspective that a human life can reconcile itself with itself—not in the future, not in hindsight or retrospect, not at the end of it or after it, but in the midst of it, in the intangible depth of meaningfulness in it that comes with it and that holds its total value.

In the end, the spirit that is personified in the mythic image of Hades, the spirit that is required to pass the test of Nietzsche's thought of the eternal return of all things, is the same spirit that is suggested in the notion of "injudicability." To seek to affirm existence as it is, on its own terms, is to look for a sense of injudicability. Conversely, to look for injudicability in everyday life is to seek to affirm existence as is—not later but now.

For two and a half thousand years we have had a psychology that is largely derived from Sappho's "bittersweet love," a psychology about the eternal processes we imagine at the boundary between what exists outside of man and what exists inside. Such a psychology of an internal self is more readily imaginable and acceptable than a psychology of "injudicability" that is based in Hades. It keeps us on *this* side of the waters that separate upperworld from underworld. It requires no dealings with Charon and his protocol of shifting from the facts of life to the images in them. It is a psychology that is conducted under the watchful eye and the upperworldly rule of Zeus. But in the end, it is no psychology in the deepest possible and truest sense. The deepest and purest soul matter and a psychology about it have to be looked for in the underworld of Zeus's brother Hades. That is where the *psyche* has its own home, and where it keeps its bottom-line accounts of all life under the sun.

Nietzsche knew this. That is why he placed his philosophy of eternal return and the affirmative revaluation of all value judgments about existence under the sign of Dionysos, the mythic and mystic god whom legend sometimes equates with Hades. Freud knew it too. That is why, in the epigraph to *The Interpretation of Dreams*, he expressed his resolve to turn away from the gods of the upperworld for his psychology of the unconscious and to turn instead to those of the underworld. Jung also knew it. That is why he located the source of greatest resistance to depth psychology in fear of Hades. And Hillman knows it too. That is why he places his brand of psychology squarely in the domain of Hades and his bottomless underworld of images, where the cardinal rule is indeed that soul is image and image soul, and where all things stand affirmed on their own terms.

TWO

HOW TO BECOME
WHO ONE IS

NIETZSCHE, IN THE FAMOUS APHORISM 341 from *The Gay Science,* raised one of Western philosophy's biggest and most difficult questions ever—and then spent the rest of his active philosophical life trying to answer it, with important but questionable results. His question is this: How well disposed would you have to become toward your life—and how would you manage to become so well disposed—to wish for nothing more fervently than to live it again and again, "once more and innumerable times mores," without the slightest change or novelty in it, and without there ever coming an end to this process? Everything you ever experienced would return to you and keep returning to you, all in the same sequence—every pain and every joy, every thought and every sigh, everything small or large. "The eternal hourglass of existence is turned upside down again and again, and you with it, speck of dust!"

This is, in summary, Nietzsche's challenging thought of the eternal return of all things. It is, if nothing else, startling. It brings everyone who encounters the idea for the first time to an abrupt halt. Before one can begin to consider it further, or even dismiss it, the thought presents whoever comes across it with an unsettling challenge that demands a personal reaction. We are facing no small sphinx here. Like a sphinx, it may well eat you alive, depending on your response. As Nietzsche said, the thought of the eternal return of all things would change you as you are, or it would crush you.

In Nietzsche's own estimation—and humility, false or otherwise, does not appear in his writings—a philosophy based on the thought of eternal return would be one of the most radical and momentous items in the history of Western ideas. It would, in his view, change history as we know it and have known it. It would open the vista of a new historical and philosophical horizon. It would create, and require, a new prototype of human being, a type who would be driven by a different philosophical pathos. That pathos would speak another language, the language of an infectious laughter that would itself become the envy of whoever hears it. The new prototype of human being also would require and develop a different kind of health, even new ideas about what health is. Long-cherished notions about what constitutes good and evil would be cast aside. A brand new dawn would appear, the dawn of a convalescence like none that has ever been known before. And while the transformed human being rejoices in the exhilaration of this great philosophical convalescence, the ancient beliefs in the Judeo-Christian God of his or her forefathers would be found . . . dead.

A thought that would do all this is no ordinary thought. It does not even belong to the category of traditional philosophical thoughts. It is, as Nietzsche fondly admitted, dynamite, shattering all that the history of philosophy has come to view as true and good. It even shatters the notions of truth and good themselves. Perhaps the only thing more astonishing than Nietzsche's own claims for a philosophy based on eternal return is that they are not necessarily untrue. But this is only so if it is possible to develop the thought into a viable, sustainable, and comprehensive philosophy. For that to be possible, the thought must first of all be imaginable and at least potentially believable. It also must look desirable enough for anyone to want to believe it and appropriate it as a philosophical idea to live by. Last, it must be practicable. There must be concrete ways in which it can become not only imaginable, believable, and desirable but also livable.

During Nietzsche's lifetime, the challenge of working out a comprehensive philosophy based on eternal return became a task with which he grew more and more personally identified. At first the thought struck him like a lightning bolt of inspiration and revelation, totally unexpectedly, and with an almost obliterating force. At that point it was a vision that appeared out of nowhere, unannounced. Nothing had prepared him for this moment and this thought. He did not feel that he was in any way equipped to hold on to the vision or to translate it into communicable terms. The idea was at first a thought that found him, not the other way around. Then the vision and the promise it seemed to hold became more and more a personal challenge. Nietzsche felt increasingly compelled to bear responsibility for bringing the idea into the world, as a philosophy that could stand on its own two feet to argue its own case. Eventually the prospect of a philosophy based on eternal return became an all-absorbing life work from which he could not turn away, a work that consumed him as a person. Finally, he came to see it as a task for which he was chosen, without having a choice about being so chosen. It became a task that he had to accept, and did accept, as his personal destiny. It was, one might say, a case of immaculate inception. In the end, eternal return was for Nietzsche more a thought that shaped him than a thought that he shaped. That fateful and transformative power of the idea is of the essence, as we will see. By the end of Nietzsche's active life, which came when he collapsed into madness and into philosophical silence, he had not been able to formulate a comprehensive and convincing philosophy of eternal return. When his illness finally killed him, there was nothing in the way of a clear and thorough exposition on eternal return. His efforts in that direction had failed in spite of multiple penetrating and important writings on topics that were to be among the active ingredients of his philosophy of eternal return. Those writings have become significant contributions to the body of Nietzschean ideas, but they left the task of thinking eternal return unfinished.

After Nietzsche's death, there were no followers who tried to carry on with the task of articulating a philosophy of eternal return. Nor was there a body of students or a school of thought that could be guided by a clear Nietzschean agenda or by Nietzsche's own instructions. All that was there at the end were a multitude of notes and a handful of people. There were one or two now mostly distant friends who had been worried about Nietzsche even before he went mad. There was a loyal but uninspired assistant who previously had transcribed Nietzsche's texts in order to help him spare his long-impaired sight and to reduce his constant and disabling migraines. There was a devout but otherwise nondescript mother who helped nurse her now-ill son. Last and definitely worst, there was his sister, Elisabeth. Her long-standing habit of meddling in her brother's life came to a pitch when madness had made him entirely defenseless. She would have done her brother and the world a service if she had stayed away from his literary estate. Instead, and as is now well documented, she unintelligently and mostly unscrupulously began to tamper with his unedited writings. She omitted existing text, changed text she did not like, and even went so far as to add text of her own while pretending it was her brother's. Most outrageous of all was that her tampering with the texts was done to serve the anti-Semitism that she herself actively promoted but that Nietzsche had always abhorred and vehemently condemned.

During Nietzsche's own lifetime, his writings were hardly sold and generally poorly received. At times he had to use his own funds to get them published at all. His first book, *The Birth of Tragedy*, was blasted by a leading scholar in Nietzsche's own chosen field of classical philology, which was the book's subject matter. His other books, in which he reached far beyond his field of scholarship, fared no better. Some friends and former intellectual associates were disappointed by his writings. Others were confused by them and rejected them. Still others worried about their friend for writing them. Some close friends felt, and a few actually were, attacked by them. His once-intimate alliance with his friend, hero, and host, Richard Wagner, was destroyed by his writing—deliberately, to set himself free from a trap of ideas he felt he must escape.

None of this was accident. Nietzsche's personal life, like his philosophy, was marked by an extraordinary and ever-increasing degree of loneliness. There were several promising friendships with intellectual associates, but only a few of those lasted. He never married. There were no significant or even insignificant romantic relations. There was one brief period of intense erotic feelings for Lou Andreas Salome, an attractive young woman of great intellect and spirit, who later would become a close associate of Freud's, until his last days in London. She did not return Nietzsche's feelings in kind and rejected his, opting instead for a closer affiliation with a mutual friend. Nietzsche was crushed and humiliated. He vented his wounded feelings as bitterly resentful hostility, apparently operating by the motto that what we cannot have we must try to destroy. Such was the more personal side of his utterly lonely life. His professional life did nothing to make up for it. His life as a professor of classical philology, at the University of Basel, was unsuccessful and short lived. He attracted few students. His first book, as mentioned, triggered a devastating critical assault. He had begun his professorship at the extraordinarily young age of twenty-four, with a glowing recommendation and promise from his highly regarded mentor that he would be able to achieve brilliance in whatever he undertook. That so promising academic career would not last long, due to poor and worsening health. He was plagued by deteriorating sight and by excruciating migraines that put him in bed, out of commission, for days on end. When he eventually resigned from his teaching post because of his worsening health, he received a meager pension. He was told that he should stop writing if he wanted to keep what was left of his deteriorating sight.

Right! Stop writing! Nietzsche, of all people! As he would later say, there lies great danger in one's physician (and not only because of the most obvious reasons). He explained: "One must have the physician one was born for, otherwise one will perish by his physician."

It is impossible to imagine what would have happened if Nietzsche had heeded the advice of his physician and stopped writing. Obviously he would not have become the Nietzsche he was destined to become and whose writings we now have. But it is not at all clear or imaginable how the history of ideas would have evolved differently without Nietzsche. What is clear is that Nietzsche's physician did not know his patient well, that he misjudged him, and that he would have killed his spirit with his treatment. For even by then, in his first book, Nietzsche already had planted the seeds of a tragic yet life-affirming mode of philosophizing in the spirit of his chosen god, Dionysos, to whom he was forever loyal and to whom he became increasingly devoted. It would have been preposterous for anyone to expect that Nietzsche would meekly give in to his doctor's well-meant and, indeed, perfectly rational advice. Thank heaven for patient resistance.

Nietzsche's health problems, especially the migraines, were his only lifelong companions, along with the vast array of potions of questionable medicinal virtue he was always using, in unsuccessful attempts to treat himself. Rather than becoming a passively obedient patient to his physician, he became an active student of the body as philosopher. He concluded, based on self-observation, that the body's varying states of health amount to as many schools of philosophy, each grounded in its own unique physiological underpinnings. Sometimes, and more so as the years passed, he complained of being in poor shape for weeks on end, even for entire seasons. During spells of renewed vim and vigor, between migraines, he wrote for hours and walked for hours. Eventually, one of his most significant and central metaphors became that of the exhilaration of convalescence. He wrote at length about the coming age of philosophical convalescence and about the newfound feeling of health that his philosophy would bring. In writing what he did about the psychological and philosophical significance of convalescence he knew whereof he spoke.

After resigning from his teaching post, Nietzsche became a nomad, supporting himself with his meager pension and the hospitality of friends, plus packages of food and clothing from his family. He traveled light and often, typically carrying just one trunk with minimal spare clothes but plenty of manuscripts and notes. He stayed in boardinghouses and with friends. During those years he wrote and wrote—and became Nietzsche. His favorite activity when he was not writing consisted of long solitary walks, preferably in the mountains and around the lakes of the regions where he lived. With every move from one temporary lodging to the next, he was forever searching the Swiss, French, and Italian landscapes for a place with a climate that would suit his health and his spirit. He never found it—until he came to live in the place where his life as a philosopher would come to an end in madness.

His last active year was spent in Turin, a city he quickly came to love. He worked hard and in rapid succession produced a large amount of excellent writing, some of it his best. This made him love the place even more. He fully believed that his new home would restore and revive him as no other place had ever been able to do. Instead, it would become the setting for his undoing. His writing became speckled with grandiose flourishes and overreaching language. He began to lose the ability to modulate his tone. His images and metaphors grew out of control. The decline accelerated rapidly. Madness was breaking through, and then taking over. His last communications were floridly insane, even though they were still echoing with lucid, albeit now too shrill, commentary. His mind finally lost its balance, and his last penned images and metaphors were out of control with grandiosity. He was now shrieking and howling with madness. One day, in this state, he saw a horse being harshly flogged in the street. History reports that he approached the horse, put his arms around its neck in a heartrending scene of commiseration, one injured animal embracing another, and collapsed. Herr Professor Nietzsche was taken away and was never again seen or heard philosophizing. After eleven years of increasingly silent madness, he died on August 25, 1900.

It is no easy matter to take up the thought of eternal return where Niet-zsche left it and to move forward with it. It is therefore no accident and no sur-prise that, with a few arguable exceptions, Nietzsche scholarship generally has done little to advance the thought by as much as an inch. No Nietzsche student has ever produced a more or less comprehensive and viable set of coherent ideas around the thought of eternal return that also was rigorously faithful to Niet-zsche's own texts. As a result, there is no well articulated, communicable, per-suasive, or even imaginable philosophy of eternal return. With few exceptions, Nietzsche commentators have tended to conclude that even though the idea of a philosophy based on eternal return perhaps may have promised much while Nietzsche was thinking about it, it delivered little in the way of convincing argument. Many scholars have elected not to deal with eternal return at all, even though it is central in Nietzsche's thinking, as he himself insisted and as any careful reader has to see. The majority of those who have tried to come to grips with it have concluded that it fails as an idea that would have any credi-bility or relevance. From a systematic review of such criticism, it is possible to compile an assortment of recurring opinions. Most of these lead to the conclu-sion that eternal return is untenable, illogical, undemonstrable, or unverifiable—perhaps even all four at once. It usually is considered practically irrelevant even if it were proven true, which has not happened. At best what survives critical scrutiny is a set of negative conclusions, according to which it probably is *not* possible to prove that eternal return is *impossible* and therefore *untrue*. But even so, it is considered irrelevant, because if it were true then we would not and could not know about it, since such knowledge would establish a difference between the state of what is repeated and the state that knows about this very repetition. Therefore, even if eternal return is true, and nothing says that it is, it becomes a matter of complete indifference. So it would seem that, in spite of all the smoke surrounding eternal return, there is perhaps no fire after all. And yet . . .

There are certain real and common facts of everyday life that do suggest, in spite of seemingly persuasive proof to the contrary, that eternal return is perhaps true after all—and potentially very relevant and promising indeed. A case in point appears in Nietzsche's own writings, in *Thus Spoke Zarathustra*. One day, Zarathustra, Nietzsche's fictional character who teaches eternal return, makes what seems an innocent enough discovery about himself. It is the kind of dis-covery any man or woman could make—and does make, routinely. It turns out to have momentous implications. As Zarathustra was climbing the mountains, he was thinking about how often since the days of his youth he had wandered alone, and about how many mountains and ridges and peaks he had climbed. "I am a wanderer and a mountain climber," he said to himself, ". . . whatever may yet come to me as destiny and experience will include some wandering and mountain climbing." And then comes his great insight: "In the end, one experi-ences only oneself." This changes everything, even though it also changes nothing: "The time is gone when mere accidents could still happen to me, and what could still come to me that was not mine already? What returns, what finally comes home to me, is my own self and what of myself has long been in strange lands and scattered among all things and accidents."

Zarathustra's discovery of spontaneously recurring behavior and experience patterns in his personal life is archetypal—timeless and universal, as old and characteristic as humanity itself. It is the kind of discovery that everyone who lives long enough to become even minimally self-aware is likely to make at some point in time, if not repeatedly. Zarathustra's discovery is about suddenly and unexpectedly seeing a connection between self and destiny as a kind of personal mini-revelation, a private Delphic oracle. It is about seeing a connection between past experience and personal identity, between character traits and likely future history, between inner events and the particular external environment in which they play themselves out. It is about seeing a connection between seeming accidents and the unconscious but compulsive fulfillment of personal dramas, between the apparent randomness of events and their invisible yet inherent inevitability, between a personal inner world and the public setting of external circumstances that one selects to match it, and between individual likes, dislikes, tastes, or values and the social and moral circle one draws around oneself as a personal horizon. Above all, Zarathustra's discovery is about the discovery of a sense of self-identity that is autonomous, that is not in his control but in control of him, and that is as it were fully separate from him—as if it were an alien force or being. His sense of identity is simultaneously lost and regained when he makes this discovery. It is first lost as he loses the illusion of being the one who is fully, and fully consciously, in charge. At the same time, it is regained as something that is almost other than him, something to which he becomes identical by being identified with it. In the process of this simultaneous loss and gain, he first becomes estranged from himself but then better acquainted with himself. It is as if he suddenly recognized in his own familiar features those of a twinlike double never before known but unexpectedly returned home to live with him from now on, at all times. Zarathustra's discovery also shows that what Nietzsche proposes in the way of a questionable speculative philosophy based on eternal return occurs spontaneously in everyday life events. It is enacted in the form of automatically, and largely unconsciously, repeated experience and behavior patterns. The macrocosm of a universal principle of eternal return plays itself out, spontaneously and in spite of all logical argument and proof to the contrary, in the microcosm of individual lives. So eternal return turns out to be true after all. It is true not because it is proven true from the start, a priori, and as proposed, but by *becoming* a truth, a lived truth that is realized on the scale of personal life history.

It is entirely legitimate to approach the thought of eternal return in this fashion, by looking to ordinary life for its confirmation. Nietzsche himself does this. In one case, he has Zarathustra describe an adult experience as being uncannily identical to the memory of a long-forgotten childhood experience, making the new event an exact repetition of that earlier event. Elsewhere, Nietzsche writes about fixed character traits that cause the same kinds of experiences to repeat themselves again and again. So it is indeed Nietzsche himself who sets the precedent for looking at eternal return from the vantage point of events and experiences that are borrowed from daily life.

The idea that eternal return belongs as much to the sphere of lived events from everyday life as to that of philosophical propositions also is suggested by the circumstances in which the thought first occurred to Nietzsche. It first came to him in a setting that was itself marked by a pattern of rigid and literal repetition. Day after day, Nietzsche was taking the same walk, around the same bay, at the same time, along the same path and amid the same scenery when the thought of eternal return's teacher, Zarathustra, first occurred to him. The rarified idea of a philosophy based on eternal return belongs naturally in a setting where concretely lived repetition is the norm and the main event. It originates there as if that setting were its natural habitat.

Even without Nietzsche's own references to everyday experiences of repetition, and without the circumstances of the thought's origins, it would be legitimate to see analogies between eternal return as a potentially universal principle and as concrete repetition. That is because man is, by his very nature and by virtue of the human condition, an eternal analogist. The life of the individual's personal experiences is always understood, because always imagined, in analogy to external events. As Plato had Socrates say a long time ago—in the state analogy that forms the basis of the *Republic*—whatever we think we understand about the life of the soul we imagine as resemblance between the intangible events of the soul and the tangible events we see around us. Similarly, the propositions we parade as universal philosophical principles are drawn by analogy with strictly individual states, which philosophical genius transposes into universal laws. As Nietzsche put it, every philosophy, every school of thought, every morality is merely the ingenious transposition of an individual state of mind or state of health into a language that would prescribe its own beliefs for everyone. Whatever we believe to be the case about anything is what the make-believe of resemblances, analogies, comparisons, or metaphors allows us to imagine and encourages us to imagine. Periodically, someone then comes along who reminds us with a jolt how uncanny it is that, to use Oscar Wilde's way of putting it, life imitates art more than the other way around.

Nowhere in the lives of ordinary people is eternal return more real than in those compulsively repeated behavior and experience patterns that thwart their lives and that send them in despair to the offices of psychologists and psychiatrists, in hopes that they can stop these personal vicious circles. Here every individual life is, as it were, a self-contained eternity based on repetition. Every repetition compulsion places the person in the role of Sisyphus, forever doomed to go again and again through the same thing. Just as in the case of Sisyphus, eternal return is the way to spell eternal damnation—nothing but the horror of endlessly repeated futile gestures, with no way out and with no end in sight. This is indeed a case in point of eternal return having become an inescapable personal truth and law: "The eternal hourglass of existence is turned upside down again and again, and you with it, speck of dust!"

Nothing is more horrifying to the cultural sensibilities of the Judeo-Christian West than the idea of abolishing linear time and of replacing it with a principle of eternal repetition. Yet this is precisely what Nietzsche proposed in the thought of eternal return. It also is what happens in the repetition compulsions that bring psychotherapy patients everywhere to the doorsteps of their treaters. The rule that governs here is the inescapable law of repetition, the law that turns life into an endless series of reruns involving familiar and fixed patterns of behavior and experience. Time and again the individual in the grip of such a repetition compulsion sees the return of the same old scenarios from past personal history, of the same old private dramas being lived over and over. These recurring scenarios are marked by the same interaction patterns, the same types of relationships, the same symptoms, and the same unchanging personality style leading always to the same outcomes or the same automatic thoughts that are always accompanied by the same feelings. There is no longer a sense of beginning, middle, or end. There is no longer a sense of purpose or goal to one's life other than repetition itself. There is no hope for change, no prospect of a better future, and nothing to expect other than repetition itself and all that is repeated. A life ruled by such a repetition compulsion indeed would have to be seen as Hell on earth—unless one could somehow, and by an as yet unimaginable philosophical trick or tour de force, become so well disposed to one's life to crave nothing more fervently than its eternal return. Eternal repetition would have to mean eternal damnation—unless one could, as Albert Camus put it in *The Myth of Sisyphus*, imagine Sisyphus happy. In the absence of such a philosophical trick or tour de force that would make Sisyphus happy, the experience of endless repetition, with life going nowhere but in circles, becomes the supreme form and symbol of meaninglessness. It becomes the formula of evil itself. Without a way to redeem a life as it has been and as it is, the thought, and especially the experience, of its eternal return becomes the supreme form of life's nausea with itself. Many a life chokes on itself in this fashion, out of sheer repulsion. This also explains the common reaction to eternal return among most Nietzsche readers: to spit it out as indigestible. It explains as well the despair of life and the attraction of suicide, which psychologists and psychiatrists see all too often in their patients when life is overtaken by eternal repetition.

Now, says Nietzsche, this reaction of horror at the thought and at the experience of eternal return is the clearest, most elegant way of exposing the fundamental Judeo-Christian hatred and devaluation of life as it is. For if life as it is were judged a good thing, so the Nietzschean argument goes, then its eternal return would have to be seen as a supreme good. Conversely, only when existence as it actually is is judged a bad thing can the idea of its eternal repetition be seen as symbol and expression of supreme evil. It is precisely to compensate for this negative value assigned to existence that Judeo-Christian doctrine promises another existence, one that will be better than the one at hand. That better state comes at, and *as*, the end of linear history—whether at the end of the life of the deserving individual or at the end of the collective history of a chosen and deserving people. Therefore, the facts of the repetition compulsion in the life of the individual—like the idea of a Nietzschean philosophy of eternal return at the level of the West's collective consciousness—put Western men and women on a collision course with their culture's inherited sensibilities. The collision is involuntary and cannot be avoided at will. Just as it is with Nietzsche's being chosen to think eternal return without having a choice about being so chosen, so too is it with every man and woman who is overtaken by compulsive repetition. These compulsions are just that: compulsions. Which means they are inescapable. They are, indeed, as every anonymous alcoholic eventually calls them, a greater power. One could not be blamed for thinking that eternal return must be the devil's own invention. It comes therefore as no surprise to find that it is indeed with the figure of a demon who speaks about eternal return that Nietzsche first introduced the thought to his readers. So it is clear that if eternal return appears as horrifyingly satanic as it does, then this is in large part because of the Judeo-Christian negative value judgment of existence that is involved. If existence as it actually is has to be improved, and if it can only be sufficiently improved by ending it as we know it and by replacing it with an altogether very different alternative, then that is so because it is negated, judged not good enough as it is from the start, intrinsically. If eternal return feels like a horror only the Devil himself could imagine then it is because of life's nausea with itself.

And here, then, is the agenda that Nietzsche hoped to realize with a philosophy of eternal return: to overcome that fundamental, and negative, value judgment. This explains his sphinx of a question, from *The Gay Science*'s aphorism 341: How well disposed would you have to become toward life—and how would you manage to become so well disposed—to welcome the thought of eternal return and to crave for a way to make it true? Nietzsche began to answer his own question by way of a New Year's resolution, formulated in aphorism 276 of the same *Gay Science*. On the first day of January of the year 1882 he wished himself a Happy New Year. It was no ordinary wish, not even an ordinary New Year's wish. Rather, it was a great philosophical wish—not only for himself but for all people, and not only for the new calendar year but for the Great New Year of a new philosophical dawn and age. Here, in Nietzsche's view, is the best of all possible New Year's resolutions for the West: "I want to learn more and more to see as beautiful what is necessary in things; then I shall be one of those who make things beautiful." He explains what he means: "*Amor fati*: let that be my love henceforth! I do not want to wage war against what is ugly. I do not want to accuse. I do not even want to accuse those who accuse. . . . And all in all and on the whole: some day I wish to be only a Yes-sayer."

Such would have to be the great New Year's resolution of any man or woman who wishes to meet the world, and his or her own existence, with an unconditionally affirmative judgment. It involves a love declaration based on *amor fati*—the love of destiny—that affirms every thing, every event, every moment, just as it is given and for the way it is given. *Amor fati*, in turn, requires the ability to affirm "what is necessary in things." Necessity is, as Aristotle suggested, that because of which a thing or event cannot be otherwise than the way it is. It is, as Aquinas thought of it, "that which cannot not be"—"*quod non potest non esse*." But the necessity of things or events in the Nietzschean sense is not merely, in fact, not at all, their logical, mechanical, physical, causal, or otherwise determinist inevitability. It is something that is altogether deeper and more elusive than all of these. It is, first of all, something that cannot be objectified. It cannot be separated from events or things and pointed at, as if it were an anatomical feature or a mechanical part or function that can be positively identified and represented.

This elusive quality of necessity, including especially its refusal to be objectified, is perhaps best expressed in the way the Greek mythic figure of Ananke, goddess of Necessity, was imagined. Her unique feature, so the myth says, is that she has no temples that are dedicated to her, no altars where offerings can be made to her, no images that represent her, no tokens that objectify her, no symbols that stand in for her. Yet it is Ananke who is invisibly present in all that happens, precisely in the exact way it happens. She is what makes every thing and every event turn out as it does. She sees to it that everything in the world and in life is thus and such, exactly, and not otherwise. While she herself is invisible in all things, it is she who makes them visible in the precise way they are visible. She is present in what makes everything *just so*. It is easy to see that Ananke, or the invisible necessity in things and events that makes them as they are, is akin to, if not identical with, their injudicability. Ananke, or the elusive necessity in all things, is another name for their inability to be judged by any standard of judgment other than themselves. Thus Nietzsche's philosophical New Year's resolution, his wish to learn to affirm the necessity of events and experiences through his declaration of *amor fati*, is the same as the desire to catch a glimpse of their injudicability. Both aim at affirming events as they are and for the way they are. Both are required as essential ingredients in a philosophical outlook that would be based on eternal return.

Ananke, necessity, that which cannot not be, that because of which something cannot be otherwise—all these are intimately familiar to anyone who is in the grip of a repetition compulsion, even though they are not explicitly named as such. They exist as the frustratingly unnamable factor that can never be pointed at but that is nonetheless the most real aspect of any compulsive repetition. They exist as what feels like a demonic force that demands inescapable, eternally recurring repetition. They are what we, today, describe with our modern synonym for Ananke's natural invisibility—unconscious. It is no surprise that psychiatry uses the term *anankastic* personality disorder as synonym for the less mythic sounding and more strictly clinical and scientific term *obsessive compulsive* personality disorder. It also is no surprise that Ananke appears explicitly named in Freud's writings precisely in the context of his remarks on the unconscious psychology of compulsive repetition, in *Beyond the Pleasure Principle*.

There is one area in particular, familiar to Freud and to all Freudians after him—even to all neo-Freudians and to more non-Freudians than would probably care to acknowledge it—where Ananke almost ostentatiously displays her characteristically invisible or unconscious presence. It is an area where the usually unseen Ananke dramatically, almost theatrically and nothing short of awe inspiringly, demonstrates her irresistible force that compels events and experiences to take shape exactly as they do. This place where Ananke displays herself so uncannily visibly, even in her very invisibility, is in the special relationship that develops in psychoanalytic treatment between patient and therapist. Here a unique phenomenon occurs which Freud was first to name, describe, and attempt to explain. He called it *Übertragung,* or "transference." Transference is not merely a secondary feature of psychoanalytic treatment but its primary and identifying characteristic. Freud even went so far as to explicitly name it the defining element of psychoanalytic treatment. If transference is present, so he wrote, then the treatment is psychoanalytic in essence. If no transference is present, then no psychoanalytic treatment is taking place. In short, transference is, as Jung agreed with Freud in their first meeting in 1909, the "alpha and omega" in the treatment of the unconscious soul. It is the process in the relation between patient and psychotherapist in which the patient spontaneously and inevitably, but unconsciously, repeats certain old and fixed interaction scenarios, along with their associated emotions. It is the process in which personal history is compelled to repeat itself within the artificial containment of the treatment setting. All that has ever had and that continues to have special emotional significance in the patient's life is repeated in the two-person play with the treater. It is as though in transference the patient must indeed live under the command of the Nietzschean demon who proposes the law of eternal return and who says: "This life as you now live it and have lived it, you will have to live once more and innumerable times more; and there will be nothing new in it, but every pain and every joy and every thought and sigh and everything unutterably small or great in your life will have to return to you . . ."

Transference is eternal return come true. Nowhere in the world, and nowhere in life, is eternal return more unquestionably real. Nowhere is it more fateful. But also, nowhere is eternal return more promising than in transference, for here it also is the avenue toward a realization of *amor fati* and of the life-affirming New Year's resolution it entails. Transference offers Everyman a chance to achieve what Nietzsche promised but did not fulfill. It is indeed not only the diabolical curse of psychoanalytic treatment, although for the patient it is that at first and, indeed, for the greater part of the process. As Freud discovered and proposed, transference also is the means whereby psychoanalytic treatment promises to be a potential agent of cure. But here we are more interested in the potential for a philosophical convalescence than in a strictly psychiatric one.

Transference works by making visible what was previously invisible, or, as we say, unconscious. All that may long have appeared accidental in a person's experiences, and determined by unique events and circumstances, now begins to show the outlines of a pattern. This pattern, it now also becomes apparent, has been repeating itself and continues to repeat itself in identical fashion and across a variety of settings. It has remained unchanged in spite of changes in setting, changes in circumstances, and changes in the cast of players involved. Now it plays itself out in transference, and with the therapist as co-star in a variety of roles according to the scenarios being reenacted. This is why psychoanalysis and Zarathustra make the same discovery, that in the realm of personal experiences and behaviors there are no accidents. Whatever comes to us as private experience was destined to be ours. Whatever it is that comes our way is a personal psychological destiny we call a "self." Everything about that self, as Zarathustra puts it, "has long been in strange lands and scattered among all things and accidents." It is easy to see that the fixed experience patterns that become visible through the repetition compulsion of transference are about the perpetual reenactment of private metaphors that are one's personal destiny. They amount to personal equations that take ever-changing sets of variables and historical circumstances and that automatically arrange them into meaningful, but static, patterns of significance. No matter what is entered as X or Y in these equations, the patterns themselves remain the same. They are the laws whose perpetual reenactment has been, and continues to be, the stuff of one's personal history. What transference does, through the offices of the treater who helps make these patterns recognizable to the patient, is identify the equations that are at work.

These private and fixed scenarios occur not only in pathological conditions. They are as much a part of personality traits that are fully accepted, and of behavior patterns that lead to personal success, as they are a part of the more challenging repetition compulsion that brings psychotherapy patients to treatment and of the transference they develop in it. What each individual reexperiences again and again in this fashion, and what he or she suffers in the repetition compulsion that creates transference, is therefore less "reminiscences of the past," as Freud said in the early *Studies on Hysteria*, than the fixed and personalized metaphors that are his or her destiny. These fixed metaphors that are reenacted again and again, "once more and innumerable times more," become the personal myths by which each individual lives. Man the analogist and esteemer is also man the metaphorist and myth maker.

Now all ancient Greek tragedy, so Nietzsche said in his first book, *The Birth of Tragedy,* which set the stage, tone, and scope for all his later thinking, is about one thing only: the perpetual process of the universe bringing things into being and then destroying them again. It is about the world as a self-perpetuating and self-affirming life force whose great creative game is one of the unending appearance of new things and of their endless disappearance in destruction. It is about existence as permanent impermanence. Every individual tragedy is a variation on that theme, a case in point. Behind each tragedy, Nietzsche went on to say, and as the defining feature of tragedy itself, is the interplay of Apollo and Dionysos. Apollo is god of plastic arts. He is devoted to the constant and creative appearance of individualized forms, events, and manifestations of life. In contrast to him, yet coexisting with him in tragedy, is Dionysos, who personifies and dramatizes the intoxicating spirit that joins all people in music, and for whom all forms of life participate in the same unifying spirit of life itself. Dionysos insists not on the individual differences that make for individual and semipermanent identities but on the oneness of all individual forms of Being. He is the mystic for whom all forms of life are one, and who wipes out all individual uniqueness. He requires the annihilation of individuality itself. Not surprisingly, his own myth is a story of being endlessly reborn and endlessly destroyed. After Dionysos, who serves as prototype, every tragic figure, each individual hero on the theatrical stage, so Nietzsche continued, is an incarnation of this endless interplay between Apollo and Dionysos. Every tragedy is, on the one hand, about the drive toward individuation and the impermanent permanence of all manifestations of life, and, on the other hand, about the spirit of Dionysos, who affirms existence itself and who says Yes even to pain, sorrow, death, and destruction. Above all, Greek tragedy is about what Nietzsche described as the greatest seduction ever, the eternal seduction that "seduces us into a continuation of existence." It is the formalized and ritualized expression of man's desire and insistence to be perpetually seduced in this fashion, under the spell of Dionysos, even though existence surrounds us everywhere and daily with reminders that all existence is impermanent. Tragedy is, first and last, about the human affirmation of Being and of man's participation in Being. In sum, Greek tragedy affirms everything, including impermanence itself, instead of devaluing everything worldly for being transitory, and instead of thereby creating the need for a better and permanent world elsewhere and at some other time. It is a cultural or collective declaration of *amor fati.* This explains Nietzsche's early decision, and his lifelong goal, to make his philosophy a form of life-affirming, tragic philosophizing in the name, and under the sign, of Dionysos. He never turned back on that decisive goal.

The same theme that unifies all Greek tragedy is present at the heart of transference and its repetition compulsion, in spite of the endless variations of all the scenarios that are repeated in it. For the repetition compulsion, too, is about permanent impermanence, and about the human value judgment that judges permanent impermanence. What is at stake in transference and in the eternal return that fuels it is, like classical Greek tragedy, the human confrontation with the drama of discovering the impermanence of all things. Eternal return, in its lived form as the repetition compulsion of transference, is a case in point of the essential plot that defines all tragedy. The repetition compulsion, as a means that allows man to become reconciled with his life, is itself an enactment of the Dionysian spirit within whose power it lies to affirm existence in spite of all human suffering. Freud explains what is at stake.

Compulsive repetition, so he suggests, is a paradox of man being reminded, again and again, of his ultimate vulnerability, even while he is simultaneously trying to reject that realization by repressing it. This paradox itself is reflected in the paradox of transference, in which the fixed experience and behavior patterns that are unconscious and therefore invisible to the patient are plainly visible to the observing treater who watches them unfold in his presence. The source of the repression that keeps these patterns unconscious is not only the dread of the emotional pain that is associated with memories of past events. Beyond that, the source of the ongoing repression is the dread of mortality or impermanence itself, the ultimate in vulnerability, of which personal emotional drama and trauma are the harbingers. Unconscious compulsive repetition represents a stalemate in this confrontation between the recognition of human mortality and the repression of that recognition. It serves at the same time to help the individual forget what he or she wants to forget and to remind him or her, again and again, of what he or she means to repress.

What is reenacted here, in the lives of ordinary men and women, is nothing less than the myth of Sisyphus. Punished by the gods to exist forever in Tartaros, the deepest pit in the underworld, he must eternally push a rock up a hill, only to see it roll down time and again in an absurd scenario of eternal repetition. Sisyphus earned this fate as a result of his persistent attempts to cheat the immortal gods and to be like them by trying to avoid his own death. He personifies the lifelong history of resistance against the acceptance of death. Homer tells how Sisyphus put the mythic figure of Hades, or Death, in chains, thereby making it impossible for him, or anyone else, to die. Ares, god of warfare, could not tolerate this. He went to liberate Death from the hands of its would-be conqueror, thereby defeating Sisyphus in spite of his cleverness. Yet before being sent to Hades, Sisyphus instructed his wife, Merope, not to bury his corpse. This was yet another trick, for without proper burial of the corpse, no soul can settle in Hades for good. Arriving in the realm of Death, Sisyphus then successfully pleaded with Persephone, queen of the underworld, to let him return to life on earth in order to avenge his death. Sisyphus thus escaped the underworld yet again, and then simply refused to return to it. Finally, the gods lost their patience with him, and so Sisyphus earned his famous punishment of an absurd existence of eternal compulsive repetition in the deepest pit of the underworld. His humanly absurd ambition to escape death thus met with a divine, yet hellish, punishment of endlessly absurd repetition. His insistent and repeated attempt to repress death, in vain, earned him his fate of an eternity of effort expended in vain. As Camus put it, in his commentary on the myth of Sisyphus, he becomes an image of the whole human being exerting itself toward accomplishing nothing.

The Sisyphean resistance against accepting the vulnerability to death animates the eternal return in the repetition compulsion, for that resistance is not so much resistance to the suffering associated with painful memories cast into the oblivion of unconsciousness as it is an attempt to repress that of which pain and suffering are reminders, the fact of human mortality. If it is about resistance to pain and suffering, then that is mainly because they are the harbingers of the ultimate in vulnerability, annihilation. Sisyphus and the eternal return of the repetition compulsion that becomes visible in transference, and that reenacts his myth, embody the opposite of the Dionysian spirit who affirms existence in spite of pain, suffering, destruction, and death.

Psychoanalytic treatment becomes possible precisely through the eternal return of the repetition compulsion. It is indeed, as Freud said, through transference, and therefore through the repetition compulsion that makes transference possible in the first place, that psychoanalysis holds the possibility of convalescence. But now it becomes clear that the convalescence that is at stake is about more than overcoming symptoms. What is at stake is the overcoming of man's Sisyphean resistance against accepting the impermanence of all things, and of his own life first of all. While the repetition compulsion of transference is placed in the service of the Freudian agenda of making conscious what is unconscious, this is, as Freud emphasized, no mere intellectual exercise. It is neither a matter of educating the patient about repression and what is repressed, nor one of merely making interpretations about what symptoms mean. Such a simplistic approach amounts to the blunder of what Freud called "wild psychoanalysis." Merely intellectual cleverness of this kind ends up serving as further defense against the inevitable. It has the paradoxical effect of making for more repression, not less. It is not enough for a patient to become intellectually informed about recognizable patterns of experience, and about their compulsive repetition. It is not enough, as Sisyphus learned, to be clever and armed with a bag full of tricks to ward off what cannot be escaped. It is therefore not enough to make ingenious suggestions about how recurring symptoms perhaps may be outsmarted with imaginative tricks of all sorts. But it also is not enough to simply "feel the pain," as some psychological treaters insist, possibly on the belief that if emotion per se is good then more emotion is perhaps even better. What is involved above all these is a fundamentally mysterious demand, the demand to willingly, with trust in one's heart and faith on one's mind—and as it were repeating Abraham's irrational readiness to give up his son Isaac—sacrifice oneself to a personal but also universal drama of essential vulnerability and impermanence. The convalescence that psychoanalysis holds out as promise is one that can only be achieved in one's willingness to die. Beyond all reasonable expectations, and beyond all possible explanations, it is precisely what threatens to kill in the repetition compulsion that also leads to a restoration to life, repeating the Dionysian eternal cycle of death and rebirth.

That is why treatment based on the repetition compulsion is no undertaking involving a game of merely clever trickery, with ingenious intellectual inventions and interventions. It is not meant for the likes of Sisyphus. It is not meant for those who are chronically resentful about being a mere mortal, in a universe ruled by motifs and scenarios that are personified as gods who outlast individuality and all the individual lives in which they fulfill themselves again and again, whenever they want it, and for no other reason than that they want it. The gods laugh at the ingenious trickery of Sisyphean cleverness. They are not impressed by it. They eventually become annoyed with it and use their own, and much more fateful, trickery to make the point that it is they who are the greater power.

The promise of convalescence inherent in the repetition compulsion is in the end about more than becoming conscious of what is unconscious—which may even be irrelevant. It is about being finite and limited, a mortal after all. It is about not being able to be everything. It is about only being able to be who one is and must become, and not someone else or something else. It is about not being able to be fundamentally different from who one is and who one must spend a lifetime becoming. It is about no other existence being possible, in spite of all long-lasting efforts to deny this, reject this, repress this, or escape this. It is about abandoning the narcissism of hoping against hope that one can somehow, with the right magical trick, become immortal—"deathless," a god.

The individual who goes through this transformative process is often rewarded with the discovery that Zarathustra makes. The horror of seeing oneself become estranged from oneself, or from who one thought one was or should be—by autonomous forces that seem alien, that are totally outside the realm of one's control, and that govern one's existence—this horror is overcome with a new found sense of personal destiny. More importantly, there also is an acceptance of the task of becoming who one is. At the level of everyday living, or at the level of the slow process of psychological treatment, this comes down to the transformative alchemy of making peace with the personal differences in character and in the history of one's experiences that make one both unique and uniquely vulnerable.

Another way to imagine these matters, and a deceptively pedestrian way of putting it, is as Nietzsche did in a seemingly flat-footed remark. It is a remark one must, as always with Nietzsche, take as a metaphor built from the images of everyday living. For that is how one thinks on behalf of the soul, by developing an ear and a knack for metaphor. As Aristotle put it in a comment on the art of dream interpretation, the person best suited for this art is the one who has the gift to listen and to speak metaphorically. With that in mind, one may glean what Nietzsche means when he counsels: "It is sensible for anyone to develop further in himself the *talent* upon which his father and grandfather expended effort and not to turn to something completely new, otherwise he will make it impossible for himself to achieve perfection in any trade at all. That is why the proverb says: 'What road should you take?—the road of your forebears.'" This is not, contrary to first appearances, erroneous Lamarckian evolution theory about the inheritance and furtherance of acquired and frequently practiced traits. It certainly is not about simpleminded vocational or behavioral counseling. Rather, it is about alchemical confidence and faith that gold can be made from anything, because it is inherent everywhere and because alchemical gold making is precisely about working with what is at hand.

This, then, is what the repetition compulsion can do. It can provide the means for human nature to come face-to-face, and come to terms, with the essential fact of the human condition. It provides individual human beings with an opportunity to face the sphinx of the thought of eternal return without being eaten alive by it. It provides each person with an opportunity to develop an affirmative view of existence and to come to a personal declaration of *amor fati*.

THREE

SPLENDOR BEYOND
GOOD AND EVIL

THE PRE-SOCRATIC GREEK PHILOSOPHER, Heraclitus, said that "to the gods all things are good and beautiful and just," and that "it is men who call some things good and others bad." What separates gods from humans in this view is less the usual matter of immortality than a matter of value judgment. To us humans there are many things in the world that do not seem so good and beautiful and just at all but that look rather bad, ugly, and unfair, if not outright evil. There is too much suffering in the world, making human existence, even under the best of circumstances, difficult. Sometimes it seems frankly too much to handle. One does not have to be insane or clinically depressed to have felt despair at some point in time. A little suffering can be overlooked. More than a little can be accepted in good faith as long as there is enough happiness to make up for it. But too many individuals, and too many peoples, know more suffering than can be compensated for with any such consolation prize. One great personal pain—and everyone comes to know at least one—is enough to leave emotional scar tissue that remains forever raw to the touch. One Holocaust per history is too much to still speak about everything in creation being good and beautiful and just. Since we are humans, not gods, it is difficult for us to say that everything always looks so fine. Ah, but the very thought of such a possibility!

Nietzsche was drawn to nothing less than the thought of that very possibility. He did not envy the gods their immortality, as Sisyphus did, but he wanted human beings to be able to see the splendor that gods could see beyond all human distinctions of good and evil. He took it upon himself to meet the challenge of thinking this thought head on. He did so in the boldest fashion, and as one who, for the sake of this self-appointed and almost, by definition, superhuman task, set himself apart from virtually everything and everybody in the Judeo-Christian West's history of ideas. This made him among the loneliest Western philosophers and human beings ever. The one kindred spirit he sometimes mentioned was the distant Heraclitus himself. Other than Heraclitus there was no human being with whom he could identify, or who he felt could possibly identify with him. The only figure who could serve as his model, and who did so throughout his entire career as a thinker and writer, was Dionysos. This god of life's perpetual cycles of death and rebirth who affirms all of existence, in spite of all eternal fluctuations of pain and joy, in spite of his own legendary story of perpetual dismemberment and rebirth, became Nietzsche's *spiritus rector*, his guiding spirit.

Nietzsche thought that much of the history of Western philosophy after Heraclitus was responsible for depriving man of the means to live up to his maximum potential, by depriving him of the ideal of that potential. He thought this was especially the case for that vastly greater part of Western philosophy that was grafted on Platonism and shaped by Judeo-Christian hopes for an otherworldly and afterworldly life. As a result, said Nietzsche, Western men and women were confined to an existence they could only imagine as wanting, as not good enough. Existence was considered wanting because of the impermanence of all things. This was held up as proof of their ultimately negative intrinsic value. Existence was judged less than good enough because of the inability of all things and all events to justify themselves by themselves. So wanting was it felt to be that a better, a perfect, a perfectly immaterial existence had to be dreamed up. That other life, so it was hoped and believed, would compensate man after his earthly life for all the worldly imperfection endured for so long. Supernatural redemption became necessary, and the noblest thing anyone could possibly strive to become was an improver of the world and an improver of mankind itself.

So imperfect was existence felt to be that nothing worse could be imagined than the thought of having to live one's life over and over again, just as it had been, and without any change in it or escape from it. For many men and women the thought of such an endless existence based on eternal repetition would have to be the most demonic idea and the most horrifyingly meaningless form of existence that is at all imaginable. One probably would curse whoever even suggested the thought, and curse the thought itself—unless, for one reason or another, one could say to whoever proposed it, and as Nietzsche imagined: "You are a god, and never have I heard anything more divine." Such a response, if it were humanly possible, would bring one closer in spirit to what Heraclitus had long ago identified as a divine prerogative—the ability to see all of creation as inherently positive in value, and therefore self-justified.

It was Nietzsche's hope and agenda to formulate a philosophy that would make this possibility a human possibility. That is what is behind the great New Year's resolution he uttered to himself and to the world one day, and with which he intended to mark the dawn of a new age, for a new type of human being: "to learn more and more to see as beautiful what is necessary in things," and so "to become one of those who make things beautiful."

Halfway or so between the ancient, pagan Heraclitus and the postmodern, anti-Christian Nietzsche stands Augustine. Almost a millennium after Heraclitus, and a millennium and a half before Nietzsche, he expressed a thought that links him to both. In his autobiographical and contemplative *Confessions* he addressed his God in prayer in this manner:

> For you evil does not exist, and not only for you but for the whole of your creation as well, because there is nothing outside it which could invade it and break down the order which you have imposed on it. Yet in the separate parts of your creation there are some things which we think of as evil because they are at variance with other things. But there are other things again with which they are in accord, and then they are good. . . . And since this is so, I no longer wished for a better world, because I was thinking of the whole of creation. . . . Though the higher things are better than the lower, the sum of all creation is better than the higher things alone.

The central idea in Augustine's prayer—"I no longer wished for a better world"—is equivalent to Nietzsche's declaration of *amor fati,* or love of all that was and is. It virtually is identical to Nietzsche's desire and declaration of intent "to learn more and more to see as beautiful what is necessary in things." Augustine, prince among Christians, was motivated by the same desire, preoccupied with the same thought and aiming at the same goal as Christianity's later and self-styled fiercest opponent. Instead of a clash of titans we have an unexpected communion of spirits. Nietzsche and Augustine aimed at changing not the world but themselves, particularly their way of evaluating the world. They did not aim at transforming the world for the sake of improving it or otherwise making it a better place in which to live. Their aim was to transform their perspective on it, their attitude toward existence in it. Above all, they aimed at changing the value judgment that man had learned to place on the world and on existence.

What makes a transvaluation of the value judgment imposed on the world possible, and what makes all the difference for both Augustine's and Nietzsche's purpose—for here again they are in agreement—is the distinction between what Augustine called "the sum of all creation" versus "the separate parts." By themselves some parts of existence look good, while others look ugly. Only from a perspective that is more panoramic and that encompasses a sense of the whole can all of existence be affirmed. For Augustine all of creation is one self-contained manifestation of Being that is perfect in itself and in its totality. It is perfect in spite of the appearance of parts that seem good and others that seem bad. The perfection of the universe cannot be broken down, in Augustine's view, neither by anything outside of it nor by anything inside of it. For

Nietzsche, all things and events are endlessly varied partial manifestations of an underlying and fundamentally Dionysian spirit that is present everywhere. For him, all fragmented things are united in the spirit of a multiform but nonetheless unified force that animates the universe and all life in it. Even the distinction between pleasure and pain falls away for Nietzsche. It is overcome by a Yes-saying spirit that affirms all. In sum, in both Nietzsche and Augustine, the totality is even better than the best parts.

But even though Augustine and Nietzsche have much in common in their desire to overcome the devaluation of the world in the court of human judgment, their proposal for a solution differs—substantially and irreconcilably. Nietzsche would have us affirm impermanence itself. He insisted that we lift ourselves up, as it were by our own bootstraps, by making a purely human reassessment of the world's value. But he realized that man, as he found him—thoroughly Christianized in his prejudice against existence—would have to radically change in order to reassess the world in this affirmative fashion. This explains the need for a new prototype of man, and for the figure of Zarathustra, who presents this new type in outline. Nietzsche would have man claim his natural birthright and would have him reach for the vision of a world that is affirmed in its totality. But Nietzsche himself ran out of steam and became mad before he accomplished his goal of a viable, affirmative philosophy for the new prototype of man to live by. Augustine, in contrast to Nietzsche, did not think that man could come to a purely affirmative view of the universe on his own. A previous type of human being, living a life now no longer possible for man, had been able to see the world's sheer splendor without impediments. That earlier human condition, so Augustine imagined, was long lost. It had been lost when man turned away from God. In the human condition as we know it since then, the soul has become permanently turned away from the sight and the contemplation of the perfection of God's universe. Ever since that time man has only been able to see what we now call "history," which includes what psychotherapists everywhere now tend to consider the bedrock of the soul's reality, psychosocial history. If the soul is ever to see that perfection again it would have to be returned to the contemplation of the divine. To regain the lost original condition, or to return to the soul's original perspective and view, so Augustine suggested, is man's ultimate good. His soul's deepest longing is to find itself restored to that old but lost vision of splendor and perfection. But, so he also suggested, man himself, man by himself, is incapable of bringing about that change in the soul's constitution and therefore in the human condition. Such a change in man requires divine intervention, divine redemption.

In summary, then, Heraclitus had thought that a purely affirmative view of human existence on earth was imaginable as a divine prejudice but not achievable as a human reality. Augustine saw it as a theoretical human potential but felt he could not promise it because it depends on the gift of divine intervention. Man can accept such intervention when it is given, but he cannot bring it about at will, by his own efforts or simply by wanting it or demanding it. Nietzsche insisted that man, on his own, can achieve a purely affirmative judgment of existence, one that is modeled after Dionysos, god and mystic of life's self-affirmation. But Nietzsche failed to deliver on his promise of a philosophy that succeeds in doing this. So the Heraclitean division that separates human beings from their gods, due to irreconcilable differences in perspective and prejudice, remains in force. And yet . . .

Brief glimpses of what the world begins to look like from a perspective that is somewhat better capable of viewing the larger picture are nonetheless possible—even from the human position. One utterly human instance of this potential is the biblical figure of Job. Job was a legendary figure even in his own time, and before the ordeal that turned him into the hero of the book that is named after him. He was the wealthiest man in his region. He lived an exemplary life and followed the laws of his God and his society. His community revered him. Not surprisingly, he was regarded, and he regarded himself, as a man whom God had blessed. And Job said thanks for all of it, all the time, in pious fear and in the full knowledge that his fate was a gift from God's hands, not something of his own doing.

Then one day, in a wager with Satan, and for no apparent reason other than just to make a point, God knowingly offered Job up to Satan, who set out in short order to bring Job down from his good fortune and to test his loyalty to his God. One by one, and in quick succession, Satan took away all that was dear to Job. And so he lost his wealth, his herds of animals, his stables and buildings, even his servants and children. Still Job remained pious. Satan then proceeded, again with God's permission, to torment Job in person, by covering him from head to toe with painful boils and leaving him in a constant state of agony while also withholding from him the relief of death. Even so, Job still tried to hold on to his legendary patience and piety, but at long last they gave way.

Giving voice to all his pain Job cried out the most heartrending cry of anguish that is at all possible for a human being and screamed the most blasphemous curse thinkable: "God damn the day I was born! . . . Let it never have been created!" Continuing in the same painful vein, he then impotently wished that he could undo the very day of his own creation, and thus the fact of his forced participation in creation: "On that day let there be darkness. . . . Let it sink back into the void. . . . Let chaos overpower it. . . . Let black clouds overwhelm it. . . . Let the sun be plucked from its sky. . . . Let the other days disown it. . . . Let the Serpent blast it with eternal blight. . . . Let its dawn never arrive . . ." This is nothing less than a precise scenario, by a blaspheming human being, for a kind of Genesis in reverse that is aimed at undoing God's own work and will. Job, the eternally pious man of long and legendary patience, had become more blasphemous than even the militantly anti-Christian Nietzsche would ever manage to be, even on his worst day.

Job's unsurpassably pained curse has to be the most intensely hostile condemnation and rejection of creation that is at all possible. If personally slapping God in the face is at all doable, then this is the way to do it. It also is the most intensely felt expression of self-hatred that is at all imaginable. But it is simultaneously the most self-tormenting wish any man or woman can possibly express, and whose torment lies in the fact that it will never be granted. For one has no choice, and can have no choice, in the matter of being chosen to be born and to participate in all of existence. It is precisely because it is a wish that cannot be granted that the act of wishing it as it were doubles one's original pain, out of sheer impotence.

From that impotent outcry of pain, anguish, and outrage, Job went on to make the second wish that cannot be granted to any man or woman who is old enough to wish it. That second wish is the wish to have died immediately at birth. By expressing that second wish, Job only intensified the feeling of impotence that is expressed, and automatically redoubled, in his first wish. For not only is every human being incapable of not being born, he or she also is incapable of becoming less than fully involved in creation, as a fully engaged accomplice to the fact of existence, before he or she is even old enough to realize it. With this second wish, Job therefore doubled his pain again and quadrupled his original pain.

Then he went yet one step farther, by wishing that he could at least be released from pain by death. If I could only die, said Job, then at least "I would be at rest, I would be sound asleep . . . (for in death) . . . the troubled are calm . . . the exhausted rest. Rich and poor are alike there, and the slave lies next to his master." This wish, too, is not granted, and so his pain is once again doubled, and his original pain has now, as it were, become eightfold in its intensity. For death is not simply an over-the-counter pain relief measure, one that can be obtained and administered anywhere, at any time, at will. Nor is it simply a generic equalizer, one size fits all. Death does not come when one wants it. It first requires a personal destiny to be fulfilled. As Freud, too, would discover, and write in *Beyond the Pleasure Principle*, many centuries after Job's story was first told but also in the context of close encounters with great and deep human suffering, once one is born, dying is anything but easy. The more involved one becomes in the everyday business of living, the more difficult dying becomes. Thus death cannot be counted on at just any time. It has its own sense of timing and its own schedule to keep. It requires, as Freud insisted, a whole lifetime to accomplish it. There are no shortcuts. Nor will just any death do. Every single life must first go through its entire, individualized destiny before it arrives at the particular death that belongs to it. Every life, so Freud went on, is therefore a detour on the way to its own death, an individualized detour for a specific death and for none other.

At the heart of Job's outburst is the pure and simple fact of human suffering in a creation that is no paradise and that often seems governed by arbitrariness and meaninglessness. This can lead even reasonable people—and pious ones, such as Job—to conclude that life is unfair, that existence is full of ugliness, and that the universe is perhaps a bad place to be. What makes Job such a deeply moving figure—among the top ten or top five of all time heroes in sheer humanity—is his willingness to name, and thus feel, human suffering in its most unadulterated fashion. He even goes so far as to reject everything in the way of human consolation, hope, and rationalization that is offered to him. For that is precisely what he does to the well-meant counsel from his wife and from his three well-meaning friends, Eliphaz, Bildad, and Zophar, who try to console him. These well-meaning would-be comforters personify not only the specific arguments they propose to Job but beyond that also the totality of familiar and accepted articles of belief in any established worldview and religion. They personify what Jung considered the use of belief and knowledge as defense against genuine personal religious experience. Compared to his friends, who are mortified by Job's blaspheming and who call upon overlearned and often formulaic and sometimes frankly flat and stale religious wisdom, Job is left without any soothing man-made conveniences. And so, after God and Satan are done taking all his possessions and creature comforts away, and after he loses his children along with the hope they represent to any parent, he is left with only two more or less personal possessions, a body covered in painful boils and a pot shard, which he uses to scratch himself in an attempt to distract himself from God-given pain by inflicting self-administered pain.

Job's pot shard is a thing of little apparent meaning or value in itself, but it is loaded with psychological significance. Among other things, it serves as stark contrast to all the ideas with which human beings try to comfort themselves and try to provide comfort to other human beings who are in agony over their existence. It is the antithesis of all the important, but often ultimately impotent, words of accepted and overlearned religious wisdom and knowledge. It is all the leftovers of all human accomplishments condensed into a small piece from a mass of rubble. It is what would later reappear in Freud as the idea of residues from life past that are grating on the tormented soul's raw nerves.

Finally, when the impotence of Job's cries of pain and outrage is shown to be matched only by the impotence of human rationalizations and accepted belief, Job's God talks back to him, in the form of a Voice from a Whirlwind. Job's pained curse has struck a chord at the heart of Being itself, and it resonates with the sound of a response. The reply is a stinging rebuke of the quintessentially human demand for clear and understandable justice. But beyond that, and in the end, more importantly, it is a reminder of an issue that is larger than the human demand for justice in this world we must inhabit. The Voice from the Whirlwind replies with these words: "Who is this whose ignorant words smear my design with darkness? Stand up now like a man; I will question you: please, instruct me. Where were you when I planned the earth?" But this is not about Job being buffaloed by an overpowering force of intimidation. It is not about

Job being pounded into humiliation. It is about Job—or any man or woman—being called and prepared for the revitalization that is afforded by the discovery of true humility.

That difference, between humiliation and humility, is cardinal. Missing it is missing the crux of the Book of Job. For Job's story, as the next scenes show, is about being reminded that creation, as it is plainly visible on any given day of the week, is a many-splendored thing. It is, in modern parlance but on a biblical scale, about therapeutic "cognitive restructuring" by a kind of existential reality testing. Above all, it is not about being battered and crushed and pulverized into dust, but about being called and prepared to see that even dust—and even being dust—is as much a part of the miracle of creation as anything else in it is. It is about discovering that miraculousness is everywhere, and about being reminded of what often is difficult to see, the mystery in the seemingly obvious and the obviousness of mystery everywhere.

After the Voice from the Whirlwind makes its opening statement, there follows a catalog of images from nature that can be observed everywhere. They are images of mysteries and miracles that are daily on display for everyone to see and to appreciate: the wind, the seasons, the weather, animal instinct, the flight of birds, rain, natural rhythms and cycles, color, life, death, snow, thunderstorms, blossoms, the strength and grace of animals, grain, bird feathers, and many others. Each image is concrete, compact, bursting with miraculousness. The most miraculous thing of all is that it is all there every day—also on the worst day of one's life.

Then the Voice from the Whirlwind, by no means deaf to human complaints made in earnest, draws what is for Job a new and radical conclusion, one that is nonetheless as old as creation itself but that too much human thinking keeps forgetting. The conclusion is this: "Am I wrong because you are right?" This is a more precise and polite way of restating the rebuke that precedes it: "Do you dare to deny my judgment?" Both replies serve as reminders that even though human intelligence may inquire into the forces that animate the world, those forces ultimately remain beyond the grasp of rational inquiry, because they are mysteries, miracles—which means they are irrational. Questions of justice and injustice, as measured and shaped by human concerns and by human thinking, are not unreasonable on their own terms. Yet they pale against the backdrop of a universe in which births and deaths, creation and destruction, coexist on a daily basis as a matter of routine.

In the end, Job is not given an answer to his demand for intelligible justice. He is not given an explanation or a justification for all that appears so unjust. In the staging of his story he remains, in effect, unaware of the wager between Satan and God that caused all his suffering. But in spite of this—in spite of his lack of conscious insight—he is given something that turns out to be more satisfying than any reply to his arguments and on his terms could ever be. He is given a glimpse, a reminder—readily available in everyday life but equally readily overlooked—of some of the finer points of that same and seemingly so ordinary daily life. Instead of being given an earful of absolute divine knowledge about good and evil, Job is shown a glimpse of splendor. He is silenced by the display of polymorphous splendor in everyday life of which the Voice from the Whirlwind reminds him and which surrounds him everywhere: "I have spoken of the unspeakable and tried to grasp the infinite . . . I had heard of you with my ears; but now my eyes have seen you. Therefore I will be quiet, comforted that I am dust." The hearsay of accepted belief and of overlearned knowledge is here dismissed and replaced by the immediacy of glimpsing a mystery and a miracle that ever so briefly reveals itself in its bright splendor.

The transformation that happens here—and transformation is the essential plot of the Book of Job—does not take place at the level of Job's arguments. It is not the logical result of those arguments. Rather, it works by shifting away from the rhetoric of rational analysis and toward an attitude more suitable for revelation. That is what the test questions from the Voice of the Whirlwind, such as, "Does the rain have a father?," are about. They are not about seeing whether Job knows the answer or can guess the answer. This is no riddle by a sphinx who eats you alive if you do not know the answer. The kind of intellectual insight into sphinxlike riddles of which Oedipus is the legendary master is not what is at stake here. There are no answers here, certainly not answers based on reason. The questions that the Voice from the Whirlwind presents to Job show the limits, and, at some level, the futility, of reasoning and of intellectual prowess. The end result of the interrogation is neither that Job receives a reply to his questions in kind, nor that Job himself is persuaded by a form of argument. Rather, the mode of discourse is itself transformed—from a polemic about intelligible cosmic justice to a poetics of revelation. With that change in mode of discourse comes a change in the way Job tells the story of existence to himself. His perspective shifts, from a humanistic viewpoint that takes reason as the measure of all things to a divinely inspired vision. And with that transformation, Job, if ever so briefly, transcends the Heraclitean division that separates human from divine by restricting the view of the former to dichotomies of good and evil and by reserving as an exclusive right for the latter the vision of splendor.

Another man, Nietzsche's Zarathustra, comes to a similar vision of splendor that lies beyond the human dichotomy of good and evil. But he arrives at it via a different route. Job offends his God to his face by his condemnation of his own creation. This is a surgical strike that serves to blast creation as a whole. Zarathustra goes one step farther. He declares the same God whom Job would accuse altogether dead. He blasts the alleged creator, but not the world itself and not existence in it. By declaring the God of Christianity dead he means that all the man-made beliefs and especially the value judgments that are associated with the image of the Christian God in his remote heaven have lost their validity. This is what Nietzsche means by nihilism: the necessary loss of value of all previously held values and of the beliefs built on them, until they are replaced by newly established values. For nihilism as loss of previously held values is, as Nietzsche understood it, a transitional condition. It is not a permanent loss of value—which he would reject as the death wish of a creature that has lost all capacity for desire and all will to live. Nihilism as a transitional and transformative phase and pivotal point is necessary, in his view, in order to arrive at a revaluation of all previous value judgments concerning existence—but this time sans promises of a better world elsewhere and outside of history.

Zarathustra rejects all promises, and all promisors, of future consolations. He wants existence in this world redeemed in value here and now, on its own terms or without importing into it extraterrestrial beauty and goodness and justice. He wants to end the underhanded devaluation of existence that is perpetuated by all wishing for a better world. Instead of the promise of joy later, he insists on its potential here and now—and here and now only. "To be sure," he says, "except ye become as little children, ye shall not enter into *that* kingdom of heaven. (And Zarathustra pointed upward with his hand.) But we have no wish whatever to enter into the kingdom of heaven: we have become man—*so we want the earth.*" This is the most radical possible "return to the things themselves," as phenomenologists like to call it. It is more radical than any such return that they propose, because it rethinks Being and existence as value.

It is only when Job is tormented to the limit, and when he has rejected all offers of comfort by rejecting beliefs that no longer have value for him, that the Voice from the Whirlwind or from the world itself speaks to him, and that its revelation of mystery and miracle begins. As Jung suggested, only when the defense of belief is abandoned, and only when a human being thereby makes himself most vulnerable, can genuine religious experience begin. A similar transformation that occurs only in extremis, when human suffering is most intense and when the overlearned formulas of consolation have lost their value, appears in Nietzsche. In *Beyond Good and Evil,* he put it this way:

> Whoever has endeavored . . . to think pessimism through to its depths . . . , whoever has really . . . looked . . . down into the most world-denying of all possible ways of thinking—beyond good and evil— . . . may just thereby, without really meaning to do so, have opened his eyes to the opposite ideal of the most high-spirited, alive, and world-affirming human being who has not only come to terms and learned to get along with whatever was and is, but who wants to have *what was and is* repeated into all eternity, shouting insatiably *da capo* (once more)—not only to himself but to the whole play and spectacle...

The original judgment of rejection is transformed into affirmation. Instead of seeking happiness in another and presumably better world, elsewhere and at some other time in the future, there is now an affirmation of life as is. The transformed attitude now wants this life, this world, this history. It wants life, world, history just as they have been, and just as they are, with nothing in them resented for not being different. It wants the same world, but minus the notion that it will only be good enough if, when, and after it has been improved. This is, indeed, as Nietzsche said, the most affirmative affirmation of existence that is at all attainable. It is identical to what Augustine had in mind when he said, "I no longer wished for a better world, because I was thinking of the whole of creation."

Job and Zarathustra are alike in the transformation they undergo from a world-denying to a world-affirming vision and judgment. But they also are profoundly different. They differ not only because one is, and remains, deeply religious and personally connected to his God, while the other makes himself militantly irreligious, even a willing accomplice in the death of the same God. That much is obvious. They also differ in their humanity—and that difference matters perhaps even more. Job is utterly imaginable. This makes it possible for him to be the Judeo-Christian West's prime hero of sheer humanity. Zarathustra, in contrast, is truly difficult to imagine, perhaps even fundamentally impossible to imagine. This makes him an altogether new prototype of man. That is why Nietzsche speaks about him as a superman. Zarathustra is superhuman not because he possesses human qualities to a superior degree but because he surpasses all that is known to be human precisely in order to become an altogether different form of human being. He is the prototype of a human being for whom being human has itself become transformed and has come to mean something other than all that was previously familiar. But Zarathustra exists only on paper, in and as Nietzsche's writings. Beyond these, there are no readily identifiable forms of human life, no personality type, that can be pointed at and that can serve as example of what Zarathustra represents. Because Job is imaginable, he also is imitable. Because Zarathustra is difficult and perhaps fundamentally impossible to imagine, he also is difficult and perhaps impossible to imitate.

This question of imitation matters. It is crucial. Because it is true that life imitates art, more than the other way around, the question of imitability determines whether something matters in life. If the figure and type of Zarathustra never makes it beyond the drafting table of Nietzsche's writings, then the form of human life of which he would be the prototype is rendered null and void— by its own practical irrelevance. Zarathustra, teacher and preacher of a strictly affirmative philosophy, may well be his own worst enemy for that reason. This makes for Nietzsche's great and decisive dilemma: how to get beyond Zarathustra, his draft for a new kind of human life in the same world? Nietzsche knew the problem, but he never seems to have found a solution for it. He thought he held the formula of a new form of human life, based on the affirmative spirit of eternal return, but he failed to make Zarathustra, its teacher, humanly imitable. No *Imitatio Zarathustrae* exists that provides guidelines for how to live the life of which Zarathustra speaks. This means that Zarathustra's philosophy fails to be

true—by failing to become true, by failing to be made true. That he had to fail
was perhaps inevitable, and Nietzsche knew that as well. For any imitation of
Zarathustra—and Zarathustra himself rejected followers who would be imita-
tors—would establish a link of identity between imitator and imitated. But
because Zarathustra was to be so different as to be suprahuman, any resemblance to or identification with the old type of man would threaten the radical
novelty of the new prototype. This conundrum—the need for imitability and
the simultaneous rejection of imitation—makes for a trap from which escape is
anything but obvious or easy. A solution would require both identity and difference—simultaneously.

In the end, Nietzsche accomplished a greater clarification of the Heraclitean distinction between human and divine than Heraclitus himself articulated. He also made a more fully defined and a more deeply felt statement about
the fundamental human longing to overcome the Heraclitean dichotomy. But
he did not, at least not convincingly, deliver on his promise to bridge the gap.
With the figure of Zarathustra and with the promise of Zarathustra's proposed
affirmative philosophy of eternal return he came close to defining a formula
and outline for a new form of human existence. But that new form of human
life falls short of being sufficiently fleshed out to be persuasive. We see no
believable human character emerge from Nietzsche's writings—other than
Nietzsche himself, and he is even more problematic than Zarathustra.

Aristotle, writing in his *Poetics* about what makes for good poetic creativity—good invention and composition—spoke about plot and character having
to be mutually defining and mutually reinforcing. A plot is only as imaginable
and as convincing as its characters are coherent and convincing for it, and vice
versa. Plot and character are inseparable. Taken one step farther this means that
plot equals character, and that character defines plot. Not surprisingly, this rule
applies not only to the art of fiction writing but to life as well. As Heraclitus
said, not so long before Aristotle made his observation: character is destiny.
Now Zarathustra shows a plot—the bridging of the Heraclitean gap between
human and divine—but the necessary character remains inadequately defined.
The plot of Nietzsche's creative philosophizing succeeds or fails with the definition of a character type that can pull it off on the stage of the world. Does
Nietzsche, in the end, succeed in this? That case cannot be convincingly argued.
Does that mean he failed? I think not, at least not automatically. But we need
to look away from Nietzsche first, and look at something that is not Nietzsche,
before he can become more believable.

Before moving on, however, it is time to briefly back up. What Heraclitus
held to be at least a theoretical possibility, albeit a divine prerogative, Augustine
thought to be a lost state of consciousness which the soul was destined to
recover but could only recover with divine intervention. Job, pushed to the
limits of human suffering and questioning, and thereby exposing the human
condition in its raw essence of utter vulnerability, was able to catch a few brief

glimpses of the divine spirit that is everywhere present. Nietzsche, filled with a longing to bridge the gap of the Heraclitean distinction, created in Zarathustra the outline of a type of human being who would fulfill that longing. But what about the unlegendary men and women of everyday life?

Now and then—infrequently, and typically only for brief moments, but with the awe-inspiring and overpowering force of a personal revelation—contemplative disciplines such as psychoanalysis participate in this long and deep preoccupation that distracted Heraclitus, Nietzsche, Augustine, Job, and Zarathustra. Those moments come when they want, not when we want them to come. They are a local whirlwind that speaks in its own voice, and at the level of lived experience, about the miracles that surround us. During these moments it is sometimes possible for every life, even every ordinary and unlegendary life, to briefly catch a glimpse of how it stands affirmed in the precise way it turned out—not only for the good things in it but also the painful ones. Everything that ordinarily seems like fragments of personal history, some perhaps good and beautiful, but others painfully not so, is here briefly united in a sense for the totality of it all, a totality that is better than even its best parts. There is, on those rare occasions, an acutely felt sense for the necessity with which all fragments come together. At those fleeting moments every ordinary life can look miraculous and magnificent—in spite of even the longest litanies of personal failures, painful experiences, terrible tragedies, irreversible mistakes, bitter disappointments, or other shortcomings one so often and so habitually resents in one's life and in oneself. These moments are less man-made than they are, as we say, God given. They cannot be produced at will. In this sense, Augustine was right. They require something more than a deliberate ego trip, in which one is propelled by human steam only. Such moments are truly gifts, and because of their very nature they are experienced in precisely that way. All that can be produced by human effort here is the receptive disposition that can recognize them as the gift they are and that can respond to them in kind—with awe, with gratitude, and mostly with the realization that something extraordinary is being displayed before one's very eyes, right in the midst of one's perfectly ordinary, everyday life.

This is when depth psychology is at its best, when it truly comes into its own. At such moments it reaches beyond its usual, and more restricted, significance as a technical craft of symptom management, or as the practical know-how for behavior change. Here psychology stops being about mind and is once again about soul. For as millennia-old tradition has it, it is soul and not mind that is the dimension of existence where things historically unique become equal to things that reach beyond the purely historical, the strictly individual and personal, and the seemingly only temporal—even the exclusively human.

The ancient Greek oracle at Delphi instructed man to "Know Thyself." This has to be one of Western history's most monumentally misinterpreted ideas. Today we take it to mean, as if it were the most obvious thing, "Know your inner thoughts and feelings," "Know who you really are," "Know what motivates your behavior," and all the rest. "Know Thyself" has come to mean, as Freud put it to us in his own oracular fashion, "Where the unconscious is there consciousness shall be." Nothing could possibly sound more compatible with our psychologically minded age and culture than the ancient wisdom that says "Know Thyself." And yet Delphi's "Know Thyself" originally meant nothing of the sort. It meant—and this has to be news to modern, psychotherapized man—"Know that you are human, not a god." It means, "Know where human cognition about everything ends and where recognition of the godly begins." It means, "Learn to recognize how local and situational manifestations of the divine—and not just your automatic thoughts, your repressed memories, and your neurotransmitters—shape the experiences of your life." It means, "There are always two sides to every coin, the strictly human side and the godly side." It means, "In everything you can and do understand there also is something you do not and cannot understand." It means, "In whatever you say there is something that remains unsaid and that cannot be said and will never be said." "Know Thyself" means, in short and most of all, "You are not alone and you are never alone, so learn to know the Other who walks with you at all times." And we can safely take it to mean, last but by no means least, "Psychology as a modern science will forever be insufficient to meet the deepest human needs, which are the needs of the soul, as long as it does not make room for the subtle, the mythic, the archetypal Other in all things and in everyday life."

But the divinely Other to which the categorical imperative of "Know Thyself" points is no metaphysical Other. It is no extraterrestrial Other—no alien being of any kind, not even a Father in a distant Heaven or a *deus absconditus*. The Other is first of all—and as Job realized—about taking another look at the all too familiar and the seemingly all too mundane. It is about beginning to glimpse the endless surplus of significance that is present in all events assumed known. The Other to which "Know Thyself" points is about the ancient idea of sensing the "nonpresentable form" that is present in all things, and that shapes them in the precise way they present themselves. It is about developing a nose for what else is in the air besides the obvious and the identifiable, about sensing that there is always more to come in all things said, that there is more to everything than meets the eye. The Other that is everywhere present is the wearer of the endlessly changing Dionysian masks who makes himself visible in those masks but who nevertheless is neither only the masks themselves nor a figure that hides behind them. Such an endlessly shape-shifting and subtle being can only be called a spirit, a genius, a god. Hence, to "Know Thyself" means being open to seeing genius in all things.

This Other is sensed more in the act of taking another look than it is in anything thus seen. It is therefore not about anything newly discovered per se. Thus the Other is not automatically to be found, or sought, elsewhere—in the newest fascinating biochemical findings from psychiatry, in the newest ingenious model of mind from academic psychology, in the latest idea or school of thought from theoretical and philosophical psychology, or in the latest easy-step program. It is not about any new findings that, as so often happens, first become newfound facts, then newly touted fads, and finally, temporarily and until the next intellectual season, the new psychological uniforms we all have to wear by collective cultural edict. The Other is about the act itself of always taking another look—and another look, and another. It is about always stopping to look again and again at all that is already known. Looking for the Other in all things is about standing still, and about only so beginning to make psychological progress. It is about the endlessly repeated "How does it feel?" from psychotherapy practice. But that question is relevant not because emotion is itself of primary importance. Nor does feeling matter as much as it does because it is the only way to gain true insight. It is as relevant as it is because it forces every Joban consciousness to stop and take another look—a good look, often the first close look ever, at things a person has long had on hand and in mind and has perhaps for too long considered already fully known.

But that Other is not only a private and privately unconscious alter ego or an introjected inner voice or mental representation. It is not primarily about inner mental pictures of fellow human beings from past history. Even though literal persons make it easy, and tempting, to think that they are the great Otherness that is at stake, these literal and even significant other persons, and the interpersonal psychology that is based on them, are not the core of the soul's affairs. The Other is me and my life as usual, but with an added sense of connection to the mythic, the imaginal, the symbolic, the eternally sacred and elusive, the metaphoric side of all things. It is the bottomless depth of psychic significance that inheres in everything that seems only literal, physical, historical, interpersonal, and otherwise uniquely temporal and personal. It is I, doing my usual rounds, on my same and familiar ego trips, but with an added sense that I am not completely alone as I go, even when solitary. It is about feeling surrounded everywhere by the genius of spirits that inhabit all places and circumstances, and that animate all things and events. The Other is all the well-known facts of my life but with an added sense that there is always more to them than meets the eye, and that this "more" remains forever elusive—real in spite of being insubstantial, purely psychic matter that is embedded in all concrete matters yet that is itself intangible.

"Know Thyself," as "Know that you are human, not a god," is, as Job discovered, no put-down of the human condition by overpowering forces that treat us like puppets on a string. It is a "lift-up" that lifts the human spirit through a reminder that being human means being able to see the mythic side of things, not just their immediate practicality and relevance for a sometimes inflated human ego. "Know Thyself" puts every human ego in good company by surrounding it with its betters. This, too, Job experienced firsthand.

A collective cultural failure to "Know Thyself" in the ancient Greek sense leads to a kind of alienation on a large scale. It makes for a shared malaise in which the feeling of intimacy with psychic Otherness, for which the soul is the ideal means, is lost. Otherness then becomes too exclusively and too restrictedly the literal other persons around me—the significant other, the interpersonal other, the social other. When that interpersonal and social paradigm of Otherness fails to carry the larger-than-interpersonal burden of meeting the soul's deepest needs, as it must, then Otherness assumes literal forms that begin to look deformed. For it then assumes the form of abnormal psychology, psychiatric condition, psychosocial and developmental deviance, social maladjustment, and personal failure. The more the sense of images animating all life diminishes, the more freakish the world begins to look. As Jung said, the gods, when deprived of their rightful place in everyday life, become diseases.

When "Know Thyself" becomes too one-sidedly self-cultivation, for a life that is considered an interpersonal affair before anything else, then a particular kind of psychic alienation may become the norm. We may, in part, have modern and popular self psychology to thank for inadvertently promoting alienation from the sense of mythic images animating everyday life. We may have modern popular cultural ideas about self and ego to thank, not for improving life by reducing loneliness, as some psychology too readily and unrealistically promises to do, but for bringing a new kind of human loneliness into being. That new kind of loneliness is not in the first place a problem of personal, interpersonal, or social psychology. It is not primarily about family, relationships, and other communal connections coming unglued. It is about disconnecting the human from the mythic by misinterpreting what the oracular command, "Know Thyself," means.

But conversely as well, when depth psychology is applied to the affairs of everyday life, but always with an eye toward the mythically Other in all things, then we can expect that every ordinary existence may sometimes reveal images of splendor. This splendor surpasses all that can possibly be accounted for by psychosocial history. In the end, it becomes apparent that depth psychology is not only, not even primarily, about the strictly human. It also is about the Other than only psychosocially human in everyday life. While individual circumstances and history must be our starting point, they are not what is solely, ultimately, and foremost in interest. There is no other place to begin than in strictly individual events and experiences, but they are not the matters that are of prime and final concern. They are of concern not only for their own historical sake but also because they are the masks which the many-faced but always life-affirming spirit of Dionysos wears.

The approach to everyday life that takes "Know Thyself" to mean its original "Know that you are human, not a god," and that would translate this ancient imperative into a modern psychology, this approach is no far-fetched idea. It requires no far-flung metaphysical speculation, and no forced reasoning that strains common sense in order to make an otherwise unimaginable point. There is nothing inherently unnatural in looking for mythic presences in everyday life, even though it goes against certain habits of modern thought that have become second nature. Looking for a mythic Other in every situation is an idea that is inherent in depth psychology itself, as a naturally built-in potential. It is depth psychology's own *telos*—its purpose, that for the sake of which it does what it does, that for the sake of which it exists. It is a development that occurred in depth psychology's own modern history. It occurred when Jung added to Freud's notion of the personal unconscious his own idea of the collective unconscious. Jung added to my psychological life—which Freud had taught me was strictly mine, privately, developmentally, and historically—something that was other than mine alone, something that had archetypal significance.

The shift in focus from Freud to Jung brought about another way of looking at the same things that Freud had first seen. For between Freud and Jung the drama of Job's revelation reenacted itself. There blew a whirlwind that raised new questions about ideas concerning the life of the soul that were rapidly becoming accepted as familiar dogma but that did not and could not tell the full story. Jung heard the whirlwind, responded to it as Job did, and saw the spectacle of the collective unconscious. Freud, insisting on the psychoanalytic shibboleth of a strictly personal unconsciousness, refused to hear the voice in the whirlwind. Perhaps that is the deepest reason why Freudian psychoanalysis and the therapies derived from it often are only incompletely satisfying. These treatments, in spite of their unquestionable contributions to human self-understanding, often must fail to show the soul what it longs most to see: not only the images of significant others from psychosocial history that have been personally internalized, but the significance of a mythic Otherness that is part of the human condition and that lies beyond all psychosocial history.

FOUR

NOW AND ALWAYS

THE CONTENT OF the unconscious is timeless, is not temporally ordered, is not changed by time, and the very idea of time cannot even be applied to it. So said Freud, in *Beyond the Pleasure Principle*, where he writes about the psychology of unconscious and compulsive repetition. And yet his method for the psychological analysis of unconsciousness is nothing if not a historical enterprise. It is historical in its subject matter (childhood development and its implications for adult life), in its method (personal recollection based on free association), and in its theory (the analyst's speculative reconstruction of the patient's forgotten past). How can this be? How can psychoanalytic treatment be both historical and ahistorical, simultaneously?

That the content of the unconscious does not change over time becomes apparent in transference, the uncanny phenomenon that defines psychoanalytic treatment and its derivatives. Transference, in which the patient repeats in his or her interactions with the therapist all the significant emotional experiences of his or her childhood history, is itself based on the repetition compulsion. That, in turn, involves an unstoppable force that insists on repeating again and again certain fixed and unchangeable behavior and experience patterns. As Freud himself alluded, though without beginning to appreciate the implications, the repetition compulsion is, as it were, a concretely lived enactment of Nietzsche's idea of the "eternal return of the same."

It is this "eternal return of the same" that drives most psychotherapy patients into treatment. The resistance to change they encounter in these unchanging experiences is itself the greatest source of personal distress, which ranges from the neurotically and characterologically troublesome to acute despair. It is as though unseen and demonic forces are at work that thwart life with unchanging and unchangeable unpleasantness. These forces cannot be shaken off at will. They interfere with one's plans, efforts, hopes, and desires at every turn. They are behind the desperate plea for help that brings even the proudest of men and women to the therapist's doorstep, with a humble acknowledgment that overpowering forces are at work and that special strategies are needed to deal with them. But the discovery of overpowering and seemingly demonic forces is not confined to psychoanalysis and its derivatives. It is familiar knowledge on the street as well. In Alcoholics Anonymous (AA), and in treatment modalities that are derived from it, there is a routine insistence on the idea of a "higher power," a power greater than that of the familiar self. There is an insistence on recognizing that recovery from compulsive behavior begins with the acknowledgment that the individual's life is not in his or her control. That control, so it is suggested, rests in the hands of another power, a power that may be imagined in endlessly different ways—as long as it is acknowledged.

The crucial point here is that the idea of this power has to be understood for what it is—psychological realism, not religious fervor. It is more about the soul's own empiricism than about religious belief. The alcoholic has to discover that he or she is not alone, that there is another presence in his or her life that must be recognized. There also is the second and equally important insight, that this other presence may be imagined as one likes, as long as it fits with one's individual life and experience. This means that the great empirical reality in the life of the alcoholic soul, the subtle but powerful Other that governs it, must be approached with, and known through, imagination. This is not because it is unreal. On the contrary. It is because it is experienced as more real than any literal thing or event that can be pointed at. The only way to know this presence is to look beyond what is literally given and toward something that is invisibly present in it. This requires faith in the imagination. To become a recovering alcoholic, so AA implies, demands before anything else that one become a more actively imaginative alcoholic. The recovery is first of all a recovery from poverty of imagination. While the brain damage that often results from lifelong alcohol abuse can lead to confabulation, the involuntary making up of events that never took place, the beginning of alcohol rehabilitation requires itself an active imagination about fabulous powers that, like mythic events, are never literal but nonetheless real. Thus an alcoholically sickened imagination can only be avoided and treated by a convalescence that begins in actively training the imagination itself for a more mythically based sense of psychic well-being.

The insistence on the presence of greater powers that can only be known by being imagined is no irrational belief that eventually is best countered with common sense. It is not something that begs to be contradicted by more soberly rational approaches, such as that of Rational Recovery, the competing alternative to AA, which dismisses the idea of a greater power. Rather, the insistence on an active imagination devoted to developing a sense for a presence in the alcoholic's life that is other than his or her own familiar self, and that is the greater power in it, is a spontaneous recovery of ancient Greek sensibilities. When a Greek of Homer's days was taught that he or she must "Know Thyself," as the categorical imperative from the Delphic oracle said, that meant, "Know that you are human, not a god." It referred to the sense that any human situation or experience can only be properly understood by recognizing the presence of an archetypal or mythic factor in it. "Know Thyself" meant that a subtle mythic presence and dimension must be actively imagined into every aspect of one's daily personal life.

(As an aside, Greek creativity went into decline during the same period in which a sensibility for the mythic was replaced by a preference for rational ways of thinking. "Rational Recovery" represents a modern turn away from the irrational, in favor of the strictly rational. This is especially so in its use of the so-called "Socratic method" of strictly rational thinking for trying to overpower the compulsive side of the soul. It is good to recall that this was the precise method whereby an entire civilization sent itself into decline. One pays dearly for killing one's gods and for trying to eliminate the irrational side of life that is their turf.)

Soon after beginning psychoanalytic treatment, when the initial hope for a quick cure starts to fade, transference begins to develop. The unseen demonic forces of the repetition compulsion seem to redouble their efforts. It becomes apparent to the patient that instead of anything changing in the therapist's office as a result of his or her intervention, every complaint and symptom almost mockingly reasserts itself, in exactly the same way as usual. Instead of finding change, the patient finds that everything is becoming more the same than it ever was. This often is accompanied by disappointed, discouraged, and outright angry feelings and thoughts that the therapist is "just like everybody else," that "nothing is ever going to change," even with therapy, that the patient "may just as well give up."

When the patient gets wind of the repetition compulsion as a real though intangible and elusive thing that shapes his or her life and that defines his or her destiny, a kind of panic may set in. It becomes apparent that life is not entirely unfolding on the plane of knowable events that can be controlled. The patient begins to realize that the soul that animates his or her life operates on an altogether different plane, where time and events unfold in a different and uncontrollable manner. The facts and acts of life seem to have little impact on this second realm that coexists with ordinary time, and that is the soul's true home base. There is now clear evidence of unstoppable scenarios that unfold at their own pace—compulsively and strictly under the governance of their own laws. In comparison to such fixed and unstoppable scenarios, the conscious facts and acts of life often seem to be little more than renewed editions of old plays. They are ancient dramas and tragedies being perpetually reenacted in everyday life—always in modernized garb, and with modern stage props and accents, but forever repeating the same old song and dance. "There's nothing in this world can make me joy," is how Shakespeare's King John complains: "Life is as tedious as a twice-told tale, Vexing the dull ear of a drowsy man."

It is no accident that the metaphor of renewed editions of old and unchanging stories is as prominent as it is in Freud's writings on the repetition compulsion and its insistence on the "eternal return of the same." This accounts also for the shared habit, in every school of depth psychology, of casting its theories in the form of timeless motifs that are borrowed from the world's myths, religions, literature, and art. Even a cursory look at Freud's psychoanalytic notions shows a small procession of figures from mythology. Oedipus is there, and Narcissus, Eros, Ananke, along with others. Jung's analytical psychology, as a second-generation development in modern depth psychology, is even more heavily steeped in imagery from myth, religion, literature, and art. And in the third generation, the archetypal psychology of James Hillman, such imagery has become not only the primary but the sole material. As Hillman insists, after Jung first explicitly stated it and after Freud had already dramatically demonstrated it, soul is image, and image is soul. Lastly, even those forms of psychology that try to do away with esoteric notions, for the sake of a presumably more rational approach, end up inadvertently elevating their own concepts to the traditional mythic status of minor gods. These concepts, precisely because they appear so convincingly rational, are not only routinely reified. They also become, to some degree, deified. With little Latin in their language and less Greek, many such contemporary popular psychologies nonetheless have their own legendary figures: Children of Alcoholics, Enablers, the Introject or Inner Child, Co-Dependents, Trauma Victims and Survivors, Multiples, Borderlines, and all the rest. These seemingly very real but nonetheless equally mythic figures might as well have stepped straight from Homer's Greece of mythic fame right onto the contemporary psychiatric unit or into the community mental health clinic. There they now gather, in a ritual circle called not the Parthenon or the Pantheon but the Morning Community Meeting or the Support Group. It is fitting that instead of developing ever-new paradigms, as many natural sciences do, depth psychology frequently proceeds by turning to old ones. For in the realm of soul, the facts of contemporary history are most effectively elucidated not with truly new ideas but with timeless images of old ones. Progress is here often made not by making leaps forward but by recognizing how new history often finds a way of standing still in time precisely by reiterating old motifs, despite all appearances of novelty and of constant change.

Freud's claim that the unconscious is timeless not only says that it does not change over time. It also suggests that the very sense of timing and even the sense of linear time itself are absent from it. That means the unconscious life of the soul is altogether indifferent to the time of day. It implies nothing less than that the soul, in its insistence on timelessness in the psychology of unconscious and compulsive repetition, ignores the greatest discovery of the Judeo-Christian West, the paradigm of linear time itself. Along with that, it here dismisses the entire history of thought that has tried to make sense of the universe by imposing this paradigm on it.

The sense of timing is lacking in the life of the soul in unconscious and compulsive repetition insofar as the autonomous imagination that animates it ignores the waking or conscious ego's temporal orientation. The soul ignores the ego's insistence on the importance of historical or temporal sequencing. That helps clarify why one of the cardinal signs of severe psychiatric disturbance is disorientation to time: the patient believes that he or she is living in a time frame that is altogether different from the actual time of the situation at hand. The unconscious soul has taken over here and has wiped out the conscious ego's compass by wiping out its temporal orientation. The conscious ego so depends on its orientation to linear time that this is the first thing we ask about upon awakening every morning: "What time is it?" We disentangle ourselves from the cobwebs of sleep and dreams by reorienting ourselves to the time of day. It is no accident that psychoanalysis ushered in the dawn of our contemporary psychological mindedness with Freud's wake-up call about the psychological significance of dreams. One of his first suggestions was that dreams serve to keep us asleep, and thus to ward off waking ego consciousness. If dreams had their way in this attempt, our entire existence would remain devoted to the unconscious life of the soul. From the point of view of dreams, and of the unconscious soul, public enemy number one, in this Freudian view, is the sound of the alarm clock in the morning.

The idea that the unconscious life of the soul is not temporally ordered suggests that customary frames of reference that use time as first principle of order do not apply to it. Notions about temporal sequencing of any kind—such as progress in time, the serial unfolding of events, plus many others—are incompatible with unconscious psychic matter, because it ignores them. The incompatibility between the conscious ego's temporal orientation and the unconscious soul's atemporality is a daily experience. One familiar occasion where it manifests itself is in attempts to recall dreams upon awakening. No dream can ever be accurately told as a sequence of events. All that happens in dreams happens in complete disregard for temporal logic or sequencing. This leads to the inevitable and familiar frustration of never being able to get the account of a dream right. As we say, "You had to be there" to get a sense of what it was like to be in the dream. Dreams are not truly accessible through hindsight. They are the historian's nightmare, precisely because of their inability to be accurately recounted.

A great deal about what is brought to psychological treatment is related to disturbances in temporal sequencing. The very notion of "disorder" has become the central metaphor in the vocabulary of textbooks on psychopathology. The American Psychiatric Association's standard text on abnormal psychology is a manual about "disorders." We no longer have "mental disease" or "mental illness" in the title of this catechism of the soul's life. The conditions of the soul are recast as problems of disorderliness. Tell a psychotherapist about the disorderliness in your life—in your love life, in the chaos of your household, in the way you are messing up your career and your health—and he or she will tell you about your mental state. Psychological treaters are always looking for the disorderly loose ends in life—loose associations, loose-lipped comments, loose impulse control, losses not followed up by a restoration to previous orderliness, the too-loose-fitting clothes that are supposed to hide a body's figure, even complaints of loose stool.

One case of the soul's disregard for orderly temporal sequencing is the reappearance of emotions from past experiences that are felt in the middle of contemporary situations, even though the present has no readily visible connection to the past. Here, feelings, thoughts, and behaviors related to events from historical time zones other than the present take over the current situation. This unexpected emergence of untimely feelings, thoughts, and behaviors that are associated with past events brings about a sense of disorder in the expected usual flow of things. It ruins the mood of the moment with displaced emotions and thoughts. These emotions and thoughts are called "displaced" precisely because they originally belonged to circumstances other than those presently at hand. Due to the soul's indifference to all temporal order, they are now attached to, and reenacted in, the present situation. Psychological treaters view such ill-timed feelings, thoughts, and behaviors as sure signs that some significant unconscious factor or other is entering the picture and calling for attention. The soul is, as it were, casting a shadow play on the surface of any currently available situation. But this is not simply about "games people play." It is about the soul's own dramatic plays, which it writes with the blood, sweat, and tears of daily life. These shadows that the soul casts on the affairs of the day bring their own agendas, about their own affairs—and these are characteristically at odds with the waking ego's conscious intentions.

The sense of poor timing, this disregard for the waking ego's plans and for its need for order, is dramatically portrayed in the literary figure of the double. This fictional character was most prominent in the literature of the late nineteenth and early twentieth centuries. Not accidentally, this coincided with the discovery of the modern unconscious. The double, who appears as an uncanny duplicate image of the story's protagonist, personifies the perpetual ill timing or untimeliness of unconscious matters. He is the protagonist's alter ego. He typically assumes the form of a twin, a look-alike, a detached shadow, a mirror image, or a painted image of the ego that has become animated and autonomous. He unexpectedly appears at every turn to thwart the protagonist's intentions and plans. Every tale of a protagonist and his double is invariably about these disruptions that occur in this fashion, disruptions that eventually lead to the protagonist's ruin and death.

The figure of the double says in the dramatic image of a personified idea what Freud said in the conceptual language of psychoanalysis. Both suggest that the unconscious soul in compulsive repetition will again and again wipe out all sense of order that is based on the paradigm of linear timing. This is no minor matter, and by no means only a clinical one. Quite the contrary. It has momentous implications, universally. Although the significance the double has is first felt at the level of individual life, that significance reaches far beyond the life of the individual and touches the level of collective cultural consciousness and history. As it goes in the microcosm of Everyman's individual life, so it goes in the macrocosm of collective history. And so it is that the God of Judeo-Christianity, who invented linear time itself, meets his Opposer in the eternally returning demonic double of unconscious repetition, who wipes out the very faith that Western man has learned to have in his future orientation. It is as though the untimeliness of personal unconsciousness, personified as a double, is Everyman's own built-in and ever-present latent Antichrist. It is no accident that we sometimes speak about the unconsciousness in our lives as though it were a personal double who looks just like us but whom we call our "evil twin." And it is no accident that Freud came up with the idea that the first objective of dreams is to keep us asleep, so that the unholy figures in them can go on to do their ungodly things without being interrupted and kept in line by a more or less civilized waking ego.

The disordering of the sense for temporal sequencing, and the mixing of disjointed time zones and sequentially incompatible situations, also occurs in what psychological treaters since Freud know as "regression." It, too, undermines the demand that the soul should unidirectionally, single-mindedly, and monotheistically march forward only, in unrelenting devotion to an ideal that is projected into an always-distant future. Regression is dominated by a backward-looking perspective. It is always retracing its steps. It turns away from consciously stated objectives for the future and returns instead to devotions that were held in earlier days. Regression, as psychoanalytically informed treaters view it, is about unconsciously sliding back to levels of functioning that correspond to earlier or more infantile phases of development. It is considered the quintessential manifestation of temporal disorder, the hallmark of unconsciousness. Regression is the pivotal point where today's history fuses with things that remain timeless, ahistorical.

It is the very idea of regression that makes it possible for psychological analysis to be both historical and ahistorical at the same time. It was nothing short of genius on Freud's part to imagine individual development not only as linear but also, and simultaneously, as circular. Borrowing a thought he had first encountered in Aristotle, he saw development not as a series of stages in which events move forward only, with earlier phases forever replaced by later ones, leaving the past behind for good. Rather, he saw it as a process in which earlier sequences return unchanged but repackaged as later, and seemingly new, experiences and developmental phases. Personal psychological history, psychoanalytically imagined in this manner, became a process in which the ahistorical coexists with history, precisely by wearing the mask of history.

But Freud not only said that the content of the unconscious is timeless, that it is not temporally ordered, and that it is not changed by time. He also said that the very category of time cannot even be applied to it. This means that, as already suggested, one must think about the life of the soul as a process that is, at some level, so independent of the events of history that the very paradigm of linear time does not even apply to it—as it were from the start. Not only does linear time not apply to unconsciousness, because it is undone by it, as

suggested. Linear time does not enter into play to begin with, except as the historical guise that all things timeless wear. Or, for the soul, too, as for the gods of
myth, history is incarnation of things ahistorical.

This means that the usual ways of accounting for psychological experiences,
with accounts that are based on linear time, should not be applied or imposed.
The trusted narrative format of "This is happening now because of something
else that happened earlier," and all variations on it, fails in important ways to
account for the unconscious life of the soul. This has important implications. For
one thing, it undermines much of the interest in historical etiology that is so
prevalent in the theories and practices of psychological treatment. The question
of why something happens in the realm of soul is, at the deepest level, as unanswerable as it is inapplicable. This makes for the Nietzschean claim that we can
describe but that we cannot explain. All we can discover is that things are the
way they are because that is the way they are. This is our best and most profound
truth. The search for hidden beginnings and causes, in deep-seated sources, this
search that has sent us down many a path looking for psychological causation as
though it were a Holy Grail, turns out to be something of a wild goose chase.
By implication, if the psychology of unconsciousness is to be called "depth psychology," as Eugen Bleuler suggested it should be, then this is not, after all,
because of deeply hidden causes that such a psychology would ferret out.

And yet, even though the life and the events of the soul resist narration in
linear manner, the desire that they be narrated remains. As Ricoeur said, "action
is in search of narrative." More bluntly put, all life wants to be told. It wants to
be able to look in the mirror, to tell its story to itself, and to become so drawn
into the tale as to be, as Nietzsche put it in *The Birth of Tragedy*, "seduced into
the continuation of existence." But of that, more later.

Because, as Freud said, the content of the unconscious belongs to a realm
that is beyond time and beyond the very category of time, it can never be satisfactorily narrated as a historical series of events. Case history, traditionally the
favorite narrative format of psychological treaters, is almost, by definition, an
intrinsically unpsychological genre. So is psychosocial history, this preferred
form of social realism of the modern mental health industry. Attempts to
recount the events of the soul by means of case history are bound to lead to
failure, just as attempts to recount dreams are, because the narrative model of
journalistic reportage that insists on chronological order is always, to some
degree, and in an essential way, inadequate.

This necessary narrative failure manifests itself in a variety of forms. It can
appear in everything that, as psychoanalysts say, resists analysis. It can appear in
what remains forever unanalyzed at the end of every fifty-minute psychotherapy hour, and in what remains beyond analysis, even after many years of it. It
can appear in the very idea of an incomplete analysis, where the patient presumably quit too soon, but it also can be present at those points where every
analysis, and not only the presumably incomplete ones, is felt to be insufficient,
inadequate, and unsatisfying. It appears as well in what makes psychoanalysis, as

Freud said, interminable. The same sense of narrative failure appears also in what makes a patient's brooding self-absorption and analytical habits of thinking, acquired in treatment, continue after every session and after the therapy has ended. Along similar lines, but conversely, by becoming a psychoanalytically trained therapist, the naturally brooding type can turn a character trait into a full-time career, around a job that is, by definition, never done. Last but not least, the necessary failure to fully narrate existence appears in the inherent and endless dissatisfaction with Freudian theory itself, and with all psychotherapy theory as a whole. They never cease to attempt a true account of human experience, but they ceaselessly fail to fully satisfy, in spite of ever new and promising theory.

It is not only psychoanalytic treatment in particular, nor even psychological explanation in general, that is intrinsically unsatisfying in its ability to fully narrate existence. Language itself is at stake in the eternal demand for an account of life that brings all psychology into being in the first place. As we of the postmodern age have come to realize—not in the least thanks to Nietzsche's penetrating and pioneering insights into the matter—language itself reveals in the end no more, but also no less, than the built-in features of its grammar. The realities it reveals and permits us to name, describe, and account for are shaped by its grammar. All reality we find *out there* inheres in language, for the imagination in language brings everything *out there* into being—including "out there" and "being"—by making everything first imaginable and then visible in the first place. What language makes us find in nature, and what it then makes us say about nature, is exactly what it first imagines about it. It is less we who use language to speak than it is language that speaks to us and through us, and that makes us listen, so that we may see. If, as many say, it is by the grace of God that we go where we go, and do what we do, then it is largely by the grace of what is truly angelic in language that we first get the idea for all of it. In the beginning there is indeed always the word. The grammatically based imaginings of language that we call, rather pretentiously, its structures—for who can claim to know the anatomy of angels?—are not merely of linguistic interest. They have major implications. As the poet said, "Can we separate the dancer from the dance?," just because the grammar in language makes us believe that there is a subject that is separable from its predicate?

As Nietzsche pointed out, it is absurd to cling to such a fundamental belief as the belief in a subject that can be separated from its predicate, for can any deed be separated from the doer, just because the grammar of subject and predicate suggests it? We say "Lightning flashes" and believe that no one can question our truth. But is it not outright silly to believe such a truth? What else would lightning do? Could it be a subject that is separated from its predicate and that is not flashing? Where would lightning be, in its presumed self-identical permanence as subject, while it is a subject that is not flashing? Questions such as these bring out the assumptions that are present in language as its grammar. They show that these assumptions, which reveal reality to us as we see it, simultaneously mask the true mystery of everything when we name anything. These questions expose the false belief of nominalism, that language speaks the complete truth about all the things it names and points at. They expose an ever-present surplus of unnamed reality and significance, a surplus that is everywhere in everyday life and that we can never pinpoint with any kind of nominalist language, nor with discourse and narrations of human lives that are based on it.

This last point is dramatically enacted in the Book of Job. It appears there as the contrast between the unsatisfactory arguments Job's friends propose to explain his misery and the poetic images the Voice from the Whirlwind brings up. These images shatter all human arguments, even the very discourse and language that produce them. When the Voice from the Whirlwind challenges Job with such questions as "Where does darkness live?" or "Where is the west wind released?" or "Does the rain have a father? Who has begotten the dew?" Job is not expected to answer. How could he? These questions and images serve as reminders that language is not made primarily to communicate or to argue about truths and falsehoods but to simultaneously hide and reveal miracle. The poet's question (Can we separate the dancer from the dance?), the Nietzschean question (Where would lightning be when it is not flashing, or how can we possibly separate the doer from the deed or the subject from the predicate?), and the Voice from the Whirlwind's questions that leave Job speechless and awestruck—all these belong to the same category. What they have in common is their effectiveness at exposing the inadequacy of ordinary nominalist language for satisfactorily narrating existence. But they expose this inadequacy not for the purpose of landing man squarely and permanently in a state of nihilism and despair. They serve to hint at the mystery and splendor that are everywhere and that both hide behind and reveal themselves in language.

What is at stake in the failure to narrate the life of the soul in models of linear time, and what is at stake in the inadequacy of language to narrate existence as a temporal process, is nothing less than consciousness itself. Ever since Augustine, the nature of consciousness has been linked to the way we understand and recount time. Until he appeared on the historical horizon, time was understood as Aristotle viewed it. It was seen as a secondary feature associated with motion, in particular, with the movement of the heavenly bodies. Time was considered an aspect of the universe itself. It was thought to be something out there, wherever one looked and saw any kind of motion or commotion, wherever one saw things that involve movement or change. Most importantly, it was thought to be part of what we, today, tend to regard as the "external" world. Augustine changed all that. He made of time an internal affair of the individual's inner life. He made of time an affair that belongs to the individual's consciousness itself, not to the "external" world.

Augustine realized that time is both a familiar phenomenon and one that is difficult to understand. He saw that it is both an all-too-well-known aspect of the human condition and an essential part of its daily mystery. As he put the paradox in his *Confessions*, not without a sense of humor: "I know exactly what time is, as long as nobody asks me to say what it is." He considered the experience of time such an all-important feature of the human condition that he made it an essential part of human nature. He did so by transforming it from the cosmic reality it had previously been into a strictly psychological one. He internalized time and thereby became the first psychologist to make internalization itself a central idea in psychological theory. He made time a psychological and internal matter by attributing it to what we now consider "mental faculties." The past he assigned to the faculty of memory, the present he attributed to attention, and the future to anticipation. In one fell swoop, time stopped being a cosmic and mysterious affair that was everywhere visible. It became instead an internal, an individual, a psychological one. Modern psychological man, as we know him today, was conceived. Consciousness, as we now understand it, was formulated, and consciousness, as we now experience it, was formed.

Augustine reshaped man, the temporal creature, into man, the temporally oriented creature—the temporally thinking, feeling, and acting creature. Man no longer only lived in a world of temporal events. He himself became more temporal than he had previously been, in his very consciousness. He was remade in the likeness of his God who had invented linear time. His devotion to his God of linear time was no longer a devotion in word and deed only. It was now also a devotion in the very essence of his reformulated and reformed being. The divine story of a world with a beginning, a middle, and an eventual end was now no longer reflected only in the temporality of worldly events but also in every one of man's temporally imagined inner experiences. Everyday life, which had largely been a matter of temporal reflections of timeless mythic events, was recast. It was transposed into a format governed by the literary genre we now know as "psychosocial history" and "case history."

But still, as Freud's comments on time and the unconscious life of the soul imply, man, the temporal creature, kept one foot firmly planted in a realm that remains beyond time, beyond the very category of time. In that other realm, and as Freud said, his life participates in things that are timeless, that are not temporally ordered, that are not changed by time, and that cannot even be temporally imagined. By resisting confinement to the model of linear time, the life of the soul, from this point of view, also resists Augustine's internalizing move that moved time itself from out there to in here. As a result, the ancient concept of *anima mundi* or "world soul"—of an entire world full of soul and not just a body with a brain and a mind in it—survives the history of a psychology that would confine the soul to the restricted realm of the individual inner self. The soul's resistance to being confined to the linear temporal imagination is, in part, a resistance to Augustine's move that would strip the world "out there" of its psychic substance and that would place all that psychic substance "in here."

In order to regain a sense for this "world soul" that exists beyond the mind, the brain, and the body, it is necessary to find a mode of discourse that is independent of the model of linear time and of the nominalist language that serves this model. Jung implied how we can begin to think about what lies beyond the realm of linear time when he suggested that the realities of the unconscious soul belong "in a world where the pulse of time beats infinitely slowly, where the birth and death of individuals count for little." There are two active ingredients in this deceptively simple-sounding formula. The first is a slowing down against the press and speed of history. The second is an indifference to all that usually appears so important in all events from the point of view of the individual's personal interest in them. Where this slowing down and this indifference appear, there the realm that lies beyond history begins and becomes visible, and there the realm of the unconscious soul opens up in the midst of everyday life.

A prejudice in favor of the historically unchanging and the impersonal stands in stark contrast to the concerns of many forms of psychological treatment. Their emphasis tends to be on promoting change, and their cardinal measure of a thing's significance is its personal impact on the individual. It is beginning to look only natural that Jung should develop a psychology of the unconscious soul that is two tiered, with one layer being about a strictly personal and historically developed unconsciousness and the other layer about a collective unconscious. One layer concerns itself with the unique events of individual psychosocial history. The other layer addresses unchanging universal facts that belong "in a world where the pulse of time beats infinitely slowly, where the birth and death of individuals count for little." What opens up in this dimension of unchanging universal facts that are indifferent to the perpetual commotion and emotion of personal case histories is, as many of the world's myths imagine it, a deep underworld that coexists at all times with the upperworld of workaday activities. Greek myth, for one, imagines this natural kinship between the hard facts of history and the elusive ones of the soul as the brotherhood between Zeus and Hades—with Zeus as god and dominant force of the upperworld, while Hades is god of the coexistent underworld and Lord of Souls.

The Italian Neoplatonist philosophers of past centuries, who figure prominently in Jung and in Hillman, had a formula for this slowing down against the press and speed of history, and for regarding with indifference the clamor and the sound and fury of personal history. They advised: *Festina lente*. Taken literally, this means, "Hurry slowly." Taken imaginatively, "Hurry slowly" points to the paradoxical idea of moving forward precisely by slowing down. It suggests that progress is to be made exactly by standing still. By extension, it suggests the equally paradoxical idea of finding depth and profundity in the surfaces and faces of things. *Festina lente* is about recognizing the true essence of events in the precise way they appear. It is about standing still in the midst of the rush of history and about, as in Job's story, catching a glimpse of the revelation that the true mystery of creation lies in the poetic images of all its creatures. It is about standing still to catch a glimpse of the cosmic imagination that brings all things into being and that animates the very soul of the world itself, the *anima mundi*. The idea in *Festina lente* is to use any given situation or event as a point of departure to transition from the flux of time and haste toward a parallel and synchronous dimension whose realities are atemporal. Nothing changes in the historical facts, but the perspective on them changes. Everything begins to look new, even though nothing about the same old, same old is altered.

Festina lente is operative in modern depth psychology itself. Here personal and seemingly unique complaints and events from private history are transformed into timeless, universal, collective patterns of significance. Strictly clinical facts are transformed in the hands of Freud, Jung, and Hillman into the mythic ones they inherently already were from the start. Above all, everything that is otherwise regarded as mere appearance becomes sheer appearance. *Festina lente*, as guiding principle for a treatment that is suitable to the timeless matters of the soul, changes the customary uses of language. It stops viewing, and using, language as an instrument that serves primarily the flow of history and the ego's historical concerns. It lets language become a means for standing still in midstream. That way, words become a means to pluck bits of eternity from the advancing flux of time. Words begin to invite contemplation and to offer glimpses of the miraculous in the midst of the mundane. The goal of slowing down by means of language that serves psychological reflection is to sound the depth dimension that inheres in all ordinary things. It serves to make room for the perspective or prejudice that myth imagines as the underworld of Hades and that is present in every corner of the universe of everyday life over which Zeus presides.

Using language to slow down the rush of history is done by paying attention to the spontaneous, but usually ignored, imagination that is present in everyday speech. Figures of speech that appear in the narrative language of daily life are isolated from it. They are reinspected and reevaluated as being more important in themselves—because they are more loaded with the soul's own values—than for the ego's narratives in which they figure. Metaphors are likewise lifted from the context in which they appear and are given their own prominence. They are allotted more significance by themselves than as servants of the arguments and the accounts in which they are ordinarily used for the sake of the ego's interests. This way, words and figures of speech that have lost the patina of original metaphors, as a result of overuse, are once again made to shine as the freestanding images they once were and still are. The temporal sequence of events in an orderly narrative is here ignored or treated with indifference. In its place there is a mode of reflection that is in no hurry to move on, to go anywhere, to come to conclusions. This mode of reflection prefers to linger over isolated fragments of the narrative. Grammar itself is made to reveal its unspoken assumptions. In the process of this therapeutic revelation, the soul that animates language itself begins to display the valuables it cherishes by highlighting the images it favors. This way Hades is seen—and seen to coexist with daily life, just as his myth suggests.

When language is placed in the service of psychological reflection for the sake of the soul's own atemporal interests, it becomes halting. Freud knew this. He recognized the natural connection between spontaneously halted or interrupted flow of speech and the life of the soul to which it points. Hence, the psychoanalytic focus on such halting interruptions of normal speech flow as slips of the tongue, slips of the pen, the forgetting of familiar names, or the misnaming of familiar people and objects. Language here stops itself. Right where it comes to a halt, it opens up access to the underworld of the soul by showing cracks in the crust of everyday concerns. The psychological explorer gains access through these spontaneously formed openings into the deeper recesses of consciousness where the soul keeps its imaginings hidden under the watchful eye of Hades. All that happens in these forms of halting or bungled speech that have themselves acquired mythic status, as so-called Freudian slips, happens also in all manner of spontaneously bungled nonverbal actions. Wherever the ego is tripped up in this fashion, there a descent into depth of soul is provided a natural start. Depth psychology has a long tradition of beginning just there, in slips of all sorts—in all those places where the promising stories of life take a wrong turn, in everything that speaks not of ego triumphs but of alter ego interference, in every venture and adventure that becomes misadventure, in the neuroses on Freud's couch, in the psychoses of Jung's hospital work. Jung, like Freud, discovered the presence of hidden psychic material just beneath the surface of everyday language. His word association experiments, like Freud's studies of slips of the tongue and other bungled actions, pointed to the free-ranging verbal fantasies of the soul that coexist with the ego's speech and that are hidden in it. They showed that when language is released of its usual burden of having to serve the future-oriented goals of the ego, it quickly begins to deviate from its straight linear course. Whenever it does so, it begins to produce all manner of spontaneous asides. And these, so Freud and Jung agreed, form a more truthful commentary on what preoccupies the soul.

Nietzsche, in *Daybreak*, and before Freud and Jung, said that "consciousness is a more or less fantastic commentary on an unknown, perhaps unknowable text." In few phenomena is this more readily proven true than in these Freudian slips of the tongue, and in these Jungian word association experiments. Here the soul shows exactly how fantastic its commentary on existence can be. This is just as in the case of the priestess of Delphi's oracle, for whom it is only when her ordinary speech flow gives way to word fantasies and word associations that she begins to voice fateful truths. Today, and as though in accordance with this ancient oracular style, psychotherapists everywhere are listening for all manner of slippages in speech—the odd choice of expression, the hesitation in an otherwise seamless account of events, the misspoken word, the misplaced use of a metaphor, the image that stands out, the cracking voice, the note of feeling that is out of character. Another of today's versions of an oracle that speaks the truth by registering disruptions in ordinary speech is the lie detector test. Like the Jungian word association experiment, from which it is derived, and like the Freudian slip of the tongue or the pen, the lie detector test shows irregularities that appear as ripples and eddies in the otherwise smooth flow of the stream of language. These, in turn, serve to indicate the presence of unseen shapes and of deeper currents beneath the stream of surface meanings. These hidden presences in midstream are themselves unchanged by the surface flow of language that runs over them. The ripples and eddies they produce are reminders that other forces are at work in the flux of daily living besides the ego's intentions. The presence of those forces explains why everything is not always the smooth sailing for which we are eternally hoping.

Depth psychology, as we have it today—as Freudian or post–Freudian psychoanalysis of personal unconsciousness, as Jungian analytical psychology of the collective unconscious, or as Hillman's archetypal psychology of the soul of the world, which erases both Freud's distinction between conscious and unconscious and Jung's between individual and collective—is a contemporary version of the ancient formula, *Festina lente*. Its aim is to slow down and stop the press of history, in order to end the ego's obsession with the literal facts of life. A psychology with this aim in mind eventually almost turns its back on the exclusively personal perspective that takes all things only literally. It eventually abandons that restricted perspective, because it measures all things too exclusively with the personal prejudice of the ego's temporal orientation. In addition to insisting on personal awareness, such depth psychology also emphasizes awareness of the restricting personal prejudices of all ego psychology. It aims at more awareness, not only of the personal and the interpersonal but also, and especially, of the impersonal in all situations. In addition to addressing the uniquely individual, it looks for what is anything but unique. It looks, rather, for what is timeless in its commonness. It stops taking psychosocial history as the best manner of accounting for the life of the soul. It stops taking the private confessional, and the intimate journal, as the soul's true and preferred genre. In their place, it takes mythic imagination to be the soul's most natural medium. Depth psychology puts the formula of *Festina lente* into practice, and by doing that it ends up giving Everyman one firm foot in history but one foot beyond history. In-depth analysis of the life of the soul is therefore indeed both historical and ahistorical, simultaneously.

Paradoxically, then, what often starts as fascination with the unique psychological features of the individual person and of his or her private history and development is slowly transformed into a kind of relative indifference to all these. But this indifference is not the same thing as lack of interest or insensitivity. And it is not about dismissing whatever is historical in favor of something else that is not. Quite the opposite. It is about reevaluating all that is historical so that what is inherently ahistorical in it becomes a more manifest part of history itself. It is about giving up the exclusivity of only one perspective in order to gain access to a deeper and richer one. It is about letting go of the private worries I have about tomorrow in order to see what the soul is thinking about today. It is not only about finding solutions to the ego's concerns with day-to-day management but also about finding access to what lies beyond those concerns, even in the midst of them. It is about catching a glimpse of what is preoccupying the ego's alter, its purely psychic Other.

The modern "talking cure," invented by an inspired psychological treater and named so by his imaginative first patient, is truly about the natural pairing of words and soul, about the natural affinity between *psyche* and *logos*. It is simplistic to think that everyday words and language serve primarily the social purpose of communication and the personal one of individual expression. Speech comes first for soul because the link between *psyche* and *logos* comes first from the beginning, as a primordial ingredient of the human condition. The natural connection between *psyche* and *logos* often may be last to be discovered—as the discipline of "psychology" was itself one of the last of the humanities to come into being, as the "talking cure" was the last attempt in treating "nervous diseases," as psychiatry is the last specialty to be consulted on difficult cases, and as the idea of seeing a psychiatrist or psychologist becomes acceptable only when all else in life is failing. But in spite of frequently being recognized last in time, the *psyche-logos* connection is anything but last in rank. What is last to come to mind often is first as founding principle and bottom-line reality. The obvious is hardest to see.

Words and language do serve communication, but this is not, in the first place, a social affair. Words are messengers not only socially but also because a messenger is, as Greek has it, an "*angelos*," an angel. Like angels, words do more than carry strictly human messages on a purely historical and exclusively humanistic plane. Their traffic is not only two-dimensional. They introduce a third dimension, depth. The angels that words are move between the realm of mythic beings and that of humans. They link the mundane and the not so mundane, the profane and the sacred, the utterly personal and things over which I have no say. As the origin of Christianity testifies in the figure of Mary, one angelic word is enough to impregnate a virginal soul with a destiny it must bear and bring into the world of human life. The "talking cure" that links *logos* and *psyche* gives Everyman a chance to see that every word he speaks also is an angelic word spoken *to* him. The ears with which we hear are located closest to our mouth not just because vocal chords and eardrums both have to be plugged into the brain via the shortest possible route. Ear and mouth exist in close proximity because all the words we ever speak are first of all words that are spoken to us and through us. They are messengers that we ourselves, not any social other, must hear first. Every word is an angel that ties us to an ahistorical destiny, not only to a human community or to our own self-reported history. Words—even our own, especially our own—are less spoken to a social other than they are an angelic Other speaking to us. Depth psychology retransforms words into the *angelos* they always were and will be. It does this by applying the formula of making progress by standing still: *Festina lente*.

FIVE

FIRST INVENTION,
THEN DISCOVERY

"SOME SOULS ONE WILL NEVER DISCOVER, unless one invents them first."
So says Nietzsche's Zarathustra. This lapidary statement contains a whole theory
in a nutshell about the nature of knowledge in psychology and in psychotherapy. It says that imaginative invention is not only possible in these fields but
necessary. Conversely, it suggests that whatever parades as knowledge in psychology is a matter of invention before anything else, and that psychological
treatment is, and must be, about a poetics of the soul.

The scene where Zarathustra makes this statement is reminiscent of the
kind of intimate and reflective interaction that occurs in psychotherapy. It
involves a young man who is deeply preoccupied and who is trying hard to sort
out his feelings and thoughts about a certain matter that is on his mind. It also
involves another person who is witnessing this and who tries to extend a help-
ing hand. He inquires about what is on the young man's mind and offers his
own reflections. This is indeed the outline of the psychotherapy setting everywhere. But it is not restricted to formal psychological treatment. It is the frame-
work of any encounter between two human beings who are focused on matters of soul. And just as the scene in question resembles the setting of
psychotherapy, even though it is itself not about such treatment, so too is its relevance not restricted to formal treatment settings.

The young man in the scene has been listening to Zarathustra, who has
been talking to a crowd about new and disturbing ideas. The young man is later
quietly brooding about what he has heard. He is trying to sort out for himself
what significance these ideas he has just heard have, and especially what place
they are to have in his own life. Zarathustra notices the young man's turmoil
and speaks to him. He asks what is on his mind, and he then guesses precisely

what is going on in his heart. The young man, when he hears his troubling private experiences of the moment accurately identified, is both relieved and astounded. He is relieved that his experience is clearly identifiable at all, that there is someone who can make sense of what he is thinking and feeling. But he also is astounded that his strictly personal and private experience can be so well understood by someone other than himself. So in response to Zarathustra's comment he says, baffled: "Yes . . . (but) . . . How is it possible that you discovered my soul?" To which Zarathustra replies, in a departure from both psychotherapy theory and practice: "Some souls one will never discover, unless one invents them first."

What is at stake here is not only a fundamental statement about the very nature and status of psychological theory and psychological knowledge generally. It also is about the way such theory and knowledge are offered to psychotherapy patients as something that applies to their personal history and to their private experience of that history. Zarathustra makes a statement here that is lacking in psychotherapy theory. It is a statement about how any psychotherapy theory ever manages to become a personal truth for any patient. It is about how any idea about the life of the soul ever manages to become believable. Zarathustra suggests that whatever claim to veracity any psychological theory can ever make is by no means a matter of absolute truth that comes with or without irrefutable proof. Rather, it is a matter of imagination that requires as its *sine qua non* a dose of willing suspension of disbelief. Bluntly put, whatever truths there are in psychotherapy are less discovered than they are invented. Truth about the life of the soul is a matter of invention coming before discovery, because invention is necessary for making discovery possible in the first place. An immediate consequence of this state of affairs is that psychology is less about the facts *of* life than it is about fictions *for* living. It is not so much about discovering insights into the way things really are but about inventing imaginative models for what we may want to believe they are like. It is about the facts of life being potentially just as fantastic as the fictions that can be imagined about them.

The whole tradition of depth psychology may thereby be restored to what it always was and is and will be in the first place, a poetics of polymorphous inventions. This is what makes for the truly mythic nature of all psychotherapy theory. It also explains the inevitability of so much in those theories that must often at first seem bizarre and hard to believe for the layperson. That hard-to-believe bizarreness is almost a necessary ingredient. It assures the presence of active imagination, which is itself necessary, because it is what makes any treatment of soul possible in the first place. No longer do we have to insist as much as we do that our psychological theories are guaranteed factual. They must be imaginative first before they ever even have a chance of becoming factual. There must be something far-fetched about them, because that imaginative quality is psychotherapy's active ingredient. If an idea sounds all too acceptable to the patient, this often only means that he or she is incorporating it symptomatically. The patient simply adds it to his or her already rigidly established belief system without there being any new light shed on anything. A psychological idea that all too readily sounds rational and true should for that very reason be viewed with skepticism from the start. It may easily fail to do the soul any good, precisely because all it does is fortify the ego's insistence on the status quo.

The idea of the poetic nature of all psychological theory casts a different light on familiar and established therapeutic knowledge. Long-lived theories such as many of Freud's still-standing concepts—about such things as the role and the workings of instincts, the early psychological symbiosis between mother and child, triangulations between children and their parents, primary narcissism and the autism of psychosis, repetition compulsions and transference neurosis, reality testing, regression, and all the rest—all this, so Zarathustra would suggest, is a poetics of soul before it is anything else. That is why an index of psychoanalytic ideas sounds like a parade of fictional figures from ancient mythology: Eros, Thanatos, Ananke, the Titans, Oedipus, Narcissus. These are only the best-known and, so to speak, card-carrying mythic figures among them. There are other borrowings as well, from religion, from history, or from anthropological lore. Many other psychoanalytic concepts disguise their imaginative nature with modern and scientific-sounding names and terms. This includes Freud's use of metaphors and images from such fields as biology, neurology, and archaeology, or from engineering enterprises such as the winning of land from the sea by means of dams and dikes. Yet no matter how strictly rational and scientific-sounding any of these paradigms may be, they are always poetic fictions before they can ever become psychological facts.

It is not only Freud who went to the inventions of the imagination for ways to express his psychological truths. Jung did the same thing. He cast his net even wider than Freud. He included not just a few handfuls but a vast array of figures from religion, myth, legend, fantasy, dreams, visions, art, and esoteric literature. As a result, and when the momentum of Jung's theorizing imagination gets fully underway, it is sometimes difficult to see that he is still writing about the psychological life of ordinary men and women. Yet that is precisely his subject matter. Whereas Freud had convinced the world that the soul is a fundamental fact in everyday life, Jung went further and stated his view that it is not only *a* fact, nor even a fundamental fact, but *the* most fundamental fact of life. As he put it, *psyche* or soul is "the mother of all facts" of life. Making that point required arguing that imagination plays a far broader role than had previously been appreciated in modern psychology, even in psychoanalysis. Hence, the expanded space that images and the imagination occupy in Jungian theory and practice. Hillman, after Jung, broadens the role that imagination plays in psychology even further. For him, there are no facts except those of the imagination, since he views all facts as image. This is behind his unrelenting insistence, learned from Jung, that soul is image and image soul. But he goes one step farther and adds his own twist to it. Thus Hillman says, in paraphrase: if the soul is what you are after in any given thing, then stop viewing the thing literally, as a fact, and start viewing it metaphorically instead, as an image. Again, and also in paraphrase: if you want to know the psychological essence of anything, you must first see it as an image, and then you must deepen that image and enter it—by developing a sense for how it imagines itself and for how it plays itself out in the incarnate world of so-called facts. Thus from Freud through Jung and into Hillman there is an intensifying focus on images and imagination as the fundamentally poetic bottom-line realities of psychological life. In this development from Freud through Jung and into Hillman, depth psychology itself, as a whole that is larger than the figures associated with its parts, is spontaneously following a principle that Nietzsche had identified before all three. In his description of what happens in inspiration, and in all perception insofar as it is based on inspiration, Nietzsche wrote this: "It actually seems . . . as if things themselves approached and offered themselves as metaphors. . . . 'On every metaphor you ride to every truth.'" Hillman, who is not only heir to both Freud and Jung but who does his work in no small measure in the name of Dionysos, whom Nietzsche, too, had adopted as his patron saint, could not sum up his own evolved views more precisely or in stronger terms.

It is not only the ideas of such modern imaginative figures in depth psychology as Freud, Jung, and Hillman that are based on the premise of a poetic basis of mind, and of poetic invention as the soul's fundamental activity. The very field of depth psychology or the psychology of unconsciousness is itself nothing if not imaginative, in title as much as in substance. The very things that are identified in its name and subject—Depth, *Psyche* or Soul, Logos and Unconsciousness—are themselves images first. They are facts only secondarily, to the extent that they become imaginable and sustainable as psychological theory. Even deliberately Freud-free and anything-but-esoteric sounding psychologies, those that would shun all things imagistic in favor of the utterly pedestrian, remain based on poetic invention. They too require willing suspension of disbelief. Psychologies with less fantastic looking matter, psychologies that are made up of more factual-looking ingredients—such as multiculturalism, feminism, and social constructivism—are, in spite of appearances to the contrary, based on invented fiction first and on factuality a derived second. In all of this, the last and hardest layer of seeming factuality to be recognized as invented fiction is the physicality of existence. It would seem that no reasonable person could possibly argue with the hard facts of physics, and with the physical basis of all psychological experience. And yet even the facts of physics are invented fictions first. They are facts only by virtue of our willingness to view them as such, by virtue of our insistence on believing in them in this manner. For even though it is easily forgotten, science, too, offers no facts, only models of imagined factuality. It offers paradigms of potential truths, images of what reality may perhaps be like, analogies that compare things unknown to things presumed known, persuasive metaphors that tell a believable lie. These models are persuasive *while* they are persuasive and *until* they are no longer persuasive. They are considered true *while* they are considered true and *until* they are proven false by newer and more persuasive models of factuality. As Nietzsche suggested: "Physics, too, is only an interpretation and exegesis of the world (to suit us, if I may say so!)." So whether it is the often far-fetched and seemingly questionable claims of fact from depth psychology, the more readily observable but interminably arguable ones from everyday sociopolitical life, or even the hard facts from proven science, in all these there exists a factuality that can only appear wearing masks. But that factuality is not one that exists *behind* the masks it wears, nor is it one that can eventually be unmasked, once we develop the right methods for uncovering it. Rather, it exists only as the masks themselves. And it is precisely here that psychology comes upon the marker stone where all strictly rational and analytical human inquiry ends, and where the mystery in everyday life begins.

But not just any invention will do to serve as theory of soul. All fictions, and especially the inventions from psychological treatment, propose a world to live in, and a way of living in that world. For a psychological fiction or invention to be possibly true, it must be inhabitable. The person to whom it is offered, as insight and potential truth about his or her life, must be capable of being persuaded that the proposed world and the life to be lived in it are possible. And for that virtual world and the life that goes with it to be possible, they must not only be imaginable but also desirable.

Freud, in "Constructions in Analysis," wrote about this sort of therapeutic inventions that psychological treaters offer their patients. He called them, quite appropriately, and as the title of his paper suggests, "constructions." He spelled out what it takes for the constructed image of such a proposed world to be considered believable. Or rather, he wrote about what actually happens when a therapist offers his or her patient the blueprint of such a world that the patient may consider, and perhaps appropriate, as a psychological habitat. Freud's discussion addresses those critics who question the speculative psychoanalytic reconstructions of the patient's presumably forgotten past. These critics, so Freud complains, accuse psychoanalysis of operating by the rule of, "Heads I win, tails you lose." If the patient agrees with the speculative reconstruction of his or her forgotten past, so the critics say, then that is taken as proof of its truth. But if the patient disagrees, so they continue, then that is taken as a sign that he or she is resistant to treatment, and that is itself interpreted as a confirmation that the psychoanalyst is probably on the right track, and that the reconstruction must therefore be true. Wrong, said Freud. The situation is not as simple as these critics would make it sound. For one thing, psychoanalysis does not simply take the patient's yes or no at face value. The decisive factor, said Freud, is something altogether different. The psychoanalyst considers a construction true when the patient responds to it with the spontaneous recollection of previously forgotten events from his or her past, a recollection that is triggered by the construction itself.

Thus, so we can continue beyond Freud, these past events now fall into place in the construction, like perfectly fitting pieces of a puzzle in progress. When this happens, the patient takes over the narration of the reconstruction of his or her past from the therapist, precisely by spontaneously supplying the historical evidence for it. The new recollections provide the way in which the patient identifies with the construction. The patient claims it as a newly added part of the story of his or her life. It is a new wing added on to the psychic household in which he or she has been living. The successful psychological construction therefore proposes a truly inhabitable world. It offers a world that comes complete with an individualized and viable history. The patient may choose to live in this world. All the patient has to do is indicate that the construction is acceptable. That is precisely what he or she does through the spontaneous recollections. The patient appropriates the proposed world, stakes a claim to it, becomes a settler in it, and moves all his or her private psychological belongings into it—all the psychic furniture and baggage and emotional family heirlooms collected over the years and over the generations. The patient confirms the construction's reality by occupying its world—lock, stock, and barrel.

A successful psychological construction is therefore true only by *becoming* true, by being *made true*. And it is made true not by the treater or the treater's theory but by the patient. It is always the patient who must offer his or her life in support of a theory that, without such confirmation of it, has no credibility and therefore no psychological value. The make-believe of the construction turns into belief because the patient wants it so, because the patient can bring enough of his or her actual experience to bear on the construction to make it appear factual. The metaphor that every construction is becomes sustainable in this fashion. It turns into what every successful metaphor is, fiction that tells a truth about the facts of life. It becomes more than just a mad proposition, made up by the speculating mind of the treater. It acquires the features of a believable, individualized cosmology. And so it is well on its way to become part of a personalized metaphysics.

But things are not always this easy, said Freud. Sometimes the evidence of spontaneous recollections is not forthcoming. In that case, so he suggested, the analyst must persuade the patient of the truth of the reconstruction. Writes Freud, in the same paper: "The way in which a conjecture of ours is transformed into the patient's conviction . . . is hardly worth describing. All of it is familiar . . . and is intelligible without difficulty."

Not so! The question of psychology's believability, of the process whereby psychotherapeutic make-believe becomes belief, is anything but familiar and intelligible without difficulty. It is an enigma Freud never addressed.

We can begin to understand how therapeutic make-believe becomes belief by looking at it through the lens of Aristotle's theory of narrative composition, from his *Poetics*. The poetic act of creating a plot or *mythos* that is successful because it is plausible, so Aristotle said, involves bringing together the events to be narrated in such a fashion that the account of their unfolding appears both self-sufficient and self-explanatory. Transposed for psychological treatment purposes that means: the psychological plot or construction a treater offers the patient as a previously untold part of the story of his or her life must incorporate recollection, and that recollection must in some fashion be self-sufficient and self-explanatory. This already gives a hint of why a patient's recollections in response to a speculative reconstruction of the past are so important. It also hints at why these recollections serve to complete the construction, and to make it believable, by providing the convincing evidence for it. Self-sufficient, in Aristotle's theory of emplotment, and in the therapeutic reconstruction of a patient's life, means complete and capable of satisfying all that is needed in order to tell the whole story. Nothing that is felt to belong to the events of the life under discussion, and that needs to be accounted for, is left out. But also, nothing that does not belong to those same events is imposed on them. All that matters about the events being brought together in the plot is told in terms that are based on those events, and on nothing else. The account is to be done in such a fashion that it satisfies the listener precisely because it says everything that needs to be said for the sake of completeness. The plot is considered good when, and because, it says enough. Self-explanatory, in Aristotle and in a therapeutic account of a life, means that the only explanation of the events that is provided, and needed, is the internal logic of the events themselves and of the characters involved in them. A well-construed and plausible story has a plot in which the events are intelligible solely on their own terms, and as a function of the total plot in which they belong. They are felt to be intrinsically inevitable in the way they hang together. The parts in the plot form a whole that makes sense, and this sense that the plot makes requires each part. The sum total that the plot provides is the only thing that makes sense of it all, and the sense it makes of it all makes more sense than any of the parts by themselves. The characters, in turn, are so perfectly suited for the plot that the plot is, as it were, their natural course. Conversely, the plot allows for no other characters and for none of the characters to be any different from the way they are.

The question of narrative completeness goes to the heart of psychology's long-standing preoccupation with remembering and forgetting. It bears on the therapeutic importance of telling the story of one's life correctly, truthfully, and completely. A potentially therapeutic construction of the soul's life proposes to account for more of the patient's life than has so far been incorporated into the autobiography he or she has been telling himself or herself. Such a construction is accepted as true, and has therapeutic value, precisely if and when and because it accounts for more than has previously been accounted for. Conversely, what psychological treaters think of as repression amounts to the opposite of a therapeutic construction. It is about recounting less of a life than has to be told to satisfy the need for a sense of completeness. By its incompleteness, it leaves the patient wanting. It makes the patient feel like an incomplete person because it makes him or her an incompletely defined character. It makes life feel like an incompletely told, and therefore an inauthentically lived, plot. This makes for the nagging sense, the intuitive knowledge, that something is missing. The facts of life do not add up as presented. Important things are left out. The patient's life as he or she has lived it, as he or she is currently living it, and as he or she will likely continue to live it is not complete. It cannot complete itself until things that are now left out can be made to fall into place. As we can gather from Aristotle, this requires skilled poetic invention. And as we may now add, this kind of skilled poetic invention is needed, because it is precisely what has to be placed in service of the soul, so that the life it animates can become, and feel, more whole. Zarathustra said it: "Some souls one will never discover, unless one invents them first." The treatment of the soul requires an imaginative, creative, inventive talking cure, indeed, just as history's very first psychoanalytic patient knew from the beginning. The psychotherapy patient, in this view, suffers less from reminiscences of the past, as Freud had put it in an early formulation, than from narrative incompleteness. The patient suffers from insufficient, and therefore unsatisfactory, emplotment, from a personal *mythos* that does not fit, because it does not cover all the facts of his or her life. By implication, the patient suffers from a life that lacks sufficient imagination, and that therefore cannot imagine itself properly. The patient suffers, in the end, from a shortness of adequate images to contain all that a life produces, so that nothing gets lost in the recycling bin of repressive unconsciousness.

The other half of what makes a psychological plot therapeutic, besides greater completeness in the account of the soul's life, rests in the sense of the plot's necessity. Only when the events of a life are recounted in such a manner that their account gives them internal coherence and necessity are they not only confirmed in their completeness but also affirmed in their inherent value. More precisely and more decisively, only then do they acquire a positive value—for being thus and such and not otherwise, for being part of a larger whole that stands affirmed in its totality. A life that is well recounted and accounted for in this manner acquires an overall sense of positive value in spite of partial features of it that may by themselves perhaps appear negative in value. The overall plot gives to all its parts, both the seemingly positive ones and the seemingly negative ones, their necessity. Here, in such confirming and affirming therapeutic plots about the soul's life, Augustine's positive world vision from his *Confessions* has the potential of becoming Everyman's vision: "I no longer wished for a better world, because I was thinking of the whole of creation. . . . Though the higher things are better than the lower, the sum of all creation is better than the higher things alone." The patient who finds a therapeutic plot in psychological treatment may come to a similar conclusion, and he may no longer wish that life had been different. He or she may now see that even though some parts of it are better than others, the total picture of it looks better than the better parts alone. And for that affirmative vision, even the not-so-good parts are needed. They are necessary to make the whole plot hang together. In sum, then, with such luminaries as Aristotle, Augustine, and Nietzsche's Zarathustra in the deep background, the soul's talking cure works as a potential for redemption that exists in every life and that relies on its built-in poetic imagination.

What is at stake is not only of interest to the patient in psychological treatment or to the treater. A universal and timeless human issue is at hand, one that is essential to the human condition. It is dramatically portrayed in a scene from Shakespeare's *A Midsummer Night's Dream*. Toward the end of the play, when the action of the magical night is over, Bottom wakes up from the fantastic events that have happened. He realizes that something special has taken place, something of great significance to himself and to the other characters involved. He is bewildered by what happened, and he feels ill suited to make sense of his experience. He even doubts whether there is anyone at all who can do justice to it. Nevertheless, he immediately and intuitively knows that it will be important to create an account of the events, an account that will be worthy of them and that will be a good thing to tell himself and others. Says Bottom:

> I have had a most rare vision. I have had a dream, past the wit of man to say what dream it was. Man is but an ass, if he go about to expound this dream. Methought I was—there is no man can tell what. Methought I was, and methought I had—But man is but a patched fool if he will offer to say what methought I had. The eye of man hath not heard, the ear of man hath not seen, man's hand is not able to taste, his tongue to conceive, nor his heart to report what my dream was. I will get Peter Quince to write a ballet [i.e., a ballad] of this dream. It shall be called "Bottom's Dream," because it hath no bottom; and I will sing it . . .

Bottom's innocence is in some ways comic. It also is profoundly reminiscent of a universal and essential human trait. His innocence makes him a winning figure not only because he is endearing in manner or because he knows and accepts his inadequacy for the task of telling what really happened. He is a winning figure primarily because he personifies the essential human inadequacy of Everyman to tell the true tale of life—his own life, any life, and ultimately life itself. Bottom, even though he may be a comic figure, presents an issue that is anything but comedy. He is, if such a thing were to exist, preinterpretive man—and to that extent, he is incomplete. He is man as he might be if he were not always interpreting the world and his life in it, with all the potential for tragedy, comedy, or farce—as well as delusion and neurosis—that goes with the act of interpreting. He is man faced with, and going through, the facts of life, yet without a sense, any sense, of what they amount to, of how they can be recounted, of what they may be likened to. Bottom is life minus the ability to look in the mirror of reflection. He is a human voice that can produce sound but that cannot hear and understand itself. He is the sound and the fury of life—not signifying nothing but rather not-signifying-at-all. He is Everyman whenever Everyman feels that things in his life do not add up to anything that makes sense.

Having been outfitted in the play with the head of an ass that was placed over his own head as he was tricked into participating in the events of the magical night, Bottom lives up to that precise image of himself. He presents a figure of man looking like a lovable ass and playing a part in things that go completely over his head and leave him befuddled. But even stronger than the feeling of being befuddled is the urge to seek an account of events, an account that one can tell oneself and others, and that can be the story of one's life. Preinterpretive man does not exist because, like Bottom, he cannot tolerate existing as such. Everything that happens in a human life happens, as it were, with an urge to end up in a book, in the account of its own story. Bottom personifies that aspect of the human condition precisely by giving voice to the feeling of incompleteness in a life that remains untold. He turns to the figure of Peter Quince, because Peter Quince personifies what Bottom lacks, the capacity to turn the events of the magical night into a story that provides a full account of what happened.

Peter Quince is ostensibly the town's resident poet, the historian who records local events. He is the bard who turns the facts of life into legend, the troubadour who sets legends to music. But who is he for Bottom—who calls on him? What does Bottom want from him? Why does he need him? Peter Quince personifies that reflective imagination that makes Everyman visible to himself and that situates him in an image of the world that is visible around him. He is the great mirror of reflection that frames everything and that can give us of each thing at least a glimpse of its significance. He is whatever is always perhaps somewhat preposterous and blundering in the eternal search for a satisfying image of one's life, like Bottom himself. But he also is what is most serious and most deeply stirring in that search, such as man's best poetry. And the image itself that Peter Quince must provide of life as it has been and is must not only be truthful. It also must be desirable, so that one wants one's life to be an imitation of it. In sum, Peter Quince is for Bottom that self-imagination that must confirm the facts of his life and that must, beyond this, also affirm the value of his life. He is what must enable Bottom to say about the story of his own life what Zarathustra wants to be able to say about all of life: "But thus I willed it. But thus I will it. Thus shall I will it." For Peter Quince personifies the essence of the imaginative seduction that, as Nietzsche said in *The Birth of Tragedy*, "seduces us into a continuation of existence."

Peter Quince's rendering of Bottom's life matters, because Bottom's life is at stake in it. For what Bottom asks Peter Quince is nothing less than to tell him who he is. What is at stake is the process whereby Bottom becomes who he is, before his very own eyes. Peter Quince's ballad must say to Bottom: "This is your life as you have lived it, as you are now living it and as you will live it . . . *Ecce Homo*. . . . Look at yourself. . . . Behold this human life which you are." What Bottom asks of Peter Quince is nothing less than to complete him. He must complete his experience by giving it to him as a recognizable image of itself, as an image that Bottom may both behold and become. Peter Quince must complete Bottom as an individual by giving him an individual story in which he belongs. He must complete his created world by giving him a local habitat in it in which to live. As the Great Bard himself put it:

> . . . as imagination bodies forth
> The forms of things unknown, the poet's pen
> Turns them to shapes, and gives to airy nothing
> A local habitation and a name.

Today the role of Peter Quince is occupied by the literal person of the psychotherapist. But here the personification of reflective self-imagination is taken one step farther—and in the direction of a literalization of persons, a literalization that has become institutionalized. It comes in the form of designated schools for professional psychotherapy training and in the guise of licensing boards—and trade organizations, insurance boards, and now also managed care organizations that oversee the practices of its treatment providers. It comes in the form of the American Psychological Association and the American Psychiatric Association, insofar as they regulate all officially sanctioned talk about the soul, as well as all treatment of it. Together these institutional forms of Peter Quince produce massive amounts of trade literature but too few inspired ballads that Bottom might like to hum to himself, let alone sing aloud with pride and glee. By becoming a restricted trade that is guarded by its own guild, and by the paying customers who subsidize the enterprise, the function that Peter Quince personifies is not only institutionalized. It also is split off from Everyman's own everyday life. It stops being an integral part of his daily activities, and it is placed apart from them. It now keeps business hours in the mental health clinic and the therapist's office, where one goes by appointment only. The universal, the quintessentially human, the essentially poetic activity of life-affirming imagination by which we keep ourselves enamored with and seduced into a continuation of existence is handed over to a class of designated specialists. The diplomas on their office walls certify their exclusive rights. These include, foremost, the right to make up the myths about the life of the soul, and the right to prescribe these myths for everyone else to live by. The idea that Peter Quince personifies for Bottom is thereby paradoxically turned into its opposite. For Bottom, so he and we expect, ends up with more than he has before turning to Peter Quince. The sense of added value in his life, which Peter Quince gives to it, makes Bottom want to sing about it. Today's psychotherapy patient, in contrast, often ends up with less. Rather than bursting into a life-affirming song, the patient discovers the stammering speech of the psychotherapy confessional, with Freudian slips and other bungled speech shaping not only the story line but the genre itself. The patient's story is not about to be handed back to him or her set to verse or music in any way, nor is it turned into a legend worth living by, and worth passing on. It does not become a personalized tune to hum along while at work or maybe even to sing in select public settings on the right occasion, as it is for Bottom. Rather, it becomes an obsessive refrain to silently and privately ruminate about at all hours of the day and night, and that is entitled, "What my therapist said . . ."

Freud consistently argued in favor of lay analysis and against the professional regulation of psychoanalysis. He also argued against a reduction of the role of psychoanalysis to that of a handmaiden of medicine in general and psychiatry in particular. These arguments are even more relevant now than they were in Freud's day. The main point is that the business of the soul belongs to the human domain, not to anyone's exclusive professional turf or to any regulatory board and regulated class. The only specialization required to attend to the soul is the specialty of being human, and that is a corner of the market staked long ago by the poets among us. As Aristotle said, poetry is more universal and more universally true than any kind of history—including, therefore, clinical history and psychosocial history—can ever hope to be. This accounts for the predominance in depth psychology of images that are borrowed from the world's best poetic imagination, for those images serve better than anything else as psychology's bottom-line theoretical concepts and constructs. So if the construction of theories and treatments of the soul is a matter of inventing fictions to live by, if depth psychology is a poetics of the soul, and if discovering psychological truth is about inventing viable worlds to inhabit, then it is, indeed, as Zarathustra suggests: insight into the soul is a kind of knowledge that starts with imagination. And that is precisely what the depth psychologies of Freud, Jung, and Hillman are all about. But there is, as Hillman notes, a crucial point to emphasize here. What matters is not so much *what* invented plots Freud and depth psychologists after him recognize in the actual lives of everyday men and women. What matters far more is the fact *that* they discover and rediscover the primacy of poetic invention for psychological theory and knowledge—and, above all, for life itself.

The task after Freud is not so much to argue where he may have been right and where he was wrong, and where we should improve on him. Those who make that their foremost concern are at risk of missing the mark, by misperceiving it. Nor is dismissing Freud and depth psychology altogether, in favor of a psychology purged of fantastic ideas, in the soul's or psychology's best interest. Rather, the task after Freud is to add to his wealth of fantastic and mythic ideas more of the same. This is precisely what Jung and Hillman appear to have understood and to have done better than most of their post–Freudian colleagues, many of whom insist on improving psychoanalysis by focusing more on removing its technical flaws than on expanding its imaginative reach. The future of depth psychology and the welfare of the soul, as Freud knew, do not depend on degrees in psychology and psychiatry, nor are they automatically well served by them. They do not necessarily require or benefit from tighter control over the curriculum of education in psychology, nor from more regulation and stricter laws governing psychological practice. They require, instead, more active imagination. Above all, they require a faith that such active imagination must come first, and a resolve to make it come first—in psychology as in life. If by nature and by method psychology in general and psychotherapy in particular tell their truths by telling made-up untruths, then the job is to work against excessive rationalism, excessive literalism, excessive scientism. The job is to work against what Oscar Wilde, in an essay with the same title, called "the decay of lying." Positively stated, the job is to work for a kind of psychology that is first and last, and unapologetically, a poetics of the soul. As Zarathustra suggests, and as the case of Freud's psychoanalysis argues, before anything else and for all depth psychology to come, the truth about the life of the soul has to be invented before—and so that—it can be discovered.

Nietzsche's philosophy and psychology, which were the wellspring of so much in modern depth psychology, were guided by his historical New Year's resolution from *The Gay Science* "to learn more and more to see as beautiful what is necessary in things," so as to become "one of those who make things beautiful." That New Year's resolution can now be reformulated to suit the purposes of the soul and of depth psychology. Such a reformulation can then become a psychologist's New Year's resolution: to learn more and more to see as imaginative what seems only literal in things, to become one of those who make things begin to show the life of the soul in them that animates them. Nietzsche would have been well pleased not so much with the hard-nosed scientific pretensions in Freud and even less so with the metaphysical ones in Jung but with the boldness of imagination in both. He would have approved of the desire to *want* to make such imagination into a hard-nosed science all its own, just as he would have approved of the desire to *want* to make it into a metaphysics for a more psychologically informed world. But he would have adamantly rejected all *belief* in any absolute claims of depth psychology, whether scientific or metaphysical. The same man who gave us a first version of what Freud would later insist on calling "*the* Unconscious," and on treating it as though it were some sort of mental organ, was also the first to reject that very notion—because he rejected all fixed, objectified, and definable "entities" that parade with a "*the*" in front of them, and that are designated by a noun to create the illusion of thing-like objectivity and of permanence.

All this has implications for the so-called "body of knowledge" of depth psychology, no matter what school. In the natural sciences, this body of knowledge is the same for everyone everywhere, from the start. A law of physics or chemistry is universal in this manner. In depth psychology, by contrast, a truth is a truth only insofar as it becomes one in the lives of individuals. As the case of Freud's constructions in psychoanalysis illustrates, a truth becomes a truth only insofar as it can be made into an integral part of the individual's life, into an appropriated piece of private psychological property. There is no universally true body of knowledge that can automatically be counted on here. There are only truths that are embodied in particular human lives. That means everyone ultimately has to discover his or her own psychology. That, in turn, implies that everyone also has to *invent* his or her own psychology. Borrowing from existing psychologies or from other disciplines is possible, but whatever is thus borrowed must be thoroughly personalized. It must be customized, not simply taken off the rack and mistaken for something that is ready to wear. This makes for the paradox that a truth in depth psychology often is simultaneously novel and ancient. The legend of Oedipus is a case in point. The motif of his tragedy is both as old as humanity and as alive as ever. As a psychological truth, however, it must not just be known as a long-established fact. It must forever be dramatically rediscovered, again and again, with every analysis of every new patient to whom it applies. And even within every analysis where Oedipus, or whoever, holds sway, the ancient knowledge must be discovered as brand new on a daily basis. Psychology by rote learning and routine practice can do nothing therapeutic for anyone. Curiously, this discipline that is so preoccupied with memory and with remembering needs one thing even more than these. It needs the ability to always start in, of all things, forgetfulness. The practicing therapist must in some respects, and on a daily basis, continually forget what he or she has learned. Therapeutic skill rests in the ability to truly discover, not just to know. And for that, one must always be ready to forget, and to reinvent.

When Aristotle wrote, in his *Poetics*, about the relation between life and the poetic inventions that provide accounts of it, he settled on the idea of imitation—in Greek, *mimesis*. Many informed Aristotle commentators, and more Aristotelians by silently accepted tradition, fail to appreciate that this *mimesis* is, as Ricoeur emphasizes in *Time and Narrative*, about the activity of imitating, not about the relation between an original and copies of it. What matters most is not so much the product of any imitation but the activity of production itself. With Freud's psychoanalytic constructions as well, it is the activity of recollecting bits of history that fall into place in the construction that matters, not the recollections or the bits of history per se. This is also why in Jung the emphasis is not just on imagination but on active imagination, on the activity of imagining. And it is why in Hillman the emphasis is on ways of seeing rather than on things seen, on pointing to the depth of archetypal significance in all things rather than on pointing at bottom-line things called "archetypes."

What drives contemporary men and women toward psychotherapy in general and depth psychology in particular is the same thing that makes Bottom turn to Peter Quince. It is the drive that is expressed in a line from a popular song, "I wish I could find a good book to live in." But this "wish to find a good book to live in" is not about longing to escape reality in favor of a life of fantasy. Nor is it about the nostalgic wish to return to a lost, and perhaps idealized, place and time, or to circumstances thought of as "the good old days." It also is not about finding a better life or better conditions for a better future. Rather, it is about something altogether different that lies beyond all these. And yet, that different something that is being sought is to be looked for in no other place than the here and now of the way things are. The desire to "find a good book to live in" is, as science fiction fantasy puts it, about "boldly going where one has never gone before," to a place and a life that remain to be discovered, because they have yet to be invented, confirmed, affirmed, and inhabited. It is about moving from a strictly literal or factual world into a world of images. That does not mean abandoning this, the only world we have. On the contrary. It is about still wanting that same old world, but enriched with the added significance and value that are inherent in the images and the imagination that sustain it, and that animate all life in it. It is about adding to life in this, our given world, a sense for the unfathomable depth and wealth of images that coexist with it and that form its basis and determine its worth. Finding one's "good book to live in" is about turning toward the image world one must enter for the sake of finding where and who one is destined to be. But again, this is not for the purpose of finding a new place with a new life and a new identity, or even different habits. It is about coming into one's own by more fully becoming who one is and who one has been. It is about finding that one can go nowhere but where one already is, and where one has been and will likely be. It is, as in the case of Freud's psychoanalytic constructions, about arriving where one has been all along and where the facts of one's life fall into place. And it is about unpacking one's psychic belongings so that one can move them into that place that has been theirs from the start. It is, in sum, about a return home to one's natural psychological habitat.

Finding one's "good book to live in" is about the homecoming of a prodigal son who must travel far and long in order to arrive back at his starting point—a case of eternally returning to the same. That starting point is not only his ultimate destination but also his original and final destiny. The return home of such a prodigal son becomes a cause for affirmation as well as a means of affirmation. His return to the place from which he started is no defeat. It is defeat only in the eyes of an eternally childlike ego that, like Icarus with his wings of wax, would flee from attachment and from the laws of gravity that bind one to the world, and that may even seem like a prison. Paradoxically, it is this eternally puerile ego, more so than the prodigal son, that is truly alienated from the ground of its origins, and that mistakes psychological alienation for freedom—freedom of choice, freedom to go anywhere and be or do anything, freedom to defy and deny anything that carries any weight and that might dampen one's spirits or restrict one's movement. It is Icarus who believes that only the sky is the limit. But the story of his crash is all too familiar. What goes up into the thin air of repression must come down. Icarus, unlike the prodigal son, fails to make a soft landing. He makes no provisions for landing anywhere at all. He goes and gets high but has nowhere to go—no destination, no place to call home, only aspiration for height and flight. Icarus, unlike the prodigal son, never returns home. Going and getting nowhere, he eventually crashes somewhere far off the mark and far off at sea. And when he does so, he makes . . . not even a big splash.

The drive to return to the home base where one originally and always belongs is the driving force in nostalgia. Nostalgia, homesickness, is no mere childish sentiment. It is an essential aspect of human nature and an essential feature of the human condition. It is a condition for which man is eternally seeking a cure. That cure lies in a return, an eternal return, toward where one belongs. If the sickness in homesickness is about being away from where one belongs, then the cure and convalescence involve returning there. As Heidegger has pointed out, in "Who Is Nietzsche's Zarathustra?," the etymology of the word "convalescence"—in German *genesen*—connects it to the Greek words *neomai* and *nostos*. Both of these are at the root of the word "nostalgia." Convalescence has to do with returning home, with homecoming, with going back to where one belongs—and being separated from which is a sickness. The prodigal son cures himself of his sickness by the eternal return home. Psychologically speaking, convalescence is about satisfying the longing to turn into the person one is, and must be, by turning to the context of images where one finds a home base for all that makes up one's person. It is about going full circle in one's life and about finding that one is who one is, and nobody else. It is about discovering that this is, after all, who one has always been, and must always be. It is about time and again returning to being the same person one has so often proved to be, because it is who one must forever become. It is about becoming not another person or a new and improved one but the same person as before, though now more so. Convalescence is about developing an improved imagination for *why* things are the way they are, precisely by developing a better sense of just *how* they are the way they are. As Freud noted, what psychoanalysis does is not change an existing person into a different one but allow a person to be who he or she is by becoming who he or she already was.

It is no accident that the idea of psychological convalescence, as a theme about becoming who one is, should turn up in connection with the idea of psychotherapy as a process of "finding a good book to live in." For convalescence, understood as homecoming, is about things other than symptom removal and symptom reduction. It is about fulfilling the promise that is inherent in every life. In that sense, psychological convalescence, by "finding one's good book to live in," is about being called to the promise of a new existence, in a state or state of mind yet to be invented, discovered, affirmed, and inhabited. But this discovery of a new psychological state is ultimately the rediscovery of an old and familiar life and world to which one returns once again. It is about being seduced not into just one more and ever more new affairs but into a continuation of the same existence, as the same person, but now as one whose being is redefined as a constant becoming of who he or she already is. Convalescence is finally about discovering that one is being chosen—without having a choice about being chosen—for a promised corner of the universe, under a new sign, but for a future that is already here in the present of all that is already given. It is about appropriating that lot and about saying yes to it by getting busy and getting underway toward fulfilling the promise. These suggestions are not meant to mock traditional religious ideas or to trivialize them. On the contrary. They are meant to gain a fuller recognition of what happens when a person assumes the role of Bottom and takes up a new idea—such as a construction from psychoanalysis—to try on for personal wear. When such ideas are tried on for personal wear, they become like a set of imaginative clothes the person wears. And these imaginative clothes, precisely because of the stories that unfold in the wearing of them, do make the man or the woman. They transport the wearer to the image world that goes with them.

In the end, the cases of the young man whom Zarathustra addresses, of Bottom seeking a ballad of his own life from Peter Quince, and of the patient of modern depth psychology seeking an imaginative construction of his or her own life to inhabit—all for the sake of "finding a good book to live in"—point beyond themselves. And they point not only toward an imaginative and poetic basis of all psychology, and of the life of the soul, as has already been repeatedly suggested. Beyond that they point toward something larger. These cases imply that everyday life, insofar as it always wants to be narrated and then lived as an imitation of its own narrative, is about recognizing that the universe itself needs to be constantly reconstructed and reinvented. To that end, it must be endlessly rediscovered, recollected, reconfirmed, reaffirmed, reappropriated, and reinhabited. And with that we are back at the Augustinean notion that the soul's ultimate longing is to return to the contemplation of, and the identification with, whatever it is we mean by the "eternal," the "archetypal"—or Being itself. Perhaps this is the true *telos* or purpose of all depth psychology: to encourage and embolden men and women to seek their way home to their natural habitat in the realm of the imagination where they ultimately belong.

SIX

To Find a Good Book to Live In

"THERE WAS NO FOG IN LONDON," wrote Oscar Wilde in an essay on what he called "The Decay of Lying," "until the impressionists started to paint it." Theories about human nature and the human condition, and especially the psychological treatments that are based on them, have a similar effect. Once such treatment gets underway, patients begin to develop symptoms from the textbooks of their treaters. Those who enter Freudian therapy start reporting Freudian thoughts and symptoms, even Freudian dreams. They also develop Freudian views about themselves and others, indeed, about life itself. In contrast, patients who enter Jungian treatment develop Jungian ideas, symptoms, dreams, and views. But if instead of entering Freudian or Jungian treatment, a woman enters counseling with a therapist who is largely feminist in orientation, then her own views on life and the world, including the way she thinks about her personal experience, are likely to become dominated by that perspective. The implication is clear: beware of the views about human nature and the human condition to which you subscribe, and beware in particular of the psychological treatment you enter, because you will end up living the plots or myths that are inherent in their theories. If you enter psychoanalysis, you will begin to view life in a tragic mode, based on the model of classical Greek tragedy, because that is how the centerpiece of original psychoanalytic theory is cast. If, however, you enter Jungian analysis, you will discover that your personal experiences reenact the dramas of mythological characters, and that what seemed strictly personal and unique is neither. But if instead of seeing a Freudian or a Jungian analyst you consult a counselor with a special interest in trauma theory, then that will have its own consequences. You soon will discover a hundred ways in which you have been ill treated, if not outright abused, and a thousand ways in which those past experiences perpetuate themselves in your current life. And whether you ask for it or not, you will receive dozens of suggestions to cope with it all.

In the end, it is in psychological treatment as Nietzsche suggested it is in philosophy: "There are no philosophies, only philosophers." Original philosophies are personal confessions that are based on personal experience and personal conviction. They dress up and parade as truth for all and as law that would be imposed on everybody. The converse also is true. Exposure to, and contamination by, any philosophy may turn a person into the type whose private confession managed to establish itself as the philosophy that bears his or her name. Similarly, a psychological treatment theory is less about any definitive truth per se than it is about a mode of life that knows only its own prejudices and ways of reasoning. It seeks to impose itself, prejudices and idiosyncratic ways of reasoning included, on everyone. It wants to become officially sanctioned moral dogma and practical categorical imperative.

There is no such thing as philosophical or psychological innocence. One cannot be without some kind of psychological and philosophical prejudice, and without the perspective that prejudice determines. The soul is no blank slate, no *tabula rasa*. It is, as Freud and others have suggested, a polymorphously imaginative, uninhibited, irresponsible, unsocialized, inventive, and eternally playful child. It is like a child who knows more and who spontaneously comes up with more than any parents ever suspected about their little one. Innocence of mind or neutrality as a philosophical starting point is something one loses as soon as one becomes engaged with the act of philosophizing—which is *in utero*, at the moment of one's conception. It begins even before that, when the two philosophizing beings called "parents" come together—and before that, when their parents come together, and so on, *ad infinitum*. In the end, innocence is something one never has in the first place, because it is the one thing that does not exist in this world, which for that very reason is anything but a peaceful paradise of the unprejudiced. As the biblical story of the world's creation has it, innocence only exists in the human condition as a negative—something that exists only in the form of its absence. Paradise forever lost, by definition, from the beginning.

Because Eros unites not only all prospective parents but all humanity, he presides not only over every human conception but also over all that humans conceive or over all concepts they bring into the world. This childlike, cherubic creature who darts through the air to go anywhere he wants is anything but innocent. Irresponsibly shooting his troublesome arrows here, there, and everywhere, and behaving like Freud's own mythic "polymorphously perverse child," he creates havoc wherever he creates new life. The air we breathe every day is abuzz with his mischief. By no means does all of it give us reason to wax sentimental about him. If lack of innocence is a bug that is everywhere in the air, then its middle name is Eros. Because Eros loves nothing better than to dart about in the airspace between two people who are within sight of each other, the setting of psychotherapy, where two individuals come together with nothing but air in between them, is an environment in which he thrives. Psychotherapy is the last place where one should even begin to expect innocence.

A common and not unreasonable assumption is that psychological treaters practice their trade as value-neutral technicians. Few common beliefs are more naive, because few institutions are more value driven than psychology in general and psychological treatment in particular. But this is not the result of anyone's deliberate doing. Nor is it a state of affairs that should or even could be stopped. It is inherent in the process itself. It is a necessary part of it. When a person enters psychological treatment that person expects an unbiased ear. The treater is to serve as a blank screen on which the patient may project his or her troubles. The treater's office serves as a place where the patient may freely lay out what is on his or her mind, so that treater and patient may look at it in shared interest. The treater's training and mannerisms contribute to the expectation of neutrality. The treater argues with nothing the patient says and rejects nothing said, rendering no judgment. The atmosphere of neutrality is further accentuated by the treater's seemingly minimal personal involvement in the process. The treater invites the patient to speak freely but speaks only sparingly, showing interest in the patient's emotions and thoughts but not displaying her or his own feelings or discussing her or his own thoughts. The treater asks questions and invites the patient to reveal himself or herself but makes few statements and no personal confessions at all. Direct questions the patient asks are more likely to be deflected than straightforwardly answered. As the popular image has it, questions presented to the treater are met with more questions in return.

The atmosphere of interested neutrality produces what every psychological treater since Freud knows as "transference." Transference—from the German *Übertragung*, meaning "carrying over" or "bringing across"—is about transporting psychological material from one place to another. It is imagined as taking psychological matters from one's private life, outside the treatment setting, and bringing them into the new and, until then, at least, more or less neutral place of the treater's office. Conflicts, feelings, thoughts, and behaviors that normally belong to relationships outside psychotherapy are thereby relocated or transferred to the place of treatment. They are, in effect, reenacted there, with the therapist serving as a player in a role the patient unconsciously assigns to him or her by projecting it on him or her. All this happens not in spite of the treater's assumed neutrality but precisely because of it. Ever since Freud, psychological treaters everywhere have viewed transference as the best way to get to know the soul in action, in its purest, most direct manifestation. For it is when the soul is on the move in this fashion, and actively doing its thing wherever it goes, especially in the therapist's office, that it best shows its true features. Transference shows the soul unfolding itself right in front of the treater's eyes, right there in the office. It shows the soul in full transparency and *in statu nascendi*, in the process of being born into the world of everyday life.

While there is, indeed, a substantial element of neutrality in psychological treatment, and while the facts of transference seem to behave as though the

therapist were a screen on which the patient projects all manner of psychological affairs, that screen is by no means blank and free of its own inherent shadow
play. On the contrary. The treatment itself, by the very choices of the plots or
myths it accepts as its theories, contributes to shaping what the patient experiences in psychotherapy. What the fog of the impressionists was for Oscar Wilde
and his contemporaries, the ideas from psychological theory are for us today.
America's leading magazine of popularized psychology is therefore aptly named
Psychology Today. That name not only suggests the goal of popularizing the theories of the day for informational purposes—that is its most obvious and, seemingly, its most innocent function. Beyond that, and precisely by the very act of
shaping how modern men and women understand and view the life of the
soul, this also shapes and, thereby, to a degree, implicitly foretells how they will
experience the soul in their own lives. It is not the former function but the
latter that is the more significant one. Many currently accepted notions that
define our modern experience of soul are brought to us through a delivery
system such as *Psychology Today*, as well as other means of mass marketing ideas
and beliefs. Opinions about what constitutes desirable and undesirable lifestyles,
about what is normal and what is abnormal behavior, or about what prized
individual traits are versus dreaded character flaws—all these are invented fictions first. They become accepted facts of life through the process of popular-
ization. Yet the real facts of soul are less those that are explicitly identified in
psychology's theories, and then popularized, than the hidden notions that
remain unstated in the theories themselves. The real unconsciousness in Oedipal triangulations is less that immature men forever long to possess their mothers and do away with their fathers, and all the variations on that theme. The
more subtle unconsciousness in Oedipal psychology—one about which psychology itself often is at least partly unconscious—involves an almost automatic
habit of narrating existence in the mode of classical Greek tragedy. This tends
to put every patient through the wringer of classical tragedy, whether that genre
applies to his or her life or not. This more subtle unconsciousness within Oedipal theory itself elevates Oedipus's own premier talent, the capacity for clever
insight, to the status of wisdom. In the process of this near idolatry of only one
form of intellect, it becomes prone to disregard many other viable modes of
knowing about the soul in which insight plays no role. It makes for a way of
thinking about oneself, and others, that is based on what Ricoeur, in *Freud and
Philosophy*, where he calls psychoanalysis a "hermeneutic of suspicion," has diagnosed as a pathos of distrust. It implies that "Know thyself" no longer means
"Never forget your place in the world as a mortal being surrounded everywhere by things immortal" but, rather, "Take a good look at yourself, because
we have found the enemy, and it is us, meaning you."

"Have you noticed," wrote Wilde, "how the French landscape is beginning
to resemble the paintings of the impressionists?" He might as well have been
writing about the effects of popularized psychological belief. The plots contemporary men and women live in, and the facts of life they factualize by identify-

ing with the fictions in them, are shaped by the theories from today's psychology. Those theories are the modern myths by which we live. It is, indeed, as Oscar Wilde so famously wrote: "Life imitates art far more than the other way around." Wilde has influential company to support his claim that life imitates the facts of the imagination more than the other way around. At the end of Plato's *Republic*, that founding text of the Western canon of philosophy, Socrates tells the story of Er. It serves to make the same point that Wilde would make again more than two thousand years later. Er, so the story goes, was a soldier. One day he was killed in battle. His body was found and placed on a funeral pyre, according to traditional Greek custom. On the twelfth day after his death, just when his body was to be burned, Er revived. He began to tell the story of the strange things that had happened since the day he was killed in battle. When he died, his soul separated from his body. Together with other souls, of other dead men, Er's soul traveled to a strange place. There he and the other souls saw four openings. Two of the openings led up and into Heaven, two led down into a kind of Hell deep inside the earth. The souls of good men entered into Heaven, those of bad men went into the earth. Er also saw souls that came out of the four openings, after having been in Heaven or in Hell for a thousand years. Those that came from Heaven told tales of blessings and pleasures they had experienced there. Those that had been in Hell told tales of pain and suffering. All the souls that came out of the openings were then led to yet another strange place. There they saw images of various forms of life that men live on earth. Er and the others were told that souls about to be born into the world must choose one of those images for their next incarnation. Among the many images from which souls had to choose were heroes, kings, athletes, craftsmen, soldiers, farmers, and others. But only the external images of these life-forms were visible during this choosing of lots. The true nature of the destinies that belonged to the life images remained invisible. These invisible destinies often were entirely different from the promises the images appeared to suggest, and much more unpleasant. The choice of a life image was fraught with danger, due to the potential for deceptive appearances. The true destiny that every image held, and that would become the reincarnated soul's destiny on earth, would only become manifest after the choice was made, after the soul had become identified with the chosen image for its rebirth into the world. The hazard in this choice, which was compulsory, lay in the possibility of being deceived by false appearances. So says and so ends the myth of Er. And so also says and ends Plato's *Republic*, for it is with the story of Er that Socrates ends this long philosophical dialogue that lays down the foundation for so much subsequent Western thinking.

That this text should end with Er's story has a rather momentous significance many Plato commentators have tended to ignore. In order to appreciate the significance of the story of Er, one must appreciate that terminal position. This, in turn, begins by appreciating what comes before it. The list of questions Socrates addresses in the *Republic* is long. It includes many of the questions that have kept philosophers after Plato busy for centuries, for millennia. They remain as relevant now as they were to Socrates and his students and followers. Even today, these questions Socrates raised keep showing up in elections, in daily newspaper editorials, in churches and schools, before the Supreme Court, in family arguments, in trials, and everywhere else. They address such matters as how one can know the true nature of anything, how one can tell truth from mere false appearance, how any kind of real knowledge is possible at all, what determines whether human behavior is ethical or not, what makes people truly happy, what justice is, what should be taught in schools, who should govern and how, what the best organization is for a society, what the benefits and risks of role models and hero worship are, and whether there is a place for censorship, and, if so, what the standards of censorship should be. The story of Er, which concludes all this, occupies, therefore, no minor position. It is the end point to which all of the dialogue's philosophizing leads. By its position alone, the story of Er states a fundamental fact of Western consciousness. But first there is the content of the story itself.

One person who would not fare well with the compulsory task of select-ing a lot by choosing an image to identify with and to live by is Don Quixote, a man who is so enchanted with the images from his beloved books about chivalry that he becomes tempted to imitate them by enacting them. Eventu-ally he becomes wholly identified with them and makes his fateful decision to become himself a knight. With his heart full of hope and his head filled with images of wondrous scenes and adventures, he rides off on horseback to pursue his calling. His life, from now on, will be one of chivalry. It will be dedicated to right all wrongs, to slay dragons wherever they may be found, to rescue damsels in distress. Once he gets underway, all manner of adventure awaits. In one of these, as everyone knows, he sees in the turning sails of windmills the moving arms of giants. As behooves a self-respecting knight, he stops to do battle. So begins the comedy of what many scholars regard as history's first novel. There follows a concatenation of personal disasters that become Quixote's true lot as soon as he gets underway in his chosen identity. The alluring images of grand chivalry lead him on, and into his true destiny. The result is masterful comedy for the readers of Cervantes's novel *Don Quixote*, but painful personal experi-ence for the story's unstoppable protagonist. As the story unfolds, Quixote sees in all the adventures that befall him further confirmation that he has selected the right path in choosing to become a knight. The reader, of course, sees a comically deluded fool of a man.

Don Quixote's story, like Er's account, is a statement about an often painful archetypal fact of the human condition. He is not alone in having difficulties with the choice of image with which to identify. All of life, of every human life, is a matter of identification with and imitation of images, just as the story of Er suggests. And all of it is about the difficulties associated with that choice. On the face of things it may seem madness for Don Quixote to mistake windmills for giants and himself for a knight in shining armor. But beyond that, there is an even greater madness—that of thinking that human life should, or even could,

be lived without identification with and imitation of images. This is precisely
what the figure of Quixote and even more so the facts of psychological transference illustrate in great detail. They say that fantasy-free reality does not exist
in any human life. They say, as Quixote's windmills illustrate, that it is human,
quintessentially human, to always live in a world that is filled with animated figures whose gestures point beyond the situation at hand. As in the case of
Quixote's windmills, these animated figures that are everywhere allude to entire
universes, full of promises waiting to be pursued. As Er's account has it, this is a
compulsory, necessary part of life in the human world. This is indeed what
makes transference not only possible but also unavoidable and essential to the
life of the soul. It explains why Freud suggested that, even though transference
occurs most visibly in psychological treatment, it is not restricted to that setting. It is everywhere in everyday life. The soul factor in life is, as the word
"transference" implies, about *Übertragung* as a process and a lived myth of being
transported. Perhaps this also explains the central emphasis in all psychotherapy
on being moved by emotion—which lifts us up, gets us down, makes us feel
beside ourselves, sweeps us off our feet, puts us on cloud nine or deep down in
Hell, makes us push people away or draw close or become aloof, makes us
introverts or causes everyone to displace their feelings all over the place. Without spatial metaphors psychology would be out of business, because they are
the soul's primary business. Transference, as Freud saw, is the soul's natural and
preferred activity.

The essential transport that moves the soul is between the location where
the literal facts of an event are situated and the image world to which they are
transported—and into which the persons involved are themselves transported.
If depth psychology makes only one contribution to human self-understanding, it is this—that we are where we are not, that the life of the soul is about
always being in two worlds at once. It is about simultaneously being in the literal world where the physicality of existence situates us and in the world of
images to which we are constantly being transported, whether we are aware of
it and like it or not. When Freud discovered the facts of *Übertragung*, which was
to become the great myth that determines so much in modern psychological
treatment, he stumbled upon a first principle in the life of the soul and recognized its central role in the human condition. It comes, therefore, as no surprise
that Freud's discovery of transference is consistent with the very first discoveries Western consciousness made about the life of the soul. Those first beliefs,
too, were directly related to the idea of the soul's fundamental mobility. From
Homer's *Iliad* and *Odyssey* on, it is apparent that this mobility, and, in particular, this mobility between the world of literal facts and the second but coexisting world of images, was the first thing that was identified about the soul. The
Homeric version of *Psychology Today* that was implied in the *Iliad* and *Odyssey*
had it that the life of the soul is first and last about a double of life that is intangible and invisible in life, even though it coexists with it. It insists that a human
being has a life not only in the realm of the literal physicality of existence but

also among the images that are the world's insubstantial and inherent depth dimension. This second and strictly image-based or purely psychic dimension was imagined as the realm of Hades, Lord of Souls and god of the Underworld that is their domain. The swiftest means of transport available to this double life of soul is through the play of suggestive and imaginative allusion that is present in all things. A windmill can become a giant, as it does in Don Quixote's eyes, through the rotating movement of its sweeps. They can suggest the gesticulating arms of gigantic creatures and meet Don Quixote halfway in his belief of being a knight in a world that is populated by giants who must be slain in battle. As Ortega y Gasset emphasized in his *Meditations on Quixote*, there is nothing exceptional about this. Life is always this way. It is full of allusions to things, events, and possibilities that reach beyond what is immediately present to physical sense perception. Once again we are back at what Nietzsche said in writing about inspiration as the basis of all perception, which is always based on imagination: "It actually seems . . . as if things themselves approached and offered themselves as metaphors . . ." To this we may add what Nietzsche had his Zarathustra say: "On every metaphor you ride to every truth . . ." This is how we find our daily truths: by being imaginatively transported into the world of an invented fiction that is created through the play of pretense that every metaphor is and that every event and situation plays for us Don Quixotes. This makes all of everyday life a practice of riding the metaphors that existence offers in endless supply. Quixote's horse, Rosinante, is only one of these.

But a windmill is also a windmill, even if it looks like a giant. Quixote's literal world of La Mancha does not confirm and sustain his beloved worldview of chivalry. Not every *Übertragung* or transference fantasy can be successfully put into action, just as in the myth of Er not every one of the images available for psychological identification lives up to its promise. Not every metaphor works, because not all metaphors speak a convincing truth about the believability of the resemblance between two different things. Freud, in "Observations on Transference-Love," describes how such failure of transference fantasy works. What he says sheds light on every Quixotic drama of an unbelievable and therefore unsustainable metaphor that collapses when one tries to enact it. He illustrates what happens with the case of a female patient in psychoanalytic treatment. As a result of transference fantasies she projects on the more or less neutral figure of the analyst she unconsciously turns him into an object of sexual desire. She becomes infatuated with the treater on the basis of what Freud calls "transference love." The patient is like Don Quixote here. She sees in one or two isolated aspects of the analyst's appearance or behavior certain allusions to a host of possibilities she imagines, and it is with those imagined possibilities that she becomes infatuated. Like Don Quixote, she is ready to enter the world of those possibilities through concrete action. She is tempted to enact her unconscious fantasies by entering into an actual and physical relation with the analyst. As in the case of Don Quixote, and of many of the promising but deceptive images from the myth of Er, the outcome of an attempt to enact the patient's erotic fantasy image would be disastrous. It would prove that the world and the circumstances as they actually are do not confirm and support the erotic image and the fantasied love scenario that is based on it. It would fail to sustain the metaphoric pretense that equates the actual person of the treater with a fantasy person he is not. The allusion that one or two of the treater's gestures or attributes make to the figure from the patient's unconscious fantasy life would, like Quixote's fantasy of giants, find its breaking point. Just as the metaphor of grand chivalry collapses for the self-appointed knight from La Mancha, so too does the misperceived promise of romantic love fail to become materialized reality for the woman in psychoanalysis. This, so Freud's account implies, is the difference between a life that lives up to the promises that inspire and animate it versus a life that suffers shipwreck over unsustainable fantasy images. The difference is about unrealizable scenarios. It is about plots for whose enactment the world as it is fails to provide the setting and the props. It is about love fantasies that cannot be consummated because there is no ground for them, and no future. It is about allusions to analogies that cannot be persuasively argued because the analogies do not exist. It is about resemblances that do not withstand the close scrutiny of reality testing. In the end it is about metaphors that do not work, because their play of pretense that there exists an affinity and identity between two different things cannot be played. In the final analysis, it is about identifications that cannot, and that will not, be borne out by the facts of life. Freud rediscovered what Er, too, had come to see in his journey into the hidden realm of soul that exists separately from the body's anatomy and physiology. Living the life of unsustainable images is a quixotic tragicomedy that twentieth-century depth psychology rediscovered in the form of all manner of transference love. And we, too, like the critical bystanders in Quixote's adventures, have called it "madness," the madness of neuroses of all sorts that gave rise to psychoanalysis and to every form of psychological treatment that resembles it.

In contrast to all this potential for error from the world of Er, all this quixotic madness from the world of La Mancha, and all this neuroticism from the world of psychological treatment, it would seem that living a life of sustainable images with which to identify must be a form of art. This art of choosing sustainable images to immerse oneself in and to live in is personified in the figure and the life of Claude Monet, the most popular of the great European impressionist painters. Monet single-handedly painted more London fog than anyone else. He may well have added more fog to London's cityscape than England's industrial pollution ever did. More than any other painter of London's everyday life, he captured what it means to be surrounded by fog and to have a view of the world and of life that is always colored, shaded, and distorted by fog. It took the outsider's view of a Frenchman to show Londoners the world in which they lived. But Monet's work went a step farther, beyond painting. It went on to suggest that all men and women, and not just the impressionist painters among them, live in the worlds they paint.

Monet's painted London fog is not just about fog. It is about the ever-present and inevitable perceptual fluctuations and impressions that are the result of the colors, shades, and reflections that shape our experience of the world. And it is not only about literal colors, shades, and reflections, nor is it simply about visual effects. It is about existence itself being a perpetual process of coloring, shading, and reflecting through which everything is constantly alive, even in its supposedly static and unchanging being. It is about the ways in which everything is constantly active, making its own unique and constantly changing impressions. It is, finally, about discovering that without this active and constantly changing life of animated appearances, nothing exists, or can exist. So many of Monet's paintings seem to make the point that a thing, any thing, is inseparable from the reflections or shadows it casts. They go even one step farther and suggest that a thing exists only by virtue of the ongoing competition or tension between it and its reflections and shadows. They seem to argue that a thing without reflections or without shadows would be no thing, nothing. Painting, for Monet, was about capturing that fleeting activity, that endlessly moving play of those reflections and those shadows, that tension between reflection and thing reflected. His art is about capturing the presence of that subtle double that coexists with everything, and without which nothing can exist. It is about coming to a halt and standing still in awe of that very game of doubling that all things bring about, and that almost appears to be their very reason for being.

But Monet did more than paint. His life as a painter came to be about more than capturing on canvas the reflections and shadows that all things cast, about more than showing the imaginative game of doubling they play. It also was about becoming increasingly devoted to actively responding to this animated world in kind. This he did by beginning to reshape or recreate the physical world around him, according to the images that the things in it created and cast. That devotional activity became the drive behind his ongoing development of the garden and the lily pond at his home in Giverny. That garden and the lily pond in it were thereby transformed from an ordinary garden, with an ordinary pond, into the legendary Monet Garden and Lily Pond at Giverny. They became not only literally famous as Monet's own fame developed. Independent of that popular fame, they also became a physical expression of what they always already were, inherently and potentially, but what they managed to become more manifestly, because Monet recognized their inherent potential destiny. It is as though he sensed the garden's own desire and as though he then devoted himself to realizing that desire. Throughout the years during which he lived at Giverny, Monet continuously developed both garden and lily pond further, while he kept painting them at the same time. A spiraling devotional activity was set in motion. The lily pond led to paintings of itself, and those paintings then in turn led to further development of the pond itself. Painting and thing painted began to develop in lock step. They became what they always already were in the first place, fundamentally and manifestly inseparable. Monet understood this mutuality that exists between a thing and its reflections and shadows, and he increasingly dedicated his whole being to it.

A repetitive and circular process of ever-deepening active meditation came into being in this fashion. This became the centerpiece of Monet's existence. His life became both an illustration of, and a case of devotion to, the mutuality between the imaginative reflections that everything in every life casts and the urge to bring forth those reflections in concretely lived form. It is perhaps here that Monet's true genius lies, for his genius was not only about being an inspired painter. Nor was he simply also a spectacularly successful and legendary gardener. The totality of his genius lies in the sum of these, which is larger than both separately and than both merely added up. Monet became a legendary incarnation of man as a meditative being whose life becomes dedicated to the subtle depth dimension that is present in every scrap of every day and that wants nothing more than to become manifest or incarnate. By the end of his painting career, Monet created a work in which art and life were fully intertwined by becoming full circle in each other. He painted a series of enormous canvases of his by then almost mythic Lily Pond, with the idea that they should be arranged in circular fashion to surround the viewer. The paintings, so arranged, were to give the viewer the sense of being in the midst of a world with water lilies on all sides. The paintings thereby stopped being something to merely look at. They became what they always already were in the first place. They became what all painting, all art, and all imaginative activity always is. They became a means of transport that moves the literal person into a double and subtle world of images. This was Monet's version of transference, or *Übertragung*.

All men and women live in the worlds they paint. That is what Monet's Lily Pond suggests. The point of Monet's genius, and of what makes his genius relevant, may well be what his famous pond of water lilies suggests about this. It tells every man and woman: Don't just passively accept someone else's world; make it your own as you see fit and so that it does justice to all that is in it. It says: Live in your given or chosen corner of the world and love it with all you have of resources. It counsels: Become devoted to the place where you are with all you can muster of reflection, meditation, and energy. Monet is unique insofar as he was spectacularly successful as a painter and as a gardener—and he knew how to run a famously sumptuous country kitchen as well. But he also personifies something that is universal, and universally accessible. He embodies something that happens in every life, but for which he is a superb model, the archetypal image. And therein lies an even greater attraction than in his paintings alone. His work and his life provide the outline of a universal and timeless theme, the theme of the impressionist relation that every person has with his or her own Lily Pond—with whatever it is that serves as one's personal Lily Pond. That personal Lily Pond can assume many shapes, including many ordinary ones. It can be the endless process of a lifelong relationship with a spouse or with family. It can be a program of study or training followed by a professional career in one's chosen field. It can be the process of raising children and running a household.

Or it can be a long-term hobby or personal project that becomes a lifelong love affair. In each of these the active ingredient is the endless mutual exchange between vision and action. The secret of success here lies in the perpetual active interplay between idea and deed, between ideal and compromise approximation, between virtual and actual, between the promise of perfection and the imperfections of reality. Here, in such an ongoing mutual exchange of active interplay, and just as for Monet, the sharp but fundamentally artificial line, between vision and fact, between hope and deed, and between image and thing, begins to fade—until it eventually disappears. One discovers that one lives in a world in which the distinction between idea and fact is altogether gradually dissolved. That is what Monet suggested in his late and large paintings that surround the viewer and that place him or her inside the painted world.

Monet's artwork is doubly inspiring when his paintings are arranged to show series of the painter's meditations on the same theme. The viewer may then see, lined up next to each other, several paintings of London's House of Parliament, of London's Charring Cross Bridge, Venice's reflection in the Grand Canal and, of course, the famous Water Lilies in the Pond at Giverny. The reaction that overcomes the viewer often is one of wanting to act, to do something, not just to contemplate. The power of that inspiring invitation to act, to do something, and to be not only moved by images but moved to action comes from the willed repetitiveness in Monet's work. It is what moved Monet to act on endlessly elaborating his Lily Pond. One Monet painting is a work of art, a still life. A series of them on the same theme begins to act like an engaging invitation to participate in life itself. By the very act of willed and repeated engagement, these series on the same theme show how a human being surrenders to the world of images he or she inhabits. It shows a surrender of observing devotion to something that is first passively allowed, then expected, and, finally, actively encouraged to dominate one's attention more and more. Ultimately, the invitation to surrender in this fashion becomes what it was destined to be from the start. It becomes the occasion of surrender to a powerful presence in one's life. At first, that presence disrupts and intrudes on one's life. Then, with one's growing and eventually full consent, it begins to take over one's life. Finally, one *wants* one's life to be taken over by it. It is as though the spirit of Zarathustra were speaking here, saying: "But thus I willed it. Thus do I will it. Thus shall I will it." It becomes a promising and sustainable impressionist transference love that says: "Ravish me."

A series of Monet paintings on the same theme shows the act of painting more than it shows any particular object painted. It shows not so much single works of art that are done and arranged as a series but the painter's devotional single-mindedness as a way of being. It shows the fundamentally miraculous experience of being attentively present at that particular corner of the universe where one happens to be historically located—and where one may decide to plant one's easel and oneself in front of it. It shows the painter, the archetypal attentive human being, as personification of that very act of being present—and of choosing, deciding, wanting, and willing oneself to be present. In the end, Monet's work, especially his repetitive work, shows the human being as painter abandoning himself or herself to the act of affirming existence. It is a model that shows the potential of every man or woman to be a virtual Job with a painter's brush in hand, overcome with awe at the fact of any and all being. This is how Being luxuriates in becoming manifest as splendor. Mere appearance becomes sheer appearance through contemplative repetition. This is, indeed, as Nietzsche would recognize, the most affirmative way of being that is at all attainable.

Monet, in spite of his legendary stature, does not dwarf ordinary men and women through intimidation. Rather, he emboldens the viewer to want to be more attentively, more devotedly, but also more actively present. To paraphrase what Nietzsche said about the art of classical Greek tragedy, Monet seduces the human spirit into a continued contemplation and affirmation of existence. But he does even more than that. He makes the seduction a mutual affair, an affair of active and willed mutuality, for Monet emboldens the human spirit, seduced by the world's images and imagination, to actively respond to the world itself. He counters Eros, the seduction of the world, with Anteros, responding Eros. He does this by stirring men and women to want to act, not just observe. Monet's own ongoing development of his garden is a case in point of being drawn into action by images and of letting imagination lead and shape one's action. Everyman's own version of his lily pond, whatever form it takes, can do the same thing.

Monet's paintings and his Lily Pond and Garden make a comment on the practice of depth psychology, particularly on the role images and active imagination play in it. Freud's lifelong insistence that depth psychology should be protected from becoming a handmaiden of psychiatry or medicine and his lifelong arguments in favor of lay analysis had less to do with professional turf or qualifications than with something else. It was, beyond these, an insistence on the primacy and autonomy of the imaginative basis of the life of the soul. And so it was also an insistence on the imaginative basis of the very field that names itself after the soul. To this we may now add that the dependent relation between psychotherapy patient and treater is not so much about the person of the treater having such extraordinary significance and responsibility. Nor is it in the first place about the patient being so uniquely vulnerable in the hands of the treater. The dependent relation affecting therapist and patient is about the fact that all psychotherapy rests on a ground of fiction, and that this ground supports both treater and treated. The true responsibility of treatment does not lie firstly and most prominently in the hands of persons. It lies in the realm of the imagination itself, which is transpersonal and impersonal. It is in the facts of the images themselves that govern the therapy process, and in the acts of the imagination, that the burden and the active ingredients of psychological treatment rest. Wranglings over primacy among schools of psychological treatment or among professional disciplines engaged in it may in some ways be dismissed, because they are in a fundamental sense misleading and, to that extent, beside the point and irrelevant.

The same thing may be said about the struggles for control by examining boards, licensing boards, registration boards, education boards, ethics boards, and insurance boards. The question never was and never will be which school, which discipline, which board, or which commission has the facts of the soul right. Rather, the overriding issue is that whoever claims to have the facts of the soul is at risk of being had by some unsuspected aspect or other of the fictions in them, just as the myth of Er suggests. And there is the rub.

That myth of Er, we can now finally say, by being placed at the end of Plato's *Republic*, suggests where the discipline that concerns itself with the fundamentals of the soul belongs in the context of the Western tradition of thought. By making its concluding statement one about the imaginative basis of everyday life, Plato's *Republic* says something fundamental about, and for, psychology. It implies that such a discipline must see and reach beyond all the arguments about the state and its social organization, beyond ethics and education, beyond what is proper conduct and what is not, beyond who should govern and how, beyond how social life should be organized and why. The *Republic*'s final statement about the basis of everyday life in purely psychic images suggests, as Nietzsche would later say, that psychology is the queen of sciences, and that it should be at the heart of all philosophizing and serve as the bottom line of all human reflection. In the final analysis, Plato's *Republic* is about the soul, first and last. The analogy Socrates introduces early on in the long dialogue, the analogy between the soul and the state, serves to magnify the image of the soul itself and to provide a vocabulary to speak about it. This founding text of Western thought is not at all primarily about the state and social life. It is not, in the first place, about good citizenship, proper individual development, and the right conduct. It is about the soul. The state, good citizenship, justice, education, and all the rest, by being only parts of the soul analogy, are in some ways handmaidens of the soul, not the other way around. This also suggests that a discipline that concerns itself with the life of the soul, such as modern depth psychology, should not lose its own identity by placing itself solely, or even primarily, in the service of good citizenship and, hence, of the state. It should not stare itself blind on adaptive behavior, social adjustment, education, and proper individual development. Rather, it should place itself in the service of the poetic imagination that constitutes the soul's underpinnings and that is the ground of existence. Poetics and poetic imagination, viewed this way, are not merely or primarily refined entertainment that serves to embellish the daily life of the cultured class. They are the very foundation of citizenship itself, for all classes of citizens. Responsible citizenship begins with poetic sensibility and active imagination. Creative citizenship makes every man and woman a painter who creates worlds by working out images in which to live. Psychology as social hygiene would make one world more inhabitable. Psychology as poetics would make endlessly more inhabitable worlds.

PART II

THE METHOD

SEVEN

MAGICAL REALISM
IN EVERYDAY LIFE

"SHE BECAME A VIRGIN AGAIN FOR HIM." So goes a line from a story by
Gabriel Garcia Marques about two long-separated lovers who eventually are
reunited. It expresses more tender emotion in one image than any long description of the reunion could possibly convey. Like every good metaphor, it manages to tell a truth by telling a lie. Unlike most metaphors, its truth is doubly
true, because the lie it tells is a double lie. For it is not only not true that "she
became a virgin again." It also is impossible in the first place, by definition. Precisely here lies the genius of the image. It is the genius that characterizes the
style of writing and the literary genre of magical realism that this image represents. It makes the impossible and the unbelievable seem true. Not only that. It
makes it look perfectly normal and self-evident.

The image of "she became a virgin again," like all magical realism, ignores
and defies the laws of nature—and it does so convincingly and effortlessly. It
turns accepted truths and beliefs upside down. In their place, it posits new laws,
laws that are based not on nature but on imagination. And all of this is done
with a flick of the wrist—without even breaking a sweat, without a second's
hesitation, without apology, and without so much as a semblance of explanation. No explanation is needed, because the image and its truth are self-
explanatory.

Magical realism may be described as a literary genre that tells stories in
which events occur that defy the laws of physics and of everyday reality and
common sense but that are nevertheless accepted as truths in their own right.
The stories are filled with accounts of how utterly unbelievable, impossible
things are routinely happening in the midst of perfectly ordinary events, all of

it as though it were the most natural thing in the world. In a typical case, the straightforward account of some entirely plausible event or other is suddenly interrupted by such an image of what must seem a stark impossibility. This image of the impossible appears like a piece of fantastic magic that seems to have been lifted from a fairy tale and transplanted into a series of historical or, at least, historically possible events. Nobody in the stories is ever surprised about any of it. Everybody sees, understands, and accepts the fantastic events without the slightest doubt or even puzzlement about them. This is exactly the great appeal of magical realism: the spontaneous, almost natural-seeming happy marriage of impossibilities and possibilities. Such is the world of Gabriel Garcia Marques and his fellow writers of magical realism. What makes magical realism succeed is the deep sense of veracity that accompanies the flickering pieces of magical reality that insert themselves into history. They happen before one's unprepared and disbelieving-yet-nonetheless-believing eyes. The automatic, reflexive sense of disbelief is immediately, spontaneously, willingly suspended— before one has even begun to think about it. By the time critical thinking sets in, the magic has already been done, and one has already involuntarily fallen under its spell. No amount of reasoning is quick enough to prevent it. The same fantastic image that one immediately recognizes as unbelievable one also, simultaneously and in spite of everything, accepts to be utterly true, truer than anything else that could possibly be said about the matter at hand.

Magical realism is not only a special genre of literary fiction, it also is a fact of everyday life. It is just as much a part of everyday life as is its opposite, which is easier to spot—common sense. Common sense needs no definition, no description, no example. Everyone knows it. It is a good thing to have and a bad thing to lack. Most people practice it much of the time—automatically, without having to think about it. It is Everyman's own philosophy for everyday living. Common sense is probably as old as practical reason itself, because it is essential to survival in everyday life. It has a good reputation and needs no defense. It requires no explanation, and certainly no justification. It does, however, need to have its archetypal patron saint identified. In the history of psychology that archetypal patron saint of common sense, or at least one representative version of it, is none other than Jocasta, Mrs. Oedipus herself. Paradoxically, but not surprisingly, the mythic queen of denial by common sense is the same figure who is destined first to be her son's mother, then his unknowing bride, and finally the mother of his children—who are therefore not only her son's children but also his siblings, just as they are simultaneously her children and her grandchildren. Along similar paradoxical lines, it seems almost fitting that it should be, of all people, Oedipus himself, the great guesser of riddles who can outsmart even sphinxes, who should find himself in such a fantastic family arrangement that would confound the average unsuspecting genealogist.

Jocasta's mythic career in common sense and practical reasoning begins when her husband Laius and she first learn from Apollo's oracle at Delphi that their son will one day kill his father and marry his mother. In an understandable attempt to avoid this terrible prediction, they respond with practical thinking that is grounded in the logic of common sense. Their solution is as simple as it is turns out to be naive and tragically flawed. They abandon their young son to the elements of nature, hoping that this will make him, and the threat of their nightmare, go away. As they and the whole world eventually discover, whatever is cast away into the oblivion of things repressed comes back to haunt all who participated in the repressing. Jocasta's tragedy turns out to be about relying too much on common sense, and about having too little regard for the images that govern human lives. It is about paying dearly for this psychological imbalance. Her moment of shattering truth comes when it dawns on her that, perhaps all along, she has counted too exclusively on common sense. At that horrifying moment of truth, it becomes apparent to her that she has been too lacking in a sense for the magical realism that penetrates life, every life. She discovers firsthand that this other reality, this fantastic and magical reality, is what ultimately shapes lives. When the story of Oedipus and Jocasta is approaching its end, Oedipus is on the verge of discovering that the man he killed years earlier, in a fit of what we now call "road rage," was none other than his father. This means he also is about to realize that the woman he subsequently married, the dead man's widow, is his own mother. And it means he is about to find out that the children he fathered with her are therefore his siblings as much as they are his offspring and his own wife-mother's grandchildren. Just when all this is about to become horribly clear to him, he recalls the prophecy, made to him years earlier by the Delphic oracle but long since forgotten, that he would one day do all these things. The sudden recollection fills him with terror and horror. Now, all these years later, and when he is on the verge of realizing that everything has turned out as foretold, it is Jocasta, until then equally unaware, who has the first terrifying intuition concerning all that is about to be revealed. Yet she still tries to hang on to common sense, one last and futile time. Seeing the terror and horror in her husband's eyes, she tries to reassure him—and herself. Turning to Oedipus, she says: "Fear? What has a man to do with fear? Chance rules our lives, and the future is all unknown. Best live as best we may, from day to day. Nor need this mother-marrying frighten you. Many a man has dreamt as much. Such things must be forgotten if life is to be endured." That, of course, is precisely what the whole tragedy and the whole psychoanalysis of unconsciousness that is based on it are all about: that forgetting or otherwise ignoring the images that form, inform, and deform our lives is something we, like Jocasta and her family, do at our own peril.

Freud, who based himself on the psychological life of his patients and on his own dreams, rediscovered what Jocasta had to learn firsthand, and at the cost of excruciating personal agony and the terror of tragedy. Like Jocasta and Oedipus, he discovered that in the realm of soul there are no accidents, no chance events. Everything in this realm is shaped according to blueprints that are formed independently of conscious ego control. As Nietzsche's Zarathustra put it, also at a moment of personal discovery: "in the end, one experiences only oneself. The time is gone when mere accidents could still happen to me; and what could still come to me that was not mine already? What returns, what finally comes home to me, is my own self and everything of myself that has long been in strange lands and scattered among all things and accidents." That the tragedy of Oedipus and Jocasta happens to be about parricide and incest is by no means the most significant part of the story, even if it is the most shocking and theatrically effective one. It is not the aggression against the father per se, nor the sexuality with the mother per se, that matters most. Viewing the play that way, and deriving an entire psychology from this, risks missing the most important point. The essential event is one of discovery, of a sudden revelation in self-consciousness. For although many things seem to be going on in the play's total action, only one thing is really happening. The content of the Delphic oracle perhaps could have been about a theme other than incest and parricide. The story of its inevitable unconscious fulfillment could then have been accordingly reimagined and rewritten. The essential plot, however, would remain unchanged, even if there were no parricide and no incest in the picture. At least theoretically, things could perhaps be different that way, and that theoretical possibility is all that is needed to indicate that we should not stare ourselves blind on the play's aggression and sexuality. By the same token, the question of parricide and incest certainly intensifies the essential plot. It does so by playing a fantastic trick on customary human notions the plot brings into dramatic question—notions about such important human matters as one's origin, one's identity, the power or powerlessness of one's ideas and choices, and one's always so unexpected yet in some ways all too familiar and all too long known but long avoided destiny. The essential plot of the Oedipus story is about becoming who one was and is and will be—by virtue of an origin that transcends the biological, the historical, and the otherwise literal facts of life, and by virtue of a destiny that transcends one's choices. It is about becoming who one is destined to be, seemingly paradoxically, and certainly surprisingly, through a series of conscious actions that aim at very different goals, goals that cannot help but inadvertently fulfill the inescapable plot of who one must be. It is about how the unavoidable unconsciousness in everyday life is a matter of enacting images that tend to remain unrecognized until they have completed their built-in destiny, just as the myth of Er suggests. And even then, as Shakespeare's Bottom from *A Midsummer Night's Dream* testifies, and as every patient in psychotherapy experiences firsthand, it is by no means easy to identify exactly what happened and what is going on. The Oedipus myth is about discovering that life, even and especially ordinary life as one sets about living it every morning with the best of intentions, is about ending up enacting images that are fundamentally too fantastic to be handled with common sense or practical reason. That is why these images, such as those of the Delphic oracle in the case of Laius, Jocasta, and

Oedipus, look so fundamentally unnatural, even polymorphously perverse, as Freud would say, when they are exposed to the light of day.

The tragedy of Oedipus and his family is about discovering that the truly powerful images that shape lives are not the conscious mental pictures that serve as road maps for daily living. For those brands of today's psychology that may sometimes perhaps rely too much on common sense, this means that rational techniques, such as cognitive therapy, though they have a legitimate place and use, are in the end no match for anyone's Delphic destiny. Apollo, who presides over that, does not take kindly to being mistaken for a doltish figure who can be easily outwitted. Laius, Jocasta, and Oedipus are there to tell us that. In the end, the myth of Oedipus is about realizing that "Know Thyself," which also falls under the Delphic oracle, means learning to understand that it is other than strictly ego designs that are being worked out in life—which is little more, but also no less, than the setting and the props for those other designs. The Greek term for such self-knowledge was *sophrosyne*. It referred to a kind of humility, a sense of place on the part of humans in relation to the immortal facts of existence that are personified as gods, and that are everywhere in the air we breathe every day. The myth of Oedipus is the *paradeigma*, the example par excellence, of this idea. It is about discovering that the images of these plots cannot be manipulated by human intellect and cleverness. They cannot be countered with simplistic methods, because they derive their fateful power from forces that are other than strictly personal and humanistic, and other than based on chance and on the laws of nature. The Oedipus story is about finding out that these forces, and the images whose shapes they assume, cannot be outsmarted. Even Oedipus, especially Oedipus, famous for guessing monumental riddles with clever insight, is no match for this.

(As an aside: It is doubly tragic to walk away from the Oedipus myth, as some popular psychology does, believing that cleverness can be an adequate response to the fundamentally tragic basis of human psychological destinies. Freud had to address that issue by pointing out the fundamental flaw in what he called, in a paper named after its subject matter, "Wild Psychoanalysis." By that he meant the failure to appreciate that, as in the case of Oedipus, what matters most in human lives is not so much the content of anything repressed but rather the ongoing act of repressing it. Missing that cardinal point in psychological treatment can and does make lives worse, not better. What is at stake can begin to be appreciated by a careful, actual reading of Sophocles' play, which portrays a case of a massively sustained labor of repression and of its gradual, painful, long-drawn-out unraveling. The fact that one can nowadays become a psychologist, a psychoanalyst, or a psychiatrist without having to read this so central human story at all carries its own risk of inducing a lack of *sophrosyne*.)

Jocasta personifies the commonsense attitude that ignores the reality of the fantastic imagination that governs lives. Her attitude places its faith exclusively in reason, and in explanations that are based on the identifiable laws of nature. She personifies the literal-mindedness of the man in the street who insists on having the facts, nothing but the facts. Her mind-set fails to realize that there are no such things as facts apart from interpretations based on imagination. She also is the authoritative voice of reason that patronizingly dismisses modes of thinking, knowing, reflecting, and valuing that differ from common sense. It is Jocasta who speaks every time someone says things such as, "It's all a matter of statistics," "It's all biology and genes," "It's always about race," or some such generalization. Above all, Jocasta personifies the lack of imagination that has no capacity to feel a sense of awe about the fantastic, the magical, the miraculous nature of everyday events. Taken broadly, Jocasta's is the voice of reason and enlightenment that has no sense of its own blind spots. It lacks awareness of the dark shadow of ignorance it casts on those aspects of existence where it cannot imagine casting any light because it turns its back to them. She is that voice of enlightened reason and of self-confident certainty and *hubris* that walks blindly into classically tragic situations without having a clue.

It is to compensate for Jocasta's brand of common sense that all modern ideas about unconsciousness, from Freud and Jung to Hillman and beyond, come into being. Their primary relevance is not that they serve to counter neurotic behaviors and to avoid personal tragedy or at least social deviance and messy, miserable lives. They are not, in the first place, handmaidens of the ego, put in service of *its* plans for our future. They matter most for the sake of reconnecting what is happening in any given situation with the image-based and very real magic that is an essential part of it. That magic cannot and will not be dismissed from everyday life. It will not be dismissed by force of argument from common sense and not by cleverness of any kind. The endless and self-perpetuating debate about Freud being a fraud—because psychoanalysis is forever failing the rational tests of science and common sense—is Jocasta all over again, every time. By wanting to replace the myth of Oedipus Tyrannus and all the rest that makes psychoanalysis so fantastic with the tyranny of common sense and its variations, this debate keeps repeating Jocasta's tragedy. It keeps repeating her tragically silly advice to Oedipus, the advice to just forget or just ignore the autonomous imagination of the soul. Instead of less Freudian or Jungian fantastics and fantasy, we need more. We need more because the imagination that underlies the life of the soul has to be met on its own terms—with images. If everyday life is fantastic, it is no use pretending that it is not or wishing that it were not. As the ancient maxim goes: like cures like—*similis similibus curantur*. The imaginative side of life needs to be met with imagination.

The great appeal that magical realism exerts and the deeply satisfying pleasure that it gives are not simply a matter of regressing to a childhood mentality that delights in fairy tales. They are a matter of progressing to a postmodern mode of thinking that frees itself from the constraints of excessive and exclusionary rationalism and that restores the sense for the magical realism of everyday life. There is a series of scenes in the film *Black Robe* that shows an attitude quite different from Jocasta's, one that is more in line with the laws governing the life of the soul. It shows a North American Indian who is first seen having a recurring dream of a particular place that is filled with images of death. Later, after many years have passed, the same man is shown slowly approaching his end. Suddenly he comes to a new place in the familiar landscape where he has lived all along. In a flash of recognition, he notices that the place resembles the one from his recurring dream. Right then and there, and unlike anything Jocasta probably would have done in similar circumstances, he realizes that the pieces of his life, including his end, have come to fall into their place, and that therefore all is well. Unlike Jocasta, who fights off the potentially overpowering impact of dream images by trying to dismiss them, the man welcomes the resemblance between dream image and life circumstance. The physical location where he finds himself, and to which he responds with a deep sensitivity for the place from his recurring dream, becomes for him the occasion where his life meets up with and consummates its long-built-in destiny. Like Nietzsche's Zarathustra, and unlike Jocasta, he recognizes that the seeming accidents he encounters are anything but accidental. Zarathustra, whose discovery occurs in the middle of his life, not at the end, shows a similar sensitivity for the specific details of what is not only his physical habitat but also the true psychological setting where he belongs. He notes that he has again and again been a wanderer and a mountain climber who does not like the plains and who cannot sit still for long. He realizes that "whatever may yet come to me as destiny and experience will include some wandering and mountain climbing . . . (for) . . . in the end, one experiences only oneself." This is not simply about behavioral habits and about the statistical probability of their literal recurrence in the future. It is also, and more importantly, about the ability to recognize that elusive yet concretely enacted images are involved. It is about sensing that it is these images that are the true psychological habitats men and women inhabit in their everyday lives. When the man with the recurring dream about images of death comes to the spot in the landscape that resembles his dream place he suddenly struggles no longer. He relaxes his whole being as one who has come home. He senses that he has arrived where he belongs, and that this place in the physical world and in the realm of images is most truly his. He lies down on the very same spot and happily awaits his death. Curiously, and paradoxically, he comes into his own, and his whole being fulfills itself, in an image that, at the literal level, also means his death. This contrasts sharply with Jocasta's commonsense attitude, which either ignores such insubstantial things as dream images or regards them as threats to her plans for her life. Her reaction is what, in another context, Hillman calls a "rage to live." It amounts to a fear of life's doings and undoings that will itself eventually do her in. The Indian's reaction is about a capacity to see life even in death; Jocasta's life and rage to live are a flight from its own imagination. His is an arrival, a homecoming, in the world of images that give his life a sense of its own place in the universe; her mind-set involves a resistance against imagination that is the essence of psychological repression.

Jocasta's brand of repression is not merely an individual and personal problem, one that can be overcome with rational insight. That, in any case, may do little more than add to an insensitivity about the soul's imagination more of the same. Jocasta's brand of repression is also, besides being an individual and personal problem, a matter of the West's collective, cultural, and historical consciousness. And all talk about the life of soul is, in this context, nothing if not a collective cultural exercise in magical realism. The whole language of a psychology of unconsciousness, irrespective of the particulars of the school of depth psychology, is about a magical reality that is imagined to coexist with the commonsense realities of everyday life. Compared to the ordinary language of everyday life, the vocabulary of all depth psychology speaks of things that often must seem bizarre, far-fetched, unreal, unnatural, and ultimately perhaps all too fantastic to be possibly true. If the realities of the soul's life are anything like what depth psychology proposes about them, and that certainly would seem to be the case, then everyday life is one fantastic magical affair indeed. The way to speak about them must therefore be a form of magical realism. The verities of such a psychology, verities that are based in images of the unbelievable and the barely imaginable, add up to an alternative view of nature. This makes of depth psychology itself an enterprise that is countercultural, because it is rooted in an imagination, a language, and a logic that go against all that the reigning culture accepts as fact. That other perspective defies the laws of physics, of logic, and of reason. It makes a mockery of all that reason, logic, the natural sciences, and everything else that is commonsensical have so painstakingly established. It dismisses the high seriousness of the West's history of ideas and replaces it with the fantastic imaginings of which the soul is capable and on which it thrives. Not surprisingly, depth psychology often looks like the madness of buffoonery. Like all madness, it has a method.

The primary method in the seeming madness of all depth psychology has a name. The neoplatonist philosophers and psychologists of past ages called it a "work against nature," an *opus contra naturam*. This was the name they gave to alchemy, their fantastic discipline of trying to make gold through the magic of transforming any given material, no matter how base, into it. Alchemy stood in the same relation to what eventually became natural, scientific chemistry as the magical realism of depth psychology stands to the laws and facts of reason and common sense. According to alchemy and magical realism, and according to depth psychology insofar as it is identical to both, the unit of reality of which the universe is made is not some sort of molecule or atom, nor is it a subatomic particle or an energy pattern. The ultimate building blocks of the universe, in this view, are the images of things that may well seem unimaginable, because they are incompatible with common sense. This includes images of the apparent possibility of things that are otherwise considered a known and proven impossibility. It includes images of the surprising ultimate veracity of ideas that must at first seem far-fetched if not blatantly unreal. It includes images of the truthfulness of propositions that are patently untrue, of the stunning believability of otherwise unbelievable notions, of the uncanny factuality of events from fiction. It includes images of a previously unsuspected life in ideas that had long seemed dead, of the utter familiarity of things that were thought to be alien and out of this world. This is no business for a Jocasta mentality. Here, in this magical realism of alchemy, as in that of depth psychology, it is the rigidly and exclusively naturalistic and commonsense view on all things that often is dismissed in favor of images that are nothing if not fantastic—images of sons marrying their mothers, of grown women becoming virgins again, of men seeing their lives come into their own in places of death. The business of depth psychology, like that of alchemy and magical realism, is about making propositions that blatantly deceive precisely in order to conceive.

Now the daily practices of applied psychology—as in raising and educating children, in the organization and conduct of social life, in treatment at the hands of psychologists or psychiatrists—these practices would be nothing without theory. But this is not only, not even primarily, because practice in these fields requires operational theories. It is not, in the first place, because workers in these areas need theories that can be applied to concrete situations so that they can serve to solve problems. It is because *the act of theorizing is itself the primary and ultimate human practice. Theorizing is the quintessential human practice that supersedes all practical living as its ultimate purpose.* It exists less to serve the activities of daily living than to be served by them. It requires practical applications, because by being applied to them, it perpetuates itself, thereby confirming and affirming its imaginings. As governing principles, theories, just like gods, who are their personifications, need the practical side of daily human living to confirm their reality. As Zarathustra wondered aloud one day, rising in the morning and, as usual, standing in front of his cave to greet the sun: "What would you be if it weren't for me and my animals greeting you every morning?" Theories need practice like gods need worldly life. This seemingly reverse relation between theory and practice, between gods and humans, applies to all human conduct. It has, however, a special significance in depth psychology, where it is more readily demonstrable than in many other human endeavors. It is here, more than in most human undertakings, that we choose the theories of our life as the private theologies that suit our personal household gods. What psychotherapy patients really want is not only practical solutions for living but even more so theories, ideas, symbols, myths, and images about it—including, especially, images of the archetypal principles governing it. The unnatural and contrarian art of alchemy serves as model for this view that, in the realm of soul, practice serves theory more than the other way around. Most ostensibly, and seemingly most naturally, the practical matters of daily living are what psychotherapy is supposed to address, with an eye toward making them manageable. But beyond that, the practical matters to which psychological theory is applied serve as occasion, as pretext, as justification for the process of theorizing itself. They serve the purpose of confirming what the theory holds and, above all, what it is designed to make us behold.

Psychological treatment, from this point of view, is less about putting theory into practice than it is about putting the practices of life into theories about them. By having theories about everything in daily life—its behaviors, emotions, developmental phases, social interaction patterns, beliefs, conflicts, problems, symptoms, value judgments, pathologies—we provide a mythic context for it all. The multiplicity of our psychological theories is modern man's own form of polytheism. In this sense, all patients of psychological treatment—and, more broadly, all consumers of psychology's theory, which means everyone—not only *have* Oedipal conflicts or narcissistic traits, or whatever it may be. By having these things, or rather by being had by them at the microcosmic level of their individual life, they *confirm* them at the macrocosmic level of the human condition. They thereby make such mythic themes as those of Oedipus and Narcissus into archetypal facts, and ultimately into a part of the ontological basis of existence. Psychotherapy patients therefore do what Zarathustra does when he greets the sun every morning. They make room in the world of facts for all the imaginings from myth. This is no longer *cogito ergo sum*, "I think, therefore I am." It is, "I am, therefore what I think and believe is proven true," which means, "My life, insofar as the psychological theory to which I subscribe identifies the facts of it, identifies, confirms, and affirms the rock-bottom facts and truths of existence itself—and those facts and truths, by the way, are as fantastic as anything in fiction."

The modern psychological practitioner—and all men or women, insofar as they cannot but have, or be had by, a psychological theory—behaves, therefore, like the alchemists of previous ages. They, too, used concrete bits and pieces of daily living as their starting point, not only to feed their alembics but especially the theories they were cooking up in them. They used the factual matters and substance of daily life as their *prima materia*, as the starting point, to begin their process of active imagination. Those tidbits of daily residue, the discarded leftovers of little apparent value, served to begin their reflections on material with archetypal significance. The identified problem, the presenting complaint, the symptom, the current issue, the contemporary situation, the slip of the tongue, the latest crisis or outburst, the dream, the loose association, the recurring theme—all these are modern-day versions of the alchemist's *prima materia* that is asking for the quintessentially human act of imaginative theorizing. This is not only, not even primarily, in order to come up with practical solutions. It is, above all, for the sake of seeing what we may behold and how we may behold it. In the final analysis, nothing is of greater interest to human beings than to behold the spectacle of life. They do this primarily by beholding the personal *prima materia* that is their own life. Yet this is not only how human beings behold their own being, and beyond that other beings and all beings. It also is how they catch glimpses of Being itself. Just like the alchemist the modern psychological treater takes the presenting *prima materia* the patient brings in and begins the project of trying to make gold from it. Like his or her ancient colleague, the treater takes the matter at hand, whatever it may be, and begins to work on it by casting new light on it. The treater does this, again, as in the old tradition, by bringing the heat of interest and of ideas to bear on the material under consideration. That interest and those ideas make new things become visible in old and seemingly all-too-well-known facts. The substance of the presenting material begins to be transformed before one's very eyes in this manner. It begins to display previously unsuspected and typically quite fantastic features. Extraordinary and unbelievable things thereby become visible in the midst of, and disguised as, perfectly ordinary and mundane matters. And even though nothing changes about the literal facts of the matter, everything about it begins to look different. That is the transformative power of alchemy, this original and archetypal form of magical realism and of all depth psychology.

The alchemist's ability to transform base matter into gold depended on two key things. One was firm containment of the matter being processed, in a vessel that must be hermetically sealed and guarded against breaking. The other was the art of regulating the flame under the vessel, the heat of active imagination. It is precisely in line with this view that Jung, who more than anyone appreciated the significance of alchemy for psychology, identified active imagination as the foremost method for handling the life of the soul. And even though Freud did not explicitly take up the paradigm of alchemy, his method of free association practices its working principle. By telling the patient to voice whatever comes to mind in analysis, Freud followed the alchemical principle of generating psychological discoveries by bringing an activated imagination to bear on the matter at hand, and on all the residues of daily living. It is perhaps no coincidence that the rule of free association in psychoanalysis and derived treatment modalities became itself their famous "golden" rule. Wherever alchemy enters the picture, there images of gold begin to appear.

The practical problems that are brought to psychotherapy, like the base matter that goes into the alchemical alembic, are rarely of great interest in themselves. They often are only interesting in themselves, and even then not for long, for the newcomer in the field or perhaps for the outsider. This short-lived and, to some degree perhaps, voyeuristic interest comes from a natural curiosity about a field where the narrative genre of gossip about life's shocking, scandalous, bizarre, or otherwise fantastic displays is part of the official discourse. That sense of novelty and that curiosity wear out in time, and usually rather quickly too. Then boredom and burnout may set in. Eventually one feels that one has seen it all. One may find oneself having a rapidly diminishing further interest in any of it. A new patient's life story can then quickly become "as tedious as a twice-told tale, vexing the dull ear of a drowsy man." Every practicing

psychotherapist knows that this is when he or she is most at risk of literally nod-
ding off in mid session. Burnout can become endemic among psychological
treaters. This can be all the more the case to the degree that the necessarily fantastic imagination that forms the depth of depth psychology is reduced. That can
easily happen when the magical realism and the alchemy that are the natural
active ingredients in depth psychology are reduced to biological psychiatry and
neurology. It can happen when psychotherapy becomes handmaiden of psychiatry, when psychiatry becomes handmaiden of medicine, when medicine
becomes handmaiden of social hygiene, when social hygiene becomes handmaiden of the state, of social life, and of the currently governing forms of
political correctness. More broadly and more deeply, burnout of the active imagination that forms the depth of depth psychology happens when Plato's *Republic*—and the genre of philosophizing that is based on it and that starts in it—is
mistaken for a treatise on social life rather than being taken for what it is, an
analogy about the soul in which the man-made state image, and all derived or
related social analogies, serve to shed light on the soul, not the other way around.
Burnout of active psychological imagination is bound to occur whenever Platonism in all its hidden forms ignores this fundamental relation between the
soul, which is autonomous, and the man-made models of social life we are
always trying to impose on it. The true interest in psychological matter and the
true significance of psychological treatment as well as the only real answer to
burnout in therapy practice lie in the activity of theorizing that is brought to
bear on the practical matters that become grist for psychology's mill. All that one
gets to see in psychiatric hospitals or clinics, all the clinical psychopathology that
parades there, as well as all else to which theoretical psychology may be applied,
is what alchemists would regard as base everyday matter from which gold can be
made. These seemingly lowly matters are the starting material that alchemical
imagination transforms into the same magnificent images that also are found in
art, in musea, in literature, or in the history of ideas. The substance, the stuff, the
matter is the same. Only the editions differ. One version appears lowly. The other
is the same substance turned into gold. Freud was right in making unconsciousness the central idea of his psychoanalysis. Clinical psychopathology, and all else
that is brought to treatment, is, in the first place, about lacking vision, imagination, the capacity for reflection and for handling unfamiliar ideas. It is about lack
of consciousness, hence, about unconsciousness. Art, musea, literature, creativity,
symbolism of all sorts, and the history of ideas are about the opposite of unconsciousness, which is why they are considered golden. This explains the emphasis
in modern depth psychology, as in its premodern versions, on processes that
make imagination central as their active ingredient. It also explains the penchant
for the fantastic, the fictional, the mythic, the philosophical, and the artistic,
which is characteristic among psychology's theoreticians.

    In Freud the emphasis on imagination is personified as the polymor-
phously perverse child in his or her perpetually infantile fantasy world. In

Freudian treatment, it comes as the golden rule of free association, and as the focus on the bizarre contents and workings of dreams. In Jung, the emphasis on imagination comes as the preoccupation with myth, with alchemy, with religious symbolism. In Jungian treatment, it comes in the form of such activities as word association experiments, the spontaneous creation of mandalas, the exploration of mythic motifs, and the analogical exploration of personal facts, dreams, symbols, and rituals. In Hillman, the emphasis on imagination comes as the explicit idea of the "poetic basis of mind." In Hillman's practice, it comes as the golden first rule of "sticking to the image" that is given in every event or situation, in every scrap of life. In each of these three cases, unconsciousness is treated with methods that are aimed at activating a dormant imagination that is inherent in all things. These methods are aimed at closing the gap that separates the seemingly base matter, which tends to present itself as a problem to be solved, from the nobler and archetypal matters that are embedded in it and that are portrayed in art—or recounted in literature, expressed in symbolism, formulated in philosophy, cast in ideas, crystallized in myth, ritualized in ceremony. Whenever workers in clinical psychopathology become overwhelmed by the depressing aspect of their jobs, when a treatment case seems so hopelessly stuck that the treater is tempted to give up, when the enterprise of theoretical psychology itself seems futile and irrelevant, or when the very idea of soul seems laughable because it is always so intangible—then one can be sure that the momentum of active imagination is at least temporarily lost. The practice of applied psychology begins to fail whenever theorizing comes to a halt. Then it becomes a sphinx that eats alive whoever lacks, or loses, the capacity to imagine along on its terms. Hence, the intuitive sense of needing to reactivate the imagination and place one's faith in that activity. Hence, the real justification for the insistence on perpetually continuing education for psychological treaters.

The relevance of the alchemical paradigm is twofold. Both aspects appear in modern depth psychology. First, and like the literary genre of magical realism, alchemy breaks free from the laws of common sense, from the exclusive insistence on strict logic and pure reason. By doing this, it breaks free from many of those adventures in the history of Western thought that have tended to run aground on dualistic modes of thinking. Alchemy overcomes the thinking that insists on artificially dividing and separating fact from fiction—and truth from falsehood, essence from appearance, material from immaterial, transient from permanent, worldly from otherworldly, profane from sacred, human from divine. Alchemy breaks free from these artificial divisions by breaking free from the tyranny of the schemes of thinking that are built into the grammar, the vocabulary, and the very language at the heart of many metaphysical beliefs and prejudices. Nietzsche wrote about these language-based beliefs and prejudices. As he put it: "We think only in the form of language. We cease to think when we refuse to do so under the constraint of language; we barely reach the doubt that sees this limitation as a limitation. Rational thought is interpretation according to a scheme that we cannot throw off." Therefore, he also wrote: "We really ought to free ourselves from the seduction of words!" Alchemy does precisely that. It breaks free from the usual beliefs and prejudices that are built into the discourse of everyday life. That also is part of the reason why the alchemists insist that alchemy is not literally true—that it is not natural chemistry, that it does not describe nature as we find it in nature, that it does not pretend to be a nature science, that the gold it is after is not the literal gold that is found in the ground. Instead of all this, they offer their art as a practice of being contrarian, as the project of a "work against nature." Alchemy offers a perspective and a habit of thinking aimed at working against every usual and accepted trend—against every habitual belief, against every customary assumption, and against all ways of thinking that have become second nature and that seem so perfectly natural that we no longer question them in any way. As a consequence, there is a natural inclination to dismiss alchemy as nonsensical—pure insanity, laughable theory, crazy chemistry. This makes it all the more tempting, and so much easier, to portray the alchemist—and the contemporary theorist of depth psychology—as a buffoon, an irresponsible charlatan. Nietzsche appreciated perhaps better than most thinkers in prior history, and before contemporary philosophy of language, just how lonely, alienated, and controversial any thinker would be who would question the beliefs and prejudices of Western metaphysics at the level of the language that creates them and then perpetuates them. He also appreciated how mad such a thinker would have to seem. He fully expected that he himself would be viewed as such an unnatural creature. He welcomed the thought, because he regarded it as necessary. Zarathustra, the one figure who speaks on Nietzsche's behalf, is even more clearly such a figure who abandons ordinary categories of thought by abandoning ordinary forms of discourse. He does this for the sake of thought experiments that are themselves based on language experiments—consisting of paradoxes, seeming contradictions, and mad-sounding propositions of all sorts. Not surprisingly, Zarathustra is often and easily depicted as a buffoon, much as the alchemists were in their field and time. By making hyperbole, hyper exaggeration, their preferred mode of speech, both Nietzsche and Zarathustra create a tone and a manner of discourse that are themselves unnatural. For hyperbole is about making propositions whose proportions of image are deliberately grotesque, unreal, and laughable—gargantuan buffoonery. That is only one reason why Nietzsche, in all earnest, thought that laughter has an as-yet unsuspected and promising philosophical future.

Freud, who turned away from his early research in neurology and then from the scientific ambitions of his *Project for a Scientific Psychology* in order to develop psychoanalysis, is, in this respect, the twentieth century's alchemist par excellence. He is an alchemist, even though he did not, as Jung did and Hillman after him, make explicit use of the alchemical paradigm. Freud became an alchemist the day he became the laughingstock of Vienna's medical community

with his theories about a polymorphous and often seemingly perverse unconscious life of the soul that seemed too fantastic to be true. As soon as he became
Vienna's resident quack in this fashion, he also became an incarnation of the
figure of the Nietzschean madman. That famous madman ran into the town
square in the middle of the day, lit lantern in hand, and announced the most
unimaginable, the most unbelievable, the most impossible thing ever conceived
by the human imagination. He announced the death of God. By this he meant
that the beliefs and prejudices associated with that God, even and especially the
very categories of thought that made those beliefs and prejudices possible in the
first place, were null and void. Few madnesses in history have had a greater
impact. Similarly, few theories of nature have profounder implications than
those of alchemy, just as few propositions about human nature have been more
willing to meet the soul on its own, and, seemingly unbelievable, terms than
Freud's psychoanalysis.

Naturally, alchemy is more then mere oppositionalism and defiance for the
sake of oppositionalism and defiance. It is certainly something other than sheer
anarchy, a rejection of all *archai* or archetypal laws. Nor is alchemy a form of
madness. It is madness with a mission and a method. In the end it is, of course,
no madness at all. Alchemy's self-appointed mission to create gold by transforming base matters, any matter, into it is about something other than making
gold. It is about an act of transformation for the sake of transvaluation. This is
the other feature that makes alchemy relevant and comparable to the twentieth
century's depth psychology. As a transformative process that is aimed at the
transvaluation of all given value, and that intends to arrive at gold from any
point of departure in the matters of everyday existence, alchemy is a process of
redemption. Its aim is to take the lesser and therefore negative value of base
matter—of all matter, and of the very idea of matter or materiality itself—and
to transform that value judgment until the very transvaluation that is involved
produces gold, the universal standard and ideal of positive value. The redemption of matter and of materiality itself to which alchemy aspires takes place *in*
the world rather than *beyond* it or *after* it. It takes place in human time rather
than as an otherworldly and afterworldly event that is in the hands of non-
human powers. In this respect, alchemy is comparable to the postmodern philosophical project of Nietzsche's revaluation and transvaluation of all values. Ultimately it is an attempt to overcome the world-denying value judgment
inherent in so much of the West's history of dualistic metaphysics. Depth psychology, this form of magical realism about everyday life, involves a transvaluation similar to the alchemist's material transformation and to Nietzsche's transvaluation of values for the sake of an affirmative pathos. Depth psychology is
therefore in important ways less about the transformation of persons and of
their behaviors, of the signs and symptoms of abnormality, than it is about the
transformation of the view that regards the foibles of human living as baseness
in it that needs to be cured out of existence. Psychoanalysis and other modern

depth psychologies matter most of all because they restore the sense for the magical realities that coexist with the mundane facts of everyday life. Freud is interesting and worthwhile because Oedipus is—and Eros, Thanatos, Narcissus, Ananke, Logos, the Titans, and all the rest. Psychoanalysis is interesting and worthwhile because it puts us in touch with all of them. The whole psychology of our unconsciousness about the life of the soul is interesting and worthwhile because it activates the human imagination and puts that imagination to work on the seemingly base matters of everyday life. Depth psychology, through its active ingredient of alchemical imagination, transforms these prosaic and seemingly dull matters into the rich substance that makes up the bulk of the soul, whose reality is nothing if not fantastic.

Schooling, study, and training in depth psychology do matter. They matter greatly, because such a psychology does not come naturally. To be healthy, experienced in life's ways, and perhaps even wise by nature are not enough here, nor is being in touch with nature or at home with nature's ways. If purely natural man could possibly exist he probably would be unpsychological to a profound degree. If Freud taught us anything that has been confirmed and reconfirmed it is that the soul is anything but natural, and that becoming a psychological creature is anything but a natural process. He also taught us that in order to think along with the soul, we must begin to think in unnatural ways, about things that often seem unnatural and that go against what we like to think of as our nature. Oedipus proved his point. What Freud taught us is that soul comes into being and comes into its own—both in the life of the individual and in the craft of psychological treatment—precisely when nature itself is given up as our natural ground. Nature alone, pure nature, does not necessarily or automatically nurture soul. This nurturing of soul requires the added active ingredient of imagination. One can sit under a tree for hours or days, or live in a forest for years on end, without necessarily doing a thing for one's soul. Truly psychological schooling involves learning to develop a degree of imaginative suspicion about thoughts and ideas that seem purely natural, that come only naturally or from purest nature, and that smack of too much nature worship. What seems all too natural, purely and exclusively natural, may well lack the ingredients that make it food for the soul. But depth psychological schooling is not, on those grounds, a purely technical activity either, simply because it has a penchant for going against nature and against all that seems all too natural. Psychological training has less to do with acquiring technical knowledge and skill than with learning to practice the imaginative art of theorizing. This kind of training is especially needed in matters where nothing but natural-mindedness and practical know-how seem to be called for.

If, like alchemists, Freud, Jung, and Hillman turn to the collective imagination of myth, religion, art, literature, and philosophy in order to ground their psychology, then the student and practitioner of this field can do no less. For that reason alone, all truly psychological treatment has to be multidisciplinary.

But this is not because it takes a psychiatrist plus a psychologist, a social worker, a nurse, and an occupational therapist to say and do all that needs to be said and done. It is because it takes images, multiple images, from many different angles and viewpoints, and always more images plus the active ingredient of an active imagination, to see what may be seen. All men and women who have an interest in depth psychology are drawn to its theories out of an intuitive sense about their fundamentally alchemical nature. They sense that these theories deal with the matters of daily living in order to reveal images of universal facts and verities. They expect to discover not simply facts of behavior and mental life but archetypal facts and laws governing the human condition. It is no accident that depth psychology's most inspired theoreticians have always had a penchant for the images from art, literature, philosophy, religion, and the history of ideas. These modern myth makers are themselves among the active keepers of those traditions—precisely by making those traditions explicitly relevant to the mundane matters of everyday life. Like the alchemists, who are their natural forebears, they operate on the basis of the prejudiced view that the soul's own gold is potentially everywhere—not for the taking but for the making.

EIGHT

IMMACULATE CONCEPTION
IN EVERYDAY LIFE

"FOLLOW YOUR BLISS," said Joseph Campbell, America's popular teacher of the world's myths and of their universal, timeless relevance. He explained: "Follow your bliss, for if you follow your bliss you will come to bliss." Campbell's prescription may be the treatment of choice for what Henry David Thoreau diagnosed forever as the "quiet desperation" that marks the lives of many men and women. That quiet desperation comes from living a life based on obligation instead of desire. In Nietzsche's way of thinking, it comes from living under the tyranny of a centuries' old dragon who, in a thousand ways, commands, "Thou shalt." The categorical imperative, "Thou shalt," silences every creative "I will." This makes for the condition of quiet desperation, of a lifelong, personalized culture of self-hatred and hatred of life itself. Campbell's prescription to "Follow your bliss" provides a way to escape the dragon's tyranny. For "if you follow your bliss," said Campbell, "you put yourself on a kind of track that has been there all the while, waiting for you, and the life that you ought to be living is the one that you are living . . . I say, follow your bliss and don't be afraid, and doors will open where you didn't know they were going to be." Following the law of one's personal bliss can prevent and cure quiet desperation through the transformative power of an inspiring idea. The inspiring idea serves as the active ingredient of a personal morality that is grounded in it and elaborated from it. Answering the call of such an inspiring idea, by accepting the challenge and responsibility of realizing it, is a way to follow one's bliss.

The word "bliss" comes from the Sanskrit word *ananda*, meaning "rapture." That means "bliss," via *ananda* and "rapture," refers to ecstasy, transport, joy, delight, pleasure, and happiness. In its association with ecstasy, it connotes gladness, intoxication, and enthusiasm, as well as trance, frenzy, or inspiration. Taken together, these words point to an unusual state of consciousness. But while the experience of bliss is perhaps unusual, it involves several familiar components. These component parts of bliss include, first, deep pleasure or joy. Second, they involve a state of being filled with an energy that has a life of its own that is almost separate from the person experiencing it. Third, there is a feeling of being so moved as to be transported from the place and time of one's literal circumstance to an altogether different place in a separate time zone. Fourth, there is a sensation and a belief that this unusual state is somehow induced, as it were by a potent agent. It is clear that states of bliss are no everyday occurrence in any life. But neither are they such rarified states as to be restricted to an exclusive elite of the lucky few, the esoterically initiated, or the otherwise exceptionally endowed. They do not have to be artificially produced by special means or in rarified conditions. Quite the contrary. Every life knows its moments of bliss. For many people, they may occur only sparingly. For others, they are by no means rare or exceptional. They belong to Everyman's ordinary lot, because they are an essential ingredient of the human condition. They are part of the extraordinariness that belongs in every ordinary life.

To follow one's bliss means to let oneself be guided by such an experience of rapture. It means accepting the experience as a gift and then cultivating it. One begins to do this by letting the experience serve as an initiation into the mystery of a deep source of joy. To follow one's bliss amounts to letting that deep source of joy become one's fundamental and sustaining philosophical pathos. One accepts that pathos as the a priori, the categorical imperative, the self-grounding ground that determines one's personal perspective. It becomes the self-moving movement—the true *auto-mobile*—that moves one forward in one's actions and that, in the process, moves one to the core of one's being. To follow one's bliss means accepting the stirring emotion of bliss in order to move on with one's life toward a genuine fulfillment of itself. It involves letting the animating mystery of inspiring ideas be the central argument with which one affirms existence, including one's place in the universe. Most importantly, to follow one's bliss means letting that which enraptures one's entire being serve as cornerstone and standard of one's personal morality and of the task of one's life that one sees in front of oneself as a personal challenge. It means hearing, recognizing, acknowledging, and answering the call of that for which, and by which, one is called. Following the call to bliss means inscribing that call over one's doorway, as a law to live by, and as a cipher that guides one's interpretation of existence and of Being.

Accepting the call of one's bliss is a sign of genius—not genius as superior intelligence but as genie, as spirit that emerges from being bottled up in a dormant state. It is about something that is latent or virtual, a potential that urges and presses to be realized. It is about a spirit that wants nothing more than to animate a life and to shape the decisive choices that are made in it. Genius, in this sense, means a life's *spiritus rector*—its inner voice and personal calling. It is the idea behind the seemingly reckless and selfish advice, "Do what you like. The money will follow." Following the call to bliss is the beginning of true vocational training. In ancient Roman religion, a *genius* was imagined as the ruling spirit that determined and perpetuated the life of a household, an individual, or a group of individuals united by a shared activity or interest. He placed his stamp on the atmosphere hanging over the household, the individual, or the group. He watched over all events taking place under his sign and under the roof where he made his home. He marked successive generations in a family with the shared patterns of habit and style that made the clan into a mini-universe all its own. He was the factor held responsible for visiting the sins and the dramas of fathers and mothers upon their sons and daughters. But he also passed on talent and title, as well as inherited sensibilities. He served as a household god who was an intangible but real and undeniable presence and part of everyday life. He was worshipped on such occasions as one's birthday, on holidays and special occasions of all sorts, or in ritualistic acts performed nearly automatically and as part of established routines. The subtle spirit of genius is what determines the unique atmosphere that hangs in the air in every household, every building, every organization. It is what songs hint at in describing how cities such as Paris or New York awaken every day. It is the characteristic impression that even a stranger in these cities quickly learns to recognize—in the sounds, the commotion, the perfumes, the food smells, even the dust in the air. It is the almost palpable subtle substance that is present in individual or collective ritualized behaviors. Manifestations of genius are everywhere, stamping all things in unique and unmistakable ways. This genius is nothing less than the Emersonian god who is present in every day, and who is indeed the very day itself.

Following the call of genius in one's experience of bliss means entering the domain of powerful forces that shape one's days, in big ways and small. Because the genius in an experience of bliss fills a person with a spirit that can dominate a whole life, it also can be a source of dramatic upheaval. Just as such a spirit can maintain the existing habits and balance in an established universe, so too can it unbalance and destroy these. That is its shadow side, the other side of the coin. This may mean a violation of one's life as one has lived it. It may mean an abandonment of familiar ideas, habits, and values. It may involve a severing of personal attachments previously held dear and a departure from places and perspectives long cherished. The Greek myth of Persephone personifies this kind of upheaval at the hands of an overwhelming and disturbing spirit. It tells the story of how young girl Persephone's childlike innocence is forever lost one day when Hades enters her life like a bully from Hell who is as unwelcome as he is uninvited and unexpected. His agenda is strictly his own. He insists on taking her away from her mother Demeter in order to make her queen in his underworld. He is what every mother warns every daughter about. The Hades spirit that descends on Persephone transports her into a wholly other realm. That also means a wholly new mode of being. She is forcefully separated from the familiarity of her mother's home life and from her mother's universe. Without asking for it or wanting it, she is installed in a new world. She is facing a set of new ideas, values, beliefs, and habits. Not only that. As newly appointed queen of this universe, she is assigned an unfamiliar position, with new tasks. No wonder this mythic motif is commonly called "the rape of Persephone."

Nietzsche experienced such an uninvited visitation by the spirit of an initially disturbing idea. In his case it was the overwhelming moment of inspiration that gave birth to the idea for a philosophy based on the thought of the eternal return of all things. The figure of Zarathustra demonstrates the initial resistance that is characteristic in the face of such violently disturbing visitations. When the thought of eternal return first comes to him, he tries to resist it—to push it away, to avoid it, to distance himself from it. He does not want to think this thought that comes to him like an intrusive and repulsive idea. He is horrified by the thought itself—and doubly horrified because it has chosen to visit him: "Huh! Let go! Huhhuh! Nausea, nausea, nausea—woe unto me!" This is Persephone's rape all over again. Zarathustra makes himself perfectly clear in the way he says No. He does not want this. He fights back. No one can accuse him of being ambivalent, of giving mixed messages. But he is no match for this force that overwhelms him. Writes Nietzsche: "No sooner had Zarathustra spoken these words than he fell down as one dead and long remained as one dead." The probable diagnosis seems clear enough. We are dealing with a case of philosophical traumatization. The rest of Zarathustra's story is about the process of his transformation. His initial horror and resistance in response to eternal return are transformed. They are finally abandoned altogether, because they have become the opposite of resistance and horror. The transformation turns Zarathustra into the willing teacher of the philosophy of eternal return. This is one case in which the original pathos of saying No is transformed into a pathos that says Yes.

Nietzsche's own life, after the thought of eternal return first came to him, shows a similar reaction of acute distress. In his autobiographical *Ecce Homo,* he wrote this about the experience of intense inspiration: "Afterwards I was sick for a few weeks." And also, "the years during and above all *after* my *Zarathustra* were marked by distress without equal. One pays dearly for immortality." The remainder of Nietzsche's philosophical life was devoted to trying to work out the details of his proposed philosophy of eternal return. The story of Zarathustra, therefore, like the life of Herr Nietzsche trying to work out a philosophy of eternal return, is about a transvaluation in which an initially negative value judgment is transformed into an affirmative one. In both cases, the transformation and transvaluation are initiated by an overwhelming spirit that occupies a human life without its consent. The scenario being reenacted is that of Persephone's transformation from unwilling bride into willing queen of the underworld. This transformation brings a new balance, even to the disrupted world of Persephone's mother, Demeter. What at first appeared a clear-cut case of brutal violation turns out to be—because it becomes—something altogether different. Persephone is not only, not even primarily, victim. She also is queen of the Land of Souls.

Following one's bliss, as a reenactment of the myth of Persephone, is about working out the story of transformation that is initiated by the ravishing spirit of a stirring idea. It means working out the transvaluation of values that is triggered by a spirited visitation that brings visions of a new outlook, from a different perspective. It means making room for something that, like Hades or the thought of eternal return, seems to appear out of thin air. If such a visitation is to lead anywhere at all, instead of only being disruptive, it requires an eventual consent to the fact of being chosen, even though it is a case of being chosen without having a choice about being chosen. That means consenting to the task of bearing the fruit of the inspiring idea, consenting to the challenge of bringing it into the world in concrete form. One must become devoted to nurture it with all one has of passion, patience, will, talent, time, energy, blood, sweat, and tears. It means accepting the seed of a complete philosophy that comes to one in the embryonic form of a personal, life-altering experience. Following one's bliss, understood this way, is Everyman's form of Immaculate Conception. As with the biblical figure of young Mary, it is about being chosen to bring into the world the concrete materialization of an idea for which one feels completely unprepared and unsuited. It involves disbelief in the face of a seemingly mad proposition for which there is no ground in any known reality, and no place in one's life.

Ideas that make for such Immaculate Conceptions do not belong in the life one has lived, is currently living, and expects to go on living. If these ideas are at all conceivable, it is only in the context of a life other than one's own. They may perhaps belong in other people's lives, but not in mine. That is why they are met with the reflex reaction of incredulity. There may even be an outburst of laughter at the impossible, the preposterous idea. What Freud called a "construction" from psychoanalysis offers a patient a virtual life story that is potentially believable precisely because it is plausible. In contrast, the proposition made by a spirit whose house call is about a personal state of Immaculate Conception seems unbelievable and undoable—not to mention uninvited and unwelcome. A construction from depth psychology offers a myth to live by. In contrast, a proposition about Immaculate Conception looks like a mad idea that has no chance of a viable future. And yet the experience of disbelief in the face of the idea of Immaculate Conception is not exclusively biblical and confined to the case of Mary hearing she is to bear a child-god. It is a universal theme whose relevance reaches beyond religious beliefs in general and beyond Judeo-Christian tradition in particular. At the pedestrian level, where ordinary people live their workaday lives, this biblical visitation has utterly mundane analogs.

Here it may be something like: "What? Me? Write a book?" or, "What? Me? Build a boat and sail it around the world?" or, "Me? Get out of this ghetto and go to college and law school and get into politics?"

Following the call of one's bliss involves more than suspending purely intellectual disbelief in the face of an idea that seems unimaginable. For even if it were imaginable, the idea would still be unacceptable, because it is incompatible with how one has always understood one's life. And even if it were considered personally acceptable, or at least theoretically possible and maybe worth considering, it would still remain socially unacceptable, because it is preposterous in light of one's established social identity. Finally, even if it were accepted for personal consideration, preposterousness and all, there is still the critical objection that one believes oneself to be singularly lacking in what it takes to make the idea bear fruit and to turn it into a reality. And yet in spite of all this, the first step required is a deliberate act of suspending disbelief in the face of an unbelievable idea.

Nietzsche's struggle to appropriate the thought of eternal return illustrates the point. It also shows the intuitive realization that if the unbelievable notion were to be believed, then all of life would be radically altered. As he wrote in a letter to a friend: "I don't know how I came to this . . . it is possible that the thought has come to me *for the first time*, the thought which splits the history of humanity into two halves . . . I have had to produce courage for myself since discouragement approached me from all sides . . . I am still far from able to speak and describe it. *If it is true*—or rather, if it is believed to be true, then everything changes and turns around and *all* previous values are devalued." This passage makes several points that apply not only to Nietzsche's experience with eternal return but to Everyman with respect to his personal moment of transformative inspiration. It emphasizes that the inspiring thought is not deliberately fabricated, but that it is a visitation that comes unannounced and autonomously. The thought of eternal return came to Nietzsche, not the other way around. It came because *it* wanted to come, not because he wanted it to come. And it is a thought he could not just *have*. He had to *undergo* it. It was less he who had to work out the thought than it was he who had to let the thought itself do its work on him. It was more a thought that had him than a thought he had. Nor did he understand how the thought came to him, how it entered into his thinking. All he could do was identify the conditions under which it came to him. It was a foreign element for which he initially could not imagine any room in his life, in his self-image, in his view of the world. Trying to actively imagine the thought into his life had already required from Nietzsche a great deal of courage. This included, not in the least, the courage to tolerate extreme loneliness. Nor was outside help available, for thinking the thought was, in the end, a strictly solitary affair. Nietzsche had to produce all the necessary courage by himself. He felt that he must become prepared to enter alone, and to live by his own wits, in the new and different reality that the thought would bring about. History would be forever changed if and when the newly conceived inspiring thought were to become more imaginable. It would be cut precisely in half. One half would be everything that came before the thought, the other half everything that came after it. And with that would also come a different morality. That would mean other values and a philosophical pathos shaped by a theme first conceived in willing suspension of disbelief.

What makes such experiences of conceiving new ideas a form of Immaculate Conception is not only the lack of preparedness for them or their initial unbelievability but also the wholly unnatural and seemingly magical way in which these conceptions announce themselves. They are never planned. It usually is impossible to pinpoint precisely how they enter into anyone's system. All that can be said about them is that, one fine day, they announce their presence. It is as though they must have been conceived while one was busy doing other things. By the time one learns of their presence in one's innermost being, they are already identifiable in embryonic form. By then they are already firmly planted deep inside one's most intimate sense of oneself. One has become host to an unknown spirit, without having realized it. From now on the inspiring concept is incapable of being shaken off at will. Any attempt to shake it off at this point does violence to the newly transformed being one has already started to become.

These transformative concepts typically do not enter into a person's system through his or her deliberate thoughts and activities. Rather, they tend to stand out from all this as something that was never there before, and that was neither planned nor willed, but that has suddenly appeared, as though out of nowhere. There is a distinct feeling that some unexpected alien spirit has laid this claim on one's person. It lets one know, after the deed is done, that life is going to be different from now on, that it is going to be about bearing this newly conceived fruit. This unnatural *modus operandi* is reflected in the original meaning of the Latin *genius* as "begetter." That inspiring begetter may do his work disguised in a variety of forms, and he may announce his deed in many ways. He may assume the shape of a sudden flash of insight or a vision of extraordinary things that lights up in the midst of ordinary circumstances. He may announce himself through the whisper of a voice that speaks up in some situation or other that deeply stirs a person in his or her most intimate inwardness. Or he may appear as the lightning-quick glimpse of an idea that flashes up and that is, at it were, caught in mid flight. Paradoxically, the extraordinariness of Immaculate Conception can occur in the most unexpected setting of all, the ordinary setting of one's routine obligations. Here the very thing that ordinarily keeps a person tied to the dragon who speaks of nothing but "Thou shalt" unexpectedly makes room for the liberating inspiration of "I will." This makes it possible for Immaculate Conception to occur in those things one must do, must undergo, must not try to avoid or deny, or must repeat again and again. It may occur in all that one cannot escape, because it is what forms the circumstances to which one belongs—the origins from which one originates, the past as it has been, the present as it is, the facts as they are. That means Immaculate Conception and the potential inception of bliss it engenders happen in the most unexpected of places and circumstances: the here and now of existence as it is. In biblical imagery, this is expressed as Immaculate Conception happening to young Mary, the bride to be, for it belongs to the natural and expected facts of life that Mary, the future bride, is facing the mysteries of marriage, child bearing, and child rearing. What makes her conception immaculate is precisely that her divinely inspired visitation and revelation happen in a set of circumstances where only natural, ordinary events seem to be at hand. This is the mythic and psychological theme of Immaculate Conception: that nothing is as it seems, that nature involves more than the natural laws of physics or physiology, that where two people or things come together in ordinary or natural history there the mystery of a third dimension, and of an altogether new reality, opens up. As modern semantic theory puts it, the meaningfulness of words and of signs generally—and of all things, insofar as everything is a cipher—lies not so much in the words, signs, or things themselves. It lies in the difference that emerges when two or more of them are brought together. The miracle of meaningfulness happens in the space, the depth, the bottomless abyss that is created between things when they are joined. This is the trade secret of Eros: that one thing alone is no thing, nothing.

The twosome from which inspired meaningfulness emerges takes many forms. It can be the most readily imaginable pair, such as two people in a close encounter, but it also can be one individual in an unexpected event that serves, as it were, as another being, and whose encounter forces unanticipated change. Broadly taken, the third and inspiring factor in any twosome is the potential for previously unimagined significance in any situation that ordinarily seems flat or two-dimensional. In Mary's biblical story, the events ultimately complete themselves in her own ascension into Heaven. This concretizes and dramatizes the move in the direction of a third dimension, the depth dimension that is inherent in the flat surface appearance of all things, and in everything that seems all too natural and only natural. Every life unveils its immanent sanctity, the fulfillment of its innate extraordinariness, when it is imagined not only naturally, and strictly historically, but also with an eye toward the intangible matter in it that gives it importance. The third dimension to which Mary ascends and through which any life fulfills itself is the dimension that legend, myth, and religion imagine as that region of the human condition that is inhabited by gods, spirits, and other unnatural beings. It is the realm of the personified images, symbols, principles, and laws that govern the human condition. This is the region of depth that contains a life's underpinnings of images whose concrete enactment we call "individual case history." That realm where the unnatural beings from myth, religion, and legend belong is not up above and far away. It is in the sense of bottomless significance that surpasses all identified meanings in any given matter. It exists as divine immanence in the profanest, the dullest, the flattest of events or facts.

One prosaic and ostensibly unholy arena where a third dimension opens up, even though only two dimensions are visible, is ambivalence, the state of being simultaneously dominated by two separate but diametrically opposed emotions, thoughts, or impulses. What defines ambivalence is precisely the insistence that the two opposites must coexist side by side at all times, rigidly locked in mutual enmity, but with each insisting on the constant presence of the other. The word "ambivalence" means, literally, "two valencies." It refers to the simultaneous existence of two values that would cancel each other out. That pair of opposites may come in an endless variety of forms. Ultimately, it is an archetypal pair with which humanity everywhere is all too familiar: Good and Evil.

Ambivalence presents itself as a problem of choice between two mutually exclusive options: either-or, this versus that, I do but I don't, Yes but No, I hate her but I love her. The essential dilemma is that no choice is possible, precisely because the two valencies insist on coexisting in spite of their mutual antagonism. This makes ambivalence a mad proposition, and a truly maddening way of being. In clinical psychology and psychiatry, it often is considered the core of schizophrenia. Here it tears apart the very fabric of the soul, leaving only fragments of a life, but without a sense of cohesion that can unify them into a more or less stable whole. In the psychology of individuals not beset by schizophrenia, it is a major source of chronic inner conflict. Here it tears at the seams of the images individuals have of themselves. In their social life, it tears apart those whom it simultaneously brings together. Even in individuals who are free of disabling conflict with themselves or with others, ambivalence is ever present as an always, at best, precarious balance between opposing forces.

At the origins of Western culture itself there is a core drama of ambivalence. Homer's *Iliad*, this founding literature of so much future Western imagination and thinking, is a story of human ambivalence. At the heart of its epic action is the paralyzing stalemate between the besieged city of Troy and the army of Greeks who are trying to sack it. And at the heart of that stalemate is the ambivalence of one leading man, Achilles. Paralyzed by conflicting emotions this one man who can tip the balance of the conflict is sitting out the war. He has been offended to the core by an incident he took as an insult against his personal and public image. In reaction, he has become paralyzed by emotional conflict, unable to decide whether to aid his beloved fellow Greeks or refuse his assistance in rage over their insult. Because of his personal paralysis, the war itself grinds to a halt. Neither side can tip the scale and win. The conflict that one man has with himself spreads among the camp of all the Greeks. They too become divided among themselves and against each other. As Homer put it, it was "as if two contrary winds were blowing." A better description of disabling and ultimately schizophrenic ambivalence is hardly possible. The word "schizophrenia" does not refer to a split personality, as popular lore has it. It refers to divided *phrenes*. *Phrenes* does not mean person or personality. In Homeric Greek *phrenes* means what is commonly imagined as the seat of the *thymus* or "breath-soul." It alludes to the soul not as literal breath but as immaterial breathlike substance. "Schizo-phrenia" alludes to a divided "breath-soul." And that is itself best described as Homer put it in his metaphor of the divided Greek camp as one in which "two contrary winds are blowing." Schizophrenia is therefore best described by its core of an ambivalent soul breath that is divided within and against itself. Heraclitus said that all events in the universe are the result of *polemos*—conflict, strife, war, struggle. He did not have our term *ambivalence* available as a notion. Even if he did, he probably would not have chosen it instead of *polemos*, for *polemos* most commonly, though not by definition, refers to conflict between two separate entities. "Ambivalence," in contrast and by definition, refers to conflict between two forces within one entity. Yet even so, Heraclitus would have to agree that ambivalence, this one manifestation of *polemos*, which today makes up the bread and butter of so much psychotherapy, is a persuasive and currently central case in point of his general theory of universal conflict and strife at the heart of existence. Perhaps, one begins to wonder, it is the essential experience of conflict within the human condition.

In everyday life, and as psychotherapists hear about it, ambivalence is expressed in statements such as, "I could kill her for what she did, but I can't stand to see her feel hurt," or, "I would like to settle down and have a family, but I'm not ready to give up my freedom," or, "I would like to quit my job, because I feel so bored and stifled in it, but I don't want to give up the security." The true resolution of ambivalence in these situations does not come from deciding which option is good and which bad. No such decision is possible, because the paralysis of two opposing options is of the essence in ambivalence. But even if a choice could be made, it would be no real solution. The real solution, if it can be reached (and the more severe the ambivalence, the slimmer the chances), comes from the spontaneous emergence of a third that deepens the situation at hand. Seemingly magically, and wholly unexpectedly, this third idea offers a way out of the conflict by opening up a new direction to follow. More often than not, this third is unrelated to the two options given. Typically it is not even rationally or naturally explainable. It tends to involve an altogether different issue, one that belongs to a totally separate category of things or events— such as a child-god born to two ordinary humans.

Beyond ambivalence as a personal conflict there is a kind of ambivalence that is impersonal. It is essential to the notion of following one's bliss. It is the ambivalence that is implied in the word "ravish," such as in the mythic theme of the "ravishment of Persephone." The word "ravish" connotes two opposite valencies. On the one hand, there is the pleasure associated with such meanings as charm, fascinate, captivate, delight, entrance, fill with rapture, enchant, enthrall. On the other hand, it involves the dramatic displeasure associated with such meanings as deflower, rape, violate. Following one's bliss is therefore filled with ambivalence. It is no psychological picnic. The council to "follow your bliss" is therefore no "feel-good" exercise for the bored, the malcontent, or the lazy. Its third and truly decisive element, the third that belongs to every ambivalent twosome, is neither necessarily pleasant nor unpleasant. It can be either, it can be neither, or it can be both. For the third matter, and what really matters as the decisive third, is the notion of transport. It is the experience of being so dramatically moved as to be transported from one's original perspective in and on the universe to an altogether different one. This can be a pleasant experience, such as in the meaning of being transported in delight. It can be a negative experience, such as in the meaning of being abducted, snatched away, or taken out of one's senses. It can also be a neutral experience, and it can be a mixed one. In each case, the truly decisive matter is that of things no longer being the same. The same old world is the same no more, if for no other reason than that one now experiences it from a new position. That new position offers another perspective on everything. The seed of bliss that makes for the potential of immaculate psychological conception in everyday life is therefore always a mixed bag because of the inherent ambivalence in it. It always presents itself as implicitly problematic. That is its first challenge. This challenge is not resolved until it is dissolved—in the third dimension of ambivalence. For that resolution to occur, one must first be willing to undergo the heartfelt and sometimes heartrending dilemma of ambivalence about seeing one's all-too-familiar life ravished by an inspiring idea.

Ambivalence tends to hide, and to remain unresolved, behind the resistance against being moved and transported to a new and third perspective. The hallmark of such resistance is an impoverished imagination, one that is unable to think in other than two-dimensional ways. When such two-dimensional thinking reigns, then all things are judged to be only good or only bad. They are either black or white, superior or inferior, the best or the worst, adorable or despicable, perfect or worthless. The corresponding action is similarly and flatly dualistic. It is a matter of all or nothing, either-or, in or out, an unconditional Of Course or a categorical No Way. Such rigidly and exclusively two-dimensional imagination is aimed at sidestepping ambivalence. It insists on seeing only half of everything. It insists that every coin of ambivalence has only one side. It avoids the coming together of any twosome for fear of the third it may engender. This is the surest way to dismiss the possibility of inspired conception out of hand. The call to bliss, the inspiring visitation of genius that begets spirited conceptions, can thus be altogether avoided in this manner. The archetypal potential for this avoidance is personified in the biblical figure of Joseph, Mary's husband to be. Joseph can reject Mary in her state of bliss. He can insist that her life, his life, their life—all of life—has room only for what is strictly rational and purely natural. He can insist on rejecting, and thus avoiding, all that is not customary and predictable, all that is not socially correct and acceptable, all that is at all mysterious or inexplicable in any way. Such rejection of bliss, on these grounds, amounts to splitting off and rejecting that part of life that can allow inspiration to fertilize existence. It amounts to turning a blind eye to the way extraordinariness and mystery routinely introduce themselves into the fabric of everyday life.

It is through the inspiration of bliss, and through a cultivation of the feeling for mystery, that the sense of divine incarnation—of the spirit of gods and other legendary creatures living among humans, and of every day being miraculous—can enter into Everyman's life. Immaculate Conception through the discovery of bliss is how new devotions are born. It is how inspired imagination begins, how men and women find themselves beginning to nurture ideas for fantastic possibilities. The human capacity for Immaculate Conception turns existence into a vision and a riddle. It becomes a vision, because it is about seeing previously unimagined and seemingly unbelievable possibilities. It becomes a riddle, because it is about the challenge of working the vision of those possibilities into a viable plot and plan to live by, concretely. Not surprisingly, this is exactly how Zarathustra described the moment of inspiration that revealed to him the potential for a philosophy based on eternal return. He called it "a vision and a riddle." The whole of Nietzsche's own remaining philosophical life, after the moment of inspiration that gave him the figure of Zarathustra and the thought of eternal return, became devoted to that vision and that riddle.

As suggested earlier, the ambivalence inherent in the potential for bliss reflects an archetypal ambivalence that is fundamental to the human condition. It is the ambivalence that sets apart, and that sets opposite each other, all things valued as Good and all things devalued as Evil. The dissolution of that twosome comes through the inspiring vision of a third view that sees beyond Good and Evil. But conversely too—and this is the new twist—the moral self-righteousness that cannot imagine and judge in other than dualistic Good-versus-Evil terms is itself perhaps a failure to come to grips with the essential ambivalence at the heart of the universe and at the heart of the human condition. *The morality of Good and Evil is itself a moral failure* in this view. Its moral flaw would be one of an impoverished and stifled imagination, one that cannot see the third dimension that potentially opens up in every twosome and that reaches beyond Good and Evil. This is precisely what gives Zarathustra his name. He is named after Zoroaster, the ancient moral philosopher who was first to think Being in terms of Good and Evil. In Nietzsche's view, he would therefore presumably also be the first to recognize the inadequacy of that very perspective. He would have to be the first to see the need to overcome it. Hence also the title of the post–Zarathustra book that sheds a good deal of light on Zarathustra, Nietzsche's *Beyond Good and Evil.*

Once Immaculate Conception is accepted as idea, the task becomes one of practical personal dedication. It becomes a work of endless puzzlement that involves disentangling the riddle of a vision and turning it into concretely visible things. This is less a problem to be solved than an opus to be endlessly worked. Such practical personal dedication and such imaginative puzzlement are a means to overcome the dichotomy of Good versus Evil. They involve a pathos and a perspective that are affirmative first and last, in spite of all real and apparent contradiction between pleasure and unpleasure. Here even the dichotomy of pleasure and pain is overcome. We are in Nietzsche's realm of what lies *Beyond Good and Evil*, and in the domain of the soul that lies, according to Freud, *Beyond the Pleasure Principle*. One utterly familiar case in which practical human dedication overcomes the dichotomy of Good and Evil is in unconditional motherly love. It happens also in other human endeavors that, like motherly love, have the stamina to overcome adversity, disillusionment, betrayal, discouragement, pain, injustice, hardship, misfortune, and everything else that periodically tempts even the best of men and women to throw in the towel. But even here there remains a core of ambivalence. This is sometimes poignantly illustrated in the pained complaint of even the most devoted mothers. As they can sometimes be heard to say: "I love my children to death, but I sometimes hate what they do so intensely that I think it's going to kill me."

There is another form of resistance against the ambivalence in the call of genius. It lies in the false belief that the fruit of an inspiring idea that is to be nurtured into existence through devoted labor must be fully and unambiguously envisioned in advance. No such definitive advance knowledge is possible, because new gods and spirits come into being precisely to bring previously unimagined things. It is the spontaneous unconscious imagination in the life of the soul that is the true begetter or genius, not the conscious ego that pilots us through daily life. This is the difference between talent and genius, as James Russell Lowell described it: talent is in a man's or a woman's power, genius is that in whose power a man or woman is. This helps explain the characteristic blindness that often accompanies even the clearest vision in all truly creative processes. It also serves to provide a warning sign. It warns that if the necessary blindness of a creative endeavor begins to weigh down the ego, with personal feelings of being in the dark or of being lost, then this may be because the ego is trying to take over the leading part from the genius that is putting it to work. Such ego weariness sets in when the mind begins to believe that it must and can do, albeit perhaps with great and heroic effort, what the soul does effortlessly. This kind of weariness also can befall any person when a creative process takes a turn that was not anticipated. It happens to a parent when a child grows up to pursue interests and values not previously held by the parents or the family. It happens when a professional career veers off course, leading to an uncertain future of new and altogether different interests. Along similar lines, the difference between talent and genius explains why every student has to become other than an imitator of every teacher, for the student is driven by a different spirit than that of the teacher. It also is why what works for one writer may not work at all for another writer, even though both may be dealing with the same subject matter. And it is why the success of one person cannot be taken as goal or measure of success for another person. It is why all genuine creating is solitary, even when it belongs within a shared tradition. In all these situations, one principle governs: the fruit of what is begotten through Immaculate Conception is made in the image of the begetter, not in the image of the human laborer, no matter how talented or dedicated. Therefore—and this is a weighty implication that can only now be fully stated—what is good for a man or woman, and what is a good thing for a man or woman to do, no one can ever know in advance. Neither accepted psychological and developmental theory, no matter how insightful, nor accepted morality or dogma of any kind, no matter how well rooted in biology, natural philosophy, or religious faith, can ever dictate in advance what will be the right thing for any man or woman to be, to want, and to do. As Nietzsche said, man is always "the as yet undetermined animal." That explains his test question about this all-important psychological, moral, and philosophical issue. As he has Zarathustra put it: "Can you give yourself your own evil and your own good and hang your own will over yourself as a law? Can you be your own judge and avenger of your law? Terrible it is to be alone with the judge and avenger of one's law." A developmental psychology that would claim to know what is good and evil for all men and women and all psychology built on such developmental theory are meeting their match here.

One case that illustrates how "terrible it is to be alone with the judge and avenger of one's law" is the life of Michelangelo. His work earned him the epithet of "divine" and "angel," rare but not unheard of epithets in his day. But as the first artist ever in history to be considered a human genius, he became the model for all individual creative genius thereafter. The overpowering, awe-inspiring, and driving force in his work and in his personality was known among his contemporaries as his *terribilita*. There is more than a kernel of truth to the popular notion that a human life inspired by genius becomes a terrible thing to put up with for all who are involved. The *terribilita* of nurturing the fruit of Immaculate Conception into being often comes in forms that make it especially terrible for the laboring ego, because it creates a sense of ruin. One such form is that of an unfinished work. Another is that of thoughts and feelings of failure, even while the work is still in progress and shows positive signs of fruitfulness. These thoughts and feelings show the fundamental difference in nature between that from which the call of genius emanates and the ego's strictly human response to it that attempts to carry out the call. To stick with the case of Nietzsche, his philosophy of eternal return was never fully worked out. By the time madness silenced him, he had drawn up several outlines for a philosophical "transvaluation of all values" based on eternal return, but the promise of that undertaking remained unfulfilled. Even before madness set in, Nietzsche himself was already critical of what he had accomplished, judging it merely the entrance to a larger structure that remained to be built in future writings. Many Nietzsche commentators have critically agreed that his promised philosophy of eternal return failed to materialize, finding it in balance much ado about nothing. The *terribilita* of such crucifixions at the hands of a devastating judgment, whether self-inflicted or externally imposed, belongs as an intrinsic potential in every call of genius. It is a potential that can befall any inspired human devotion and effort. It is the cruel sacrifice that any human ego can be asked to make to the supreme and pitiless master it serves. An even more terrible fate can come with the call of genius when the fruit of the ego's labor and devotion is itself destroyed. Then all that seemed full of promise turns into ruin, leaving only brokenheartedness and inconsolable grief. The most extreme version of this theme is the most terrible thing that can happen to any human being: the loss of a child. This is the greatest cruelty that can befall anyone: the destruction of what has been brought into being with one's own blood, sweat, and tears. It is what is presented in Michelangelo's *Pieta,* and it is what is asked of Abraham when he is told by his God that he must sacrifice his son, Isaac.

But while Immaculate Conception is a potential in Everyman's life, this potential also has its own pathological shadow existence there. Wisdom therefore warns: Look for what is divine in your life, but do not mistake yourself for a god, because your first toothache will make you feel and look like a fool. Just as Don Quixote finds that not everything that looks like a giant is a giant, so too is not everything that seems like a good idea an occasion of inspired Immaculate Conception. And even though established laws concerning individual psychological development cannot spell out in advance what precise shape a life should take for its own good, those laws cannot be simply ignored, anymore than the laws of gravity can be dismissed. Not every notion that comes to mind is a seed of bliss to come, a call and a sign of genius, the cipher of a viable and justifiable personal morality. Nor can just any established morality be arbitrarily thrown to the wind, to be replaced at will by the first tempting idea that comes to mind, and that emanates perhaps from nothing more than sheer narcissism or sociopathy. What may perhaps be privately regarded as proof of one's personal genius or divine personal calling, and what is perhaps worshipped for those reasons at the ego's own altar, may be no more than false divinity. One characteristic form such false divinity may assume is that of grandiose delusions. Here the ego becomes overinflated and declares itself genius, king, descendant of gods, or perhaps even a new god. It places the royal, the divine crown on its own head, and all the world is reduced to nothing but applauding audience. What makes grandiose delusions grandiose and delusional is the misattribution of grandeur, the personal appropriation of impersonal magnificence. They are about mistaking the magnificence that is everywhere in the air for personal grandeur. That way lies the madness of overinflated self-importance. The insanity of grandiose delusions does not lie in the magnificent content of grand ideas per se. Nor does it lie in devoting one's life to grand ideas that engender a sense for the inherent magnificence in ordinary events.

Delusional grandiosity lies in the idea that it is the person who is magnificent, simply because he or she associates with what is grand. Here fusion of categories leads to confusion of categories. Here "Know thyself," meaning "Know that as a human being you are always in the presence of divinity," is mistaken to mean that humans must aspire to become gods themselves. Hearing the call of something grand and magnificent does not mean that the person who hears the call is magnificent or ought to be considered grand. It is the blindness of a pathologically impoverished imagination for which nothing magnificent exists anywhere within sight that is most at risk of concluding that one's own person must be the only thing that can possibly be magnificent. What is needed for protection against grandiose delusions, this ultimate in ego trips, is the humility of true receptivity. This is what makes every life virginal and fertile ground for Immaculate Conception. Such a virginal fertility is one that must be regained again and again, so that one may remain open to the visitations of genius. It protects a life against the madness of self-importance and self-inflation, and it prevents the false pregnancies of hubris.

NINE

HERE AND NOW

"STICK TO THE IMAGE," says Hillman again and again, following Jung's original suggestion. It is archetypal psychology's Golden Rule, in the same way that the principle of free association—to say everything that comes to mind in connection with what is being examined—serves as Freud's Golden Rule for psychoanalysis. But while these practical guidelines are similar in this respect, they differ in others. Freud's rule serves the psychoanalytic program of "Where the unconscious is there consciousness shall be." It exists so that we may discover what is unknown, because it lies hidden in what we think of as the unconscious. Hillman's rule, in contrast, exists so that we may begin to see what is already fully displayed about the life of the soul in the precise way in which a given situation presents itself. Freud's rule exists to uncover the hidden value judgments in the moral economy that governs what we imagine as man's inner life of mental processes. Hillman's rule exists to cast a reflective light on the soul's valuables as the soul openly displays them in all things. The psychoanalyst's job is to rethink man's accepted knowledge about his inner life. He or she is hired in the employ of the ego and serves to help make the patient's life more livable. The archetypal psychologist works to make the ego reimagine the world as the soul inhabits it. He or she works in the service not of the ego but of something that is other than ego. The job here is to make more room in the world not for the ego but for that other. Psychoanalysis encourages man to talk more freely about himself and to become more articulate and more insightful about his inner life. Archetypal psychology lets the always well articulated images that are present in any situation do all the talking. Here the patient is encouraged to become not a better reporter on man's inner life but a better listener to all that the universe has to say about itself through the many voices that are everywhere in the air. Those voices are not hallucinated ones that spring from my disordered mind and that are commenting on me. They are the phenomenal voices that are inherent in all things and that are commenting on those things and on *their* adventures in the world.

The rule of sticking to the image serves to let the soul matter in any situation speak for itself, about itself, and in its own language. This is to prevent psychology and psychiatry from doing all the talking for it, with preconceived theories about it that are superimposed on it. It is to prevent psychotherapy patients from too obediently imitating the textbooks of their treaters. It serves to hear all things as the soul's own figurative speech. Sticking to the image means taking a situation as it presents itself, without introducing anything extraneous. This differs from the rule of free association. There the patient is told to voice everything that comes to mind in connection with the matter under analysis, even though it may not be included in the original matter under consideration. The rule of free association makes all matters grow in psychological substance by a process of accretion, by adding imported and superimposed layers. In contrast, the rule of sticking to the image makes matters gain in significance by a process of deepening the sense for what is given, without adding a single layer of extra matter to it. Sticking to the image works through a method of amplification. This consists of enlarging the images inherent in the matter under consideration. That, in turn, reanimates the sense of the latent life in those images. Sticking to the image, by amplifying the images in a given matter, increases the sense of its psychic significance, so that it may reveal its own true magnificence. This is archetypal psychology's own form of *Magnificat*, for it is about magnifying the sense of value, of the presence of the soul's own valuables, in all events. Sticking to the image is a rule about taking all things, all of existence, and all of the universe as they are. It is about sticking to the here and now of life as it is. Everything, in the precise way in which it presents itself, is thereby regarded as a way in which the life of the soul reveals itself. As Jung first suggested, and as Hillman repeats after him: Image is soul, soul is image. That means, if one wants to recognize the psychic substance and significance in things, one must see them as images—images that are inherently complete, as well as precisely defined in their own terms. They show bits of psychic life that are in their own way self-contained, self-sufficient, self-regulating, self-governing, self-explanatory, self-justifying, and self-esteeming. Sticking to the image is a practical application of the phenomenological agenda to "return to the things themselves," as they are lived. This stands in contrast to focusing on the necessary material conditions that need to be met to make experiences possible, and that presumably explain them. The purpose of sticking to the image is to develop a sense that all is valuable as it is, meaning as it is lived here and now.

The "image" in "Stick to the image" is nothing more and nothing less than the actual event or experience itself, as it is told, as it presents itself, and as it looks in everyday life, *but now taken figuratively*. That is what Nietzsche meant when he said that "all things present themselves as metaphors" and that "on every metaphor you ride to every truth." When a psychotherapy patient comes to the office in a foul mood and reports a dream of overflowing toilets, the rule of sticking to the image keeps the treatment session closely involved with that mood and that dream image. It looks at them as though they were a direct but metaphoric statement about the present condition of the soul. Treating that mood and that image becomes an exercise in actively developing a more imaginative sense for the presence of "overflowing toilets" and "crappy moods" in the patient's life. The mood and the image are amplified and explored from the inside. They are taken as a condensed description of an entire psychological universe, and of a whole way of being in that universe, complete with its own philosophy. Treater and patient alike thereby begin to recognize the theme of "overflowing toilets" and "crappy moods" in other experiences in the patient's life. The mood and the dream image provide the soul's own vocabulary to speak about such matters as "dumping a load of crap on everything and everybody," or about being "dumped" by a partner or an employer and "feeling like crap" about it, or about feeling and thinking that therapy itself often seems like "a pile of crap," and that the therapist is "full of it." This generates a more actively imaginative, more differentiated, less rigid, less compulsive, more naturally impersonal, and less self-accusing sense of what may otherwise only feel like the mess one has made of one's life. It provides a more therapeutic way to think and talk about feelings of nausea with one's life or about a pervasive self-loathing that turns everything foul. It may help articulate more precisely what it is like to have no control over uncontainable foul moods that spill over everywhere, soiling and spoiling everything. It may lead to more deeply felt reflection on such timeless and universal themes as inevitable decay or the eternal return of all things to elemental being. The purpose of sticking to the image is to develop a better sense for how an "overflowing toilet" and a "crappy mood" constellate a way of being that has its own internal logic, with its own points of view and perspectives, its own characteristic processes, and its own habits of thinking, acting, and feeling. It is about patient and treater developing an expertise in the philosophy and psychology of overflowing toilets and crappy moods. Sticking to the image is a craft of psychological miniaturism, a way to think along with the soul's own aphoristic style of philosophizing. Sticking to the image also is how psychological matter stops being only, or mostly, something inside me—in my head, my innermost feelings and thoughts, my memories or my introjects. The matter under consideration becomes something that contains me and sustains me, including my worldview and way of being. It becomes something that is in the air, something that has many names, because it wears many different masks. In the end, sticking to the image is about, as we say, beginning to "appreciate" what the life of the soul is presenting. "Appreciate" here means both "to value" and, most importantly, "to increase in attributed or assigned value." It is about the alchemical work of turning psychological daily residue—the "crap" left over from everyday life—into valuable soul matter.

But sticking to the image in this manner is not in any way about being able to identify or claim "the right image" or "the true image" or "the correct image"—the one interpretation that is the bottom-line psychological truth. There is a stronger emphasis on the activity of becoming more imaginative than on any identified image or on any particular psychological interpretation. That means an image, in this approach, is no allegory, where once we get to the message inside the envelope, we can throw away the envelope itself. The realm of the soul's imagination is a polytheism, as Hillman emphasizes. No one image rules above all others, and at the expense of all others. Here no hypothesis is ever promoted to hypostasis. No one image is ever anything more than adjectival or qualitative in the way it tries to describe the life of the soul. Nothing is objectified and solidified in a noun, thereby suggesting permanent, absolute identity of any kind. Here, metaphor is protected from becoming metaphysics by the very activity of producing ever-more metaphors and images.

Sticking to the image is a formula for developing a genuine self psychology. But the self that becomes manifest through the rule of sticking to the image is no strictly human inner self. It is a self that is larger than the body. As Jung said, in sharp distinction from Freud, for whom anatomy is destiny, and in whose view all psychology is ultimately grounded in the body, the greater part of the soul exists outside the body. And as Nietzsche's Zarathustra suggested, before both Freud and Jung, the self that becomes mine in my personal life and history lies out there, to be discovered by me in strange lands and scattered among all things and seeming accidents. Soul, in this approach that equates soul and image, is not *mea anima*, my own inner self on whose behalf I become selfishly obsessed with *mea culpa*, with what I did wrong and how I can correct it to make everybody's life better. Soul, in this view, is not just "in me." It is also, as Zarathustra said, "over me." It is not a purely human and humanistic soul. It is the soul of the world, the universe—the World Soul or *Anima Mundi*. The soul factor in things, their psychological significance, is, according to this approach, in how they actually already *are*. It is neither in how they could be, potentially, nor in how they should be, ideally. But neither is it in what came before them, historically, or in what triggered them, causally. It is not in what may come after them, predictably, and not in how they may turn out, finally. It is not in what might have been instead of them, wishfully, or in what may perhaps replace them, alternatively. It is not in how they should be, morally, or in what can be done about them, hopefully. Nor is it, for that matter, in the way they are construed socially, in how they are maintained politically or reinforced underhandedly, in what consequences they may have culturally, or in what explains them economically. And it is not in what makes them, to a greater or lesser degree, adaptive developmentally, well adjusted socially, effective behaviorally, rewarding personally, or desirable for whatever reason. The soul factor in things, according to this approach that takes all things as image and that equates image and soul, cannot and should not be reduced to or identified with any of these. But neither is the soul factor in a situation all that may well be part of its necessary material condition, such as the state of the body or the functioning of the brain. It is not in how things in the mind are triggered physically. It is not in how anything is activated biochemically, programmed genetically, transmitted neurologically, or induced iatrogenically. While all of these may be involved as necessary material conditions in what gives an event its psychological significance, none of these, nor any combination of them, is itself that significance. None of these material conditions is itself what makes anything matter. The soul matter in an event is what turns the identifiable event, and all its identifiable parts, into something that has an importance that can itself not be described in terms of the parts. It is the element of importance itself in all that matters.

The rule of sticking to the image is a way of "returning to the things themselves" in order to let them explain themselves, and justify themselves, according to their own terms. It is a way of insisting that every experience is its own goal, that it does not need to be completed, justified, redeemed, or otherwise rationalized by anything lying outside of it. Looking for the psychic value of a thing outside of the thing itself is a way of devaluing it by splitting off its value—before one has even come near it, and before one even realizes it. "Can we remove the idea of a goal from a process," Nietzsche asked, "and then affirm the process in spite of this?" He answered his own question: "This would be the case if something were attained at every moment within the process." Sticking to the image is about realizing that objective. It aims at deliberately and self-consciously *not* pursuing anything that, like a "goal," serves as a locus of value on which value is projected but that lies outside of the process, the event, or the situation itself. Sticking to the image keeps the locus of the sense of value in the situation itself, not outside of it or in any other way beyond it. It makes of all psychology situational psychology. It makes of all therapeutic theorizing an occasional work of imaginatively responding to the *genius loci*, the local god or situational daimon who inhabits the matter at hand. Here, again, archetypal psychology puts into practice what Nietzsche proposed, and what he had Zarathustra suggest. Says Zarathustra: "'I want heirs'—thus speaks all that suffers; 'I want children, I do not want myself.'" This focus on what is *not* at hand, at the expense of what is, is in Nietzsche's view the dead giveaway of a fundamental pathos of resentment against life as it is. It is, still according to Nietzsche, the Christian West's almost reflexive judgment, one that judges existence to be so lacking in inherent positive value that, without a drastic improvement, brought on by an external and otherworldly source of redemption, it can never be considered good enough. Nietzsche's ambitious idea of redemption, in contrast, is about a redemption from the very need for such otherworldly redemption that is based on a devaluing judgment of existence. Zarathustra sums up the problem, as well as his solution for it. It is a solution that is echoed in the rule of sticking to the image: "To be sure: except ye become as little children, ye shall not enter into *that* kingdom of heaven. (And Zarathustra pointed upward with his hand.) But we have no wish whatever to enter into the kingdom of heaven: we have become man—*so we want the earth.*" In another formulation of the same idea, Zarathustra puts it more simply, more directly, and more strictly positively: "Remain faithful to the earth." From this follows his great categorical imperative for the individual in his or her individual existence: "One must learn to love oneself . . . so that one can bear to be with oneself." One way to put that Nietzschean ambition into practice is the rule: "Stick to the image."

Psychological treaters are trained to consider a diagnosis of personality disorder when they see patients who are almost exclusively focused on other matters than on the way things are with themselves. Patients with such personality disorders tend to be rigidly fixated on their own perceptions about the world around them. They have little sense of their psychological life, which they prefer to avoid. They often are described as "externally focused." They come across as unreflective and unimaginative about possibilities other than those that belong to their own inflexible ways of thinking. Their focus elsewhere, at the expense of attention to their own psychological states, comes in characteristic forms that are almost instantly recognizable. "If only my circumstances were different," they sigh. "If only I were dealing with other people," they complain. "If only I could find another job," they grumble. "If only certain things had not happened," they lament. "If only my family had treated me differently," they accuse. While such laments are common and often legitimate, and while they do not automatically indicate a personality disorder, the chances that such a diagnosis is at play increase to the extent that this sort of lament is almost exclusively the only thing a person has to say about his or her life. Such endless complaints about life not being different from the way it is can easily become a source of chronic resentment. This can generate endless frustration—and bitterness, cynicism, dissatisfaction, restless fretting, unsatisfied ambition, unending ruminations, discontent, depression, and slumbering, chronic anger with periodic volcanic explosions. Each of these complaints can ruin the good weather of many an otherwise fine day. They continue to be generated as long as the person insists on wishing to be elsewhere, rather than where he or she is at. They are a sign that the patient is alienated from the life of the soul in the here and now of where things are at. They are ever so many incarnations of the early Job, who is stuck in an angry, accusing, futile, and misguided insistence on a different world, a world that would be run according to a different plan.

Perhaps few ideas are as naturally predisposed to foster alienation from the life of the soul in the here and now of the way things are as the founding notion of linear time that is at the origin of the West's Judeo-Christian culture. That idea's active ingredient, and the great implicit devaluation of existence as it is, is the notion of history leading to a future that is hopefully different and better than the present. It is about history leading to a more valuable life in the future, in a place and circumstance that are portrayed as a promised land for a new, a different, a more promising state of being. This divinely inspired founding idea, at the heart of Judeo-Christian consciousness, always points to where we are not. It points to a distant time, place, circumstance, and state of being that are idealized, and compared with which the life that actually is, here and now, must seem less than good enough—hence, essentially and inherently bad or evil. In the everyday world, the theme of a more promising existence comes in such formats as the idea of progress, of a better and more democratic world, with more opportunity for more people. It is found in the hope for endless economic growth, for revolutionary scientific breakthroughs in medicine, for rapid and endless technological advances, for increased longevity and better health for all. In the life of the individual, there is no end to the fantasies of a more promising existence. Here it comes as the ideals of fast professional advancement, better personal relationships, improved self-esteem, more effective treatments for everything, a brighter mood thanks to improved mood elevators and mood stabilizers, smarter children who do even better than their parents, and, at the end of it all, perhaps not the certainty of a heavenly afterlife but at least the assurance of a golden retirement with free access to prescription drugs. Never mind that, at some level and in some fashion, each of these fantasied and promising improvements on life—whether at the scale of religious belief, social ideal, or personal goal—implies a slanderous devaluation of existence as it is here and now: "I want heirs, I want children, I do not want myself." Sticking to the image would undo that slanderous devaluation. It is a way in which, with perhaps Zarathustra in the lead, the not so meek go marching with the intent to inherit the earth—not later, but now.

Sticking to the image is a way of siding with the life of the soul that is actually taking place, instead of siding with the ego and its demand for a more promising future. Nowhere is this difference clearer than in the way the rule of sticking to the image views the realm of personal feelings. As the common caricature of the psychotherapist has it, he or she is always intensely interested in feeling: "How do you feel?" "What makes you feel this way?" "How long have you felt like that?" Were it not for feeling, psychotherapists would hardly be able to conduct their business. Their entire enterprise might well run out of business. And yet feeling is by no means everything in psychological treatment. Even though feeling is held to be central for very good reasons, it is nonetheless not the most important thing. Even more important than feeling, though intimately connected to it, are a keen sense of image and an active imagination. The unconsciousness that modern psychotherapy has been trying to replace with consciousness for a hundred years now is, in this view, largely a problem of poverty of imagination.

Feeling points to psychological significance but is not therefore itself what is most significant. If a man or a woman has strong feelings about something, he or she takes that to mean, and rightly so, that something significant is at hand.

But then that same person tends to make a characteristic error of a misattribution. Since the sense of significance that is in the air touches us personally, we have learned to conclude, with a reflex reaction that has become second nature, that it must be our person itself that is the locus of significance, the site where whatever is the matter matters. Then a second error tends to occur. Since our person is regarded as the site of psychological significance, we have come to conclude that it must therefore be our person itself that is of prime importance—at least as far as we, personally, are concerned. This Western tradition that emphasizes personal feeling and that places psychological significance inside the individual person is long. As discussed earlier, it finds much of its origin and early definition in the personal lyric of the ancient Greeks, with Sappho's poetry and its emphasis on personal, inner feeling as a decisive case in point. The novelty of that poetry, and its huge success and impact, was in the fact that it provided Western man with the root metaphor of an imagined inner psychological space. That inward location is the arena where the events of life, including the external machinations of the gods and other forces that govern it and that fill the air, have their impact. Love, this so central theme in all psychology, is a mysterious force the Greek imagination attributed to the god Eros, but its impact on man, so Sappho suggested in her famous metaphor that became a founding paradigm, is like that of a "bittersweet" taste. That means, it is a personal affair. Most importantly, it is an inner reaction. As seen earlier, the fact that the notion of a "bittersweet" reaction that is both personal and inner now seems almost trite, because it has long been considered self-evident, only goes to show the fundamental ways in which it has developed into an unquestioned truth. It became an accepted truth, even though its origin is in the literary invention of a metaphoric image. As previously discussed, Sappho's fiction of an inner life that may be compared to a bittersweet taste in the mouth became psychology's belief in an inner self as a fact of life. And thus fiction crystallized into fact, for this is what every good metaphor, over time, always tends to do: it tends to become a metaphysics precisely because it is convincing. So much is this the case with Sappho's metaphor that today many, if not most— including those who ought to know better—almost automatically consider it madness to even cast doubt on the assumed factuality of such an inner self. And yet, from the beginning and always, the notion of an inner self is fiction first and last, even though we insist on making it into a fact that we would like to keep forever beyond questioning.

The rule of sticking to the image proposes a different relation between feeling, person, and locus of psychological significance. Rather than focusing on inner, personal feeling, it is aimed at developing a better and more impersonal feeling for focusing on the here and now—with an activated imagination and with a sense for the inherent depth in every here and now. Whereas the emphasis on feeling places psychological significance inside me, the emphasis on image reverses that sense of interiority. It turns the notion of psychological inwardness inside out. Instead of placing psychological significance inside me, it places me inside psychological significance. Image stops being psychological content and becomes psychological container. No longer do I have it inside me. It has me inside itself. No longer do I carry psychological significance inside me wherever I go. Rather, I am held and sustained inside the enveloping depth of significance in the image itself. It is no longer I who transfer feeling but I who am transported by images, and that is what I am feeling. First, my personal feelings are restated as those of a protagonist, the identified patient, whose role I play in a psychosocial story that is no longer mine alone, for it also is that of my family and my community. Then, and already much more imaginatively, I am recast as only one character in scenarios of dramas called "family dynamics." These scenarios and dramas play themselves out in the repetition compulsions that shape my life and that make up my personal psychological destiny. Ultimately, and because in the final analysis all things are always to be viewed mythically, I stand identified as a concrete participant who, in the flesh, partakes in a mythic drama. This is truly a case of "participation mystique" taking place in everyday life. At this final level of significance, where everything becomes most significant precisely by becoming mythic, and where fictional plots become personal realities, I am a person who is chosen to embody archetypal themes that can only be spoken of in figurative language. Hence, Narcissus, Eros, Oedipus, and all the rest, whether ancient and venerable or modern and pedestrian. Bottom-line psychological matter becomes visible when the facts of personal history are sensed as fictions that serve as metaphors for human lives. Psychic truth telling begins and ends with the telling of poetic lies. That my experience of love is "bittersweet" is only one in a long series of inspired lies.

The shift in emphasis, from personal feelings contained inside my bosom to a feeling for impersonal significance that contains me, bosom and all, becomes archetypal psychology's way of restating what Nietzsche said. It is another way of saying that the world and existence in it justify themselves as an aesthetic phenomenon. In contrast, the emphasis on inner feeling in a treatment that locates psychological significance exclusively inside the person is, from this point of view, a defense against the images that shape and animate the person's life. Feeling itself can be a defense against imagination. Feeling points to me and makes me focus my attention on myself. Image points away from me and makes me see things other than myself. In feeling, I almost cannot help but view myself as the personal reference point of any drama that touches me personally. In image, I see that I am only one actor among others, perhaps only a stage prop, and that the drama itself comes first. In feeling, the world seems to close in on me. In image, a world opens up before me and around me. In feeling, I am prone to project myself all over the place, even in places where my projections do not belong. In image, I myself am projected into places that are the natural psychological habitat where I belong. Feeling makes everything subjective. Image makes everything objective, including all that is private and subjective. In the focus on feeling, my interest is in my sense of well-being. In the focus on image, my feeling of personal well-being is dismissed as secondary, or even irrelevant, in favor of a more transpersonal sense of psychological being. In feeling, the focus is on the impact the world has on me. In image, the focus is on the place I have in the world. In feeling, there is a focus on my personal plans and intentions. In image, the focus is on the plans and intentions of something other than me, something whose plans and intentions supersede mine and claim me for their purpose, all the while ignoring how I feel about any of it. In the focus on feeling, I am naturally inclined to seek what I regard as justice. The focus on image reaches beyond the very categories of justice and injustice and shows me glimpses of mysteries in creation that are beyond good and evil. In the focus on feeling, I cling to what I think I know about how the world should function. In image, I am presented with previously unknown and unimagined laws governing the world's functioning. In feeling, the main interest is in my feeling good. In image, what matters most is learning to see that everything created is as it should be, even though much of it may not make me feel so good. In feeling, I regard the world as already fully created, so to speak once and for all, with everything in it already fully identified and assigned its proper name. In image, I am witness to some of the mysteries that go into the world's ongoing creation and that are involved in the process whereby every created thing acquires an identity and a name that best suits it. Personal feeling is strictly profane. Image provides glimpses of what human beings have always and naturally considered sacred. In feeling, I am focused on linear history—what happened in the past, what is happening now, and what I want or do not want to happen in the future. In image, linear time stands still—everything happens simultaneously, as in a timeless painting or a universal and eternal symbol. In feeling, I am identified with the early Job, who demands that his God justify himself and his creation. In image, I am identified with the later Job of the same legend, who can briefly see glimpses of the miraculous wherever he turns and looks.

Feeling, according to the rule of "Stick to the image," serves to draw attention not to itself but to an image that is insisting on being imagined into my life. The personal call that feeling is, is not, first of all, a call to attend to one's person, and to one's personal needs. It is a call for one's personal presence in, and one's personal attention to, a concretely enacted image that is playing itself out as a piece of life history. Feeling is evidence that one is being drawn into something larger than oneself. That larger something is not merely an interpersonal drama, with actual persons. Nor is it only an unconscious family dynamic, about real-life people whose representations go on living in the private world of my inner mental life. What one is drawn into is an imaginal universe, peopled with figures who are caught in plots that can only be known by being imagined.

The shift in perspective and worldview that comes with the shift of emphasis from personal feelings to impersonal images has practical applications—with moral implications. The emphasis on personal feeling makes me feel personally responsible for the events in my life—if not for bringing them about, by unconsciously and perhaps compulsively setting them up, then at least for figuring out ways to handle the situations in which I find myself. Hence, psychotherapy's insistence: "What do you do when you feel like this?" Image, in contrast, makes me less personally the heroic figure who must alone be burdened with responsibility. In an approach that puts image first, before feeling, it is the image itself that bears the burden of responsibility for the situation. In this view, it is the image, not me, that contains the information, the knowledge, the know-how needed to respond in a way that is consistent with the image in the situation, and, therefore, appropriate to the situation itself. My moral responsibility therefore shifts in focus. It is no longer a responsibility for the situation as such but a responsibility toward the image in the situation. Holding the image in a situation responsible for the situation and holding myself responsible to the image in the situation rather than to the situation itself also means shifting the focus of my faith. When I feel held personally responsible for events or for handling them, then I must have faith in myself personally, in myself first of all and, ultimately, in myself alone. I must have faith in my ego, in my coping skills, in my problem-solving abilities. But when images are seen as the bearers of responsibility, then they become the locus where I place my faith. By extension, when feeling and the personal management of feeling are held to be central, then I am placed in charge of my life, but then I also am on my own, alone. In contrast, when image is central, *it* is in charge, and then I do not have to be so alone. The image is there, as it were, as an autonomous presence that can clarify a situation for me. It can be my guide in the situation, it can help me with the matters that matter to me so personally and so intensely, it can be a source of encouragement. In brief, the image governing the situation can be my mentor telling me what to do.

Because a psychology that makes feelings central emphasizes feelings that I must have alone, in the privacy of my solitary inner life, it is partly that same psychology that is inadvertently responsible for making us all feel more alone than is necessary. Which means that the psychology of feeling has itself become partly responsible for creating desperately lonely and forlorn psychotherapy patients—by alienating them from the images that are the basis of their lives, including their feelings. By making feeling come before all else, it disconnects patients from this truest *spiritus rector*, this guiding spirit that is the real genius of their life, and whose ingenuity is always more inspired and more inspiring than any ego can ever be. Psychotherapy is often fondly described by its practitioners as a "holding environment," a metaphor derived from the biology of a mother holding and caring for her helpless and vulnerable infant. It is tempting for therapists to conclude that it is they who are doing the holding in this holding environment of treatment. Yet as seasoned therapists know, it is precisely when the treater eventually and invariably fails the patient in some important manner, thereby jeopardizing the alliance with the patient and thus the treatment itself, that the most significant and possibly most therapeutic events of the process tend to take place. The only thing that can do any holding then, and the only thing that can save the treatment, is not the person of the therapist but a shared sense of something transpersonal holding both treater and treated. That *tertium quid* that holds the twosome of treater and treated is a dramatically enacted and acutely felt image that serves as container, not only for individual feelings and individual persons but for the treatment process itself. While the feelings in such a treatment crisis point to an event of great psychological significance, it is not those feelings themselves that are that significance. Nor is it any longer the person of the treater who is handling the situation. Something else is the elusive significance that is at stake, the container that is doing the holding and the spirit that is guiding the process. That something else that guides the process here does not hesitate for one moment to sacrifice both the patient's feelings of well-being in treatment and the therapist's feelings of competence for doing the treating. These are the times when the patient's hopes may be crushed, along with the treater's ego. Many a therapy process comes to a premature end in these storms. Something primordial is at work and is taking over.

"The experience of the Self is always a defeat for the ego," wrote Jung, in *Mysterium Coniunctionis*. The reference is to the encounter between the conscious ego and the realities of the life of the soul about which the ego is unconscious. This is a way of summing up the difference between an emphasis on image and an emphasis on feeling. It serves to highlight that a psychology of image stops being a psychology that is placed in the service of the ego. The shift in focus, from feeling to image, amounts to a certain deliberate indifference to the intentions, agendas, values, and sensibilities of the ego. It favors an interest in something that is independent of the ego, something that is fully autonomous. It makes for a shift in mind-set that ends up following an altogether different logic than that of the ego, a logic that to the ego can often only appear illogical, if not outright mad. The shift from feeling to image does nothing less than sacrifice the ego on the altar of something that demands just this sort of sacrifice, something whose very essence is precisely about demanding this sacrifice. It requires a great psychological leap of faith that abandons everything cherished as rationality, everything that seems common sense, even everything that is revered as humanism. All of it is abandoned in favor of something that is nothing if not irrational, something that unapologetically and without explanation parts company with common sense, something that appears anything but humane. This leap of faith is nothing less than an act of surrendering the individual human will to a Greater Will. A psychology that surrenders feeling and ego to image does nothing less than reenact Abraham's willingness to sacrifice his son, Isaac, to his God—just because that God demands it, for no apparent good reason.

Isaac, so Abraham's God had promised, would be the seed of a chosen people who would eventually live in a new state, a new state of consciousness. Because of that promise of a brighter future Isaac served, as any child does to any parent, but this time magnified to biblical proportions, as an extension of Abraham's own ego. Isaac personifies all the ego's hopes for a better future of bright expectations and of promises fulfilled. He is a case in point of the desire and hope that Zarathustra described as saying: "I want heirs. I want children. I do not want myself." Abraham's willingness to sacrifice Isaac, when and because the voice of his God demands it, is the archetypal act of faith in a destiny of the soul that supersedes the ego. It is an act of faith in the greater will of an autonomous and intangible double, a double Jung imagined as a Self that supersedes the ego's conscious will. This other will operates under a set of laws different from all those of which the ego can ever be aware. This act of faith is the ultimate declaration and fulfillment of *amor fati*, or love of one's destiny, that is at all attainable. But by abandoning common sense in this fashion, and by his very willingness to go against the tide of all that seems reasonable and human, Abraham also is willing to commit an act that, at the level of feeling, can only evoke pity and horror. There is pity for the child sacrifice, and there is horror at the thought of an act that seems as far removed from humanity and from divinity as it is possible to imagine anything. Here, in Abraham, humanity and divinity conspire to override all rules upon which a more or less intelligible world, based on reason, common sense, and humanism, could possibly be built. In the face of such pity and horror, the human spirit becomes virtually speechless. What little voice remains can only speak of that pity and that horror. One case that resembles the Abraham-Isaac pair in this respect is Shakespeare's Othello. Looking at the dead and brutally sacrificed Desdemona, whom he himself has killed in a fit of jealous wrath that is almost biblical in proportion, Othello gives voice to his sorrow: "The pity of it, Iago. The pity." Another and more contemporary case appears in Konrad Lorenz's *Heart of Darkness* (as in the film version of that story, *Apocalypse Now*). Here the central figure names the brutal sacrificial slaughter he has been witnessing by its most heartfelt name: "The horror. The horror. The horror."

Abraham is not stopped by feelings of pity and horror. He goes beyond them. He is willing to sacrifice not only his own son, meaning all that is near and dear, and all that the future holds of promises. He also is willing to sacrifice his own identity, his self-image as a human being who, like all human beings, must live a life that is no picnic, in a world that is no paradise, even under the best of circumstances, and who therefore has ample reason to be familiar with feelings of pity and horror. Abraham abandons the morality of personal human feeling. In the process, he is willing to become a monument of apparent inhumaneness, a personification of seeming heartlessness. He embodies the utter brutality of which perhaps only the life of the spirit, and of all forms of idealization, is routinely capable as a matter of course. Here good old Abraham seems to have become pure evil. It is as though in Abraham-Isaac, just as in the case of Job, God has given humanity over into the cruel hands of Satan—or Othello-Desdemona into those of demonic Iago.

Where the quintessentially human feeling of pity is abandoned, and where the seeming horror of pitilessness appears, there one worldview comes to an end and a new one takes its place. The worldview that comes to an end is that which corresponds to a psychology placed in the service of the ego. The horizon that opens up is that of a psychology that takes the soul, not the ego, as its primary concern. The sacrifice of the ego that is made for the sake of the transition from one worldview to the other is echoed in the seemingly casual, if not cavalier, manner in which the ego is spoken of from this other vantage point. Hillman puts it this way: "In the realm of soul the ego is a paltry thing." Nietzsche is just as casually dismissive: "As for the ego . . . that is only a play on words." This must indeed be, as Jung put it, a defeat for the ego.

In what must be one of Western literature's, Western history's, Western religion's, and Western morality's starkest paradoxes, Abraham, this founder of the Judeo-Christian religion of mercy, and Nietzsche, who would undo Christianity if he could, are joined in their readiness to abandon pity as a prime virtue that safeguards man's humanity. This oddest of odd couples is united in their readiness to sacrifice pity for the sake of a Greater Will. They are both ready to dismiss the human ego as a paltry thing, as though it were, indeed, no more than a mere play on words. Just as Abraham found that he must overcome pity for the sake of the fulfillment of his God's plan, in spite of everything that cries out about the horror of it, so too did Nietzsche find that we must overcome pity. But in his mind we must overcome it not for the sake of a God who exists mostly outside of the world but for the sake of a philosophical pathos and perspective that would affirm the world itself. That Nietzsche was acutely aware of the reaction of horror with which his proposal to overcome pity would be met is clear. He showed a deep appreciation for the natural feeling of horror at the seeming unnaturalness of his suggestion. He even explicitly identified pity as not only the last but also the hardest thing for man to overcome. We must overcome pity, said Nietzsche, because in spite of seeming virtuous, it is an underhandedly malevolent act and pathos. It is underhandedly malevolent, because it implicitly slanders life for being as it is. It involves a judgment that whatever actually is should not have been. Pity says that whatever has happened should not have happened. It says that existence as it has been and is, and may well continue to be, should not be. It suggests that man is not up to his own existence. Pity implies that man needs, and deserves, something other and better than the world in which he exists. It insinuates that the universe is not good enough for man, and that, in turn, he is not fit for it. This kind of pity, says Nietzsche's Zarathustra, is Buddhist in essence: "It sees a sick man or an old man or a corpse," and it concludes on that slim basis that life "must be refuted." That is why, in his view, Buddhism's highest ideal is freedom from the suffering that comes with everyday worldly life. "One thing I teach," said the Buddha: "suffering and the end of suffering. It is only ill and the ceasing of ill that I proclaim." The method for achieving that goal is based on a strategy of detachment from complete absorption in or identification with the daily concerns of practical living. The potential ultimate reward for a life devoted to such detachment is a state of nirvana, meaning complete release from pain and suffering through detachment from the ordinary impact of all earthly realities. The image of the ultimate human good, in this view, is a state of being that is released from the eternal process whereby all living things are born into this world. While it is inaccurate to portray Buddhism as a life-negating orientation, as Nietzsche was tempted to do, it is entirely accurate to say that the Buddha's central objective is the end of earthly suffering. In this respect, it is not entirely unfair to suggest that Buddhism is at least initiated by a sentiment that is not unlike what Job expressed in his initial outcry of anguish over life's cruelties and over the very fact of his birth into this world of suffering: "God damn the day I was born. . . . On that day—let there be darkness; let it never have been created." Buddhism partakes in that condemnation of the pain of existence and magnifies that condemnation into a complete worldview. Nietzsche's view of Buddhism is, therefore, not unjustifiable.

Nietzsche offered the pathos of a philosophy of eternal return as a way to convalesce from the life-negating illness he considered pity to be. Now we can see how Zarathustra concludes the statement cited earlier. "'I want heirs'—thus speaks all that suffers; 'I want children, I do not want *myself.*' Joy, however, does not want heirs, or children—joy wants itself, wants eternity, wants recurrence, wants everything eternally the same." This pathos does not want to escape the suffering of everyday existence, as Buddhism and all pity do. It does not want to end this difficult existence. It does not want to replace it with another and better existence, in the future of another world or of a different life in this world. It wants the here and now, fully affirmed as it is. It wants that here and now so much so that the greatest possible good it can imagine is to make of every moment an eternity unto itself, with everything before it just the same, and everything after it the same. "What?" said Nietzsche, in *Beyond Good and Evil,* "and this wouldn't be *circulus vitiosus deus?*"—eternal return as a divine principle and law? The rule of sticking to the image sides with Nietzsche on the matter of pity. It counters pity by insisting that every life and every moment in it already have their self-affirming value built right into them, in the precise way everything is as it is. The categorical imperative to "Stick to the image" insists that every life not only has the right but also the obligation to declare its own inherent values. These values are present in it in spite of all pitiable appearances to the contrary. Sticking to the images in the facts of life is the opposite of detaching from them.

When therapeutic psychology becomes carelessly unquestioning about itself, especially in its insistence on improving life, it can inadvertently turn into a method of institutionalized devaluation by means of pity. It can become a form of systematic pity whose procedures are placed on semi-scientific footing—and whose agenda is sanctioned as mental and social hygiene, whose methods are regulated by trade organizations and licensed by state boards, whose practices are paid for by insurance plans, and whose virtual availability to all ensures that its gospel is taught everywhere. "We have invented happiness," says what Zarathustra calls the "last man." This "last man" is someone whom the Nietzsche scholar, Laurence Lampert, takes to be modern, therapized man. Says Zarathustra: "Everybody wants the same, everybody is the same: whoever feels different goes voluntarily into a madhouse"—or, we might add, in psychological treatment. Therapeutic man will change and improve himself if it kills him. He will change and improve himself *until* it kills him. There is nothing he is not willing to "work on" or "work through." Yet all this going into psychotherapy for the sake of change and improvement may, in certain ways, paradoxically and inadvertently, become the beginning of the end. It may potentially become the real undoing of one's life—by a systematic but underhanded form of devaluation through pity.

Half of the skill of psychological treatment is knowing the difference between what is changeable and what is not. It is the same skill that is involved in recognizing when the human ego meets up with something that is larger than it, and whose agenda supersedes and defeats it. It is a practical version of the rule "Know thyself," meaning "Know what is in your control and what is not." The inability to recognize what is unchangeable has vast moral, and demoralizing, implications. It perpetuates a pathos of resentment against the life that is by holding out the seductive promise of a life that is not. It keeps feeding a hostility against life as it is that may well end up at war with the universe itself. The inability to recognize what is unchangeable is an inability to recognize the soul's own reality. It is an obstacle in the way of a life's fundamental capacity to affirm itself. It mistreats the soul by flatly and flagrantly ignoring it. It is perhaps no wonder that a century of psychotherapy aimed at producing a new and improved kind of man has, in spite of everything that has been genuinely useful about it, often left us more wanting than satisfied. It is perhaps no wonder that even though we have become well acquainted with the psychopathology of everyday life, and with methods for managing it, psychology has nonetheless often tended to get us farther away from having a sense for the soul in everyday life.

Sticking to the image in a given matter begins by becoming more imaginative than one has been about it. A case in point—and one that can repeat itself in any life—is Zarathustra's discovery about the self-repeating patterns that shape his behavior, his experience, his sense of who he has been and will be, even the habitat where he naturally belongs. Zarathustra starts off with what is by no means always easy, the observation of the obvious or a statement of what is all too familiar: "I am a wanderer and a mountain climber . . . I do not like the plains . . . I cannot sit still for long . . ." At this point, every statement still begins with "I." This is the beginning psychotherapy patient doing what the treater tells every patient to do: talk about himself or herself. As every therapist knows, and as most therapy patients eventually discover, when enough "I"'s line up, they begin to form a pattern. Zarathustra, like every man or woman in psychological treatment, begins to recognize the outline that is formed when all the "I"'s he is thinking about line up. This is the first step toward self-recognition and self-acceptance: "Whatever may yet come to me as destiny and experience will include some wandering and mountain climbing." Then there is the personal discovery of a transpersonal law. This is the discovery that nothing in any human life is as accidental as it often seems. Says Zarathustra: "In the end, one experiences only oneself. The time is gone when mere accidents could still happen to me; and what could still come to me that was not mine already?" Finally, there is the full realization of the complete autonomy of individual psychological destiny. This involves the discovery that the destiny of the soul is nothing but reality itself, the reality that includes not only the person and the person's sense of self but the whole wide world around him or her: "What returns, what finally comes home to me, is my own self and what of myself has long been in strange lands and scattered among all things and accidents." Zarathustra's view has broadened from the strictly personal "I" of his private experience to the transpersonal reality of the universe in which he is now truly beginning to belong by, for the first time, discovering his proper place in it. From a psychology of ego and of an inner individual person, a *homunculus*, he has moved to a psychology of the soul of the world itself—of the *anima mundi*. This is, in a nutshell, the psychology of the prodigal son. He too finds his true self, his true destiny, and his true destination by finding out where he belongs. He belongs not elsewhere and always on the go, forever preoccupied with doing other things. His true home is in the here and now of where he is. His proper place is that same place that he and Everyman are perpetually poised to abandon: the *hic et nunc* of life as is.

Freud's method of free association, we can now see, becomes ultimately therapeutic not when and because, like the prodigal son, it abandons its starting point and pursues everything that comes to mind, no matter where it leads. Free association leads to the convalescence of psychological homecoming when and because, after roaming wide and far in every direction, it returns to its starting point of the patient's experience here and now—but with a changed view on all things old and familiar. As noted earlier, Jung wrote that "The experience of the Self is always a defeat for the ego." He did not say that the ego is thereby altogether destroyed, or that it ought to be destroyed. Quite the contrary. What is at stake reenacts the drama of Isaac not having to be sacrificed after all, and of the prodigal son reaching his surprising destination not just in spite of getting lost but as a result of getting lost. All that is destroyed or that needs to be lost and sacrificed is the ego's rule, and the ego's insistence on ruling. What must be given up, with full consent, is the ego's habit of imposing its will and its fantasied delusion of control. The ego is defeated in its beliefs but it is not altogether destroyed. Rather, it is transformed. It becomes something that is simultaneously wholly new and yet also the same as before. This is precisely what Freud said about psychoanalysis: it does not change people, it allows them to become who they are. The transformation of the ego is about linking it to something that resembles it like its double but that, like a true double, has a life of its own. That other self is in the ego's true likeness, even though it is immaterial, and even though it can only be known by being imagined. It is the ego's fundamental origin and ground. The transformation of the ego is about establishing a linkage between the familiar sense of oneself and the elusive soul factor that brings the sense of self into being in the first place. It is about recognizing that personal sense of self as an incarnation of the soul's own creative imagination. It is about establishing a sense of kinship with the elusive factor that supports a person throughout personal history, that determines his or her destination, that delineates his or her destiny, and that, as any guardian angel does, preserves the person throughout life, for a particular death and for none other. This transformation of the usual sense of oneself is about the familiar facts of one's life beginning to look uncanny, that is, animated with a sense of having a soul of their own. It is about those facts becoming both strange in appearance yet at the same time more intimately known than before. It is about the familiar sense of oneself coming into its own in spite of, and owing to, the very dread of its defeat.

The key ingredient in this transformative process is the linkage between ego and something that is other than ego, and that is therefore often called an "alter ego." That linkage historically has been imagined as a kind of embrace or sense of union—between things historical and things timeless, between things visible and things invisible, between what is tangible and what is intangible, between the literal and the metaphorical, the factual and the mythic, the sacred and the profane, between all that is mortal and all that is not. It is no accident that depth psychology has always been preoccupied with love's embraces. But as the historical development from Freud to Jung and Hillman shows, that same depth psychology was bound to find out that the embrace that is at stake is not first and last a biological fact. The embrace or union the soul is after is not, in the first place, an act from nature, making the physical body the last step in all psychological theorizing. Rather, it is an embrace that takes place in the realm of the imagination that rules all things—including the physical body and all its acts.

TEN

IT IS ENOUGH
AND IT IS GOOD

MODERN PSYCHOLOGY'S SCIENTIFIC METHODS of inquiry yield findings that often can be fascinating, even practically useful, but that nonetheless do not fully satisfy the needs of the soul. Whenever science answers one question, it also raises new ones. That is, of course, its nature. Scientists are perfectly happy with this arrangement, and for good reason. It leads them to ever-new opportunities for inquiry, and thus to new findings. It is precisely the failure to find definitive, final answers to its endless questions that keeps the scientific enterprise going. Scientists are therefore forever on the move, especially in areas of basic research, without arriving at a final destination or without staying anywhere, at any newfound point of view, for long. Everything can be a point of departure for them, but few conclusions are permanent points of arrival. Most science remains perpetually underway toward discovering new horizons, new territory, new promises. And while it is forever underway in this fashion, it is perpetually and hungrily searching for new knowledge, new models, new paradigms. Scientific wisdom, in any area of fundamental research, must be constantly updated. No rest, ever. Paradise lost, for good.

The central metaphor that defines all science is one of searching—in Latin, *quaerare*, which yields the English query, quest, question, inquiry, inquest, inquisition, and more. Other images and metaphors that define scientific inquiry—exploring, analyzing, testing, probing, measuring, examining, quantifying, investigating, and all the rest—all these are derived from the root metaphor of searching. They involve a sense of the fundamental endlessness of the scientific enterprise, and they imply the characteristic inability of science to be fully and finally satisfied. The images and metaphors that shape the scientific enterprise involve a spirit that contemplative tradition long ago described as a *cor irrequietum*, a heart that is ever restless. Such a heart is always underway and on the move, forever reaching and yearning for an end to its own restlessness. This heart at the heart of science is restless, because it is on an endless journey, a pilgrimage of compulsive searching. It is on a *peregrinatio animae*, the eternal wanderings of a perpetually wandering soul. As Augustine, in *Confessions*, already said about all science, even before science as we now know it came into being, it is driven by "a kind of empty longing." By that he meant a longing that cannot be fully and finally satisfied with the results of its own activity. And so it must always move on.

Modern psychology, to the degree that it often emulates models and methods of scientific inquiry, especially quantitative ones, is for these same reasons at risk of failing to completely satisfy the searching soul, even though its methods and findings often are fascinating and useful. Insofar as modern psychology follows methods of inquiry that are based on models of scientific research, it is at risk of being driven and guided by a *cor irrequietum*. It is at risk of developing a chronic heart condition marked by permanent restlessness, with a heart that yearns for an end to its restlessness but that can not only not reach, but that can also not offer, rest. If modern psychology can only be such endless searching, as it threatens more and more to become, then all it can do is take us all, collectively and individually, on a journey that turns out to lead nowhere final but to endlessly more restless journeying. It would make all psychological analysis interminable indeed, as Freud suggested—an endless *peregrinatio animae*, analysis for the sake of analysis. This mythic motif of tireless questing is already enacted in the endless questioning in many modern methods of psychological evaluation. Here the mode of discourse is itself reshaped in its fundamental format. It is turned into a permanent question mark. All interaction becomes inquiry: Who is the patient? What is the identified problem? Who else is involved, and how? What is the history? What the etiology? What are the identifiable stressors? The dialogue and the evaluation are shaped by a regimen of endless questions. And if those are not enough, then there are more rigorously scientific methods of inquiry, with long questionnaires of all sorts, personality inventories with hundreds of questions that are scored and analyzed by computer. It is perhaps enough to give anyone a *cor irrequietum*, a nervous heart condition—not just those among us who are plagued by nervous diseases.

Greeks of Homer's day, in spite of their practical categorical imperative of "Know Thyself," had no formal psychology. They did not even have a word for psychology, and certainly had no scientific psychology. They went to oracles instead of psychotherapists with questions about their lives, and they walked away from them with answers. Today, religious peoples still go to their temples or shrines and turn to their divinities to have their prayers answered, in the knowledge and expectation that no prayer goes unanswered. And children everywhere, now as much as ever, turn to their parents and elders for answers about anything and everything, in absolute faith that an authoritative answer will be forthcoming. Yet many consumers of modern psychology often turn to soul treaters with questions about their lives without receiving satisfying answers. What they receive instead are often more questions, questions that are based on the latest method of questioning but that do not give the soul what it seeks. There is no reason why we should be satisfied with methods of psychology that cannot produce satisfactory answers. We should not hesitate to say that such treatments of the soul may be, in the final analysis, less than good enough. Something else, something more, something less empty and more fully satisfying is needed before we can be truly content with psychology's offerings.

Poetic imagination, in contrast to scientific inquiry, makes boldly declarative statements that can and do leave one satisfied. It satisfies by producing moments of revelation and inspiration that, if ever so briefly, silence all questions and all questioning. It temporarily stops all questing. Poetic imagination succeeds in satisfying by yielding moments of what the ancient mystic philosopher and psychologist Plotinus, in *Enneads*, called *amplexis*, by which he meant an embrace or union—a kind of falling together or coming together, a coincidence or agreement—between the realm of all things ordinary and historical and a sense of something that is, as it were, an extra dimension of significance that inheres in them and that is both their origin and the ground to which they seek to return. This embrace or union, this amplexis, is about developing a sense of getting in touch with, and of being touched by, something that amounts to more than all that can possibly be said about the matters of the everyday world. It is about moments during which the plainly and ordinarily human suddenly appears transformed into a more glorious image of itself. The workaday world is, as it were, transfigured and looks even better than its Sunday best. It is as though, by the gift of an alchemical trick, everyday life becomes identical to an enriched double image of itself. Amplexis is a moment during which the ordinary unexpectedly gives away a glimpse of its inherent and fundamental but usually hidden extraordinariness. It is an occasion on which otherwise unbelievable images—images of things usually presumed unreal or otherworldly and perhaps too fantastic to be true—are made concrete and real. They become credible, luminous apparitions that turn up in the middle of the events of everyday history. Amplexis expresses the magical realism of a deeply satisfying embrace or union between the utterly human and the mystery in it—between the mundane and the unbelievable, between the eternally elusive and what is close at hand. The idea of such an embrace or union serves to identify those moments in the life of the soul when the heart is filled to overflowing with feelings of complete satisfaction. These feelings are derived precisely from the personal experience of such a coincidence of things historical and timeless, of the unique and all that is universal. It is about those moments when ordinary men and women feel, among other things, that they are Everyman or Everywoman, and beyond that Humanity itself, catching brief, reflected glimpses of the ground of all beings and of all Being.

Such moments of amplexis are cases of revelation that belong in everyone's life. When they do occur, all familiar knowledge about the human condition falls away, and it is replaced with an inspired vision. Stale accepted wisdom, received doctrine, even all authority and all sources of authority are shed like worn clothes. They are replaced by a discovery that all things, even the seemingly mean and paltry, appear to have become miraculous—that the obvious is full of mystery, that unfathomable depths are present behind the flat surface of all things. Amplexis is about discovering that splendor sometimes can be seen where nothing even remotely splendid had seemed to be at hand. These moments reenact the discovery of splendor all around that Job makes when he has rid himself of all hearsay and of all received knowledge that is paraded in front of him by his friends. In these moments, one can, like Job, find oneself nakedly facing reflected glimpses of Being itself. One is stripped of all that was previously known and cherished, and one finds oneself freshly clothed in the sense of radiance that emanates from creation itself—from the least suspected corners of it, from the least things in it. At such moments of amplexis and of complete satisfaction, the heart says, as Augustine put it in his *Confessions:* "It is enough and it is good," *sat est et bene est.* When such an embrace or union is taking place, then the soul is truly satisfied. For at those moments the seemingly profane matters of everyday existence are united with the ground of their being that gives them their value. This is what ultimately makes them worthwhile. It inspires human beings to affirm existence and to be, as Nietzsche put it, "seduced into a continuation of existence."

Modern psychology has long been fascinated with identifying those elements in everyday life that make it satisfying, and whose absence makes it unsatisfying. Developmental psychology in particular, along with the psychotherapies that are based on it, has been especially fascinated with what it takes to make a life experience, and a whole life, satisfying. This has led to an endless fascination with questions about what constitutes good or satisfying infant and child care. Hence, the important idea of Good Enough Mothering. Hence, also, the objectification of that concept as the Good Enough Mother. These notions have become modern psychology's formula for the active ingredient of a good life. But beyond that, the notions of Good Enough Mothering and the Good Enough Mother also have served to implicitly define the very essence or idea of the Good itself. What Plato eventually had to acknowledge he could not define—the essential, universal, absolute, pure idea of Good—modern psychology often seems to imply it has been able to identify—as Good Enough Infant and Child Care. And with that, the West's psychology has come to walk in lockstep with the West's dominant—and, to many, often domineering, because often more dogmatic than mystical, more reactionary than visionary—religion, according to which Good is God, and God is Good, because he is a Heavenly Father, a Divine Parent.

The child's initiatory experience of The Mother as source of all Good becomes, according to developmental psychology and all treatment based on it, its historical prototype and standard of all later goods and satisfactions. By implication, any less than good enough aspects of that original experience become prototype of all later dissatisfaction. Future life experiences, being to a large degree repetitious variations of infantile core experiences, are shaped by and measured against this original and initiatory standard. Every individual's early childhood experience of this first standard of value sets the tone for the quality of life to come. Hence, psychotherapy's fascination with the childhood origins of the patient's current life experience: If you are unhappy now, that must be because the way you were raised then was not good enough. The therapeutic improvement of the human lot depends in this view on correcting what can be corrected about that historically first encounter with the incarnation of the Good.

Notions about what constitutes a Good Enough childhood experience are unquestionably fascinating, and they can be useful in applied forms of psychology such as psychotherapy. Yet in spite of everything that makes them worthwhile, they are, in one important way, less than good enough to fully satisfy the soul. While they are *about* the particulars of what is required to satisfy concrete childhood needs, the notions in themselves are still less than good enough to speak in satisfying ways about the deepest needs of the soul. In order to satisfy the soul's deepest needs, these notions themselves have to meet one requirement in particular. They have to meet the requirement of serving the possibility of amplexis. They have to be able to promote a sense of embrace or union between the historical life of the individual and the life of the archetypal realities that are embodied in it. As is implied in the idea of amplexis, the soul is traditionally imagined as that aspect of everyday life that partakes of both the utterly human and of a depth dimension that gives everything human its greatest possible significance. That depth of significance in all things remains beyond words and beyond concepts. It is always more than words can say or concepts can grasp. It is that surplus of significance that can never be definitively told in any language or medium. This is no metaphysical speculation of any kind. It is everyday observation of the most ordinary kind. For with everything that matters greatly to us—love, pain, joy, longing, loneliness, fear, outrage, or despair— there is the inescapable feeling that no words can ever express all that needs to be said about it to tell the whole story. No account of any significant event will ever do it justice, and no factual explanation will ever give a truly satisfactory explanation. In the daily practice of psychological treatment, where human beings go to contemplate their most valued psychic matters, this is expressed in the seemingly so prosaic yet profoundly true complaint that "Nobody really understands." A related sentiment appears at the level of the soul's collective and cultural life. Here it comes in the form of the common philosophical despair about the impossibility of language itself, and of all systems of signification, to provide an accurate and satisfactory account of anything.

Contemporary psychology is at risk of failing to satisfy the soul, because it often inquires into only half of the soul's natural life. The strictly historical and seemingly factual half of the equation is often all that it considers relevant. As a result, psychology itself makes it difficult for anyone to be prepared for the sense of amplexis. For with our eye on only half of what goes into an embrace or union, it becomes impossible to imagine an embrace or union at all. This is the significance of much of contemporary psychology's shift in interest away from an embrace between the historical aspects of things and their mythic other half and toward areas of inquiry that may well be fascinating and useful for practical living but that do not necessarily satisfy. Not even all that can possibly be said about etiology, family history, trauma history, differential diagnosis, neurology, sociology, psychodynamics, defense mechanisms, developmental failures, brain chemistry, DNA, and everything else can ever make up for the lack of a sense of amplexis. With no other half to embrace, because psychology itself turns away from it, there can be no sense of amplexis. There can therefore be no Augustinean sigh of contentment—no "It is enough and it is good." Much of the subtle but undeniable dissatisfaction that psychology itself inadvertently generates in the process, and that has, to some degree, become a collective, iatrogenic condition, is then placed in the lap of the presumably less than good enough mother. Or it is placed at the doorstep of the allegedly less than good enough parental house. Or it is projected on whatever other historical circumstance that is under suspicion of having failed to meet the needs of the child or the person. But it is not necessarily that mother or that parental house or whatever other circumstance that has failed to satisfy. The failure to fully satisfy lies in large measure in the failure to embrace the subtle other half that goes with every human life. And for that failure, modern psychology may perhaps only have itself to blame.

What psychotherapists call the "regressive pull" to return to earlier phases of infantile development—with mother's lap and breast or even her womb as signpost on this backward road—this "regressive pull" seems to be one strong case of the soul seeking to embrace something else beside the historically given world. Another case is perhaps that of psychotherapists and their patients becoming embroiled in intimate relations with each other. Driven into each other's arms by the powerful currents of strong emotions, even sensible treaters and patients are here sometimes effortlessly swept off their otherwise firmly planted feet. It is not enough to interpret these instances of the soul seeking embraces beyond the boundaries of accepted relationships as cases of abnormal mother-child development. Nor is it enough to explain them on the basis of mix-ups resulting from misleading projections. Much as such explanations offer, they nonetheless do not tell the whole story. To take the unconsciously fantasied figure of the mother or the sexualized fantasy picture of the patient or therapist for what the soul really desires may be a case of mistaking the soul's projections for its project. One can imagine, instead, that what the soul really wants here is neither the real persons themselves nor even their distorted and projected fantasy forms but an embrace and union with the elusive configurations of significance of which those persons, and all fantasy figures based on them, are historical embodiments and resemblances. The impulse to return to earlier developmental phases and the impulse to enact sexual fantasies in literal embraces between treater and treated are perhaps, in a way, only human, all-too-human trifles compared to the Good Enough Embrace the soul seeks. Explanations for these impulses that are based on ideas about unconscious projections have unquestionable value for practical living, but they fall short of accounting for all that is at hand and for all that needs to be said about them. It is, indeed, more as though what the soul really wants, the only thing that fully satisfies it, is a sense of the embrace between the historical facts of human lives and their other half, their image-based and, ultimately, mythic other half. And if such an embrace is what is at stake, then a psychology that would do it justice must itself contain ideas for such an embrace, and it must have the capacity to accommodate the need for such an embrace. That is why such a psychology needs Plotinus's notion of *amplexis*.

Since the case of therapists and their patients becoming engaged in intimate relations is then not only a matter of projections, it also is not enough to make these projections conscious in order to handle all that is at stake. If even well-prepared treaters can fall under the spell of this compulsion, then it is perhaps not because they fail in their awareness of transference and countertransference. Rather, it shows that projection theory alone, in spite of everything that makes it persuasive, is not quite enough to deal with all that is in the air. It is almost as though we are witnessing a fairy-tale scene in which the hero must cross the path of an invincible dragon or magician. No degree of human preparedness and know-how is ever a match for such encounters. What is required is something more mysterious than that. Likewise, what is at stake in the impulse to enact sexual fantasies between treater and patient is more than, and different from, all that can be rationally accounted for by projection theory. This should come as no surprise. As soon as we enter the realm of compulsions, we encounter forces that resist all efforts aimed at thwarting them. These compulsions act, as Freud and every commentator after him has observed, as though they were demonic powers. By extension, it is not only a matter of individual treaters failing those patients with whom they become intimately involved. It is a matter of the psychology of projection itself failing the treaters as well. It sends them into confrontations with matters of soul in individual lives and in the world at large with notions that are, in important respects, not quite up to the task. This is a case of the fairy-tale hero who is armed with all the accoutrements of chivalry but who lacks a sense for the magical realism that is involved in encounters with invincible dragons and magic. But beyond failing both patients and treaters, the psychology of projection also fails its one great patient, soul itself. For the soul wants to embrace. It exists to embrace. It is its function and task and destiny to embrace.

Freud appreciated the soul's insistent desire to embrace. Hence, his libido theory and his pansexualism. By placing libido and pansexualism at the center of his theoretical imagination, and at the heart of all human activity, he made his account of the soul a story about the human quest for a great embrace. He knew that in this quest the soul looks at everything with the same predisposed and desiring eye. He recognized that it sees in all things an endlessly varied plurality of potential candidates for the Great Embrace. But the same realization also made Freud insist on a treatment method based on deliberate privation of the impulse to seek literal embraces. Each and every desire must be acknowledged, because it shows where and how the soul is at work. Yet none must be satisfied literally, in the flesh, lest we lose sight of the elusive soul factor that manifests itself, but that also perpetually hides itself, in the mask of these impulses. Even more importantly, we may now add, desires that surface in psychotherapy must not be satisfied in the flesh, because what the soul desires is not flesh but amplexis, an embrace of what is image in the flesh. That is why we need free association in Freudian psychoanalysis, active imagination in Jungian analytical psychology, and an ear that hears all things as metaphors in Hillman's archetypal psychology. Above all this is why we need more rather than less imagination, fantasy, idealization. For these are not necessarily and automatically falsehoods, whose true names are illusion, projection, distortion, cognitive error, or overlearned automatic thought. The imaginings of the soul that are encountered in regressive and transference or countertransference fantasies are not, in the first place, about mistakes that must be corrected. They may be viewed as signs of the soul's straining to reach and embrace the other half of any given historical matter. For what the soul desires, in this view, is not less imagination but more. What is wrong about trying to literally satisfy the presumably incestuous desires that project themselves on therapists or patients, other than what is obvious and easily understood, is not in the first place that those desires are incestuous and based on too much fantasy. What is wrong here, in this view, is that the literal gratification of those desires would not be good enough, because the objects of desire have not been imagined well enough. What is problematic about these imaginings is not so much that they are unconsciously projected and distorted idealizations, but that they have not been sufficiently reimagined in terms of ideals that are less psychosocial than mythic in character. They have to be considered for what they are, which is truly fantastic, perplexing, and baffling. They are incapable of ever being known in advance, based on preconceived notions from established theory. They are equally incapable of being explained in retrospect, based on persons from psychosocial history. What makes a psychology based exclusively on projection less than completely satisfying is that fantasy material encountered in transference and countertransference is more complex, more mysterious, more elusive, and ultimately richer in value than anything that can be historically accounted for based on known and knowable persons or events and on their internalized mental representations. It is not mother's lap or breast or womb that is the end of the line. That would not be good enough. It would never satisfy the soul's deepest desire, for it would be no more than a family affair, made up of all-too-familiar family dynamics. It would not be a satisfying amplexis.

Transference does not only mean the projection of inner feelings and thoughts on outer objects, as we have come to know it from psychoanalysis. It also means, as seen earlier, "transport" or "transportation." It means being lifted and carried away from one place and deposited elsewhere. What psychotherapists call "transference analysis," then, no longer serves only the analysis of the body's unconscious sexual desires. It also has to serve the embrace the soul seeks. Such transference analysis must therefore involve that sense of being transported elsewhere. But the "elsewhere" that is involved in the soul's search for a good enough embrace is not, as previously emphasized, literally another place. It is not in another world with a different life, or at least a different set of circumstances. It is not about a promised life away from here or about a promising state of mind at some other time in a better future. Nor is the "elsewhere" the soul seeks in the transports of transference metaphysical or otherwise beyond worldliness in any fashion. It is still in one's lived world, just as it is, here and now—but with that here and now transposed. The historical or literal facts of the situation at hand are transposed to the dimension of the intangible images that are inherent in them and that give them their concrete shape. The facts of the matter are gathered together once again or "re-collected." Then they are transposed into the seemingly fictional but very real, even if fantastic, accounts where those same facts make more sense than before. They make more sense here, because they are cast in their own most imaginative terms. Now they speak about themselves with an imaginative logic and with a language that fits them. All things now fall into place, because of the convincing sense that their imaginative story is indeed where they belong. It also is where their protagonist belongs with them. The facts and their protagonist find their true home base when they are thus transferred and returned to the plot or *mythos* that is their natural habitat. In the end, and as Plotinus suggested when he said in the *Enneads* that all things desire to return to their origin, the facts of the soul recollect us, not we them. They recall us to where we belong, to where we always already are, to where we always were in the first place. If the realities of transference have anything to tell us, it is this—that we are where we are not. It says that the soul roams well beyond the boundaries of the body, and that it takes us along for the ride. As Jung put it so precisely, the greater part of the soul is outside the body.

This kind of recollection that uses transference to put us in our place, by showing where we belong and where we must turn, is made possible by listening to the facts of life with an ear for metaphor. It requires an ear for analogies—for resemblances, likenesses, and connections between seemingly unrelated things. It involves, above all, the capacity to see identities between nonidentical things, even between categories of things that seem to have nothing to do with each other. What Aristotle said about the craft of dream interpretation applies here as well: what is needed is the ability to recognize similarities between seem-ingly dissimilar things and classes of things. And thus in line with what he also said in this context: the person best suited for the task is one who knows how to handle the uses and workings of metaphor. Every plain, hard fact assumed known has to be listened to again, but this time it has to be heard as a metaphoric statement of fact. That way the person who is caught by the facts, or rather caught in rigid literal-mindedness about them, can find those facts and himself or herself along with them re-collected, re-located, and re-situated into a realm of images where both they and he or she naturally fall into place. It is no accident that the Greek word *metaphora* refers to moving, relocating, transport-ing. In today's Athens, trucks are driving around with the word *metaphora* painted on their sides to advertise their company's preparedness for the job of moving household furniture. Along similar lines, it is not surprising that one sometimes hears psychotherapy being spoken of as a process of "having one's psychic furni-ture moved around."

A deliberately and persistently metaphoric mode of thinking that is aimed at developing a sense for psychic transport, and ultimately therapeutic move-ment, may seem far-fetched. To transpose the literal facts of everyday life into metaphoric statements about the life of an insubstantial soul may seem far removed from treating concrete situations at the level of the practical concerns about them. But that is exactly the point. The kind of transference analysis or imaginative transposition that is at stake is about changing perspectives precisely by shifting positions. It is about looking from a shifted viewpoint at matters that are familiar and assumed known but that also are suspected of being psycho-logically underimagined and therefore so unknown that we rightly call them "unconscious." Yet it is not those unimagined or insufficiently imagined matters themselves that are unconscious. It is we who are unconscious about them. The sense of transference or transport by means of imaginative transposition is needed and is, as psychoanalysis has always indirectly held, the active ingredient of treatment, because changing perspective is exactly what is required. It is required so that the other half of any given reality can come within clearer view and closer reach, and so that the soul's desire for amplexis may be satisfied. For such transport brings the deeply longed for sense that here are indeed substan-tial and worthwhile things to embrace. The shift in position takes place when a situation begins to look different as a result of being looked at differently. As the perspective on the matter changes, so too do the feelings and thoughts about it. This is how true soul treatment is set in motion and moves along, moving its patient with it. Something becomes unstuck and shifts loose, making the move-ment of truly moving emotion possible. This is not merely a temporary waxing of sentiment. Nor is it only an intensification of familiar but still largely blind personal feeling. It is truly life-altering or transformative movement. Nothing has changed, yet everything is different—everything looks different, and every-thing feels different. The same old world is the same no more, even though nothing about it has changed. The same old person is renewed as well. The person is different by now being more clearly, more profoundly, and more satisfyingly the same than he or she ever was. That change that makes all the difference, in spite of not changing anything, feels truly good. Nothing more is asked for. Nothing more is needed. This is enough. When an imaginative process brings about this kind of psychic movement—whether in treatment or outside of it—then it is truly good enough. Then the heart sighs a great and deep sigh of contentment: *sat est et bene est.*

This kind of transposition of transference content and of the idea of transference itself that moves away from literal persons and facts, not only to fantasied internal representations of them but to altogether figurative personifications and timeless events, this move has implications for how we understand family psychology. That governing social paradigm that always occupies so much space in our usual imaginings about the life of the soul we now begin to view with growing skepticism. It begins to look more and more like a colonizing force that has grown accustomed to imposing its rule and its imaginings— at the expense of the soul's own sovereignty. Rethinking transference as transport and transposition to the ground of the soul's imagination has implications for how we think about social relationships and for what we expect from them. It changes our theories about what makes relationships satisfying or not. Most importantly, it redirects us in our search for satisfaction itself, because it redefines what we mean by satisfaction. This change involves casting a different light, from a different angle, on the enterprise of searching for good family feelings to live with or for a good household to live in. That search acquires an added and different meaning. So does the idea of family therapy and couples therapy, and of all psychotherapy that it is based on family models that presume to account for the life of the soul. Even the very idea of the family of origin, the family where everything presumably starts, comes to mean something other than mother and father, siblings and grandparents, and all past generations. In the end, the shifted view of transference, as a process of transport and transposition to a dimension of images, challenges the dominance of the social paradigm of family that tends to govern psychology. All this happens because the very idea of family and of origins is relocated to another plane. This shift in view on family, family psychology, and family therapy occurs because we also begin to look elsewhere than in the usual places to understand true psychological origins. Such true origins, from this perspective that is based on the idea of transference as psychic transport, do not lie in the biological family of origin or in the extended family. They do not lie in the idea of multiple family generations, or even in the culture of the old country and its old-fashioned ways. Bottom-line psychological origins do not originate in the ways of the elders of the clan. To look for one's most original origins, for the deepest grounds of family life and family love, and even for the idea of family life itself in all these literal and historical places alone is, in a way, to look for the foundations of family feeling in all the wrong places. Contrary to accepted psychological dogma, it is not, in the first place, one's historically first family that is first in psychological significance. And it is not the biological family of origin that is anyone's truest origin. Something else is first and origin.

The family of origin, like every other and later relationship that may or may not resemble it, is only one particular form of something else that is larger than it and that precedes it. That larger and more primary something is the sense of belonging. But—and this cannot be said quickly and emphatically enough—it is not, in the first place, about social belonging as a social fact of life, and with life itself understood as a social affair first and last. It is about a sense of being situated and contained in, as well as shaped by, a context of significance that is larger than the sum total of one's individual person and one's social persona—larger than all one's social experiences. The sense of belonging that is at stake is derived from the mythic quality of events, persons, and things, not from their sociology. Family, family relations, family feelings, and family life are facts of the collective and impersonal imagination before they are biographical facts of anyone's personal and social history. Oedipus, this central family figure of so much founding family theory, is a legendary or mythic fact before he is a fact from anyone's individual social history. Having an Oedipus complex, which psychoanalysts say we all do our whole life long, means being perpetually embroiled in the stuff of legend before it means coming face-to-face with any of its particular psychosexual and social implications. Oedipal triangulations and tribulations that are repeated throughout adult life and that reenact set patterns of interaction first established in childhood are more impersonal than strictly personal. They are more fictional than purely historical—more imaginal than literally factual, more collective than uniquely individual, more atemporal than developmental, more ritual than clinically pathological. My mother is ultimately more important because she embodies for me and confronts me with universal and timeless mothering than because she is mine socially, historically, uniquely, and developmentally. She matters in the end more as representative of the Great Mother in the Sky than as my Mommy Dearest.

Family of origin is the first historical and social encounter with the sense of belonging to, and of being contained and shaped by, something that is larger than oneself. But the fact that the family of origin provides the developmentally first encounter with that sense of belonging is not enough to conclude that family of origin itself is therefore of the order of rank of first causes, of founding principles, of true origins. Nor is such a conclusion justified by the additional fact that the sense of belonging is all too readily construed as social belonging, or by the fact that psychology has done so much to reinforce this social sense of belonging before and above anything else. The family of origin is itself no origin in a truly original way. It is where the sense of origins is originally encountered, but this initiation that comes with the first family is an introduction to something original in the more fundamental sense of something autonomous. That something original and autonomous that is more fundamental and that goes beyond family of origin itself is something that is truly *sui generis*—in many more ways than one. It is not only self-generated but also self-contained, self-governing, self-serving, self-regulating, self-justifying, self-esteeming, and, ultimately, self-explanatory as the most bottom-line self psychology there is. Family of origin points to all these things in addition to pointing at my mom and my dad, my brothers and sisters, even our grandparents and their ancestors. Family origin, in spite of seeming so personal, is ultimately impersonal, because it is transpersonal. It is beyond any given set of persons. It goes beyond personal relationships, personal affairs, personal feelings, and personal or interpersonal problems. It reaches beyond the internal organization of personality and beyond the external manifestations of personality disorders. It goes altogether beyond the very category of person, because it reaches beyond the notion of personhood.

The word "person," along with all the other words and ideas that are derived from it, comes from the word *persona*. This referred to the mask that ancient Greek actors wore in the theater in order to identify them as the mythic figures they were portraying on the scene. The word *persona* itself comes from *per* ("through") and *sonare* ("to sound"). These word origins suggest that the theatrical mask the person of the actor wore on stage was a medium through which myth voiced itself. It was a way through which gods and other fantastic figures managed to find a way and a place for themselves in this always physical and historical world of our everyday human life. That means "persons"—and personal affairs, personal relations, personal feelings, and all the rest—are the theatrical *persona* or dramatic mask through which there sounds the voice of something more hidden than the literal facts and events. They serve up something that is simultaneously masked by the facts but that presents itself through them. It wears those facts as ever so many face masks through which it makes itself heard, seen, felt, and recognized as incarnate. It is how imaginative matter becomes present in the flesh in this world of the flesh that is the favorite playground of all mythic beings. All seemingly so personal matters are not in the first place, nor in the final analysis, about personal projections. They are, for that reason, not fully, not sufficiently, not satisfactorily served by exclusively personalistic psychologies of projection. Nor are they, in the end, about any kind of humanistic psychology, one that puts the human person and all things ostensibly human first. Personal matters, in this view, are about the ways in which mythic beings project themselves and the substance of their mythic matter onto the stage of our world. They are the masks with which impersonal matter enters upon the scenes of private lives.

The developmentally first family from my psychosocial history and from my personal story as I tell it to myself and to others is not first—not by a long shot. It is the first instance I encounter, and thus my first personal experience, of what is archetypally first. But first in this archetypal sense does not mean historical first or otherwise sequentially and temporally first. It means first as primordial, first as more fundamental than anything else, and therefore first in order of rank. Archetypal first means first as deeper, more profound, than anything that can be known and said. It means first as ground of all consciousness, but also first as eternally beyond all possible forms or models of consciousness. It means first as autonomous categorical imperative, as first principle, as first commandment, as formative principle, and as ontological basis of all the soul's reality. Above all, and before anything else, it means first as second to none by any measure or standard. The founding principles of my life are not my mother and father, my brothers and sisters, even our grandparents and their history of multiple generations of ancestors. All these historical foundations and firsts may provide the first personal sense of foundation, but they are not, for that reason, the foundation itself. They are not themselves first, simply because they first introduce me to all that always was and is and will be first. What is truly first is the great spoken and unspoken imperative in every first family—"Because I say so!" That is the true and founding first principle. No psychological analysis can undo that, nor should it even try. It cannot be undone and it does not need to be undone, for what speaks through this first commandment is not truly, certainly not only or primarily, a historical person in the social role of Dad or Mom. Nor is it the inner and distant voice of their own parents and of prior generations that speak through them. It is not even the voice of the sociological institution of family itself or of family tradition and collective cultural heritage. The voice that commands "Because I say so!" is the voice of none of these, even though they all pick up its language, its accents, its idioms. What speaks through the persona of immediate and remote family alike, and through all collective tradition, is the compelling mythic command to enter creation and to become devoted to it with life and limb—to love it with body and soul, and to work in it every day of the week, with every breath one takes and with every act one undertakes. What is at stake is the command to go forth in the world in order to become immersed in its polymorphousness, and ultimately to feel and to be polymorphous with it and in it. This commanding and even domineering voice that speaks its compelling categorical imperative through all personal, familial, and social experiences originates in, and speaks up on behalf of, creation itself. It is monumentally, divinely indifferent to personalistic prejudices and perspectives, and to every personal feeling or opinion I may have about it. It speaks *through* the persona of all things personal, but it speaks *about* all manner of things transpersonal and impersonal.

Family psychology and the psychological analysis of the individual that is based on family psychology are never final and definitive. They are never finished. We are never done with family, because family is never done with us. But if psychological analysis is interminable, as Freud said, then it is, in the first place, because the gap between what is historically first and what is archetypally first can never be finally, definitively bridged. Analysis of the individual's life that is based on family models is never done, because not even all that can ever be said about the historically first family can ever say all that matters as much as it does on an archetypal level of significance. And yet this is not necessarily and automatically proof of the failure of depth psychological analysis itself. On the contrary. It points to ways in which it can be most successful. By being interminable and always incomplete every family analysis, and all analysis of the life of the individual that is based on it, points not so much *at* family itself but *beyond* it, beyond everything historical and beyond everything literal that can be known and said about any family, even about the very idea of family itself. Every actual member of any given family thereby ultimately points away from the person, and toward the dimension of archetypal first principles in which he or she participates. Every family member points to more than only literal case history. Therefore, what makes family analysis interminable is neither the analysis nor the failure of analysis but family itself. Family analysis is interminable because family is bottomless in its polymorphous imaginative basis, not merely endless in its personal sequelae and sociological implications. The actual members of a family, these persons we know all too well yet also not at all, eventually must be unburdened of the weight of carrying history and the world on their personal shoulders. It is not they who lead us into the world and through it—or astray in it. All they ever do, including how they do it, is done in the name and under a sign of more primordial figures who precede all persons in origin and who reach beyond all historical analysis. These more primordial figures come before all history, even before the very idea of history itself. It is those figures, who can only be spoken of figuratively and mythically, who are our true first family.

But it is not only images of mothers and fathers, brothers and sisters, uncles and grandparents that count here as the mythic figures that make up the soul's own family. It is all figures of fiction, all configurations of the imagination, insofar as all those images are the forms and shapes behind all persons—behind all relatives, behind all relationships, behind all relationship patterns and dynamics and experiences. But these figures and configurations of the imagination that form the soul's own family, and that may well be personified as mythic persons, must not be thought of as objectifiable metaphysical persons or personlike entities. Nor must they be thought of as perhaps figuratively personified but nonetheless objective and identifiable factors of any kind. They can only be known by being imagined—and they must be imagined so that they may be loved. We are close here to the profound mystery that Pascal identified when he said that earthly things must be known to be loved and that divine things must be loved to be known. We work on that mystery, the mysterious relations between knowing and loving, through active imagination. For these images that make up the soul's own family of origin can never be fully known in any absolute way. They are always known only by approximation. They become known in this fashion through figurative speech, through speech that can only allude to bottom-line matters that are themselves bottomless and elusive. And they remain elusive like this, even while they also are concretely embodied in the here and now of all the situations, events, and personal or social experiences of everyday life.

If the actual persons in the family must be unburdened of the weight of history, then this means that the sense of historical family can and must itself be unburdened of such things as blame, guilt, shame, and responsibility with which personalistic thinking tends to burden them. It means that those categories of personalistic experience, and others that are related to them, become themselves inadequate at a certain point, and thus ultimately irrelevant if one wishes to go beyond that point. They become inadequate, because they are too much grounded in and tied to the social sense of literal persons—the patient and his domineering father, passive mother, controlling wife, or seductive mother-in-law. What is at hand in everything that feels so personal in the interactions with these persons becomes itself at some point impersonal. It becomes so impersonal that, from that point onward, it is best thought of as timeless and universal—or archetypal. With this appellation, that all things seemingly personal become at a certain point archetypal, one reaches not only beyond individual or family history, one reaches also beyond the very category of historically based psychology—and that includes perhaps especially developmental psychology, this favorite genre of contemporary psychological treaters everywhere. These categories and these psychologies are by no means dismissed. On the contrary. But they are given a different role to play. They become stepping stones that lead beyond themselves. They point toward a depth of soul at the heart of all being that is, as Heraclitus suggested, without bottom. That is why we can never reach the end of it, making all depth psychological analysis interminable, because it is archetypal. The deep archetypal dimension in the daily life of the soul is the avenue through which the soul embraces its true origins of first principles. It is therefore no surprise that the word "archetypal"—from the Greek *archai*—in its root meaning refers to "original" or "the originals." The bottom-line origins of the facts of the soul are less to be found in the historical first family than in the archetypal basis of images that underlies all life, including all family life and all ideas from family based psychologies. The archetypal substance in all things that is its psychic active ingredient can never be firmly grasped or definitively defined, because it cannot be objectified—even though it is always concretized or incarnate. That subtle substance that makes up the archetypal origins of all things can never be pointed at and can only be pointed to, through a language of images.

The practice of using family based psychological theory in the search for good family feelings to live with, in spite of everything that can and should be said for it, is at risk of leaving the soul less than fully satisfied if and when it does not also look for the archetypal depth of significance in all things. By focusing exclusively on redeeming family history with psychotherapy focused on literal persons, by going to counseling with a limited agenda of improving the current situation at home through changes in personal and interpersonal behavior patterns, and by interminable analyses of the internalized family figures that make up one's inner personality, we may be left less than fully satisfied *because we are not reaching archetypal depths*. A historical and sociological approach to family psychology is at risk of leaving the soul in an important way empty-handed, because it encourages everyone to look one-sidedly and often exclusively in the direction of social paradigms—at the expense of a sense for the archetypal origins of all things. This ignores the soul's own family origin in the realm of the imagination, the realm of the images underlying all of everyday life, including its sociology. What the soul desires at its deepest level of inwardness is neither the right person nor a better personality. It does not seek more satisfying personal relationships or personal improvement. What it longs for most is a fulfilling sense of amplexis, a sense that a life is embracing the archetypal double that is its true self and that can only be known by being imagined and loved.

ELEVEN

SEEING IS BELIEVING

THE TERM *ARCHETYPAL PSYCHOLOGY*—in contrast to Freud's "psycho-analysis" and Jung's "analytical psychology"—was coined by Hillman in 1970. As Hillman discusses in *Archetypal Psychology: A Brief Account*, the modern use of the notion of "archetypes" is itself usually and rightly associated primarily with Jung. It was he who reintroduced the term to the West's vocabulary of ideas after it had been absent from it for centuries. Prior to Jung, the term was virtually lying discarded on the rubbish heap of ancient ideas presumed dead. Yet before Jung, it was already Freud himself, even though he did not speak of "archetypes," who had spontaneously reverted to the practice of naming the processes in the unconscious life of the soul after mythic images from the world's storehouse of literary fictions. This trinity of Freud, Jung, and Hillman is no accidental trilogy. It reflects three aspects of one tripartite issue, an issue that involves the way grammar affects how we think and how we act.

As Nietzsche noted—being among the first to give this matter of the influence of grammar on thinking and behavior its proper psychological and philosophical weight—we think only in the categories that are provided by the structures of grammar. That means *what* we think is not only determined by *how* we think, or how we think we think. It is also, and before anything else, determined by how the grammar of our language makes us think, precisely by giving us the very categories of thought with which to do our thinking. Thus grammar shapes how we think, even before we have thought a single thought, before we have begun to think about thinking anything at all. Our ways of thinking up psychology, of thinking about the life of the soul, are a case in point. Since how and what we think affects what we do and how we do it, it is worth our while to see how grammar affects the way we treat the life of the soul.

The three issues that are at play here involve three categories everyone knows from grammar school. They are adverbs, nouns, and adjectives. Because

grammar makes up differences between adverbs, nouns, and adjectives as a manifestation of the soul's own imagination, we who would be interested in the
psyche's logos—in talk about the soul that concerns its logic and logistics—can
do no less than take a closer look at these differences. For it is those differences
that are differentially personified in the modes of thinking and the modes of
psychological treatment we identify as "Freud," "Jung," and "Hillman." Briefly
put: Freud's psychoanalysis is a psychology built on an adverb, Jung's analytical
psychology is one construed on a noun, and Hillman's archetypal psychology is
an exercise in the use of an adjective.

Freud must be credited with introducing the practice of not only naming
the clinical facts of psychopathology after mythic figures, which began long
before him, but of recognizing the active presence and acute relevance of archetypal themes in Everyman's daily life. His psychoanalysis is, before anything else,
an insistence that understanding the soul begins by looking for its basis in the
motifs from the mythic imagination. We must see and say, Freud suggested, that
Eros, Narcissus, and Oedipus are alive and well and living next door—holding
down jobs, raising children, and doing all the other things we all do every day.
He showed all who would be psychologists that understanding the life of the
soul is a matter of thinking and speaking *archetypally*. Here *archai* serves as root
for an *adverb* that qualifies *how* we practice psychology. And *how* we do that,
Freud implied, is by reverting the subtle stuff of unconsciousness in everyday
life to the fictions from myth that are enacted in it. The small band of famous
mythic characters Freud selected to animate his psychoanalytic theory serves to
argue his point.

It is to Jung's credit that he explicitly named these timeless and universal
patterns in the life of the soul by their proper name of *archai,* or "archetypes."
We must see and say, Jung suggested, that all psychology is, in the final analysis,
about bottom-line facts called "archetypes." These bottom-line facts he thereby
identified by a *noun* that names *what* it is we are after in analyzing the life of the
soul. His psychology is therefore often called a "psychology of archetypes." Jung
then proceeded to offer his catalog of archetypes that, in his view, govern the
life of the soul. That catalog went on to exist after him as the popularized metaphysics of the soul called "Jungian psychology." But while the world owes Jung
an immense debt of gratitude for reintroducing the ancient yet eternally serv-
iceable term and notion of archetypes, we also have popularized "Jungian psychology" and, to a certain extent, Jung himself to thank for a crucial and
common misunderstanding. That misunderstanding is about mistaking archetypes for substantive or objectified entities. It takes and mistakes archetypes to
be things, or at least thinglike things, whose being is similar to that of quasi-
physical beings.

Hillman views the world and life in it as fundamentally archetypal in quality, but he emphatically rejects all notions and all metaphysics of substantive or
objectifiable things that ought to be called " archetypes." His brand of psychol-

ogy is about describing and typing all things, including the notion of "archetypes" itself, as "archetypal." He creates a psychology that is centered around an
adjective. That adjective seeks to describe the first *qualitative* characteristic of the
life of the soul. Hillman takes all matters as masks or metaphors that serve the
adjectival purpose of alluding to the most fundamental quality of the life of the
soul. That fundamental quality, in his view, is its basis in a poetic or creative
imagination. Hence, and in direct contrast to Jung's "psychology of archetypes,"
his choice of the term *archetypal psychology*. This choice serves to indicate the
adjectival twist he gives to modern depth psychology's own historical development. If the idea of "archetypes" is as crucial to depth psychology as it is, and as
Jung spent his life arguing, it is more in an adjectival than in a substantive
manner. So Hillman has come to insist, in the manner of a student who went
beyond his master. We must see and say, suggests Hillman, not that archetypes
are things, but that things are archetypal. It is that distinction, between archetype as noun and archetypal as adjective, that makes all the difference. Not surprisingly, and as will be seen, that difference is itself . . . archetypal.

    The foregoing chapters consistently have used the adjectival descriptor
"archetypal," never the noun "archetype." This has been no accident. This book
is meant as an exercise in the *practice* of archetypal psychology, which works
more by thinking archetypally than by talking about archetypes. It is not meant
as a volume of information or a compilation of facts and critical questions
about things called "archetypes" and about theories of archetypes. It is not an
attempt to convince the reader of a set of facts concerning the role of "archetypes" in everyday life. It is intended as a more or less orchestrated maneuver
consisting of a series of essays that attempt to describe a qualitative aspect of the
life of the soul that is invoked by the adjectival appellation "archetypal." That
means nothing in the foregoing chapters has been meant to argue that archetypes are identifiable and objectifiable entities with certain characteristics.
Everything so far has been about trying to see how all things are characteristically archetypal. It is not about any Kantian noumenon or *Ding an sich*, a "thing
in itself" called an "archetype." It is about a phenomenal world in which all
things may be seen to be archetypal. It is not about taking literally anything said
to be "archetypal," not even the views of archetypal psychology itself or anything said in the foregoing pages. It is about viewing all things phenomenally
and phenomenologically as archetypal realities in the life of the soul, even
though the notions of "soul" and "archetypes" themselves must never be objectified. Just as it is with the notion of "soul" itself, which, as Plato had Socrates
say, cannot be known with human knowledge, so too is it with the notion of
"archetype" as noun, as noumenon, as *Ding an sich*, as thinglike thing in itself.
There may or may not be such things as "archetypes." Such knowledge is not
only beyond the scope of these chapters but also beyond the scope of what is
humanly knowable. It would indeed take some kind of suprahuman knowledge
to answer that question. Hence, and just as in the case of the notion of "soul,"

the idea that it would require a divine kind of knowledge to say anything about "archetypes" per se. But the good news, the truly good tidings, is that this does not even matter. It is, for all practical human purposes, a matter of complete indifference. Whether or not "archetypes" exist, and whether or not we should therefore "believe in them," is irrelevant. What does matter, the only thing that matters, and greatly so, is that all things can be seen to be archetypal. All we have to do is look at them as Freud first did—archetypally. The world is archetypal, because we may see it archetypally. The archetypal quality of the world is real, because the act of viewing it archetypally is feasible. The adjective is possible and refers to something real, because the adverb is humanly doable. To sum up, then, the life of the soul is not only real but also essentially archetypal—in spite of the fact that neither the soul nor archetypes necessarily exists. Whether they do or not is in any case irrelevant. It is a matter that is alchemically dissolved in its own solution, even before it can become an artificial problem that must be solved or a critical question that must be resolved.

Viewing things archetypally begins by shifting positions—from believing to seeing. But this is not merely about a shift in the *content* of any belief. It is not about abandoning one belief or set of beliefs in favor of another. It is about a shift involving the very *activity* of believing as a fundamental act of consciousness. Archetypal psychology begins by deliberately giving up the essential ingredient of all belief, which is the familiar and trusted ground of accepted knowledge. Archetypal inquiry is precisely *not* about any such accepted knowledge, in any of its variants—whether established creed and dogma, demonstrable theory and documented fact, even scientific evidence of any sort. It also is *not* about assumed underpinnings or conditions of any kind. Nor is it about causation in any form. It is about deliberately abandoning all these, and about seeing what is then left to see. The archetypal approach to discovering the life of the soul in everyday life is about looking squarely into the face of whatever presents itself *as it presents itself*. It is about seeing a living face in all things. It is, as Hillman puts it in one phrase, about "facing the gods," about recognizing the genius of *daimones* that are everywhere in the air in all situations. Looking at things archetypally is about reanimating the sense of *anima* that became psychology's own taboo when "animism" was declared not only primitive and un-Christian but also irrational and unscientific. Thinking archetypally is about assuming an attitude that can allow itself to be stunned by the very looks of whatever one is looking at. It is about developing a mind-set in which one can be filled with awe at the sight of sights that have long been looked at, and that have long looked familiar, but that suddenly acquire a new and newly animated look. In the final analysis, the activity of looking at things archetypally is about abandoning not only all established knowledge but also all belief in the world as a fundamentally intelligible or knowable mechanical process. It is about looking once again at the same old world of everyday life when that belief in its rational intelligibility is given up, and about seeing what is then left to see.

What is then left to see is the heart and soul and mind of creation itself—the *anima mundi*.

Job is one case, the great and legendary case, of making that shift from believing to seeing. His story is about what becomes visible when belief and hearsay about the world are abandoned, and when the fundamental unknowableness of the universe is rediscovered by having one's sense for it restored. Job's legendary encounter is about returning to a capacity for authentic experience by abandoning all prefabricated beliefs about experience. It is about discovering what Jung said about religious belief, but what can be said about all forms of belief, that it serves as defense against original personal experience. That defensive function of belief, and of the act of believing, is personified by the figures of Job's well-meaning, all-knowing, and pious friends, Bildad, Zophar, and Eliphaz. They tell him to shut up in his wounded and rageful defiance and to be quiet. They fear what he is doing. What he is doing is what all rage-filled woundedness does in extremis. He is throwing away the soothing and self-soothing beliefs with which man usually tries to reassure himself when frightened. He is rejecting the assurances with which man comforts himself when faced with the potential of being brought to grief. Job's story is about taking the risk of renouncing what solace may be derived from such familiar human conveniences and niceties. What makes Job appealing is that he does this not only out of rage-filled woundedness but for the sake of facing unknowableness itself, as close up as possible. His story is about deliberately rejecting all human claims to knowledge, precisely because such knowledge is found to be fundamentally unsatisfactory—and because something else, something more satisfying, is being demanded. Job is about taking the great risk and about facing the potentially catastrophic danger that come with not settling for an inauthentic or false sense of self. The miraculous discovery he makes at this mortally dangerous and pivotal point—a discovery that every psychotherapy patient can make, as though in ritualized imitation and reincarnation of Job—is that, contrary to all expectations, one does not automatically perish in the process of daring to be so vulnerable as never before.

Job is, in the end, about being stunned into awe-filled speechlessness by the endless multitude of miracles and mysteries that are everywhere visible in all things. A crucial point in his story is that he is reminded of the fundamental unknowableness that is everywhere in the air by a Voice from a Whirlwind. That is, he hears it from the very elements that surround him daily. The voice he hears is not one of an otherworldly being. It is the voice of a spirit that is immanent in the world, in his circumstances. Job's experience is one of theophany, of environmental or situational theology. His encounter is with a *genius loci*, the inherent spirit of genius that resides in all things and in every event. "Where is the road to light?" asks that Voice from the Whirlwind. The question challenges Job to rediscover and restore his capacity to be in awe about such a fundamental daily miracle as the visibility of all things, the visibility of anything. "Where does darkness live?" the Voice asks, raising the question of how one even begins to imagine darkness, unknownness, invisibility, even unconsciousness itself. For the very first thing we always do, as unstoppably as though driven by an inborn reflex or by second nature, is cast some kind of light, however dim, on everything we approach, thereby pushing darkness itself, and with it the deep sense of the unknowability of all things, out of sight. The Voice from the Whirlwind goes on like this, showering Job with unanswerable questions. It is as though he were presented with a series of koans, those mystery riddles from Zen Buddhism that are presented as unsolvable puzzles, impossible paradoxes, and bizarre conundrums of every sort. They serve as focus for years of contemplation, working as a purgative for all false knowledge, and for every false sense of self. "Have you seen where the snow is stored?" asks the Voice. "Where is the west wind released and the east wind set down to earth?" "Who cuts a path for the thunderstorm?" These deceptively naive questions—the kind that takes a child or a god to ask—restore elementary facts of existence to their stunning miraculousness. Or there are these unanswerables: "Does the rain have a father? Who has begotten the dew?" Images such as these restore a human mind to its innate capacity for speechless wonder, which is quite possibly the most deeply human of experiences. There are humbling reminders as well that put everyone in his or her place: "If you clap for the bolts of lightning, will they come and say 'Here we are'? . . . Do you show the hawk how to fly?" These and similar reminders of the genius in even an ordinary weekday serve to break the defensive shell of hardened beliefs, of set knowledge, of established wisdom. For the longest time in any human life, and in many lives for the greatest number of years, if not all of them, this defensiveness is virtually its own objective and goal. Yet breaking this shell is necessary in order to reveal the stunning display of miraculousness that is immanent in all things.

Just over one hundred years ago, unconsciousness, as we now imagine it, still had to be discovered and its treatment invented. Today, most adults in the Western world, and even many older children, know about it. The very notion has almost become old hat. Its basic working principles are known to millions. It probably would be difficult to find someone who is not at least minimally familiar with the idea. This development itself is in some ways paradoxical. After all, unconsciousness is, by definition, unconscious. That means it is, in the first place, unknown. Whatever happened to the original sense of speechless awe that must have filled the early psychoanalysts and their patients, who jointly discovered the modern unconscious and who, in the process, invented psychotherapy? We may have become too familiar with at least some of the secrets of the unconscious life of the soul to imagine what those first psychoanalytic witnesses must have felt and thought. We may perhaps have become just a little too self-congratulatory in our cleverness about the unconscious life of the soul. Paradoxically, our proudly acquired and sometimes self-assured knowledge about it has, to some extent, become self-defeating—precisely because the sense of knowledge undoes the original aura of unknownness that gave to the idea of unconsciousness its relevance in the first place. Our dealings with unconsciousness now often have the quality of a surprise party that does not come as a surprise at all anymore. Often the encounter with unconsciousness seems almost to have been anticipated, sometimes even with a sense of boredom. Psychological treaters in particular can easily be overcome by a sense of having seen it all. The mood of stunned and admiring discovery that formerly accompanied the occasions on which a glimpse of the unconscious life of soul could be seen has in many instances changed and become blunted, flattened. From an experience of awe, we have gone to one of blah—in less than a century. Sophocles' and Freud's awe at the drama of "Oedipus Rex" has been replaced by Woody Allen's flippant "Oedipus Wrecks." Thus do old gods often die. They simply lose their luster of godliness, due to prolonged exposure. Eventually their feet of clay crumble, until they are finally and easily pushed over by the first ill wind that blows their way. Or they fall at the first defiant hand that would knock them off their pedestal. And then word spreads that some old god or other is dead.

A common and understandable misunderstanding has it that treating unconsciousness must mean making the unknown known. It usually is thought to mean that forgotten memories must be recalled—or recurring unconscious thought patterns exposed, repressed wishes brought to light, ancient and long-buried traumas uncovered, things put away in the past dug up, personal idiosyncrasies dragged out of the closet, and any and all other hidden secrets revealed. In Freud's prescriptive formula, which for many has become depth psychology's categorical imperative: "Where unconsciousness is, there consciousness shall be." The depressions from the winters of our discontent must be treated with the mania of spring cleaning. This inherently grandiose agenda of making unconsciousness conscious may once have been right, when the psychoanalytic sense of unconsciousness was first being discovered. Today, however, hundred years later, and precisely because we have virtually lost the sense of unconsciousness itself, it has in some important ways become potentially dead wrong. Today it would seem that, in many ways, we need more of a sense of unconsciousness, not less. That does not mean we have to become once again more unconscious. Nor does it mean that we should throw out all psychotherapy that is aimed at developing more insight into oneself. It means that we need to rediscover a sense for the quality and substance of unconsciousness itself. If the idea of an unconscious life of soul is to retain relevance, and if the practice of its treatment is to retain significance and potency, then we must, like Job, rediscover unknownness itself. If necessary—and there is much about accepted contemporary psychology to suggest that it has become necessary—*we must rediscover unconsciousness by reinventing it.* That means reactivating the imagination that can imagine, and reimagine, unknownness itself. That way we can once again, and like Job, begin to see where unknownness hides everywhere in plain view, in this endless parade of events that creation puts on every day and that we know as everyday life.

Unknownness does not merely refer to absence of knowledge. It is no simple negative that is derived from a positive. Unknownness itself is a positive datum, one that needs to be experienced and, yes, known on its own terms and in its own right. What is needed for this is a reversal in emphasis. It requires an approach that stresses the awe-inspiring or "awe-full" unknownness in everything, instead of emphasizing only our awesome knowledge and know-how about it.

The point of the questions about creation Job hears in the Voice from the Whirlwind is not that he, or anyone else, should be able to answer them or even try to answer them. The point is that they show things that can only be seen when the protective box of human knowledge that closes in human experience is removed. That way the scope of human experience can become equal to the scope of the universe itself. And that way the individual's sense of soul expands to its true size, which is that of the world soul, the *anima mundi*. Once again, we come upon what Jung said, that the greater part of the soul exists outside the body. This is by no means an Eastern turn of mind. Nor is it a turn of mind designed for Westerners who, in despair and angry disillusionment, want to turn away from the West's own traditions of thought. It is not about gazing far away, because the philosophical and psychological grass is believed to be greener on the other side of the fence that keeps us where we are. On the contrary. Looking for the unknownness in everyday life is as thoroughly Western as Platonism, and as all that is derived from it. It is a turn of mind familiar to the Neoplatonist writers of past ages, who had a different attitude than we do today toward the unknownness, the unconsciousness, in all things. Not surprisingly, they also had a different method for treating it. They were psychotherapists of a different breed. Their formula for approaching the unknownness in all things was *ignotum per ignotius* or, nearly identically, *obscurum per obscurius*, meaning, "the unknown (or the obscure) through the even more unknown (or more obscure)." The idea is to approach the unknownness or unconsciousness in all situations with notions and images about things that are themselves fundamentally and explicitly unknowable. "The unknown through the more unknown" does the opposite of combating the unknownness in a given matter by imposing on it beliefs about things presumed known. It is precisely about making more room, not less, for the sense of the unknownness in all matters. It aims at resisting the temptation to colonize the territory of the undiscovered with familiar ideas and habits of thinking that would imperialistically impose themselves on everything and everybody. Today, after a century of Freud's "Where the unconscious is there consciousness shall be," we are in the paradoxical situation where, in many respects, the best treatment for the soul is to cultivate not only more consciousness but also, simultaneously, a more differentiated and more sophisticated sense of unknownness.

Patients are in danger of being ill served from the moment when their treaters, and they themselves, begin to believe that they know what is wrong with them—and this not only because of the obvious problem of carelessness due to excessive confidence or haste. Much of what is wrong with patients who enter psychological treatment is that they have become all too well and all too rigidly known—not only to themselves and those around them but perhaps especially to therapeutic psychology itself. Much of what can go wrong with patients today is that, to the extent that treatment theory and practice know them all too well, treater and treated alike may have lost the sense for the mystery and miracle in the patient's life. The potentially catastrophic price that both patient and therapist may have to pay for this is a massive loss of an imagination for the positive quality of fundamental unknownness about the life under analysis. A voice from a whirlwind is needed to restore to treater and treated alike a sense of unknownness and a sense for the unknowable. True soul treatment in any life begins by reintroducing a sense of unknownness about that life, about everything in it that has become all too familiar. It requires that the treater becomes the one who, from first to last, does not know. The treater must bring to the treatment an expertise in the matter of unknownness and unknowability. He or she must become capable of tolerating and of being inspired by a Joban whirlwind of seemingly naive but truly stunning questions. This is not easy. As psychoanalysts might put it, after the manner in which they like to characterize their profession, it is not only impossible, it is also very difficult. Rediscovering a sense of the unknownness in things presumed known about a person's life requires more than self-proclaimed open-mindedness and lack of social prejudice. And more is required than the undifferentiated innocence that ignores the precise ways things are because, at heart, it has a blind eye for the mystery in all things and no stomach for the polymorphous imagination that governs them. Ineptitude for developing a sense of unknownness betrays itself less as lack of knowledge or as naivete than as lack of ability to see anything miraculous anywhere. The ability to see and tolerate unknownness requires, above all, the capacity to feel and tolerate awe and uncertainty in a universe in which the only certainties are one's own ignorance and one's vulnerability. In the end, the capacity to recognize and tolerate unknownness matters more, and requires more, than all acquired knowledge. And all acquired knowledge must ultimately become subservient to that capacity. If a discerning, well-educated, and well-trained mind serves any purpose here, it is in its ability to become open to the vulnerability of awe-filled ignorance. Paradoxically, psychological education, training, and study serve here less to add new information to an endlessly growing body of established knowledge than to add a new sense of depth and riches to the endless differentiation of unknownness.

How can psychological treaters and their patients develop this skill of recognizing and tolerating the unknownness in their collaborative work? First of all, and as in the case of Job, who dismisses his all-knowing friends who claim to be able to explain his misery, by exposing and abandoning all sense of familiar and overlearned knowledge. That includes looking once again, as though for the first time, at the matter at hand. All the variations on what is essentially a theme of "Everybody knows we all have to have an Oedipus complex (or fear of loneliness, ambivalence, or whatever), so here's yours"—all these have to go. Instead, treater and patient alike must work in the opposite direction. They must move not from the disquiet of something that is truly unknown toward familiar and established, if not formulaic, knowledge. Instead, they must practice the rule of going from the unknown toward the utterly unknown and the absolutely unknowable. They can do so by looking for whirlwinds of not-knowing. The simplest, though anything but easy, way—and as Hillman notes, the most therapeutic one in the treatment of the soul's matters—is through interest. Interest involves genuine respect. That, as Hillman also points out, implies "re-specting." This "re-specting" is the same thing as eternally returning to look again and again at something presumed known, and beginning to see more and more in it the longer and deeper one looks. Here one refuses to stop at any one particular thing known or seen, or at any aspect of it that can be pointed at. Instead, one always goes farther, to add more and to develop a deeper sense of its intrinsic depth of significance. No knowledge is dismissed, but none is considered final. Bottom-line knowledge becomes impossible because, as Heraclitus said, the primordial characteristic of the soul is its bottomless depth. One goes beyond every mode, manner, and act of knowing, one goes ever farther and deeper than anything that becomes known. Here it is knowledge itself, not unknownness or unconsciousness, that is considered the malaise, the illness, the thing that needs treatment. True knowing about the life of the soul ends whenever psychological insight is assumed achieved and established.

(As an aside that is perhaps needed to keep archetypal psychology from being confused with other and more widely known traditions of thought on this point, it almost seems as though we are entering the neighborhood of Buddhism here and of its insistent "not quite this, not quite that" about all humanly possible insight. But the resemblance is superficial, for Buddha aimed at a state of emptiness and detachment from the ordinary world, whereas Job and archetypal psychology are precisely about being filled with a sense of miracle and mystery that is everywhere present in the world, on any given day. Job and archetypal psychology are about embracing the world and everything of the world *again*—as Nietzsche's demon of eternal return says, "once more and innumerable times more"—over and above and in spite of all the pain and suffering that come from such embracing attachment, and which Buddha would escape.)

The kind of treatment needed to cure us, where necessary, of psychological knowledge that represses unknownness itself moves, not surprisingly, in a contrarian direction. It abandons Freud's directive that "Where the unconscious is there consciousness shall be." In its place it introduces the more alchemically oppositional reflex to go against everything that is so familiar and usual as to seem natural because, by sheer force of habit, we have turned it into second nature. This approach offers, contra Freud, a categorical imperative that says something like "Where accepted knowledge exists, or is assumed, there a sense for unknownness shall have to be reintroduced." Here all insight-oriented psychotherapy that is derived from psychoanalysis may well stop being regarded as the treatment of choice, as originally promised and as often still held. The potential overvaluation of insight itself, and especially the endless and often self-absorbed obsessive pursuit of it, sometimes largely out of sheer and mere habit, may to some extent need to be diagnosed as something of an iatrogenic condition. At the very least, a continuing pursuit of insight therapy may need to be reimagined with a new insight. The new insight is that insight therapy, even insight itself, can become its own worst enemy. Such a situation can be prevented if insight can be reimagined to mean not only more understanding or clearer knowledge but also never-ending, always inconclusive, forever unfinished "in-sighting" through endless "re-specting." Only then do the sights that can be seen through insight become what they truly are—magnificent sights to behold. This is something vastly different from, and something vastly more satisfying than, mere hindsight about a moral economy whose acts can and will be held against us by the likes of Job's all-knowing and accusing friends.

Unknownness itself is no unknown. It is an essential and positive idea in all major religions, in all mystical traditions past and present, in all history of philosophy. Not surprisingly, unknownness has its own, and well-known, archetypal representations. In the biblical tradition of the Judeo-Christian West, the essential unknowableness in all things, the fundamentally unnamable ground of all Being, is represented by the tetragrammaton YHWH. This unpronounceable Hebrew four-letter word—the original unspeakable "four-letter word"—consists of four consonants without pronunciation symbols. The deliberate omission of pronunciation symbols keeps it unspeakable. This safeguards the mystery of Being from being inadequately named, from being expressed in ways that fail to do it justice. The etymological root of the tetragrammaton YHWH is associated with the verb *hawah* or *hajah*, meaning "to be." This has been related to the scriptural "I am," and thus to the metaphysical idea of "He is" or "He who is"—Being itself, Being in its most absolute sense. Historical data about related words suggest that YHWH lends itself to being pronounced as "Jaweh" or "Yahwe." Hence, the "Yahweh" of modern usage. The insistence that the ground of Being should be identified by an indecipherable cipher, a cipher that is deliberately kept unspeakable because it is too full of mystery, serves to reflect a reality that is unidentifiable because it is unnamable, meaning unknowable. Put in traditional philosophical language, historical beings are phenomenal or concrete and visible, but Being itself, the ground of all beings, cannot be named by any noumenon, any definitive name that identifies it in absolute, objectifiable terms.

These are not merely abstract matters that are relevant only to specialists. Nor are they strictly religious matters reserved for the devout, or esoteric and perhaps mystical ones accessible only to the initiated. They are as ordinary as everyday life in the workaday world itself. For as every person, speaking from his or her loneliest loneliness, eventually puts it, in a universal and true complaint about the fundamental unknowableness of his or her plight and of the human condition itself and in fact of anything at all, "You just don't understand. Nobody understands." That means none of the terms used in any psychological theory or by any well-meaning comforter, by any commentator on any human life or on the human condition itself, is ever adequate to name anyone's experience. The complaint that "Nobody understands" is legitimate, for who can really name any human experience or any human life by its rightful name? Who can say everything about it that can be said about it, everything that ought to be said about it to do it justice? As Socrates put the case, for all the West's history to come, it would take a long tale to tell the whole story, and surely a god alone could tell it. All we humans can ever manage to do is suggest images that allow us to allude to what it is like.

The idea and practice of regarding all things as "archetypal"—in a strictly adjectival sense, without speaking of "archetypes" and mistaking them for objectifiable and namable things to be designated by a noun—this idea and practice belong in the same tradition of using language itself to guard against language. They serve to guard against the creation of inadequate names and against the derivation of false beliefs that are based on them and named after them. Just as the tetragrammaton YHWH has a built-in safeguard against being mistaken for something pronounceable, namable, identifiable, or objectifiable, so too does the habit of designating all things "archetypal," without positing objectifiable "archetypes," guard against turning metaphor into metaphysics. Thus, perhaps surprisingly, *archetypal psychology itself, even more adamantly so than its critics, refuses to believe in archetypes.* Nowhere is this more the case than in the habit of representing archetypal patterns of experience in the form of images of mythic gods and demigods. Even though there are many situations that serve as reminders, and as manifestations, of these mythic realities that endlessly return to reenact their dramas in Everyman's daily life, the bottom-line truths about these figures are as elusive as the variations on their themes are endless. Yet all the same—and this is part of archetypal psychology's endless balancing act—without concrete incarnations, those same gods and demigods would be nothing.

A god wears whatever mask suits the occasion where he makes his presence felt. He keeps on finding ever-more suitable masks, in ever-new renditions of his eternally repeated tale. He never shows himself without such a mask. Nor would he, should he, or could he. Along similar lines, those well-documented human experiences that world literature hands down as descriptions of religious, philosophical, mystical, or other authentic revelations are forever depicted in the form of likenesses—resemblances, metaphors, analogies, allegories, parables, visions, dreams, epiphanies. They are never presented as bare essences without mask that can be described or defined in some absolute way. If the root word "persona" in the word "personification" means the mask that ancient actors wore to represent gods and demigods on stage, so that all would recognize them, then it is because representing, designating, recounting anything always involves such masks. A mask is not only something that presents visible and recognizable features and shapes. It also gives to all things represented—to all things present—an unfathomable depth of essence that can only appear as appearance. Masks transform mere appearance into sheer appearance. But just as a mask reveals, so too does it conceal. The persona the actor wears and the personifications of mythic motifs in the form of personified gods and demigods serve up a dual issue, a double presence, a two-faced face. They suggest that in addition to what can be seen and pointed at on stage, or in any setting, there also is a concealed dimension, a hidden depth that is unfathomable, and, to that extent, invisible or unknowable. That hidden dimension of every mask serves up endlessly new concrete features and manifestations of the archetypal theme at hand. By doing just that, without ever stopping by reaching bottom or by running out of new incarnations, it prevents anything that can be seen, pointed at, or said concerning any matter from being the definitive and final word, the bottom-line conclusion. In this respect, the notion of the Greek persona serves the same purpose as the Judeo-Christian cipher YHWH. Each serves to indicate that we are in the presence of mystery, and that mystery is inherent wherever we are, in whatever we are looking at. But each also suggests that the human terms with which we indicate that presence are not the full story, because that story can never be fully told.

Archetypal psychology is no stranger to this tradition of pointing to more than can ever be pointed at. An archetypal approach to practicing psychology speaks about more than the usual nominalist definitions of the terms it employs to talk about any given matter. Those usual definitions are not regarded as any kind of last and definitive word, and they are not accepted as decisive argument about anything. Rather, they are viewed as serving up images that, like all images, generate ever more images, and they never stop generating an endless parade of images. Just as a metaphor can only be explained by introducing ever more metaphors to do the explaining—which is itself an everyday case in point of getting to know the unknown through the more unknown or through more of the unknowable—so too does the archetypal way of viewing all things generate ever more views to behold and viewpoints to hold, or rather to be held by. An archetypal way of viewing the world looks at it as a stage filled with personas through which mythic motifs are spelled out. It sees in all matters ever so many scenes in which fantastic beings voice their legendary minds and tell their fabulous tales and truths. Every situation thereby becomes a mask that simultaneously reveals and conceals. Every circumstance turns into a dramatic stage on which unnamable beings play out their scenarios. The mask that everything becomes in this fashion is the specific form through which the situation at hand speaks about more than what we ordinarily associate with it. But again, it must be emphasized that this "more" than what is ordinarily associated with anything is still and always part of it. It is no metaphysically "other" reality that is external to it and that belongs to another category of things or to another event or experience. Rather, it is the unfathomable depth of Being that is immanent in all things. The persona or mask that everything is makes of every circumstance an opportunity to see in all things a glimpse of what Job discovers when the Voice from the Whirlwind points to some of the finer points of creation.

In the tradition of the Judeo-Christian West, the unspeakable tetragrammaton YHWH was made pronounceable, and its mystery was, at least to a certain extent, made speakable by an act of imagination. This consisted of adding to the four consonants a set of vowel signs and suggesting that instead of having to be stumped and silenced by an indecipherable sign, the reader could read the familiar word *Adonai*, meaning "Lord." Imagination thus made it possible to give at least something of a name to the unnamable, even while also still realizing that nothing about it was thereby definitively named, and to make some of the mystery in it somewhat imaginable. Later, however, in the medieval and derivative "Jehovah," translators of the Hebrew texts ignored the fact that the vowel signs were only human conveniences, added for the sake of making the unspeakable capable of being alluded to by human language and in human discourse. Disregarding the fact that the vowel signs were by themselves no intrinsic part of the unnamable name itself, they took, and mistook, "Jehovah" for the rightful name of Being itself. The challenge of walking the thin line between making YHWH—or any religious, philosophical, mystical, or psychological equivalent—speakable in everyday language, yet without mistaking anything thus spoken for the thing itself, remains a constant theme of human self-awareness. It is an original and permanent part of the conundrum of what it means to be human. It comes therefore as no surprise that psychology too has had to find a way to deal with it, and that it will never be done with having to deal with it. The entire field of psychology, whose subject matter of soul is itself an undefinable something made of ingredients that are elusive—and some say, in part, divine—this entire field is one elaborate variation on that theme. Psychology's subject matter, the soul's subtle substance, is everywhere in the air, more so than any other matter that concerns us as human beings, yet it is always intangible, and always other than anything we can point at or put our finger on. It is present in all things said, yet it is identifiable with none of the things spoken. It is alluded to in all things named but captured by no single name or noun—by no single theory and no one school of treatment. Authentic psychology, which is psychology that tries to know soul on its own terms, has to be a conscious and self-conscious enactment of this theme. This is a matter not only for theoretical or philosophical psychologists. Nor is it an issue only for academic psychologists or clinical psychologists with a theoretical and philosophical bent. It is an issue that matters to Everyman, for Everyman is, and must be, a psychologist. He must have his own theories about soul, and his own practices for handling matters of soul. No one can name the facts of soul or soul itself by their definitive name. Yet no one is exempt from having to decipher the signs, the symbols, the cryptic inscriptions of soul that are everywhere and that point to soul as the ground and substance of everyday life. For soul is the great indecipherable and unspeakable cipher of significance or value that is everywhere embedded in the text of the world's history, and of Everyman's every moment in it.

Freud taught us to think archetypally, in an adverbial way, so that we may learn to think truly psychologically. We should resist the temptation of taking the adjectival views we have on the life of the soul for the outlines of hard facts about it that can be contained in nouns. We should not mistake our psychological findings, and the declarations they inspire us to make, for definitive findings and for statements of fact. Rather, we should keep regarding the ground of all facts in the realm of soul as fundamentally unspeakable by any of the names we may give it. Let us give up on the hubris of wanting to name any kind of final and definitive psychological formula, one that would serve as our theory of everything in the life of soul, as theoretical physicists hope to do in their field. Let us, rather, stick to the smaller goal and the humbler practice of imagining ways that help us talk about something that is undefinable, yet whose story would be a shame not to try to tell ourselves as best we can. Let us remember the humility that is personified in Shakespeare's Bottom, from *A Midsummer Night's Dream*, and that speaks for Everyman:

> I have had a most rare vision. I have had a dream, past the wit of man to say what dream it was. Man is but an ass, if he go about to expound this dream. Methought I was—there is no man can tell what. Methought I was, and methought I had—But man is but a patched fool if he will offer to say what methought I had. The eye of man hath not heard, the ear of man hath not seen, man's hand is not able to taste, his tongue to conceive, nor his heart to report what my dream was. I will get Peter Quince to write a ballet [a ballad] of this dream. It shall be called "Bottom's Dream," because it hath no bottom; and I will sing it.

One way to make the text of the soul that everyday life is at least somewhat speakable, in a manner that also does justice to its inherently unspeakable mystery, is by, as in the case of the tetragrammaton YHWH, looking for the equivalent of pronunciation signs in it. These pronunciation signs in the text of everyday life are the images and metaphors that all things are. They may not definitively name the unnamable soul factor that inheres everywhere, but like a mask that a god wears on the world stage, they articulate some of its features. "YHWH" does not really mean or even sound like "Adonai," "Lord." Yet if we look at it a certain way, and if we articulate it accordingly, then it does make sense to speak of "Adonai" or "Lord." A similar strategy is good practice for psychology, and that is precisely what happens when, as Freud first did, we try to think and talk archetypally, so that the life of the soul may appear in its archetypal features. By looking at the textual data that any given event is for the inherent images that make the matter at hand imaginable, we make the otherwise unpronounceable soul substance accessible to human language and discourse. That way the stuff of everyday life becomes itself imaginable as the endlessly miraculous substance it is. It is no accident that so much in the history of practical depth psychology has depended on such vowel equivalents as the methods of free association in Freud, of word associations and active imagination in Jung, and of sticking to the image in Hillman. Every time a psychotherapist today asks a patient, in connection with an experience that leaves the person speechless because he or she cannot articulate it or talk about it, "Does this remind you of anything?," the patient is being encouraged to look for vowel signs in the matter at hand. That way, the patient hopefully can begin to make the otherwise unspeakable and unimaginable experiences of that life accessible to being spoken. This is today's mundane, but no less exegetical, method for making the unspeakable consonants of a personalized tetragrammaton accessible to human talk. It is, after all, the discipline that defines itself as a "logos" of "psyche" that proposes to treat the unspeakable unknownness of soul, or what we have been calling "unconsciousness" after all the vowel signs we have added to the name of "soul," by means of a talking cure. It also is no accident that, as Freud suggested at the end of his life, psychological analysis is, and has to be, interminable. No matter which vowel signs, or how many, we see in the soul's own textbook we call "Everyday Life," and whatever we may say about what we read there, no matter how we read it or interpret it, there is no final, last, definitive, all-encompassing word. Like Bottom's dream, every psychological event is bottomless. To think otherwise is to be, as he says, a "patched fool."

TWELVE

EVERYMAN'S OWN DOUBLE

"A LIFE IS JUDGED by the suicide it commits." So writes Richard Klein, in *Cigarettes Are Sublime*, a book that goes against the tide of political correctness by praising the virtues of cigarette smoking. But Klein's remark is neither about deliberate suicides nor about death-defying acts. It is about the proposition that the subtle pleasures of cigarette smoking may in some cases perhaps outweigh the pursuit of longevity and good health for their own sake. Whether the argument is persuasive is debatable, but that is not what matters here. What does matter is that Klein's remark becomes poignantly relevant not when taken literally, as he means it, but when it is viewed as a statement about something other than literal, physical death.

The thought that a life is judged by the suicide it commits captures a profound paradox at the heart of the human condition. But in order to see this paradox in its full scope, we must look beyond the notion of identifiable pleasures, which are the subject of Klein's book. Fortunately for us, we have a pair of sturdy shoulders to stand on as well as a guide to teach us how to look—which not only has to be in the right direction but also in the right way. But first the reader should perhaps be given a bit of advance notice about the view to which this is leading. That view is the paradox that in the life of the soul, death does not oppose life but safeguards it—all life long. This paradox only comes into clearer view when we shift perspective, from seeing death as a physical fact of nature to recognizing it as a mythic one of the soul. This change in perspective requires shifting attention from the hard facts of history to the subtle and purely psychic ones underlying them. For in the view that is at stake here, death is an ever-present and living but purely psychic, and always intangible, elusive factor that accompanies life at every turn. It is a factor that gives every life its final shape—not its terminal one at the end of its days but, rather, its defining one throughout all the days before that, and in all the events that take place in it. It is a kind of intangible still life that inheres in all the situations and features that every life develops over all the years of its entire duration. Yet this chronic and subtle presence of death in the midst of life, at every moment in it, is not simply about thoughts of the end of life being somehow on everyone's mind at all times, whether consciously or unconsciously. It is not about such things as an omnipresent fear of death—or about the denial of it, the obsession with it, the anticipated grief over it, or the endless struggle for the postponement of it. The subtle death or the subtle sense of death that is at stake here is none of these. It is about sensing the facts of life, precisely as they are, but minus the usual notions about the physicality of nature. It is, to use Ovid's way of putting it, in referring to the underworld of the soul over which Hades presides, and as Hillman writes in *The Dream and the Underworld*, about all of life exactly as in life but minus the body, the blood, and the bones. It is about what is left over when the paradigm of the literal *physis* or physicality of existence is subtracted from the way we think about it. But—and this cannot be said quickly and emphatically enough—this is not for the sake of a denial of physis or physicality. It is, instead, for the sake of overcoming the literalism in the usual ways of thinking about physis. It is to see and reach beyond the literalism that, as modern man's habitual way of thinking, tends to become second nature, in the same way that every persuasive metaphor tends to become a metaphysics.

What is left over when literalism about the physicality of existence is subtracted from the usual ways of thinking? What can there be left to think about? What remains are the images of what, in the first of these twelve chapters, was proposed as the injudicability of all things and events. What is left is the precisely formed yet intangible substance that gives to each thing its purely psychic essence. That psychic essence of every thing is the sense of its intrinsic value, its significance, its importance. What is left over and what is left to think about is the intrinsic and self-defining standard that is built into each thing, and that is the only standard that is good enough, but also the only standard that is needed, to judge each thing. Not surprisingly, and as with what is designated by the words "soul" and "archetypal," this subtle "injudicability" that is the essence of each thing has to be imagined before, and *so that*, anything can become known or said about it.

Cigarette smoking, so Klein argues, is more than simply a bad habit the surgeon general has declared hazardous to your health. It also is a complex phenomenon that involves a multitude of layers of potential significance. It has, for example, behavioral implications that have to do with the instinctual act of sucking, as well as symbolic implications that have to do with the idea of extracting a subtle essence from something in order to incorporate it into one's own being. It has biological and developmental implications involving the gratification of oral needs. It has both soothing properties and stimulating properties. It has political implications about such things as the different roles different groups of people play and the different behaviors they display. It has aesthetic properties, and it can play a role in shaping all sorts of mannerisms. The list goes on. Of course, it also kills.

Cigarettes thus being, as Freud might say, as overdetermined in their value as they are, they can therefore not be easily given up without unleashing great forces of resistance. That struggle is not only, and not even principally, with feelings of ambivalence about something that is both good and bad—pleasurable but unhealthy, life enhancing yet death dealing. The potential value that cigarettes hold is not really "ambi-valent" or "two-valued," with those two values simply and straightforwardly opposing each other. It is truly polyvalent. It cannot be adequately evaluated by a one-liner from the surgeon general printed on the side of cigarette packages, no matter how reasonable and correct that one-liner is. Writes Klein:

> If cigarette smoking were not also good for you, so many good people would not have spent some part of their lives doing them uninterruptedly. . . . One thinks of the many great men and women who have died prematurely from having smoked too much: it does them an injustice to suppose that their greatness did not depend in some degree on the wisdom and pleasure and spiritual benefit they took in a habit they could not abandon. . . . Healthism has sought to make longevity the principal measure of a good life. . . . But another view, a dandy's perhaps, would say that living, as distinct from surviving, acquires its value from risks and sacrifices that tend to shorten life and hasten dying. A life, in that view, is judged by the suicide it commits.

But Klein, even though he is perhaps looking in the right direction to better appreciate the psychological complexities of a seemingly simple act, does not look at the matter in the right way. He does not see far enough or deeply enough, because he is looking too literally. His own main point becomes more valuable when it is taken to its own inherent, but more subtle, conclusions. The suicide that is built into a life is not simply, nor even most importantly, about something that threatens to "shorten life and hasten dying," as Klein suggests. It is about something that involves the very essence of that life, its psychic definition, the living substance that animates it. In order to see this aspect of what is at stake, we must look farther and deeper than the identifiable and objectifiable pleasures that cigarette smoking gives. As another compulsive smoker put it, also in the title of one of his books—even though this one is not about smoking— in order to see the subtle death factor in life, we must look *Beyond the Pleasure Principle*. Freud's book of that title is, like Klein's book, about compulsive habits, many of which are unhealthy or otherwise self-defeating. They involve complex matters that, like cigarette smoking, are at once biological, psychological, social, cultural, literary, aesthetic, symbolic, and philosophical in their implications. And Freud's book, like Klein's, is deliberately and self-consciously provocative, even within its own and otherwise not so easily shocked field of psychoanalysis. Its most provocative thesis is about *a connection between life and death that exists in life as it is lived, at every moment in it, not just as it comes to an end*. *Beyond the Pleasure Principle* is the place and occasion in the mythic world of psychoanalysis where Freud proposed the idea that, right alongside the forces that make up the sound and the fury and the clamor of life's visible drama, there also is a silent, hidden, invisible, unconscious force *that strives toward death*. In keeping with the psychoanalytic tradition of naming the facts of life after the fictions of myth, because they resemble each other so much, this force eventually was called Thanatos, after the god of Death, who also is called Hades.

Death, in Freud's view, is not something that is external to life and imposed on it from the outside, as Spinoza had held. It is something that is, from the beginning, woven into the fabric of life. Or Death, so Freud proposed, is something that coexists with life at all times—at all points, in all events, at every moment of life, and throughout its entire duration. It coexists with life as the underworldly Hades coexists at all times with his upperworldly brother, Zeus. But Freud went even farther. He proposed that every life strives continuously, at every turn and throughout the entire length of its duration, to achieve exactly its own precisely defined death, and none other. As though to drive the radicalism of his point home, Freud spelled out what this view means for an understanding of biological evolution. As this biological evolution took its course, over its long history, so he suggested, dying became increasingly difficult. At first, when life-forms were simple, dying was easy. But as new life-forms developed, they became more complex. This also made it increasingly difficult for them to achieve their own unique death. Hence, so Freud suggested, all of life developed into an ever-more complicated but nonetheless always circuitous path to reach just the death that fits each particular case, and none other.

The paradox that Klein sees in cigarette smoking is somewhat similar to what Freud had in mind with his hypothesis of a death instinct, but the similarity only goes so far. Klein never reaches the point of seeing, as Freud did, that death is at bottom a purely mythic and psychic factor in and throughout life, not merely a biological and terminal one at the end of it. What Klein shares with Freud is the view that life is about developing and clinging to personal habits that may eventually and cumulatively kill one but that, at the same time, give life its unique shape. But for Freud this is not merely a secondary phenomenon, as it appears to be for Klein. In Freud's view, it is about far more than giving each life its unique and identifiable but still only secondary characteristics. For him, death itself is a primary principle, on a par with all that promotes life in life. Hence, his radically new model of a lifelong and equal partnership between the clamoring, easily identifiable life forces and a silent, invisible, mythic, subtle, intangible death factor that is devoted to fulfilling each life's own destiny, and none other. Freud's idea of a death factor in life leaps therefore far beyond the kind of thinking of which Klein's is a typical example. It achieves its full scope of significance by abandoning the long-held principle that every life takes on the shape it does largely because it is, before anything else, a pursuit of pleasure, of the gratification of needs and wants through the reduction of unpleasure. Freud therefore proposed the radically new notion that a life's true fulfillment does not lie in the pursuit of pleasure, as he too had previously held when he made the "pleasure principle" into the supreme psychoanalytic law. In his revised view, he suggested that the soul's deepest desire and happiness lie in a lifelong devotion to a good and unique death, one that takes a whole lifetime to achieve and that is brought about by a carefully selected and personally crafted lifelong suicide. Not surprisingly, even psychoanalysts—especially psychoanalysts, for whom the pleasure principle was received constitutional law—were taken aback.

When Freud was transposed to the English-speaking world, his psychology of Thanatos, or Hades, who in myth requires a transition across waters separating life's upperworld from its underworld, never quite made it across the English Channel and the Atlantic Ocean. Psychoanalysis and derived psychotherapies in the English-speaking world have had little use for a psychology with Freud's death instinct built right into it, at its very center. Even today in America, perhaps especially today in America, psychotherapists tend to have little theory for, and less practice in, dealing with the notion of a death instinct, or with Thanatos and Hades. Death is dealt with only when it means literal death or destructiveness and loss or variations thereof. Psychotherapy on American soil has made itself a part of the life sciences, the health sciences. Death in American psychology—whether academic, clinical, or popular—tends to be almost exclusively equated with the physical end of life or with damage done to life. There is little room for the notion of death as a purely mythic and psychic dimension of everyday life. Even the notion of "underworld" no longer means anything involving the subtleties of Thanatos or Hades. It no longer evokes a sense about a realm where the soul has its own home base in an image-filled world. "Underworld" today means death in the street, and death projected on the silver screen in the endless sagas of endlessly repetitive physical violence that feed on a paranoid lack of imagination. "Underworld" means death as crime and criminal, death as a social plague of excessive and gratuitous violence. On the whole, in American popular culture and popular psychology, death means poor physical health in extremis. And in the modern world of advanced medical technologies, death means the triumph of disease. It is the last engineering challenge, as well as the final insult that will no longer be tolerated and passively accepted. On behalf of the life of the soul, one may ask: Where does the subtle spirit of Hades or Thanatos find a place today in Everyday Life? Where is there room for a psychic underworld? But back to Freud.

From Freud's Thanatos point of view, death is not simply life's great opposite, the force that makes it come apart. Quite the opposite. It is what makes a life hang together. Yet it is not some invisible and magical master mind that belongs outside the events and facts of a life. It is what links a life's seemingly separate parts, events, and accidents into patterns of significance that stretch out over a whole lifetime. It also is what gives to each part itself, to each separate moment, its own intrinsic value. For in the myth of Hades, the underworld is not merely a kind of department of registration, where only one identifying picture is kept of each life. Rather, each bit of life, every moment, is worth a picture to Hades. This makes his realm a place of truly endless still life meditations on each thing and on each life. The Hades spirit of endlessly imaginative valuation is enacted in Monet's repetitive work. Perhaps even more recognizably so, it is what animates Andrew Wyeth's more than two hundred paintings of the same figure of Helga. What is at stake here is a devotion to the endlessly detailed self-definition and beauty of one human figure. Wyeth's Helga paintings are a case of making the reality of Thanatos or Hades visible right in the middle of upperworldly life under the sun. They are a case of showing how everyday life contains a built-in drive and capacity toward self-perception. But this is less about any kind of personal self-image or self-regard than it is about mythically based proprioception—Hades living alongside Zeus at all times. Wyeth's Helga paintings are a case of subtle and Hades-based self-assessment that is present right in the midst of all things. This kind of imaginative proprioception does not come afterward—in retrospect, with hindsight, or at the end of it all. It is built into everything as it is, in everything as usual. It is everything just as it is, but sensed differently—subtly, with a feeling for the wealth of still lives in it that are worth noting. Judging a life, from this point of view, is about walking through the day, any day, with a deeper sense for the picture-perfect and precise details of every moment and situation. Assessing a life with a Hades mind-set is about sensing the defining features and patterns that are woven into it, and that make it what it is and nothing else. It is about seeing that all the seemingly fragmented events and experiences that make up a life's history are the thread with which these features and patterns are woven.

We come back here, once again, to Zarathustra. For picking up the threads of a life and developing this subtle sense that everything is precisely as it should be is exactly what Zarathustra does when, in his moment of sudden insight, he says to himself, "The time is gone when mere accidents could still happen to me; and what could still come to me that was not mine already? Whatever returns to me, whatever finally comes home to me, is my own self and whatever of myself has long been in strange lands and scattered among all things and accidents." Zarathustra's discovery is, as suggested in earlier chapters, about more than a personal inner self. Now we also can see it as a discovery of the invisible and underworldly Hades, who presides over the destiny of all souls and over the soul factor in all things. It is about sensing the reality of his boneless realm in one's own very bones. It is, above all, about developing a sense of good faith that for everything that is, and for everything that happens, there is a place in the underworld of images that Thanatos and Hades dedicate to the soul substance in all things.

With this Hades perspective in mind, Freud's idea of a death that becomes difficult to achieve, due to the increasing complexities of life as it develops over time, is not as bizarre as it seems. It begins to make sense when we view it in light of what Jung called the psychological "complexes" that make daily life so complicated, and by which he meant the uniquely personal and unconscious patterns of significance that shape every human life into its own form. Unlike archetypal patterns of experience, which are universal, Jung's psychological complexes are personal. They are not about the archetypal Great Mother but about my mommy dearest and about my lifelong relation with her. The complications of life that constitute these private complexes are stitched together over time into individual patterns of personality style. They are made up of the scraps of life that belong to its unique individual history, and to none other. For each life, from the perspective of these personal and individual complexes, is a case of having to alchemically process its own raw materials through its own individual development. The raw materials themselves are endlessly collected from each life's historical circumstances. As Zarathustra says, they are found "in strange lands and scattered among all things and accidents." Jung's personal complexes, which together add up to the whole silently patterned identity of personal unconsciousness, determine not only the clamor and the sound and fury in a life. They also set down the limitations that prevent a life from being other than what it is. For that which gives all things their defining form and features also is what seals their inescapable destiny. It is a built-in, self-limiting imagination that takes a whole lifetime to do all its complex creative work but that also, in the same process, determines what a life will not be. It makes for the fundamental psychological impossibility in each life that contributes as much to its definition as anything else does: that a thing, an event, an experience, a life cannot also be something else, from another life. It makes every day as good as it gets. No better, no worse. Just so.

Jung spoke about this self-limiting aspect of personal unconsciousness as the "shadow" that every form of consciousness casts. That shadow may be imagined as the darkness that every light creates outside the area where it casts its light, as the unconsciousness that comes into being with every form of consciousness. We also may think of it as our own back. It is, like our back, something intimately ingrown in the complex anatomy of our life, something that is present in everything we do and experience, wherever we go. It is a defining feature of every posture we assume, of every stance we take, and of every standpoint we occupy. It is something that gives us a recognizable profile, even from a distance. Yet, like our back, it also is something we ourselves will never be able to clearly see, even though it is visible to everyone who sees us. This very back of ours that casts our shadow, and that is the shadow side of every life, is present in everything we do, think, and feel—both subjectively and objectively. This back with its backbone that holds us up all life long, and that makes us *homo erectus* in full pride and stride, this intrinsic support we count on to back us up in all we do and in all that happens to us, this back, while being strictly and intimately ours, subjectively, also is not ours at all, objectively. While it is mine, and mine only, it also is always publicly, objectively visible in the world at large, even though it never presents itself that way to me. While it is behind my sense of private subjectivity, it is simultaneously the objective subject matter of all my history. It is publicly visible for all except me to see and to know. With the same inner core of built-in psychic backbone with which I walk through my own private world, I also walk around in the world of those who surround me in life. In this sense, my unconsciousness itself finds a place in the public and objective domain. What I take to be my personal unconsciousness exists therefore in others as much as it exists in me. It exists as other people's reactions to me. It exists as their feelings and thoughts about me, including those ideas about me that they do not even tell themselves.

This shadow that every life casts through the complications of living and that crystallize into personal complexes is made of the stuff of images. It should therefore come as no surprise that, as Hillman notes in *The Dream and the Underworld*, the soul images in Hades are called *skia*, or shadows. That means the substance of which the shadows I cast as I go are made is the same substance that goes on living in Hades. It is Ovid's bodiless, boneless, and bloodless life stuff. This suggests that it is by virtue of our shadows, and by casting those shadows, that we are gaining entry into the realm of Hades, even while we are walking around in nature and in history. And so we may indeed view death less physically and regard it instead as the soul's nonphysical substance in life. Death thus reimagined purely psychically is the soul as *skia* or shadow. It is the living but subtle essence that defines a life but that also limits it. It is the lifelong Hades side of my existence. And so the permanently invisible back side of my life, including all the shadows it casts, is indeed my death image. It is, as Freud suggested and as Klein half remembered, the lifelong suicide that walks with me wherever I go.

The images that Hades cherishes are not fantasies of literal death and literal destruction. They are, rather, the subtle yet real objects of the kind of love that comes into being and that can be sensed in life when literalism about all things stops being the dominant view. Such love from the Hades perspective on life is no longer dependent on the usual sense of the factuality of all things. It is no longer dependent on this dominant view because *physis*, or nature, is no longer the leading paradigm. The love Hades personifies is a love for the images and the imagination that become incarnate in all physicality but that are not physicality itself. It is a love for the subtle matters of existence that I can only see when I look beyond my habitual belief in the literal facts of history. Death, mythically and purely psychically conceived, is that pivotal point where the strictly historical sense of my existence gives way to a sense for the subtler things in my life. Here I meet my true other half. This other half touches me personally and subjectively in all that is physical and factual and historical, yet it is itself none of these. It is what gives me a sense of having my own personal place in a world that is itself beginning to look mythic, and that thereby makes my own existence mythic. This is the deepest essence of myth. It is the imagination that goes on behind the back of life's clamor, behind its sound and fury. Myth is creation's whispered gossip about its creatures. This kind of gossip comes in endless forms, including oral tradition, literature, mythology, art, culture, philosophy, religion—and, yes, psychological theory and the practices based on it. As Nietzsche put it: consciousness as a fantastic commentary on an unknown and unknowable text.

In the end, the death that is at stake in Hades is not at all the destruction or the end of any life. It is, rather, the end of the exclusionary viewpoint that only regards the literal physicality, factuality, and historicity of life as real. What Hades wants is not anyone's destruction or end. What he wants is the end of the single-minded view that takes the very ideas of physicality, factuality, and historicity too literally as the bottom-line and only facts of life. The biggest fact of life, says Hades, the most bottom-line fact, is psychic bottomlessness itself, the infinite depth of significance that inheres in all things and that is filled with endless images—and that depth is precisely his turf. Viewed from this nonphysical or unnatural perspective, death stops being something that can and that should be done only at the end of life. It takes more time than that. As Freud said, it takes a whole lifetime, every minute of it. Judging a life, from this point of view, should therefore not only be done in late-life autobiographies. Nor should it be restricted to the end of one's days, to eulogies at funerals, or to all manner of commentary after the fact, *post mortem*. It is a matter that should not have to wait until such a late, and often too late, date. It should be started much sooner, as soon as possible. It is a matter that has to be taken up in life and done throughout it—by looking for the Hades factor in it that is its built-in psychic substance.

But even though developing a sense for Hades in everyday life should be taken up sooner rather than later, it is not child's play, or even a child's concern. That is perhaps why it receives no attention in psychologies focused on childhood development and on the themes of childhood internalizations and the "inner child" in all their variants. Nor is dealing with Hades a business for the young and the up and coming, for he contributes nothing to success in any realm or endeavor. Developing a sense for Hades may well do nothing for vocational and career planning—and nothing for improving family life, for adaptation of any kind, or for personal and interpersonal well-being. It is not for making life easier or better. Nor does it aim to contribute to social welfare and the common good. Having a sense for Hades has no bearing on making the world a better place, and it is not meant to have an effect on improving anyone's behavior. It does not aim to do any of these, because Hades is no improver of mankind. He is not in the business of offering hope for a different and better future. He does not even seek to bring novelty of any kind. Instead of that, the business of Hades is confirming and affirming the way things are and have been. He promises nothing except that he will keep and value, even eternalize, everything exactly as it turned out. He holds out no hope, because hope has no value in his eyes. He has no interest in change and, above all, no interest in change for the better of any kind. Hades needs neither hope nor change, because he is fully satisfied with everything he finds, and just as he finds everything. For all these reasons, his offerings, his viewpoint, and all that is to be seen from his viewpoint are truly not for those under seventeen. They do not need Hades. They need to work out a future—with hope in their hearts. Eventually that future will in any case make room for Hades, when he is good and ready to enter life. And that he then tends to do with a bang, often as an unexpected and overpowering intrusion. Not surprisingly, that entry is frequently imagined as a kind of violation, his rape of Persephone, by which he makes her Queen of his realm. This rape takes place with Demeter, Persephone's own mother, standing by helplessly. Or even adult accompaniment and protective guidance do nothing to make Hades any more accessible or imaginable for a youthful spirit that is innocent about him. That is no doubt why true entry into the deep domain of depth psychology—and not merely intellectualization about it—often is impossible for the young and those with a juvenile imagination. Here it may well be the right thing essayed on the wrong occasion.

But as a life gains definition, in its fullness, which also means as a life begins to show its limitations in definition that make it such and such and not otherwise, then the Hades factor in it becomes an increasingly fitting preoccupation. For that is when he becomes an increasingly near presence and an outspoken companion. One's sights become less exclusively set on the distant future and more focused on the here and now. They become focused on everything eternally recurring that has been and that is, and that is likely and largely to continue as is. For a youthful spirit that has been aiming mostly at distant and dreamed-of goals, this sudden emergence of the Hades way of looking at everyday life may herald a crisis. Everything about such a youthful spirit's familiar ways can be unexpectedly and violently disrupted in this fashion, and perhaps forever changed. Persephone's mythic innocence is here lost once again, as unsuspected impulses break into the open and ravage the usual sense of the all-too-familiar scene. The face-to-face encounter with the underworldly Hades begins.

Dante said it, in the opening line of his *Divine Comedy*: "Nel mezzo del cammin di nostra vita/mi ritrovari per una selva oscura,/chè la diratta via era smarrita"—"In the middle of the journey of our life/I came to my senses in a dark forest,/for I had lost the straight path." That means here the way of thinking that is more informed by an imagination for the deeply mythic significance of things begins neither at age seven or seventeen, nor at age seventy, but in the middle of life. It begins when one is fully in the midst of one's affairs, when one is underway and on the road to going wherever one's road seems to be going.

But this is not only, not even primarily, about chronological age and about midlife crises. It is about all states of fully absorbed involvement. It is about all conditions of feeling that one is in mid-stride, in the prime of one's momentum. Each of these states can become a place of entry into the domain of Hades, for it is when anything is most busily coming into its own, when its defining outlines seem most definitive, that limitations, too, enter into play. This is when the deepest matters of psyche can appear—and appear in their most dramatic form. The same lines of thought that define one's mind-set at any given time also are the fault lines where the firm ground of one's way of being tends to break up. When one's trusted ground underfoot breaks up along these fault lines, life as usual breaks down with it. One's usual standpoints, viewpoints, and postures can become infirm and untenable, due to a shifting foundation for one's imagination about all things. Whatever has previously provided firm footing breaks open and threatens to swallow one whole. Whoever has stood on ground long assumed solid may lose the familiar sense of balance and may be overthrown or even crack up. Life among long-standing individual and collective constructs breaks down and seems to become life among ruins. One's own antiquity, the remnants of one's prior claim to fame, comes into being precisely with these ruins. And with that, psychic archaeology—Freud's favorite metaphor for psychoanalysis—can begin. What also can begin with this is a Nietzschean revaluation of previously assumed values. And then one also discovers, again with Nietzsche, that history happens backwards, that there are untold volumes of previously unimagined and even unimaginable things that are yet to take place in the past.

The sense of *terra firma* often is replaced by a feeling of psychic landslides and mud slides during these upheavals in one's usual ways of imagining all things. Masses of wildly moving emotional matter may shift loose, lifting everything off its footing. It seems that nothing can be controlled any longer, because nobody is in control, and everything is coming down. All that may have taken long to build and that may have involved much creative ingenuity falls apart. Only masses and messes of barely identifiable psychological rubble seem to be left over, the usual sense of differentiation among all things having been virtually wiped out. One case of such upheaval appears in the nightmares that so many psychotherapies in mid-process seem to produce: images of unstoppable diarrhea and of overflowing toilets. Here, in these dreams, life appears reduced to nothing but disgusting-looking elemental psychic matter that is flowing everywhere. It seems to have been let go by normally well-ordered and controlled processes that now lose their firm hold. It is as though the soul itself is expelling the usual diet of familiar ideas and constructs, as though nothing in all that otherwise appears perfectly natural works anymore. In the treatment process itself, it may seem as though nothing is being "worked on" any longer and then neatly "worked through" and "worked out." None of what goes on in treatment at these times can be neatly stacked up and left behind in perfectly shaped little piles of fully digested feelings and thoughts—everything properly metabolized with the aid of perfect hindsight and insight. Nothing seems clear anymore. Everything seems to have become one putrid mess. And the mess spreads everywhere, on everything. It even spills over on the therapist, who feels that she or he can do nothing to help contain this big flood of dark matter. Everything in life now stinks, and nothing in it is protected from contamination by this sense of mess. Even the treater cannot keep feeling clean. All that is left when treatment becomes messy in this manner is a pervasive feeling of disgust with the emotional leftovers and the daily psychic residues that are spilling over on all sides. All the therapist's well-meant gestures of containment that are offered at this point fail. Psychology and psychotherapy themselves now reek like ever so much crap. Existential nausea, disgust with everything, is the matching sentiment. This is the nightmare of Nietzsche's necessary temporary nihilism as it may be experienced in everyday life.

The alchemists had a name for these phases of the soul that feel like an overwhelmingly messy and nihilistic state of things. They aptly referred to them as a condition of *putrefactio*. It is no pretty picture, no pleasant experience. More than a few therapists and their patients, and many in ordinary life, may not have the stomach for it. But necessary it nonetheless is—not for some other and better state after it but for the sake of putrefaction itself. For, paradoxically, in all the residual psychic matter that can easily make a mess of life, there inheres the potential for a deeper sense of things—not after them, as in whitewashing and soothing fantasies about a more pleasant outcome that will have made it all worthwhile, but right within it, inherently, in the mess itself. That deeper sense of things belongs to Hades. What is at stake is a shifting from the usual viewpoint of everyday life under Zeus to the twin but desubstantialized viewpoint of Hades. This involves a putrefaction of the ways of thinking that are based on nature and on models found in nature. That putrefaction of all nature-based ways of thinking is the deeper process that goes on beneath the surface appearances of the mess, beneath all the clinical signs and symptoms that are so easily identifiable. In the myth of Hades, the figure of Demeter, who is not only Persephone's mother but also governess of vegetative life, becomes clinically depressed when Hades erupts into life. The crops over which she presides begin to wither, threatening the life of humans who rely on them. At this surface level of events, the level of Demeter's visible vegetative decline and melancholy, anyone can make the obvious diagnosis of reactive depression. But this is not merely a process of nature, just because it affects nature's functioning and the trusted cycles in nature's own life. For Hades does not belong to the natural realities of top soil or even deep earth. He takes Persephone, and everything else that matters to him, to levels of significance that go deeper than the top layers or even the deep ground of nature. Hades brings something other than a strictly natural upset that belongs in the natural order of events. He is not something that is somehow reassuringly natural. He does not go away by himself, seemingly naturally. He is not part of a familiar process that only has to run its natural course and that will then automatically lead to some sort of cyclical renewal of life. Hades upsets not only the usual manifestations of all that seems natural but even the very idea of nature itself. He threatens nature insofar as it informs the natural view on things that always tends to become our first thought because it is our own second nature. Most importantly, he is about undoing and abandoning all modes of thinking that are built on the archetypal idea of *Natura*.

The Hades way of undoing the hold that the paradigm of Natura has on the usual habits of thinking affects not only such enterprises as psychoanalysis, insofar as it is based on the paradigm of the anatomical body and its physiological functioning. It affects all thinking according to which the ultimate basis of existence is in *physis*, and thus all thinking for which the last statement about what it means to be human must be based on the natural laws that govern *physis*. Hades therefore takes depth psychology, the care of the soul's deepest matters, out of the hands of physicians. This makes him the original and archetypal lay analyst. He does all that he does by providing the soul, and the management of its affairs, with his own medium and paradigm. That medium is the domain of images, and the paradigm that of the imagination. At the Hades level of psychic profundity, we are far from nature indeed, and our thinking becomes far from natural—just as Freud proposed when he first spoke so seemingly madly to Vienna's medical community. Depth psychology, the treatment of the soul's deepest and most essential matters, when done under the sign of Hades, is therefore truly an *opus contra naturam*, just as the alchemists said. Given the dramatic and unnatural upset that Hades brings about, it is no wonder that he often is depicted as a bully from Hell. It is no wonder that his entry into life is told as the story of a violent rape, not a subtle Immaculate Conception. What is violated when he enters the scene is less an innocent girl, Persephone, who delights in nature's beauty, than the innocence in the view that takes nature as the measure of all things—and of all good. What is ravaged is less any product of nature, nor even any particular thoughts from nature-based thinking, than the idea that nature provides the best model, the best paradigm for understanding anything and everything, including the life of soul. What Persephone's archetypally childlike mind-set must discover, like it or not, is that when the deepest dimension of soul enters into play life is no longer child's play in a cosmic nature park. Like Buddha, upon leaving the protected backyard of his parental house, the Persephone mind-set discovers that the lap of Being is no gently rocking cradle, with Mother Nature doing the rocking. "When I was a child I spake as a child," says the West's favorite Book, adding that those childish ways must be given up. Hades is precisely about giving up these childish ways. This includes perhaps, and not in the least, giving up the often-unquestioned primacy of psychology's seemingly so natural child paradigms. It also includes, and to no lesser degree, giving up psychotherapy's seemingly naturally, but often too exclusively, child-centered ways of thinking about matters of soul that are anything but child material.

The mythic Hades factor in the life of the soul has been imagined and reimagined in an endless number of ways. In modern literature, one of its manifestations is as the figure of the *Doppelganger,* or Double. Not by chance did this figure appear on the literary horizon at the same time that the modern idea of unconsciousness came upon the historical scene. Even less accidental is the fact that it was depth psychology, through Otto Rank's book, *The Double,* that first pointed to the psychological significance of this theme. Both unconsciousness and the Double are imagined as an insubstantial yet very real companion that walks with us every step of our way, wherever we go, whatever we do. They are everyday life's other, and more subtle, half. They are the underworldly and purely psychic Hades, as it were shadowing his more physically imaginable upperworld brother Zeus. The Double appears in literature in a wide variety of forms, yet in all this variety his essential features are constant. This suggests an unchanging and spontaneously recurring theme of psychological significance. He often appears as a mirror image that detaches itself from the mirror and then begins to lead an independent life. In a variation on that theme, he may appear as a shadow that does the same thing. There are stories of doubling through twinship or through mistaken identity. There are cases of reflections in water or of portraits that develop a life of their own. A Double also may appear through processes that involve the magical rejuvenation of a person, as it were in an acute regression to an earlier and younger way of being. Similarly, but in reverse, there may be doubling through magical aging, as in profound depression or in acute psychological decompensation. And there are stories about such clinical forms of Doubles as the contents of persecutory delusions, of hallucinations, of depersonalization, or of irrational fears, such as the fear of reflections in water or in mirrors. There is also the fragmentation and multiplication of personality into independent characters who are separated by amnesia, as in multiple personality disorder or dissociative identity disorder. Last but by no means least, there are stories in which solitude itself—man in his loneliest loneliness, man in his own company, man *as* his own ultimate company—is personified and assumes an autonomous life.

The recurring theme that is the backbone in all Double stories is of an exact replica image of the protagonist that detaches itself, then begins to lead an existence of its own, and eventually does so more and more at the protagonist's expense. In the process, the protagonist's life becomes increasingly affected by the Double, and then shaped into its defining and self-limiting outlines. Eventually the protagonist is undone by this shadowy twin. There are three outstanding features in all Double stories on this unchanging theme. First, there is the complete reversal of roles, and of relative importance, between the protagonist and his Double. Second, there is the gradual undoing and the eventual end of the protagonist's life as this reversal completes itself. Last, and as a surprise denouement, there is the discovery of a great and truly mind-boggling paradox, a discovery that is reenacted in the history of psychology itself as the discovery of the notion of unconsciousness. The discovery is this: the Double is not only what interferes with life, and what undoes the ego's sense of being in charge of it, but he is simultaneously what gives that life its shape and definition throughout its entire duration. The Double dramatizes the paradox that every life's built-in undoing serves, indeed, as its most life-giving factor. This last and central idea, of the death-dealing Double also being a life-giving and life-defining factor of existence, is explicitly stated in the stories themselves. One such story, "The Student of Prague," which was a film in Rank's day, illustrates all Double stories on this point. It ends with the still life scene of the protagonist's grave and of the figure of the Double who sits on the grave. Three lines from Musset's "December Night" end the story: "Wherever you go, I shall be there always,/Up to the very last one of your days,/When I shall go to sit on your stone."

Rank interprets the Double as an imagistic formulation of, as he puts it, "man's relation to himself." The Double forces the ego to become engaged in a reflective discourse and an inevitable relation with its own imagistic foundation. It is the way a life begins to tell the story of itself to itself, right in the middle of life, while the action is going on and is going increasingly clearly in the direction of its built-in destiny. Doubles are the way in which life becomes imaginable through its basis in a world of truly autonomous images. These images are at first ignored or at best devalued and denied ontological status— like shadows, reflections, dreams, and other intangible and fleeting matters. Eventually, however, as the sense of doubling in life grows stronger, these same images prove to be increasingly and uncannily real. In the end, they turn out to be the dominant reality and to have the last word, in spite of their apparent lack of ontological status. This is indeed what Klein said, even though he did not spell out the full depth of his own claim: that a life is judged by the suicide it commits.

The Double serves as an alter ego in relation to the waking ego, which runs the affairs of everyday life. The death he brings into life as a companion and a destiny is less about the literal and physical end of life than about the end of the waking ego's perspective on it and rule over it. What ends is not so much life itself but rather the psychological and philosophical prejudices of the waking ego. The Double kills by terminating the waking ego's ego trip. Most importantly, he kills the ego's hubris, the overweening pride a person may have in herself or himself. The killer is the discovery that the waking ego is not alone, but that this waking ego has an overpowering twin who demands his or her due. Once again we see that the ancient Delphic command to "Know Thyself" refers less to knowing one's own person than to sensing the presence of a subtle Other. And more contemporarily we are once again facing the admonition from Alcoholics Anonymous to develop a sense for the subtle presence of a greater power in one's life that shadows one's every moment, gesture, feeling, and thought. It is no accident that Alcoholics Anonymous views alcoholism as a disease. But here, too, just as in the case of Klein's statement that a life needs to be judged by the suicide it commits, those who would claim that alcoholism is a disease are prone to underappreciate the best part of their own point. If alcoholism is a disease, this is not primarily because of physiological reasons—in spite of the physiological findings about an underlying physiological process. It is more because of subtle reasons that belong in the diagnostic category of Hades events. Alcoholism is a disease, because the doings of a person's alcoholic Double are aimed at the undoing of that person's false belief that his or her ego is in charge. This undoing may or may not involve a decline in the person's physical health. Most importantly, however, it involves the undoing of the belief that the person is in control of his or her own life, and the discovery that something else is.

In Double literature, it is always a male protagonist who, like a diseased body turning against itself, kills himself by attempting to destroy his Double image. It is precisely in the very act of trying to kill his Double that the protagonist is himself mortally wounded—at his own hands. Edgar Allen Poe's story, "William Wilson," makes the case for all Double stories on this crucial point. The protagonist is, as usual, hounded by his Double. In a desperate moment, he challenges the Double to a duel. They struggle, and the protagonist plunges his sword into his Double's heart. At that point, the wounded Double says to the protagonist: "You have conquered, and I yield. Yet henceforth art thou also dead. . . . In me didst thou exist; and in my death see by this image, which is thine own, how utterly thou has murdered thyself." This is a theatrical image of the suicide that the Double has been bringing into the protagonist's life. It is a dramatization of the idea that the conscious ego is being unconsciously placed in the service of its own, but deeply unconscious, destiny. And thus the protagonist unwittingly carries out his own suicide on behalf of his Double. This means that the waking ego is needed and is put to work to undo itself. It is unwittingly put to work to unseat its own prejudices and to dislodge its hubristic belief in itself. It is enlisted to dethrone itself from its governance over daily life. It is made to disabuse itself of its ideas and plans for its future, and so it leads itself in the march to end the notion that it rules, and that therefore it matters most. But, so Nietzsche had already suggested in his own way, this is precisely the essence, the active ingredient, of all nihilism. For nihilism, in his view, is the condition in which ruling ideas, presiding metaphysical prejudices, governing value judgments, and controlling ways of thinking are brought to naught at their own hands, as a logical and inescapable conclusion of their own implications. It is an unavoidable shrugging off of previously held viewpoints as no longer valid, in favor of newly beheld ideas that are dawning and that are inspired by images of a greater will. What defines nihilism in this view—and this is the point Nietzsche emphasized almost as though he were speaking on behalf of the Double—is precisely the fact that it is the activity of human self-consciousness itself that is put to work to undo itself. With this in mind, it seems almost inevitable that the idea of disease would have to suggest itself to AA's way of imagining alcoholism. For here, too, and here so self-evidently, the ego is put in the service of the task of its own self-destruction.

If every life is a lifelong suicide, through a lifelong coexistence with a Double who works on behalf of Hades, then the very idea of health itself must be reimagined. If, as Aristotle said, a believable story requires that its plot and characters are mutually necessary to each other, then the same is true for every life and the precise kind of health that goes with it. The healthy life, in this view, is not the same for everyone. It should not be imagined and defined in the same way for everyone. A life lived wisely and well, with an eye toward its own health, is not necessarily a symptom-free life or a minimally symptomatic life. It is a life that develops a keen sense for the unique kind of health that is part of its destiny, and that is precisely the health with which it must carry out the task of its destiny. Every life is then not only a lifelong self-definition and a lifelong pursuit of its own death, as Freud suggested. It also is a lifelong search for the right sense of health that belongs with it. No other sense of health will do. But also, and just as importantly, no other health is necessary. Most importantly of all, each life involves a lifelong search for the right kind of physician, that is, the right paradigm that can guide how one must treat one's life and its foibles and unique health. Nietzsche wrote about the relation that exists between a person's individual health and that person's outlook on existence:

> A philosopher who has traversed many kinds of health, and keeps traversing them, has passed through an equal number of philosophies; he simply *cannot* keep from transposing his states every time into the most spiritual form and distance: this art of transfiguration *is* philosophy. We philosophers are not free to divide body from soul as the people do; we are even less free to divide soul from spirit . . . constantly, we have to give birth to our thoughts out of pain and, like mothers, endow them with all we have of blood, heart, fire, pleasure, passion, agony, conscience, life, and catastrophe. . . . And as for sickness: are we not almost tempted to ask whether we could get along without it?

Health should therefore not be so negatively defined as life minus the pains, illnesses, and idiosyncrasies great and small that make it what it is. It must be positively imagined as a certain specific and necessary condition that goes with the plot of a life. A negative definition of health ends up with a negative definition of life itself. John Donne put it this way: "There is no health; Physicians say that wee,/At best, enjoy but a neutralitie." In this view, health either does not exist in life and is fundamentally incompatible with it, or the life that is left over when all symptoms are removed from it is devoid of life. The latter amounts to imagining life in the manner of an anesthesiologist gone berserk.

The right sense of the precise kind of health that is required for each individual is, quite literally, vital. Life itself is at stake in it. Nietzsche put this bluntly, warning that there is "danger in one's physician"—and not only or even primarily for the most obvious reasons. He explained: "One must have the physician one was born for, otherwise one will perish by one's physician." His own case is a case in point. Had he heeded the advice of his physician to stop reading and writing in order to spare his failing eyesight and minimize his debilitating headaches, he might well have reduced his symptoms. He might well have lived a physically more comfortable life. Yet the treatment and any physical improvement that would have resulted from it would have been a worse fate than the identified symptoms. They would have cut him off from the very core of his life and from his destiny. Instead of following his physician's perfectly rational advice, Nietzsche followed his symptoms. He looked at them not to resent them and be rid of them but he saw them instead as ever-so-many concrete images of philosophical and psychological arguments with which he had to come to terms. That was Nietzsche's brand of "working through." It was not meant to get rid of anything but, rather, as Hades does with all scraps of life, to reserve a precise place for every mode of living and thinking. Few thinkers have so keenly sensed, and so thoroughly explored, the precise health profile that was their own lifelong Double and that became a living and autonomous Other presence in their life. In the process, Nietzsche learned to recognize many specific modes of being and forms of life, along with their accompanying psychology and their built-in philosophy, in every one of his states of health. He managed to spell out his entire philosophy precisely from this keen sense for the lively fluctuations in his health states. Even as madness was taking over, and until it finally silenced him as a philosopher, he was capable of recognizing its features as well, allowing him to speak insightfully on its behalf. One can forgive him for regarding himself as a psychologist without equal in history.

In monumental contrast to Nietzsche's sense of intimate connection to the precise health that must be his, all his days long, there is Plato's Socrates. Socrates found life, in his final analysis of it, essentially unhealthy and in need of a radical and permanent cure. He was even ready to give up on life itself for that very reason—with what must be the most momentous and historically most significant sigh of relief any philosopher has ever sighed. As he was about to drink the hemlock that would kill him, just as his sentence by the city of Athens required him to do, Socrates gave his friends his last instructions. Upon his death, so he told them, they were to offer a cock to Aesclepius, the god of medicine. That offering, he explained, had to be made to express his gratitude for being cured of life by death. With this tip of the hat to Aesclepius, in gratitude for finally being cured of the disease we call life by death, Socrates outwarned every surgeon general to come. For in this Socratic view it is not only cigarette smoking that is unhealthy but life itself, life as a whole. Death alone is an effective cure. Could it be that this diagnosis and its implicit warning were perhaps not about existence per se but about Socrates' own existence as a lifelong dedication to reason? Could it be that his lifelong dedication to reason not only defined his life, and beyond that the very spirit of reason itself, but that it also, in the same process, defined the limitations of such a life and of the spirit that dominates it? Could it be that, in keeping with the archetypal laws of Double psychology, Socrates ended up using reason in order to send reason itself on its way to its own necessary undoing with this terminal blow? Nietzsche, it would seem, had a more viable and more affirmative solution. Instead of looking for one Absolute state of Good Health, corresponding to one Absolute Good, as Socrates did without ever finding either, Nietzsche found many doable kinds of good, and many viable kinds of health.

Another positive and anything but anesthetized understanding of what health and the good life are comes from Freud. He defined them, simply but profoundly, as being able to love and to work. A few lucky ones among us are fortunate enough to find both love and good work. Many unlucky ones find neither love nor a job they can love. A solid majority manages to do at least one or the other some of the time. They at least periodically find some people and things to love and at least occasionally work that provides some rewards. But nobody, except perhaps an infinitesimal portion of the truly anesthetized, gets to "enjoy but a neutralitie." To love and to hold a job. Freud did not say whom or what we should love, nor how, and he did not say what kind of work we should do. He did, however, emphasize that the ways in which we may go about the business of our life and its built-in destiny are many, and endlessly imaginative. Like Nietzsche he implied that The Good is not one absolute thing, but that it can take on multiple forms, because it is polyvalent. And with that, in contrast to Socrates, he, too, as much as put reason—and Socrates with it—in its place as only one among many possible ways of imagining life and living existence, and by no means an unquestionably superior one.

Athens put Socrates to death, because it found him guilty of corrupting the city's youth. He allegedly did so by virtually deifying reason, at the expense of the gods, those irrational pillars of everyday life whom everyone knew and had more or less learned to live with. Yet Socrates never formally or openly denied the gods. He even made a point of paying homage to them, as was expected. Whether he did so in earnest or as an expression of his usual irony is difficult to judge. Freud, in contrast, did not hesitate to declare his disbelief in the God of his people and forefathers. Instead of those beliefs, he proposed an ambitious plan for exploring the life of the soul on its own terms. That plan was based on an imaginative analysis of Everyman's ways of dealing with everyday life. It used an imaginative, mythic commentary as its operational formula. Yet quite paradoxically for a man of his outspoken atheism, and in contrast to Socrates and his insistence on reason, Freud implied that for a life to have any chance of reaching a viable coexistence with its own destiny, it must develop a sense for the irrational and archetypal Double that accompanies man at every turn. That

Double, so Freud argued with all the force his psychoanalytic theorizing could muster, inexorably dethrones man's ego consciousness. It sends it on the last trip the ego ever imagined it would have to make, for it sends it on a trip into the imaginative basis of existence that is the realm of Hades.

It is, indeed, as Freud recalled from his classical studies and as he reminded the world in the epigraph to his history-shaping *Interpretation of Dreams*: If we cannot change the way things are in the upperworld by changing the gods of the upperworld, then we must turn our attention to those of the underworld.

APPENDIX

BACKGROUND MATTERS AND TEXTS

CHAPTER 1
THE SOUL'S OWN FUNDAMENTALISM

It has become a habit of modern Western men and women to think, or rather to assume without even thinking much about it, that knowledge about "human nature" is largely cumulative. The farther we have come in history, especially in modern history, so we tend to tell ourselves, the more we have learned about what makes Everyman and Everywoman tick. If we continue our search and research, so we then go on to assume, we will discover ever more. Our understanding of what it is like to be human, therefore, seems only to be growing.

An even more fundamental habitual assumption is that "human nature" is a more or less stable thing, something that has stayed far more the same throughout known history than it has become different. A man or a woman of, say, Abraham's days, or Plato's, is assumed to have been much the same as today's men and women. Habits change with time and culture—that we know. But "human nature" itself is generally thought to remain mostly the same. Hence, what we are after when we develop psychological theories is, by and large, knowledge about presumably unchanging facts of psychological life.

Both assumptions are open to questioning. First, knowledge about anything, including psychological life or what this book calls "the life of the soul," may not only be impossible, as postmodernism argues, but it also is not necessarily cumulative. Second, there may perhaps not only be no such thing as a definable "human nature," as postmodernism also argues, but whatever there is of such a "human nature" may not at all be unchanging.

As such writers as Michel Foucault have argued, in works such as *Madness and Civilization* (1965), *The Birth of the Clinic* (1973), *Discipline and Punish* (1995), and *The History of Sexuality* (1978), even fundamental human experiences—madness, illness, crime, and sexuality—are by no means stable and unchanging. They do change, and greatly so. But even beyond that, others argue, "human nature" itself, or what supports even the most fundamental human experiences and what makes them possible in the first place, changes. Dutch psychiatrist Jan Hendrik Van den Berg (1983), along with others, has long argued that our "human nature" as a species is anything but stable or fixed. Hence, the title of one of his central works, *The Changing Nature of Man: Introduction to a Historical Psychology*. In it he argues that, among other things, even such a presumably culture-free and defining fact of life as physical pain may not be as unchanging in essence as we customarily assume, or that something as basic as childhood itself did not always exist and came into being at some point in history. Van den Berg calls his approach to the study of psychological life "metabletics," by which he means "the study of changes." Hence, his idea of "historical psychology." Virtually his entire work is one protracted attempt to formulate and demonstrate such a "study of change" and such a "historical psychology."

It is therefore not surprising that "mind" itself should come up for review as a less than stable or unchanging fact of life. It, too, has its own history, with its own origins. Bruno Snell (1982), in *The Discovery of the Mind in Greek Philosophy and Literature*, traces that origin in the history of Greek culture. The central premise in his study is that "belief in the existence of a uniform human mind is a rationalist prejudice" (16).

Within the larger context of whatever may be meant by "mind," there is the more specific arena of what we now take for granted as the "interior" life of the person. That, too, like "mind" itself, has its own origins. And that is where the significance of early Greek lyric poetry, or what Snell calls the "personal lyric" (1982, 46), enters into play. Looking at Homer and at the lyric poetry of Archilochus, Sappho, and Anacreon, Snell argues that from Homer's *Iliad* to the *Odyssey*, there is a subtle shift, with the latter showing "a more subtle perception of the (individual) distinctions between men than its predecessor" (47). Archilochus picks up on this shift, and in his poetry "we find a more precise appreciation of the self and its distinctive qualities: and that is indeed the beginning of something new" (ibid.). Sappho goes one step farther. Whereas Archilochus elaborates on what the *Odyssey* proposes, that "different men take delight in different things" (XIV, 228), or as Archilochus says, that "each man has his heart cheered in his own way" (Snell 1982, 41), neither Homer nor Archilochus gives priority to any one such preference over another. Hence, one person's preference for horses is just as valid as another person's love of armies of foot soldiers (ibid., 47–48). Sappho, in contrast, states a clear and distinct preference. "She places that which is inwardly felt above external splendour," and she tells us exactly which thing has the greatest value for her: "that which is lovingly embraced by the soul" (ibid.).

While she is not the first among her fellow lyric poets to emphasize this preference, "Sappho was the first to put this into words" (ibid.). She goes even farther and describes that inner feeling as one she must helplessly undergo, much as all human beings must helplessly accept what the gods hand down for them. Love, in Sappho's eyes, remains something visited upon a person by the god Eros, as it had long been understood before her, "but the feeling of help- lessness (that goes with love) is her own" (ibid., 53). It is, so Snell (1982) emphasizes, "her personal property in the fullest sense of the word," one she experiences and writes about as "a sensation of having approached to the very roots of her being: she is favored with a glimpse into the uncharted territory of the *soul*" (ibid.). Not only is Sappho first to focus so explicitly on the inner person, she also states precisely why what goes on inside the person over- whelmed by love is largely beyond personal control, thereby making the person feel helpless. That helplessness is imagined as *amechania* (ibid., 62), which in today's psychological parlance perhaps might be expressed as "lacking in coping skills," or some such phrase. Sappho's helplessness or *amechania* is best appreci- ated when it is contrasted to the way the heroic Odysseus is described in Homer. He is repeatedly called *polymechanos* (ibid.). As many Homer translators put that phrase, he is a man "of many ways," meaning a man who never seems to run out of tricks or "coping skills." Going from Homer to Sappho, we move therefore straight into the beginnings of a psychology of the inner personality or of inner personhood. Thus our "inner self" is conceived by a woman poet from Lesbos, a woman made to feel inwardly helpless by feelings she owns but cannot control because they are divinely given. Writes Snell: "Sappho, with her bold neologism 'bitter-sweet,' discovers the area of the soul and defines it as fundamentally distinct from the body" (1982, 60). We are certainly a long way from our own complex and fully autonomous inner life as we now know it, and for Sappho it is still the gods who continue to rule all human matters. However, an inner world is beginning to open up: "the distress of the soul is claimed as man's private property" (70).

Yet while the "human nature" of our species may change in fundamental ways, it also has a dimension where it opens up on eternal and unchanging matters. One of the main windows through which the West has been looking for glimpses of such eternal matters is, of course, Plato and the Platonism of absolute and unchanging Ideas. As Plato's Socrates talks about them—mostly in *Phaedo, Phaedrus, Meno, Symposium,* and *Timaeus*—these absolute Ideas are the timeless, everlasting, and immutable bedrock of all temporal realities found in the historical and lived world.

The history of intellectual commentary on Plato's Ideas is as complex, rich, and endless as it is long and defining not only for Western thought and culture but for Western consciousness itself, even for the very "human nature" of West- ern man. For the history of psychology, however, and for archetypal psychology in particular, the notion of absolute Ideas traces its course mainly through the Mediterranean Neoplatonist writers, early on especially such leading figures as Plotinus and Proclus, and later their subsequent commentators in the Italian

Renaissance, such as Vico and Ficino. The still later and Germanic branch of that development eventually includes Kant and Goethe and, already much closer to us, Schopenhauer and Nietzsche. That Germanic line of development finally leads, for our purposes here, to Jung, whom Hillman, in his *Archetypal Psychology: A Brief Account*, rightly calls "the first immediate father of archetypal psychology" (1983, 2). Other branches of development in Platonic thought that lead into archetypal psychology include such figures as William Blake in England and the work of French scholar Henry Corbin on Islamic mysticism.

One name that is conspicuously absent from Hillman's "brief account" of archetypal psychology's historical background is Augustine. This is largely because archetypal psychology, in Hillman's hands, tends to avoid what is Christian—except to do fierce combat with its insistence on a monotheistic consciousness and with the monotheistic spirituality associated with it. And yet there is the fact that Jung, in taking up the notion of archetypes, roundly acknowledges Augustine's important, if not crucial, understanding of them. For us here, in our attempt to find our bearings in the intellectual terrain where archetypal psychology is situated, and especially in our attempt to anchor this book there in ground that will hold us, Augustine is a central figure. Perhaps his greatest intellectual achievement is that he, as the most thoroughgoing spokesperson of a trend in which many of his contemporaries participated as well, joined Plato's thought, especially that part of it focusing on the divine substance of which absolute Ideas are made, to Christian doctrine. As Augustine (1984) put it in *City of God*: "we selected the Platonists (by which he meant what we now call the Neoplatonists, among them primarily the mystic philosopher, Plotinus) as being deservedly the best known of all philosophers, because they have been able to realize that the soul of man . . . cannot attain happiness except by participation in the light of God, the creator of the soul and of the whole world" (X, 1). And also: "There are none who come nearer to us than the Platonists" (VII, 5). Some scholars emphasize that point by suggesting that it was "to Neoplatonism that he was converted, rather than to the Gospel" (Augustine 1953, 13, referring to Alfaric 1918).

The intangible substance that makes up the stuff of absolute Ideas or archetypes, whether in Augustine or in Hillman, is something that cannot be pointed at. As Hillman (1975) writes in *Re-Visioning Psychology*, archetypes, which he views as "the *deepest patterns of psychic functioning*" (xiii, emphasis in original), can only be spoken of metaphorically, in images: "Archetypes throw us into an imaginative style of discourse" (ibid.). Hence, "All ways of speaking of archetypes are translations from one metaphor to another" (ibid.). One such metaphor is that of their inability to be judged by anything other than themselves. This feature emphasizes their valuative aspect, their role as that which determines the inherent psychic value of all things, events, and experiences. Augustine describes that intangible substance that is the ultimate value of all things as follows: *Nullus de illa iudicat, nullus sine illa iudicat bene*—"No man passes judgment on it, and no man judges anything well without it" (1964, II, 14). He explains what he means: the intangible substance he is talking about that is the essence and ultimate value of things is "superior to our minds, which become wise only through this beauty and which make judgments, *not about it but through* it, on other things" (ibid., emphasis added). But rather than being anything like an abstract value, this is perhaps best imagined, for the purposes of depth psychology, as something we may call "existential value," the sense of value of every lived event and experience, the sense that what is at hand matters in a specific and complex way. Hillman puts this as follows: "archetypal psychology uses 'universal' as an adjective, declaring a substantive perduring *value* which ontology states as a hypostasis . . . the universals problem for psychology is not whether they exist, where, and how they participate in particulars, but rather whether a personal individual event can be recognized as bearing essential and collective importance" (1983, 11). And precisely here enters Nietzsche's notion that man is "the esteemer" (1954, 1, "Thousand and One Goals"), the creature whose entire life, and every moment in it, amounts to one long and protracted evaluation and judgment of the universe and of life in it. Nietzsche's preferred judge for this supreme act of judgment is Dionysos, and the judgment he advocates is a Dionysian affirmation of existence. This view is first spelled out in his first book, *The Birth of Tragedy* (1966b). It remains his guiding principle throughout the rest of his writings, most explicitly in such places as *Thus Spoke Zarathustra* (1954) and *Beyond Good and Evil* (1966a), but everywhere else as well. Nietzsche's most Disonysian thought, in this respect, is his idea of an affirmative philosophy based on eternal return.

The intangible or subtle substance of a thing, event, or experience that gives it its psychic reality is not easily imagined, other than in more or less vague and generalized ways. That point is illustrated in Augustine (1953) in *The Nature of the Good*. This "Good," the inherent and bottom-line positive value in any thing or event, is imagined in terms of what Augustine calls three "generic" qualities that are present in them: measure, form, and order. "All things are good; better in proportion as they are better measured, formed, and ordered. These three things, measure, form, and order, not to mention innumerable other things which demonstrably belong to them, are as it were generic good things to be found in all that God has created" (iii). Such a vocabulary makes it almost impossible to say anything more about the "Good" in all things in any specific terms. For Augustine's Christian theology, whose God, in his view, is, as it were, the logical conclusion or extrapolation of the Platonism of Ideas or archetypes, this appears to present little in the way of a problem. For an archetypal psychology of Everyman's Everyday Life, however, we need more specificity, more individualized uniqueness, to do justice to individual experiences and events. But since, as Hillman (1983) suggests, in the matter of things archetypal, one may shift metaphors, such a shift would seem to be an appropriate solution.

One way to imagine the intangible substance that is the specific inherent or internal value of all things, events, and experiences is through the myth of Hades. Hillman's (1979) *The Dream and the Underworld* is perhaps archetypal psychology's most explicit exploration, not only of the first novel dream theory after Freud's and Jung's, but even more so of the value dimension that is attached to all matters of everyday life. Imagining Hades as a psychological reality is the same thing as imagining the intangible, subtle stuff that gives to all things their psychological value.

CHAPTER 2
HOW TO BECOME WHO ONE IS

Few writers in the West's history have addressed the question of the value of existence, especially the question of the sense of that value as it is experienced in everyday life, with as much lucid and fierce energy and with as much bold originality as Nietzsche. If man is the esteemer, as Nietzsche (1954) insists, then Nietzsche himself is the Vesalius whose incisive writings cut right through Western man's philosophical skin in order to reveal the psychological anatomy of that Esteemer underneath it. As Heidegger suggests (1979–1982), in his massive, four-volume study on *Nietzsche*, the history of Western philosophy takes a new start with Nietzsche, and it becomes, for the first time, value thinking.

Nothing cuts to the bone of the matter of the value of existence like Nietzsche's thought of the eternal return of all things. Yet while it is central to Nietzsche's thought, as he says again and again, including in the late and autobiographical *Ecce Homo* (1966c), in the section on *Thus Spoke Zarathustra*, to many readers and commentators it seems unworkable, and perhaps even not worth the trouble of serious consideration. In a recent and well-received Nietzsche biography, an otherwise sympathetic and imaginative writer calls the thought of eternal return a "vapid concept" (Chamberlain 1996, 152). If someone as deeply sympathetic to Nietzsche as Chamberlain is so dismissive of the thought, then one can only fear for it in the hands of less friendly readers. In my own study of Nietzsche's thought of eternal return, I have argued that eternal return often is wrongly dismissed on the basis of its inability to be mathematically or otherwise logically proven—or to be justified in its assumptions, demonstrated in fact, verified by empirical means or, for that matter, proven relevant at all, even if it were demonstrably true, which it certainly is not (1993, 25–34). A representative sample of commentators I have viewed in this manner includes Capec (1967), Danto (1965), Simmel (1907), Soll (1973), and Stambaugh (1972). More sympathetic and positive takes on eternal return are found in such philosophical commentaries as those of Heidegger (1979–1982, especially volume 2, but as I have argued, Heidegger's final judgment of eternal return has more Heidegger in it than Nietzsche), Löwith (1997), Klossowski (1997), and Deleuze (1983).

There is, to my knowledge, and other than in my own *Nietzsche and Psychoanalysis*, no commentary on eternal return that takes it explicitly, and as Zarathustra himself does (Nietzsche 1954, 3, "The Wanderer"; and 2, "On the Vision and the Riddle"), into the arena of everyday life experiences of repetition. In this respect, and more often than not, eternal return tends to remain an idea that is confined to the speculative realm of "What if?" questions, which is precisely how Nietzsche first introduces it to his readers (1974, aphorism 341). Some commentators, even those sympathetic toward eternal return, object to taking up the idea on its own literal imagery of repetition. They must be granted that, as a cosmology of how things really are, eternal return is, indeed, not sustainable. And besides, that is neither its claim to fame nor its true relevance. And yet, when an image is central to a metaphor, one must live with that fact, and one must not wish it away and then, driven by that wish, rationalize it away. The notion of repetition is, therefore, precisely where I have placed the weight of my reading of eternal return. If the image of repetition is good enough to serve Nietzsche in the arguments he proposes with eternal return, then, conversely, eternal return has a place of choice to occupy as an archetypal image and background that can perhaps shed light on the potential significance of everyday life experiences of repetition.

Rejecting the image of repetition in eternal return would be the same thing as deleting from the myth of Dionysos the image of the god's rebirth, or from the biblical and theological view of Jesus the Resurrection, or from the parable of the prodigal son his return home, or from Job's encounter with the Voice from the Whirlwind the story of his eventual restoration. Deleting repetition from eternal return would amount to deleting Sisyphus and his rock from the myth of Sisyphus. Yet my approach, both in *Nietzsche and Psychoanalysis* and in this book, is not about reducing eternal return—neither to petty repetition nor to pathological repetition. It is aimed, instead, at returning both of these to their archetypal context, so that we may gain a sense of their fullest possible significance and implications and, hence, a sense of their inherent value.

CHAPTER 3
SPLENDOR BEYOND GOOD AND EVIL

What is today sometimes still called "depth psychology," as in Golomb's (1999) recent book, *Nietzsche and Depth Psychology* (which covers Freud, Adler, and Jung), is generally thought to have been first named so (i.e., *Tiefenpsychologie*) early in the twentieth century by Zürich psychiatrist Eugen Bleuler (in Ellenberger 1970, 562, n.308). Many early figures need to be included under that umbrella of modern depth psychology, which was then, and still is now, taken to mean the "psychology of the unconscious." Some of these are, most notably, Franz Anton Mesmer, Jean-Martin Charcot, Joseph Breuer, Eugen Bleuler,

Adolf Meyer, Pierre Janet, Oskar Pfister, Hermann Rorschach, and Ludwig Binswanger (Ellenberger 1970). To this very incomplete list of well-known early figures we should add such names as Sandor Ferenzi, Herbert Silberer, and Georg Groddeck. And still the list of figures from that past era of modern depth psychology is incomplete. In the present-day history of archetypal psychology, as we have it in Hillman's generation, are such contemporaries as Roberts Avens, Patricia Berry, Edward S. Casey, Evangelos Christou, Henry Corbin, Gilbert Durand, Robert Grinnell, Adolf Guggenbühl-Craig, Rafael Lopez-Pedraza, David L. Miller, Thomas Moore, Robert Sardello, Robert Stein, and Mary Watkins (Hillman 1983). Many other names should rightfully be included, but to do justice to them all is simply impossible here.

What all these figures, both past and contemporary, have in common, in one fashion or another, is that they all labor under the metaphor of "depth." Without that "depth," depth psychology or the psychology of unconsciousness is unimaginable and impossible, in the same way that physics would be impossible without the metaphor, if not the metaphysics, of "nature" or "matter." But of course depth psychology's notion of "depth" has nothing to do with the idea of *res extensa*, or physical space, as in Descartes. Instead, it has everything to do with the analogical use of the metaphor of a "third dimension of depth," as it is spelled out, among other places, in Augustine (Hölscher 1986). We find this psychological notion of "depth" for the first time in the pre-Socratic Greek philosopher, Heraclitus, which is why he often is regarded as the distant founding father of the tradition (Hillman 1983, 4). Heraclitus, this first Western thinker reported to have taken the *psyche*, or soul, as his central concern, made what is not only the first but also the longest lasting, most penetrating, and most comprehensive statement about that soul's essential nature or primordial characteristic (Hillman 1979, 24ff.). He described it as endlessly, bottomlessly "deep"—in Greek, *bathun*. He also defined and shaped all depth psychology to come by bringing together its three essential terms—*depth, psyche*, and *logos*—in a formulation that, in one modern translation, reads: "The soul is undiscovered,/though explored forever/to a depth beyond report (Heraclitus 2001, 70).

Aristotle reports that during the very early history of the West's searches into the nature of psyche, Alcmaeon had said of the soul that "it is immortal because it resembles 'the immortals'" (1992a, I, 2). That connection between human affairs historical and things immortal, a connection based on "resemblance," is how depth psychology in general and archetypal psychology in particular anchor themselves in what Heraclitus forever described as the eternal river of everyday life, a river that is always simultaneously the same and not the same (2001, 81).

Given that almost inevitable connection between things temporal and things immortal, depth psychology in general and archetypal psychology in particular eventually come upon the matter of value, the value of existence. Heraclitus identified the fundamental issue when he said that to a god all things are beautiful and just, whereas men regard some things as beautiful and others as ugly or unjust. As a contemporary translation has it: "While cosmic wisdom/ understands all things/are good and just,/intelligence may find/injustice here, and justice/somewhere else" (2001, 61). That matter, of two essentially different perspectives on this world that man must inhabit, becomes the great philosophical problem. It does so not only for Greek philosophy in general and in particular for Plato and all Platonists and Neoplatonists who come after him. It already had been the problem for biblical Judaism. There it was explicitly addressed in, among many other places, the Book of Job. It also would remain the central problem in the Christianity of one of its best-known and, at first, long-resistant early converts, Augustine.

The reader of Augustine's writings is well served by viewing him not only as a student of Neoplatonism until his conversion to Christianity but as a Neoplatonist throughout his entire life. It is no exaggeration to say that he not only views Plato as a near-Christian, as noted earlier, but that his reading of Christianity could not remain standing if its Neoplatonist basis were removed from underneath it. The one ingredient that has to be added in order to view Augustine's Neoplatonism from the right perspective is Paul, the Pharisee educated defender of Jewish Law, whose conversion made him the mystic visionary whom many scholars consider the true founder of Christianity, more so than the historical figure of Jesus himself. The Pauline ingredient that Augustine adds to his reading of Neoplatonism is Paul's epistle to the *Romans*, especially its view of Jesus as the model of human being whose death overcomes the dividing gap that separates humanity from the divinity that permeates and surrounds it everywhere.

Augustine's reading of Neoplatonism, with the added ingredient of Paul, is in many ways best summarized in Augustine (1963) himself, in his *Confessions*. This work is less a historically literal autobiography, even less a strictly personal analysis, than it is an artifact depicting a spiritual process of transformation (Hawkins 1985). What is transformed is Augustine himself, more particularly his way of viewing the world, with himself in it, in relation to Being itself. The result is Neoplatonism at work toward what Augustine regarded as its logical and inherent conclusions: "its methodology involves a figurative reading of the events of an individual's life" (Hawkins 1985, 28). Such spiritual autobiography—which Augustine single-handedly invented as a new genre of narrative— can be described as "the expression of what remains fundamentally inexpressible" (ibid.).

The active ingredient in this transformative Augustinean vision that puts Neoplatonist theory into Christian practice, the "trick" that makes it work, is the ability to see, if ever so briefly, beyond the usual and all-too-human dichotomy that views some things as good and others as evil. Augustine's (1963) account of arriving at the possibility of that view is what constitutes the essential plot of his *Confessions*. When elsewhere he argues in great detail that "All things are good" (1953, iii), he is in his own way rediscovering what Heraclitus found, that in spite of all appearances before the human eye to the contrary, "good and ill are one" (2001, 57)

These are the very same issues and questions that lie behind Nietzsche's writings, especially such works as *The Birth of Tragedy* (1966b), which claims the life-affirming spirit of Dionysos as archetypal model for its view, as well as *Daybreak* (1982), *The Genealogy of Morals* (1966d), *Beyond Good and Evil* (1966a), and certainly also his *Thus Spoke Zarathustra* (1954), with its life-affirming philosophy of eternal return. Perhaps the best summary of all that is entailed in Nietzsche's search for an affirmative morality that overcomes the human dichotomy of good and evil may be found in aphorisms 341 and 276 from *The Gay Science* (1974). The one aims, through the thought of eternal return, at an affirmative *amor fati*; the other identifies the ability "to see as beautiful what is necessary in things" as the prerequisite for making amor fati possible as a love to live by.

Yet with Augustine and Nietzsche, we remain largely in the realm of theoretical human models—in one case through a spiritual autobiography that is more stylized fiction than real human history, in the other through a prototype of an alternative form of humanity that deliberately sets itself apart from humanity as we know it in everyday life. In this respect, and just as in Plato, the idea of a Good that goes beyond the practical concerns of everyday life remains out of reach.

It takes the Book of Job to offer us the picture of an imaginable and very real human being in whose life these matters play themselves out—some might say at his expense, others might say with his actual life as concrete medium. Job, precisely because he is so utterly and universally human, forms a bridge between what is more or less speculative in the thought of Heraclitus, Augustine, and Nietzsche and what is concretely lived by Everyman in certain circumstances, such as those in some phases or at some moments in psychoanalysis and in depth psychology generally. To know oneself, whether as in Augustine's (1963) *Confessions* or in contemporary depth psychology, becomes ultimately to come to know the presence in one's life of something other than one's usual sense of oneself. All matters historical become a mask, as in the cult of the life-affirming Dionysos (Otto 1965). That Dionysian spirit animates, sustains, and directs Nietzsche and much of the depth psychology that can be grounded in him.

CHAPTER 4
NOW AND ALWAYS

It is much easier to underappreciate, if not altogether to forget or even to ignore, the importance that Augustinean thought on time has for the West's understanding of itself—both collectively as a culture and at the level of personal individuality—than it is to overestimate it. Just as early Greek personal lyric gives us a first differentiated sense of inner individuality, so Augustine gives us a radically novel understanding of individual, and, as he argues, inwardly located, intentionality.

Human beings have of course always known that they are mortal, that time eventually will overtake them. It took Augustine's understanding of time, in itself a radical advance over Aristotle's, to add to the sense of individually differentiated inwardness also an internal calendar of events, a calendar divided and organized according to three internal mental functions: memory (past), attention (present), and anticipation (future). From Augustine onward, that inner calendar of events is part of the human psychological anatomy. This is by no means only a matter of a subjective sense for the passing of time. It goes to the heart of the way we imagine and narrate the events of our lives. It therefore also goes to the heart of the way we talk to ourselves about who we are—or think we are.

Augustine's thought on time belongs primarily in Book 11 of his *Confessions*. He there writes the famous lines: "What, then, is time? I know well enough what it is, provided that nobody asks me; but if I am asked what it is and try to explain, I am baffled" (1963, XI, 14). The prevailing understanding of time in Augustine's day was that of Aristotle's *Physics*: "I once heard a man say that what constitutes time is the motions of the sun and moon and stars. I did not agree" (1963, XI, 23). What Augustine asks himself is, as Ricoeur puts it, "How can time exist if the past is no longer, if the future is not yet, and if the present is not always" (1984–1988, 7)? Augustine writes: "If the future and the past exist, I want to know where they are" (1963, XI, 18). As Ricoeur emphasizes, and as is crucial for psychology, Augustine's question shifts from asking *how* time exists to *where* it exists: "The question is not naive. It consists in seeking a location for future and past things. . . . All of the arguments that follow are contained within the boundaries of this question, and will end up by situating 'within' the soul the temporal qualities" (1984–1988, 10).

The upshot of this train of thought—which is not merely of scholarly relevance for philosophers of time, but which is truly a major historical event in shaping Western consciousness itself—is that we end up with a psychology of time whose language is "quasi-spatial" (12). Not only that, this quasi-spatial language of psychology is cast in images and metaphors—and eventually in narratives, including entire psychological theories—whose root image is that of an individual inner soul with internal, or, as we say today, "intra-psychic" mental faculties and mental processes that orient us in and to time and to all the events taking place in time.

Augustine's thought on time is not formed in a vacuum. It belongs in a Judeo-Christian context, in a tradition whose God created linear time and who governs it in the form of history, which he gives a beginning, a middle with a specific direction, and an end. That Judeo-Christian "creation" of linear time becomes truly an "invention" when it is contrasted to the worldview that dominated human consciousness before it. That prior consciousness, as Eliade (1999) describes it in *Cosmos and History: The Myth of the Eternal Return,* and elsewhere, is based on a concept of cyclical time, according to which all events repeat preexisting and eternal or archetypal models of themselves.

It is against this background that we must view Freud and his Unconscious. Freud was no philosopher, and certainly no philosopher of time. Yet his imaginative psychology of individual unconsciousness places him squarely within the ongoing human conversation about time. Freud's (1955a) *Beyond the Pleasure Principle* contains his important commentary on the sense of time in the life of the soul: "Unconscious mental processes are in themselves 'timeless.' This means in the first place that they are not ordered temporally, that time does not change them in any way, and that the idea of time cannot be applied to them" (1955a, 28). The explicit comment itself is brief enough, but of its implications, it is difficult to see the end. These implications are spelled out, among other places, in lived experiences of time in which the usual sense of linear and forward movement is disrupted by compulsive repetition and by the sense of timelessness it engenders.

These lived experiences of disruptions in the usual sense of linear time have more than pathological implications. They belong to the natural repertoire of capabilities in human consciousness. If, as Nietzsche (1982) suggests, "consciousness is a more or less fantastic commentary on an unknown, perhaps unknowable, but felt text" (aph. 119), then these disruptions in ordinary linear time consciousness are perhaps the footnotes in that commentary referring to matters other than those immediately at hand. They refer to those ways in which everyday life remains closely tied to matters that are perhaps less strictly pathological in their essential nature than they are mythic, pagan, and ancient— and altogether more compatible with the presumably discarded myth and cosmology of the eternal return of timeless themes of meaningfulness. A therapeutic psychology that tries to stay close to the phenomenology of time consciousness in the spontaneous life of the soul becomes therefore by necessity archetypal in its approach. Thus it is not social case history that is the genre most suitable to account for the soul's presence in everyday life. Rather, as Jung and Hillman argue throughout their writings, depth psychology becomes exegesis of the mythic imagination in all such case history. An archetypal approach to the psychology and psychopathology of everyday life therefore ends up having one foot in historical time and one foot beyond it.

CHAPTER 5
FIRST INVENTION, THEN DISCOVERY

Aristotle (1992c), in *Poetics*, writes that "the poet's function is to describe, not the thing that has happened, but a kind of thing that might happen, i.e., what is possible as being probable or necessary. . . . Hence poetry is something more philosophic and of graver import than history, since its statements are of the nature rather of universals, whereas those of history are singulars. By a universal statement I mean one as to what such or such a kind of man will probably or necessarily say or do—which is the aim of poetry, though it affixes proper names to the characters" (IX). He then goes on to emphasize that "what convinces is the possible" (ibid.). For those who might be easily bamboozled by superficialities of appearance or method, he stresses, "the poet must be more the poet of his stories or Plots than of his verses . . . it is actions that he imitates" (ibid.). As for the relation between plot and character, and also the internal logic that holds plot and character together, he says: "whenever such-and-such a personage says or does such-and-such a thing, it shall be the necessary or probable outcome of his character; and whenever this incident follows on that, it shall be either the necessary or the probable consequence of it. From this one sees . . . that the Dénouement also should arise out of the plot itself" (ibid., XV).

What Aristotle writes about poetry applies also to the theories of depth psychology. Hence, Zarathustra's lapidary statement about the intimate bond between epistemology in psychology and poetic imagination: "Some souls one will never discover, unless one invents them first" (Nietzsche 1954, I "The tree on the mountain").

What in Aristotle's text is called "Plot" is, in the original Greek, *muthos*—myth. Therefore, the theorist of psychological life is a writer of its Plots, its myths. He is a mythographer of the soul. Hence, Hillman's endless explicit emphasis that all work in psychology—theory building, critical analysis, review of literature and history, case description, diagnostics, therapeutic practice, etiology, explanation, treatment recommendations—all of it implies a poetic basis of mind. All of it is matter to be handled with a mythic imagination. And it is not only official mythology or anything explicitly resembling official mythology that is viewed as mythic. All the realities of the soul are considered mythic. Hence, all soul work itself must be mythic in essence.

"Of course," writes Hillman, "this approach in modern times started with Freud. He imagined psychopathology against a background of the Oedipus myth" (1975, 100). "But," he goes on, "Freud's method of reversion took a positivistic course; it became reduction. Instead of leading events back to their base in myth—the soul's return to myth— Freud tried to base the myths on the actual behavior of actual biological families, ultimately reducing the mythical to the pathological" (ibid.). In other words, and to reframe this in Aristotelian terms, Freud took universals and reduced them to history, rather than taking case histories and elevating them to the significance of the universals in them. Freud was no poet in this important respect. He was a historian, and psychosocial history has remained psychology's favorite genre ever since.

But there is more. In Aristotle's scheme, the hero of tragedy is larger than life ("better than the ordinary man" (1992c, XV), whereas the hero in comedy is smaller than life ("worse than the average . . . Ridiculous, which is a species of the Ugly" (V). We are once again in the domain of value here. Now Freud, by taking large mythic themes ("better" or more highly valued ones) and reducing them to the smaller size ("worse" or negatively valued) of the individual pathologies of case histories, was therefore moving psychological analysis in the direction of comedy, in spite of recognizing the features of tragedy behind individual lives. He was, in effect, practicing reverse alchemy. Hence, and this should come as no surprise, instead of Aristotle's "pity and fear" (1992c, XIII–IV), which are elicited in the audience at the Greek tragic theater, we have the devaluing snickering that is never far away among the lay public when talk turns to psychoanalysis.

Yet Freud, despite himself, is not all historian, and neither is psychoanalysis pure comedy. For psychoanalysis, despite Freud's own explicit restriction imposed on its clinical practice—the restriction to aim only at individual repressed history—has more poetics in it than is often suspected. "What convinces is the possible," says Aristotle. "Possible," in turn, means "probable and necessary." That, in turn, means "not the thing that has happened, but a kind of thing that might happen." Freud implicitly reiterates this point when he argues that if the patient does not spontaneously recollect facts from his or her history that confirm the analyst's construction, then the analyst must persuade the patient of its truth (1955b, 265). That is, the construction must be made to appear possible, probable, and necessary.

The active and therapeutic ingredient in both Aristotle and Freud—therapeutic insofar as both speak of "catharsis"—is the spirit of imaginative boldness that is personified in Zarathustra and that, also in a therapeutic setting, laughingly says good-bye to any semblance of historical factuality and metaphysical veracity: one must "invent" the soul before one can "discover" it. This imaginative boldness of spirit protects psychological theory, and the therapy talk based on it, from becoming mere psychobabble that becomes passé as soon as the first whiff of the next cultural and scientific new developments can be detected.

Psychological theory that treats soul matters with a talking cure does what it does, like a poetics, by using imagination to aim at universality and timelessness. Hence, the implication, eventually made explicit in Jung and Hillman, that it should be archetypal. But that sense of the archetypal is less about literal universality and literal timelessness than it is about a response of confirmation and affirmation, a response that says, as though in Zarathustra's words: "But thus I willed it. . . . Thus I will it. . . . Thus shall I will it" (Nietzsche 1954, 1, "Thousand and One Goals;" and 2, "Redemption"). What is at stake is what Nietzsche (1966b), in *The Birth of Tragedy*, describes as the desire to narrate existence: "The same impulse which calls art into being, as the complement and consummation of existence, *seducing one into a continuation of life*" (sect. 3, emphasis added). The same spirit that, according to Nietzsche, calls Greek tragedy into being—"Thus do the gods justify the life of man: they themselves live it—the only satisfactory theodicy" (ibid.)—also is the spirit that makes both Shakespeare's Bottom from *Midsummernight's Dream* and depth psychology's patients turn to a "Peter Quince" for a poetic construction of their life, one that can be confirmed and affirmed.

Simply living one's life is not enough. One also must tell oneself the story, the plot, the myth one is enacting and inhabiting, because only in the telling can it be confirmed and affirmed. As Aristotle, Nietzsche, and Zarathustra suggest, only in that way does one truly arrive at where one is. This is what Heidegger (1977) means by convalescence: "The convalescent is the man who collects himself to return home—to turn in, into his own destiny. The convalescent is on the road to himself" (65).

To fully appreciate what is at stake here we may, once again, return to Augustine. We do so not for his theology, his religious beliefs, or his Christianity, nor, for that matter, for our own, but for the psychology we may cull from his writings. After all, his importance lies not only in his stature as a philosopher and theologian or church father and saint, but also, and perhaps before anything else, as a psychologist and an individual engaged in a lifelong personal search for the insights and truths he needed in order to feel fully satisfied. If Augustine is read as the Neoplatonist he remained throughout his life, even after his conversion to Christianity, then also the non-Christian reader can see his point that a life only completes itself by its return to its home base in the lap of Being itself. And access to that requires not psychosocial or historical analysis but poetic imagination. Augustine's (1963) own *Confessions* may be regarded as a case in point of such imaginative poetics. As Hawkins argues, his autobiography is an "expression of what remains fundamentally inexpressible . . . its methodology involves a figurative reading of the events of an individual's life. The method of achieving this is one where events in the personal life are imposed on archetypal patterns of sacred history, and the meaning and purpose of that life is therein seen as coincident with divine purpose" (1985, 28). This is, to stay with the spirit of Neoplatonism in Augustine, empirically borne out and essentially mythic psychology first, and religious doctrine only second—even though Christian doctrine, with Augustine's own help, eventually takes the latter to support, facilitate, and elucidate the former.

CHAPTER 6
TO FIND A GOOD BOOK TO LIVE IN

"It sometimes happens," writes Havelock (1994) in his *Preface to Plato*, "that an important work of literature carries a title which does not accurately reflect the contents. . . . These remarks apply with full force to that treatise of Plato's styled the *Republic*. Were it not for the title, it might be read for what it is, rather than as an essay in utopian political theory" (3). What it is about, then, is *not* political theory. Only about one-third of the *Republic* is "political" (ibid., 18, n. 37), and even then the "political" talk and its arguments serve mostly as an analogy for talk about the soul, that is, "the polity in (a man's) soul" (Plato 1978, 608b1; also see 605b7).

What, then, is the *Republic* about? It is largely about the relation between poetry and the soul, in particular, the influence that poetry has in determining and shaping the life of the soul. It is, before anything else, and despite the great diversity of other things discussed in it, about the poetic basis of everyday psychological life. This notion of a poetic basis of everyday psychological life is not only the explicit subject matter of the myth of Er, which constitutes the second half of the *Republic*'s tenth and last book, but, rather, of virtually the entire dialogue, starting from Book II. All of it is set in motion by a practical question: How should a person act in the practical world of everyday life? That question is first formulated in Book I, at and as the dialogue's beginning. It is subsequently reformulated in the broadest terms, as the state-soul analogy that is set up in Book II and that shapes the format of the remainder of the entire dialogue. So what appears to be political matter, starting with the *Republic*'s misleading title and including all the subsequent political theorizing that is begun in the *Republic* and continued for centuries and millennia in response to it, all this is in fact largely, as I also have argued elsewhere (Chapelle 1993, 129–40), an implicit psychology about a poetic basis of mind.

Another misleading title, with a somewhat reverse fate from the *Republic*'s, is that of Freud's (1955c) "Observations on Transference-Love." Just as Plato's *Republic* seems to be talking about daily life in the public arena and about the policies that should govern it, even though it is really addressing matters of soul, so Freud's "Observations on Transference-Love" seems to be addressing only private and internal matters of the neurotic soul, even though its implications have a much broader significance for everyday life. Hence, only psychoanalytically interested treaters are likely to be drawn to Freud's paper, as it would seem to refer to technical matters of interest only to specialists in the restricted field of psychological analysis, and yet it contains matter that is of broad and universal significance in the human condition.

"Observations on Transference-Love" and related writings may be read as a twentieth-century extension of Plato's *Republic*. Just as Freud's (1955b) "Constructions in Analysis"—also seemingly a "technical" paper of restricted significance to specialists only—may be read in conjunction with, and as a practical application of, Aristotle's (1992c) *Poetics*, so too can "Observations on Transference-Love" be regarded as a practical and lived version of much that is at stake in the *Republic*. For what the man or woman in psychological analysis is going through—the compulsion to be drawn into the world and the events of transference fantasies—is more than merely a process that is generated by, and restricted to, a specialized psychological treatment procedure. Rather, each is personally enacting and living universal philosophical matters about the poetic basis of mind, matters that are at the foundation of Western thought and culture and that have shaped Western consciousness itself throughout centuries and millennia— and with no foreseeable end of that cultural and philosophical history in sight.

Freud's (1955a) important suggestion that the poetics of transference fantasies is not restricted to psychoanalytic procedure but applies also to all daily life is already demonstrated in the West's very first novel and one of its all-time favorites, Cervantes Saveedra's (1957) *Don Quixote of La Mancha*. Here all the ordinary things and events that belong in the daily life of the men and women who live in La Mancha, where the protagonist encounters his adventures, are submitted to one man's poetic sensibilities. While Freud's patients, overcome by transference, are constantly stepping from the realities of the treatment setting into those of projected fantasies of love, Quixote rides from his beloved fantasy tales of chivalry into the fantastic universe he inhabits as he travels through La Mancha. This is precisely what is said in Plato's (1978) account of Er, but this time it is enacted in Quixote's Spain.

Framing this poetics that is spelled out in Plato's *Republic*, in the myth of Er, in transference theory, and in *Don Quixote* as a problem of truth versus illusion, as so much post–Platonic Western thinking does, tends to turn the matter into a more or less artificial philosophical problem and removes it farther and farther from the psychology of everyday life. A potentially more profitable approach is one that incorporates and deliberately develops a sense of the poetic basis of mind and of everyday life. This is precisely what Monet accomplishes, both in his serial paintings and in the ongoing physical process of turning the world of his Giverny garden into a concrete incarnation of the poetic images to which it is forever alluding.

Psychological theory in general and psychotherapeutic theory and practice in particular participate in that ongoing conversation about the poetic basis of existence that Western man has with himself, with his fellow human beings, and with the world and the universe in which he finds himself. Monet provides a model for a sustainable poetics of everyday life. Such a poetics turns mere appearance into sheer appearance. It amounts to a Nietzschean affirmation of a world of appearances. True world citizenship is perhaps less in need of political theory than of a sense for the poetics of soul. True psychology is not handmaiden of social policy and social hygiene but is active imagination placed in service of the soul's own imaginative or poetic basis.

CHAPTER 7
MAGICAL REALISM IN EVERYDAY LIFE

Of all the "models," "paradigms," or "languages" for psychology, alchemy surely has to be the most far-fetched one. How can anything that, at best, resembles nothing more than primitive and grossly prescientific chemistry have any bearing on anything at all? How can it be more than self-absorbed fantasy with misplaced pretensions of high seriousness, even while it does not even seem to bother to demonstrate its relevance, if it has any at all?

When Freud first spoke to Vienna's medical community about his "discovery" that deep inside the heart of every grown man or woman there lives a "polymorphously perverse child" trying to get its seemingly unnatural ways—boys wishing to do away with their fathers in order to become sole possessors of their mothers, and all the rest—he was nearly laughed out of town and out of the world of modern and scientific medical thinking and practice. Alchemy is many, many times more fantastic in its imaginings than Freud ever was, either on that day he first lectured to Vienna's doctors or in any of his subsequent theories. And yet, as Silberer (1971), a member of Freud's eventual Vienna School of psychoanalysis, would show in *Hidden Symbolism of Alchemy and the Occult Arts*—and before Jung made alchemy central to his analytical psychology in Basel, in such works as *Alchemical Studies, Mysterium Coniunctionis*, and elsewhere—alchemy is an early form of depth psychology.

Alchemy as a tradition dates back to ancient times and reaches all the way into modernity—Eliade (1978), Regardie (1970), Waite (1970), Taylor (1974), Grinnell (1973). It is a sustained and deliberate pretense, involving unrestricted but focused imagination, about processes taking place in, and procedures applied to, everyday matters and materials. Alchemical writings are about such things as lead, sulfur, urine, and quicksilver. They are about such quasichemical procedures as heating, cooling, blackening, whitening, coagulating, and dissolving, all of them taking places in alembics, retorts, and Marie's baths of various sorts and shapes. And they are about such everyday matters as marriage, death, children and mothers, fathers and sons, births, unions of every kind and transformations, and about everything else that happens to ordinary men and women everywhere.

Alchemy's fundamental "theory" is one about a world in which matter itself—all matter and all matters—is endowed with soul, soul engaged in processes that can only be described by means of images and metaphors. Its "practice" is one of applying what are essentially ritualized and symbolic procedures to the soul substance in the matters of everyday life. It is in many ways both magical realism *avant la lettre* and postmodernism before modernism. Its genius and relevance are in its detachment from the tyranny of the naturalistic view, from the literal beliefs in materialism, and from the dominance of ways of accounting for all things that are based on common sense, materialism, and naturalism. Alchemy's preoccupation is, rather, with the subtle and purely psychological anti-matter that inheres within all literal matters and their materialist accounts.

Alchemy is above all, and despite its explicitly declared goal, not about making gold—or even golden views, golden experiences, or gilded mannerisms and lifestyles. It is, rather, about the revaluation, the redemption, of all material life and of all literal factuality in the concrete world of daily living. But this revaluation, this redemption, is neither worked by otherworldly means nor for the sake of an otherworldly or afterworldly life. It is for the sake of a revaluation and redemption that take place *in* the world, not in any way or fashion *beyond it.* It is not esoteric spiritualism or quasireligion for entering another life but magical realism for inhabiting this one. And that is precisely why Nietzsche, before Silberer's and Jung's appropriation of alchemy for depth psychology, considered the figure of the alchemist "the most worthwhile kind of man that exists... the man who out of something slight and despicable makes something valuable, even gold itself. This man alone enriches, other men only give change" (letter to Georg Brandes of May 23, 1888, quoted in Chamberlain 1996, 232, n. 10). He wants to be precisely that "most worthwhile kind of man." As he also writes, in the same letter: "I have asked myself what hitherto has been best hated, feared, despised by mankind—and of that and nothing else I have made my *gold*" (ibid.) *A depth psychology that is cast as an alchemy, as much of archetypal psychology is, is not merely active imagination for the sake of active imagination, nor only a poetics of mind for the sake of a poetics of soul. It is a practical Nietzschean revaluation of values for the sake of an affirmative theory and praxis of redemption.*

CHAPTER 8
IMMACULATE CONCEPTION IN EVERYDAY LIFE

Modern psychology, insofar as it is a science about "human nature," tries to say what man *is*, or at least what he *resembles*. It also ventures to say how man can become even better at being what he already is—a new and improved version of himself, the sanest or healthiest version ever. In combination, these two activities amount to no small undertaking. One can therefore forgive psychology for believing that this is all that it has to do in order to fulfill its task. And yet there is more. For in addition to a scientific psychology about "human nature," there also is a psychology of the process of Immaculate Conception, whereby a man or woman is, as it were, conceived a second time, this time not naturally but purely psychically, when life is already fully underway. This involves a process whereby a man or a woman becomes what he or she is destined to be—which is far more, and far more complex and significant, than merely being sane or insane. The psychology of this second, this purely psychic, this Immaculate Conception is based on magical realism, not on scientific models of "human nature." It suggests that man can yet become something that is almost inconceivably different from what he already is, or from what he is assumed to be. This is precisely what Nietzsche means when he says that "man is the *as yet undetermined animal*" (1966a, 62. emphasis in original). It also is what Zarathustra means when he says that "Man is something that shall be overcome. . . . The overman is the meaning of the earth" (Nietzsche 1954, "Prologue," 3).

This famous—or, in the hands of German nazism, infamous—Nietzschean notion of an "overman" is not about any sort of superior human being, with superior human qualities, as too many Nietzsche readers have thought. It is least of all about any kind of genetically, racially, or otherwise naturally superior class of human beings. Nor is it about a kind or a class of human being that can declare itself superior in connection with its accomplishments or its ingenuity. The "overman" is what every human being can become "over and above" all that he naturally is assumed to be—all that he is known and defined and expected to be. That "overcoming," that "over and above," is not accomplished by such means as a healthy lifestyle, exercise, body building, or intellectual, spiritual, or any other kind of training and discipline, or by whatever natural means. It comes into being in the form of the magical realism that imposes itself on "human nature" and that thereby reconceives it.

In order to appreciate what is at stake here and what Nietzsche and Zarathustra mean—and in order to begin to be able to imagine what such a psychology of purely psychic and Immaculate Conception in everyday life might look like—one may turn to the biblical figure of Abram, whose name is transformed into Abraham when his long-familiar identity is magically changed into "a father of many nations" (Genesis, 17, 4). Abram is instructed by his unknown and unknowable God to up and leave his homeland, to go to an as yet unidentified place, in a land not his own, in order to start a people that at first seems quite literally "inconceivable," simply because Abram and his wife are, "realistically" or naturally, too old to have children. What Abram is made to do is "overcome" his known life, including his known identity, and assume the uncertainty of an "*as yet undetermined*" life and identity.

The difference between a psychology of "human nature," which tends to be nearly all that modern psychology offers and can conceive, and a psychology of Immaculate Conception is the difference between the natural *conditions* of the life of the soul and the actual magical-realistic *facts* of that life of soul. Perhaps nothing of what modern psychology has to say about "human nature" can be enough to satisfy the deepest human needs as long as such a psychology has as yet to determine that, to repeat, man is *always*, permanently and by definition, "the as yet undetermined animal." While it is true that modern scientific psychology is becoming increasingly good at identifying the natural or minimal conditions that make the life of the soul possible, it has as yet to determine for itself whether it can, or why it might want to, conceive of a dimension of everyday life that is governed by magical realism.

CHAPTER 9
HERE AND NOW

If scientifically imagined psychology, which is the greater part of psychology as we have it today, has difficulties in conceiving anything like a psychology that reaches beyond nature while refraining from otherworldly metaphysics, and if this is because such scientific psychology focuses on the assumed material conditions that make experience possible but not on the elusive totality of the experience itself, then this is itself primarily because its emphasis is on material explanation, which defines the bulk of the rational tradition in the West. And if that is the way things are with modern psychology, it is largely because it has espoused the views of Aristotle (1992a), from his *On the Soul*, where the primary association of soul is with biology and the body. In turning to Aristotle, psychology knowingly and deliberately turned away from Plato, where soul is more mythically understood than biologically, and where it is more closely associated with the realm of the underworld of Hades than with the anatomy and functioning of the physical body. As Hillman (1975) writes: "Aristotle's definition of soul, as the life of the natural body . . . [allows] . . . no way to approach psyche other than in the biological and analytical ways Aristotle preferred. The Aristotelian fantasy rules Western psychology . . . it does so today whenever psychology assumes the organic biological slant toward the soul's events, or whenever it insists on empiricism" (206). Because the modern, rational, scientific, and ultimately materialist West has put most of its eggs in the Aristotelian basket of analytical and nature-based reasoning, and because it remains focused on material explanation in this fashion, its scientifically imagined psychology more often than not fails to sound the true depths of soul, depths that are nonetheless inherent in all daily activities and events, all day long, all the days of our lives.

In critical response to this approach, we have had such orientations as phenomenologically informed psychology. Its insistence on a "return to the things themselves" has been an attempt to address lived experience itself, as directly as possible, rather than remaining focused on the presumably natural or material conditions thought to be behind it. But this has largely been an epistemological exercise. Insofar as phenomenological psychology has largely remained epistemologically focused—on how to "know" the nature of lived experience as it is actually lived, and not only on the assumed material conditions that make it possible—it often has insufficiently appreciated that, as Nietzsche (1966b) first put it in his *Birth of Tragedy*, the lived world is in the first place an aesthetic and moral phenomenon. More precisely, it has insufficiently appreciated that this involves, before anything else, a value judgment about existence which man cannot stop from being made, and from seeing made, by means of his own life. Nor has phenomenological psychology sufficiently appreciated that the content of that value judgment can only be identified indirectly, by being imagined. It would therefore seem that phenomenological psychology, while being appropriately critical of the limits of scientific models for psychology, has insufficiently appreciated what in these pages is viewed as the poetic basis of mind and of everyday life, especially the valuative and self-affirming dimension of that poetic basis.

Archetypal psychology proposes that the best way to imagine the value judgment inherent in every lived event or experience is by "sticking to the images" in the identified facts of that event or experience. This idea was first spelled out as an explicit and primary method for psychology by Jung (1953–, XVI, par. 320; see also Hillman, 1983, 6ff.). Jung also insisted that "image *is* psyche" (1953–, XIII, par. 75). Both principles were subsequently taken up as a golden rule—and made virtually inseparable and interchangeable—by Hillman (1983, 6 ff.).

But these "images" are not pictures of any kind. Archetypal psychology is therefore not merely picture thinking, or what Plato (1978), in Books 6 and 7 of the *Republic*, considers the lowest form of thinking, because it is the farthest from grasping the true essence of anything. What archetypal psychology calls "images" are neither mental pictures nor mental representations, or what psychoanalytic psychology thinks of as internalized introjects. Nor do they stand in for something else, as Hillman (1979) argues throughout *The Dream and the Underworld* and elsewhere. They are themselves the soul's pure substance and visibility. But visibility is here not a visual matter, and substance not a physical one. Both visibility and substance are here more about a way of seeing than about anything seen. Nor do images refer to something that is located or generated internally, in the mind. As Hillman (1983) writes: "It is not we who imagine but we who are imagined" (8). And as Jung (1953–) writes: "this is still 'psychology' though no longer science" (VI, par. 84).

In Nietzsche's view, ever since *The Birth of Tragedy* but subsequently also throughout the rest of his writings, the world is not just an aesthetic and moral phenomenon, it is an aesthetic and moral phenomenon that depends on itself to justify itself. Hence, the important question, a question to which eternal return provides the affirmative answer: "Can we remove the idea of a goal from the process and then affirm the process in spite of this? This would be the case if something were attained at every moment within the process" (Nietzsche 1968, sect. 55). As I have tried to argue in this book and in *Nietzsche and Psychoanalysis* (Chapelle 1993), Jung's and Hillman's insistence on "sticking to the image" is archetypal psychology's unintended way of realizing the agenda of eternal return (Chapelle 1993, 225 ff.). That unintended realization of the Nietzschean agenda of eternal return is accomplished without having to explicitly rely on the notion of repetition or on lived experiences of repetition, yet also without omitting anything essential from the Nietzschean agenda of redeeming all that is of the earth, on its own terms. The argument has been, most compactly stated, that archetypal psychology puts Nietzsche into practice, and that it does so most explicitly in the rule of "sticking to the image" in all things. The important shift in emphasis this brings about for psychology—from emphasizing personal feelings inside the individual to developing a feeling for the impersonal that surrounds and sustains the individual, all without having to invoke any metaphysics, especially perhaps a metaphysics of spirit—this shift in emphasis is perhaps the greatest practical consequence of an archetypal approach to the psychology of everyday life.

CHAPTER 10
IT IS ENOUGH AND IT IS GOOD

"The origin of all things is their end as well," writes Plotinus in *Enneads*, the collection of his texts put together late in his life by his pupil, Porphyry (II, 8 [30], 7, in Plotinus 1964). The statement is meant to convey Plotinus's view, based squarely in Plato but with added and profoundly Plotinean originality, that all things are a reflection of an origin to which they strive to return, and that we can only begin to sense their deepest reality when we can glimpse that origin to which they seek to return. This idea, so the Plotinus scholar, Elmer O'Brien, writes, shapes the mystic agenda that informs much of the medieval view of the cosmos: "It was the schema that many a medieval mystic attempted to reproduce within him, in order to achieve his itinerary to God" (see the Introduction in Plotinus 1964, 20). This agenda is explicitly spelled out in Augustine's *Confessions*, which is centered around the Plotinean idea of "*amplexis*," of an embrace or reunion between the concrete matters of the everyday world in history and their divine origin to which they seek to return (Hawkins 1985, 67).

The genius and relevance of Plotinus, and the point that matters most here, lie in the fact that, as O'Brien puts it, "he manages to eliminate the conventional dichotomy between action and contemplation" (Plotinus 1964, 162). For Plotinus, each and every thing in the world strives toward contemplation—and that not only in discreetly and explicitly "contemplative" moments or activities in the life of man alone, nor only in the self-styled and exclusive class of humans that considers its lives and its practices "contemplative." In his famous "bad joke"—which is neither bad nor a joke but an inspired and bold insight by means of which he leaps beyond Plato and beyond Christian dogmatism—he proposes the following: "If, before beginning serious investigation, we were jestingly to say that all beings strive toward contemplation—not merely those endowed with reason but unreasoning animals as well, even plants and the earth that begets them—who would listen to such nonsense?" (Plotinus 1966–1988, III, 8 [30], 1). But he is not jesting. He goes even farther and includes his own bad joke: "Could it be true that in jesting we are contemplating?" (ibid.). His answer is both unhesitating and earnest: "Yes" (ibid.). And he means it: "To contemplation all actions tend" (ibid.). But he is, of course, nobody's fool, and he immediately adds: "compulsive actions drawing it (i.e., contemplation) somewhat towards external objects, voluntary actions less so" (ibid.). A little later he makes his position even clearer: "*The point of action is contemplation and the having an object of contemplation. Contemplation is therefore the end of action*" (ibid., III, 8 [30], 6, emphasis added). This is precisely what the present book proposes in the chapter on the magical realism and the alchemy in everyday life: that, contrary to the usual view, according to which theory serves practice, all the practices of everyday life serve to confirm the theories we have about it, so that we may behold what those theories hold, and what they hold out for us to consider and believe.

When a sense of contemplation within action—in the midst of action and as the intrinsic *telos* of action—is achieved, so Plotinus continues, "Then the soul rests. It seeks no further. It is sated." At this point—and this is precisely what satisfies, and what this book has been arguing as the true goal of depth psychology—"Knower and known are one. I mean this seriously" (ibid.).

The same essential idea appears after Plotinus in his most influential student, Augustine. Here it is described as the sense of complete satisfaction that is derived from the contemplation of God: *Sat est et bene est*—"It is enough, and it is good" (Augustine 1963, VII, 7). But the Augustinean or Christianized version of Plotinus can only reach its sense of fully satisfying contemplation through Christ, and through a full conversion to Christ: "Certainly now we see through a glass darkly, and not yet face to face, and so, as long as I am on a pilgrimage away from you, I am more present to myself than to you" (ibid., X, 5). For Augustine is not merely Plotinus transposed for Christian purposes, Plotinus with a Christian twist. Augustine is Plotinus with Paul grafted on. He is Plotinus plus Paul.

Archetypal psychology, more comfortable in the footsteps of Plotinus and in the imaginative Greek polytheism before him than with the often exclusionary dogmatism of Christian monotheism after him, participates in the Plotinean serious jest, this *serio ludere*. For it too produces the self-protective irony about itself that is missing in Christian dogmatism—and also in the metaphysics of Jung's psychology of objectified archetypes. As though directly, though ironically, alluding to the famous Augustinean and Christian metaphor according to which, except through Christ, we only see "through a glass darkly," Hillman (1975) picks the very image of glass as a metaphor of choice for archetypal psychology. He picks glass to describe what he calls the soul's natural act of "seeing through" the literal appearance of all things—of seeing into a depth of images, meaningfulness, and significance that are always hiding within the concrete masks that all things are (140–45).

What satisfies in the practice of thinking archetypally about matters of soul is less anything seen than the archetypal way of seeing itself. It is less about seeing something than about seeing through something. That is largely what distinguishes archetypally based psychology from scientifically based psychology, which contents itself with identifying the supposed material conditions that make an experience possible—and which then implies that consumers of its psychological theories and practices should be content with that as well. Hence, Hillman (1975) writes: archetypal "psychologizing is not satisfied when necessary and sufficient conditions have been met or when testability has been established. It is satisfied only by its own movement of seeing through" (140). That Hillman is still working in the neighborhood of Plotinus—even that of Augustine, in spite of archetypal psychology's likely protests to the contrary—

comes across in the following statements about the traditional depth psychological practice of always seeking to look deeper than any surface matter: "As we penetrate or try to bring out, expose, or show why, we believe that what lies behind or within is truer and more real, powerful, or valuable than what is evident" (ibid.). This, says Hillman, is how archetypal psychologizing "*justifies itself*" (ibid., emphasis in original). And here is the connection to Plotinus and Augustine: "we justify the activity by appealing to an ultimate hidden value that can never fully come out but must remain concealed in the depths in order to justify the movement. This ultimate hidden value justifying the entire operation can also be called the hidden God (*deus absconditus*), who appears only in concealment" (ibid.).

CHAPTER 11
SEEING IS BELIEVING

There is always a danger to any psychological theorizing, including archetypal psychologizing, or what Hillman (1975) calls "seeing through" (115–64). The danger, says Hillman, is this: "the disrepute of psychologizing may be blamed mainly upon the confusion of the tools—ideas—with the activity. Psychologizing becomes illegitimate by simplifying into psychologisms" (ibid., 141). Hillman explains with an example of something that many who are engaged with psychology tend to forget, or simply fail to realize in the first place: "by means of the idea of the unconscious we are able to see into, behind, and below manifest behavior. But the unconscious is merely a tool for deepening, interiorizing, and subjectifying the apparent. Should we take the unconscious literally, then it too . . . must be seen through, deliteralized. Without the idea of the unconscious we could not see through behavior into its hidden unknowns. But we do not see the unconscious" (ibid.). "The problem here," Hillman writes, "is the ancient one of hypostasizing an idea into a literal thing" (ibid.). But, Hillman is also quick to point out, "this is more than slipshod thinking, for it is inherent in *eidos*, idea, itself" (ibid.). It is less the person making the error who is responsible for the error than it is the impersonal idea itself that makes the person see what he or she sees, and that then makes the person become literal about what he or she sees. It is also less about the person having an idea that may be wrong than it is about the person being had by an idea that, as it were by itself, convinces him or her that it has pointed at all there is to be seen and that therefore it should govern. Hillman reminds his reader that the notion of "idea," from the Greek *eidos*, comes to us from Plato and originally means "both that which one sees—an appearance or shape in a concrete sense—and that by means of which one sees. We see them, and by means of them. Ideas are both the shape of events, their constellation in this or that archetypal pattern, and the modes that make possible our ability to see through events into their pattern. By means of an idea we can see the idea cloaked in the passing parade" (ibid.,

121). The immediate implication is that the more ideas we have to see with, or by means of, the more we can actually see. That is one of the reasons why active imagination, or the method of activating the imagination, is so important in depth psychology in general, and most explicitly in archetypal psychology in particular. This also implies that ideas, when handled in the medium of active imagination, always engender ever more ideas and keep on engendering more ideas, "breeding new perspectives for viewing ourselves and the world" (ibid.). For our common history, this means such things as where once we thought the world to be flat, we now think it round. For therapeutic psychology, there is this implication: "our ideas change as changes take place in the soul, for as Plato said, soul and idea refer to each other, in that an idea is the 'eye of the soul'" (ibid.). So Hillman concludes: "Psychologizing is in danger when it forgets that literalism is inherent in the very notion of idea. Then we begin to see ideas rather than seeing by means of them" (ibid., 141).

There is a profound humility that is implied here. Despite all the psychologizing, or all the seeing through we may do by means of a deliberately activated imagination, any account of an event we give ourselves or a psychotherapy patient in this fashion "does not mean that we now know more fully or surely what is actually taking place" (ibid.). Even though I may see through behavior and experience, and in so doing recognize a Savior complex in it, or whatever, all the while "believing that this account is more basic and valid than appearances," there is nonetheless "no surety that it *is* the Savior complex and that now I know it because I have seen it" (ibid., 142, emphasis in original). The whole point of psychologizing, says Hillman, is that it "confirms ambiguity, it does not settle it" (ibid.). The goal is not to arrive at a position or a place of certainty, a sort of central clearinghouse of all bottom-line human meaning where the truth about things can be seen displayed—and then grasped and clasped as a personal possession that I can from now on consider my privately owned property. Instead, the goal of psychologizing is to move us in such a way that we are moved to a place, a viewpoint, a mind-set where "we hover in puzzlement at the border where the true depths are. Rather than an increase in certainty there is a spread of mystery, which is both the precondition and the consequence of revelation" (ibid.).

This is, we may add to Hillman, Job all over again. It is Job stunned, silenced, awed, mystified, made dizzy by the display of miracle everywhere, right in the middle of an ordinary day of the week. The more one looks here, the more enigmatic and mysterious things become, even though, paradoxically, they also reveal their enigma and mystery more clearly and more visibly than ever before—right in front of me, right before my very eyes. When such a vision, such a revelation, is experienced and takes over, then something in the soul is the same no more. Job, though the same as before, is a profoundly changed man, living a profoundly changed yet unchanged existence, in the same yet different world.

By getting caught by its very tools, by the ideas it employs, psychologizing becomes psychology. That way psychology becomes its own worst enemy, precisely by believing it has found, exposed, and displayed objective and true things—the ego, the unconscious, repression, the case history, the diagnosis (ibid., 145). What is at stake in this shift from seeing by means of ideas to thinking we see the things themselves can be understood—psychologized or seen through—in a number of ways. Hillman's own critical ideas on the matter present one way of doing so. But Hillman's ideas are themselves not about bottom-line facts either, as he would be the first to see and admit. In this respect, Hillman is like Nietzsche, who gave us the idea of a personal unconscious but who then also was the first to reject any belief in that idea that would claim it to be fact. This self-ironic move Freud never made when he persisted in elaborating and objectifying the idea of the unconscious that he had found in Nietzsche. Rather, he spent the rest of his life arguing for its factuality, thereby turning the metaphorics of psychological analysis into a psychoanalytic metaphysics. Jung did the same with the idea of the collective unconscious and of archetypes when he proceeded to catalog those objectified archetypes and to give us his "psychology of archetypes."

One way to psychologize or see through these matters is, as proposed in this book's chapter 11, "Seeing Is Believing," through the idea of an adjective-based or adjectival quality of all things. Such an approach can see that all things have an archetypal depth of significance, even while steering clear of objectifying archetypes, as Jung and Jungian psychology have done. Another way, also removed from familiar depth psychological notions, including archetypal ones, is through the idea of looking at the identifiable facts of an event for the equivalent of pronunciation signs among them that can help allude to the always unspeakable true name of all things. Still another way, and one that steps back even farther not only from the usual theories in depth psychology in general and archetypal psychology in particular but also from contemporary Western consciousness generally, is by examining the history of the words "belief" and "to believe."

As the scholar of religion, Wilfred Cantwell Smith argues, in such books as *Belief and History* and *Faith and Belief*, what we today understand by "belief" and "believe" is by no means the same thing as what these words meant in past centuries. Today "belief" and "believe" refer to an activity of the mind that involves more or less critical thinking and that is aimed at determining whether something is going to be upheld as true (or at least temporarily tenable) or false. As Smith puts it, quoting one of his colleagues, "modern philosophers are not at their ease until they have written down a proposition on the blackboard to have a look at it" (1985, 57). This approach, involving the only meaning of "belief" and "believe" that most of us, children of the rational, modern, and scientifically thinking West, know, is by no means universal and timeless, and certainly not privileged. Rather, it is itself an idea that needs to be seen through.

"Belief" and "believe" as we now know them are very late historical developments, according to Smith. He makes his scholarly arguments on the basis of such grounds as word usage and word counts in the Bible, in Shakespeare, in the great philosophers and other writers of past ages, in leading dictionaries throughout the centuries, and in other major sources of textual material. Some of the main findings that are most to the point here, for purposes of shedding light on the archetypal way of psychological theorizing, emphasize that "belief" and "believe," prior to meaning what they now do to us, referred far more to deep and intimate (and, we might add, at least partly unconscious) matters of soul than to critical and mostly conscious ones of mind. As Smith argues, "belief" and "believe" had more to do with the German "*belieben* . . . 'to hold dear,' 'to prize.' It signified to love (it comes from the same root as 'love': German *Liebe*, Latin *libido*), to give allegiance, to be loyal to; to value highly" (ibid., 41; see also Smith 1998, chapter 6). Two things are most striking here: that we have once again landed in depth psychology's libido theory and the human act of seeking things to intimately embrace, and that this has to do with becoming devoted, life and limb, to things we value highly. Perhaps not surprisingly, Smith finds that the act of "belief" or "believing" was formerly spoken of in over ninety percent of the occurrences of the verb in contexts involving a first and a second person, only rarely the third person (1985, 52). It was more about I and Thou, intimately involved, than about a third, an outsider to that intimacy. Today, in contrast, so Smith argues, the activity of believing—especially in philosophical contexts—refers mostly to something that other people do (ibid., 53). It is now mostly something that is of interest insofar as it is fair game for critical analysis and commentary, with that analysis and commentary meant to decide, possibly once and for all, whether the belief in question is true or false.

"Belief" and "believe," in their original sense, as Smith explores them, are about what can be loved and held dear, because it is held in high esteem. And it is held in high esteem because the context of intimacy between a first and a second person in which it is at issue makes a vision of the idea in question not only possible but also trusted. It is not: I believe you because you have proven your case. It is more: I see what you mean and I value what you mean, because what you tell me shows it to me, and because I can see it as you show it to me, because I trust you. It is, as Smith puts it, a matter of declaring one's loyalty and devotion. It means: "entering—deliberately, through an act of will—into a relationship of personal allegiance" (ibid., 42). In Smith's examination of religious texts, this referred of course most prominently to pledging allegiance to God. However, the pattern is not restricted to religion, and certainly not to Christianity. Rather, and as Freud's use of libido theory argues, it is about the life of the soul in all its libidinal or "believing" activities. Smith repeatedly emphasizes that what matters most is the *activity* of *Belieben*, not the specific content or object invested with libido. If, as the book at hand has argued, archetypal psychology does not *believe* in archetypes as objectifiable things, it nonetheless devotes itself unconditionally to the act of *Belieben* the archetypal images and imagination that are the very soul of everyday life.

CHAPTER 12
EVERYMAN'S OWN DOUBLE

Perhaps the hardest thing for modern Western men and women to overcome is the idea that the physicality of existence, its material condition, is the bottom-line truth about it. The sciences of nature must have the last word, so the modern West has come to believe. This is good for the sciences of nature, but it is not good enough for in-depth dealings with the life of the soul. Understanding the physicality of existence and the natural laws that govern it is only good enough when all we dare ask for is knowledge about the assumed minimal material conditions of events. But knowledge of assumed minimal material conditions does not tell us anything about the psychic essence of events, which is subtle and metaphoric rather than physical and literal. This does not mean, however, that the only alternative that is left for depth psychology is to pursue some form of disembodied "spirituality" of any kind. For psychology's root paradigm is *psyche*, not *pneuma*, even though, as Hillman (1979) argues, Christianity has worked hard to reject the realities of soul in favor of disembodied spirit (see especially 85–90), leaving room only for a view of matter and embodied life that is devoid of soul. The price for such a rejection of soul has been willingly paid by the West's own psychology, but it has been painfully extracted at the expense of Everyman's sense of soul in everyday life. Just because the physicality of everyday life is not its ultimate reality, as Christian philosophers argue with the "near-Christian" Plato at the head of the pack, this does not mean that the soul matter of daily life is, for that reason, any less incarnate. This may seem a contradiction, but it is not. What it means is that, as Hillman (1975) puts it in discussing what he calls the "naturalistic fallacy," "nature cannot be the guide for comprehending soul" (84). This implies not only that the physicality of existence does not explain or even describe the realities of soul. It also means that nature and the way things are in nature cannot be the norm for sizing up the way things are in the realm of soul. Nature is not the measure of all things when we wish to talk about the life of the soul.

The naturalistic fallacy is as common as it is, adds Hillman, because it is all too easy, and because that very ease is itself part of what makes this fallacy so attractive and seemingly persuasive (ibid.). All one has to do is take nature as one's reference point, take all that is visible in nature as the most natural thing. But this does not work for soul, which is unnatural—even though it loves to sport with all that is in nature. For soul is neither part of nature nor subject to the laws governing nature, even though it is everywhere to be found in the midst of nature. To see just how unnatural the realm of soul is, one only has to look at dreams. There everyone can experience firsthand, on every dream-filled night, how unnatural the soul's spontaneous activity is. For the events, persons, things, activities, deeds, processes, and scenarios that occur in dreams, even though they remind us of how things are in nature, here strike us even more for the dream's unnatural and imaginative treatment of them. What we notice above all is how different from nature everything in dreams is. Dreams are the soul's own spontaneous alchemical *opus contra naturam*—the soul at work on going against nature, the soul undermining all that we take to be normative in nature, the soul effortlessly dismissing all that is second nature in our natural ways of thinking. So argues Hillman (1979) throughout *The Dream and the Underworld* which, beyond offering the first truly new dream theory since Freud and Jung, also offers the first truly new paradigm for an altogether novel approach to depth psychology. In writing about the ease with which we constantly and almost naturally fall for the fallacy of naturalism, Hillman (1975) speaks of "the inertia of following nature" (84). As he adds: "such naturalism soon declines into materialism ... (which) insists that material reality is first and psychic reality must conform with it: *psyche* must obey the laws of *physis* and imagination follow perception" (ibid.). The realm of soul, however, in contrast to that of nature, moves "from natural meaning to imaginative meaning" (ibid., 85). Psychological significance and meaningfulness are the most natural thing in the world, yet "they are not nature but culture ... nature that has gone through a process within the imagination ... *soul in the very midst of nature*" (ibid., emphasis in original).

Soul is neither mind nor matter. Nor is it the effect of one upon the other, as is proposed in psychologies of "the mind-body connection." Rather, it is a third that is neither one nor the other. But it is not a third that in any way results from any two—whether mind and body, spirit and matter, nature and something that lies outside of nature or that transcends life in nature. Nor is soul what, in quasimechanical and at least theoretically intelligible ways, "links" the two poles of any of these pairs, for by "linking" them it also keeps them apart, which means it keeps them intact as a bottom-line duality to which everything must be referred, meaning reduced. And also—this follows closely as an immediate implication—soul is not about a correspondence or lack of correspondence within any twosome. It is not about a correspondence or lack of correspondence between fantasy and fact, between perception and reality, between imagination and factual history, between emotion and reason. It is, instead, an autonomous third that overcomes these usual twosomes, a third whose very reality lies precisely in this overcoming of dualities of every sort. What Hillman calls the "fundamental intolerance of human psychology" (ibid., 175) is precisely the insistence on such endless twosomes of every imaginable kind, and on the terms that make up their duality—all at the expense of the psychic third that simply, effortlessly, and magically-realistically ignores them.

Body-mind, matter-spirit, emotion-reason, nature-supernatural, world-other-worldly, fact-fiction, physical-metaphysical, perception-imagination, truth-illusion, projection-reality, belief-truth—all these are denials of the soul's own reality, due to the "fundamental intolerance" within so much of psychology.

Soul is less in any of these dichotomies—all of which are variations on the theme of "nature" and something that is either outside of "nature" altogether or dismissed as airy nothing—than it is in the imaginative dissolution of all seemingly natural things, dichotomies included. That dissolution is what Hillman, (1979) mainly in *The Dream and the Underworld,* but in many other places as well, calls the "death perspective," which myth depicts as Hades and his non-physical, unnatural underworld of images that animate all life under the sun.

Deliberately taking up its position in that Hades perspective, archetypal psychology makes a dramatic shift in priorities: "It is not life that matters but soul and how life is used to care for soul" (Hillman 1975, 175). This is not inhumane indifference to the human. On the contrary. It is about adding to the strictly humanistic perspective a depth of meaningfulness and significance for which purely humanistic terms and prejudices tend to be too limited in their imagination. As in the realm of dreams, the "main concern seems not to be with living but with imagining" (ibid.). This is not about imagining instead of living, and with a disregard for living. It is about adding to everyday living more imagining, so that room can be created—as Hades does vis-à-vis Zeus—for a sense of the soul in everyday life.

WORKS CITED

Alfaric, Prosper. 1918. *L'Evolution Intellectuelle de S. Augustin*. Paris: I. Nouroy.

Aristotle. 1992a. "On the Soul." Pp. 153–249 in *Introduction to Aristotle*, ed. Richard McKeon. New York: Modern Library.

———. 1992b. "Physics." Pp. 118–145 in *Introduction to Aristotle*, ed. Richard McKeon. New York: Modern Library.

———. 1992c. "Poetics." Pp. 663–712 in *Introduction to Aristotle*, ed. Richard McKeon. New York: Modern Library.

Augustine. 1953. "The Nature of the Good: Against the Manichees." In *Augustine: Earlier Writings*, trans. John H. S. Burleigh. Philadelphia: Westminister Press.

———. 1963. *Confessions*. Translated by Rex Warner. New York: New American Library.

———. 1964. *On Free Choice of the Will*. Translated by Anna S. Benjamin and L. H. Hackstaff. New York: Library of Liberal Arts.

———. 1984. *City of God*. Translated by Henry Bettenson. London: Penguin.

Berg, Jan Hendrik van den. 1983. *The Changing Nature of Man: Introduction to a Historical Psychology*. New York: Norton.

Bettelheim, Bruno. 1984. *Freud and Man's Soul*. New York: Vintage.

Capec, Milec. 1967. "Eternal Return." In *The Encyclopedia of Philosophy*, ed. Paul Edwards. New York: Macmillan.

Cervantes Saveedra, Miguel de. 1957. *Don Quixote of La Mancha*. Translated by Walter Starkie. New York: New American Library.

Chamberlain, Lesley. 1996. *Nietzsche in Turin: An Intimate Biography*. New York: Picador USA.

Chapelle, Daniel. 1993. *Nietzsche and Psychoanalysis*. Albany: State University of New York Press.

Danto, Arthur. 1965. *Nietzsche as Philosopher*. New York: Columbia University Press.

Deleuze, Gilles. 1983. *Nietzsche and Philosophy*. Translated by Hugh Tomlinson. New York: Columbia University Press.

Eliade, Mircea. 1978. *The Forge and the Crucible*. Translated by Stephen Corrin. New York: Harper Torchbooks.

———. 1999. *Cosmos and History: The Myth of the Eternal Return*. Translated by Willard R. Trask. Princeton: Princeton University Press.

Ellenberger, Henri F. 1970. *The Discovery of the Unconscious.* New York: Basic.

Foucault, Michel. 1965. *Madness and Civilization: A History of Insanity in the Age of Reason.* Translated by Richard Howard. New York: Random House.

———. 1973. *The Birth of the Clinic: An Archaeology of Medical Perception.* Translated by A. M. Sheridan Smith. New York: Pantheon.

———. 1978. *The History of Sexuality.* Translated by Robert Hurley. New York: Pantheon.

———. 1995. *Discipline and Punish.* Translated by Alan Sheridan. New York: Vintage.

Franz, Marie-Louise, ed. 1966. *Aurora Consurgens.* Translated by R. F. C. Hull and A. S. B. Glover. New York: Pantheon.

Freud, Sigmund. 1955a. *Beyond the Pleasure Principle.* Pp. 1–64 in *The Standard Edition of the Complete Psychological Writings of Sigmund Freud,* vol. 18, trans. and ed. James Strachey. London: Hogarth.

———. 1955b. "Constructions in Analysis." Pp. 255–269 in *The Standard Edition of the Complete Psychological Writings of Sigmund Freud,* vol. 23. trans. and ed. James Strachey. London: Hogarth.

———. 1955c. "Observations on Transference-Love." In *The Standard Edition of the Complete Psychological Writings of Sigmund Freud,* vol. 12, trans. and ed. James Strachey. London: Hogarth.

———. 1955d. "Wild Psychoanalysis." In *The Standard Edition of the Complete Psychological Writings of Sigmund Freud,* vol. 11, trans. and ed. James Strachey. London: Hogarth.

———, with Joseph Breuer. 1974. *Studies on Hysteria.* Translated and edited by James Strachey. London: Penguin.

Golomb, Jacob, et al. 1999. *Nietzsche and Depth Psychology.* Albany: State University of New York Press.

Grinnell, Robert. 1973. *Alchemy in a Modern Woman.* Dallas: Spring.

Havelock, Eric A. 1994. *Preface to Plato.* Cambridge: Belknap Press.

Hawkins, Anne Hunsaker. 1985. *Archetypes of Conversion: The Autobiographies of Augustine, Bunyan, and Merton.* London and Ontario: Associated University Presses.

Heidegger, Martin. 1977. "Who Is Nietzsche's Zarathustra?" In *The New Nietzsche,* ed. David Allison. New York: Harper and Row.

———. 1979–1982. *Nietzsche.* Translated by David Farrell Krell. New York: Harper and Row.

Heraclitus. 2001. *Fragments.* Translated by Brooks Haxton. New York: Viking.

Hillman, James. 1975. *Re-Visioning Psychology.* New York: Harper and Row.

———. 1979. *The Dream and the Underworld.* New York: Harper and Row.

———. 1983. *Archetypal Psychology: A Brief Account.* Dallas: Spring.

Hölscher, Ludger. 1986. *The Reality of the Mind: Augustine's Philosophical Arguments for the Soul as a Spiritual Substance.* New York: Routledge and Kegan Paul.

Homer. 1961. *Iliad.* Translated by Richmond Lattimore. Chicago: University of Chicago Press.

———. 1965. *Odyssey.* Translated by Richmond Lattimore. New York: Harper and Row.

Jung, Carl G. 1953–. *Collected Works.* Translated by R. F. C. Hull. Edited by H. Read, M. Fordham, G. Adler, and W. McGuire. Princeton: Princeton University Press; London: Routledge and Kegan Paul.

Klein, Richard. 1993. *Cigarettes Are Sublime.* Durham and London: Duke University Press.

Klossowski, Pierre. 1997. *Nietzsche and the Vicious Circle.* Translated by Daniel W. Smith. Chicago: University of Chicago Press.

Löwith, Karl. 1997. *Nietzsche's Philosophy of the Eternal Recurrence of the Same.* Translated by J. Harvey Lomax. Berkeley: University of California Press.

Nietzsche, Friedrich. 1954. "Thus Spoke Zarathustra." Pp. 103–439 in *The Portable Nietzsche,* trans. and ed. Walter Kaufmann. New York: Penguin.

——. 1966a. *Beyond Good and Evil.* Pp. 181–435 in *Basic Writings of Nietzsche,* trans. and ed. Walter Kaufman. New York: Random House.

——. 1966b. *The Birth of Tragedy.* Pp. 3–144 in *Basic Writings of Nietzsche,* trans. and ed. Walter Kaufman. New York: Random House.

——. 1966c. *Ecce Homo.* Pp. 657–800 in *Basic Writings of Nietzsche,* trans. and ed. Walter Kaufman. New York: Random House.

——. 1966d. *The Genealogy of Morals.* Pp. 439–599 in *Basic Writings of Nietzsche,* trans. and ed. Walter Kaufman. New York: Random House.

——. 1968. *The Will to Power.* Translated and edited by Walter Kaufmann. New York: Random House.

——. 1974. *The Gay Science.* Translated by Walter Kaufmann. New York: Random House.

——. 1982. *Daybreak.* Translated by R. J. Hollingdale. Cambridge: Cambridge University Press.

Ortega y Gasset, José. 1961. *Meditations on Quixote.* Translated by Evelyn Rug and Diego Martin. New York: Norton.

Otto, Walter. 1965. *Dionysus: Myth and Cult.* Translated by Robert B. Palmer. Bloomington and Indianapolis: Indiana University Press.

Plato. 1978. *The Collected Dialogues.* Edited by Edith Hamilton and Huntington Cairns. Princeton: Princeton University Press.

Plotinus. 1964. *The Essential Plotinus: Representative Treatises from the Enneads.* Translated by Elmer O'Brien. S. J. Indianapolis: Hackett.

——. 1966–1988. *Enneads.* Translated by A. H. Armstrong. Cambridge: Harvard University Press.

Rank, Otto. 1979. *The Double.* Translated by Harry Tucker. New York: New American Library.

Regardie, L. 1970. *The Philosopher's Stone.* St. Paul, Minn.: Llewellyn.

Ricoeur, Paul. 1970. *Freud and Philosophy: An Essay on Interpretation.* Translated by Denis Savage. New Haven: Yale University Press.

——. 1984–1988. *Time and Narrative.* Translated by Kathleen Blamey and David Pellauer. Chicago: University of Chicago Press.

Silberer, Herbert. 1971. *Hidden Symbolism of Alchemy and the Occult Arts*. Translated by Smith Ely Jelliffe. New York: Dover.

Simmel, George. 1907. *Schopenhauer und Nietzsche*. Leipzig: Duncker und Humbolt.

Smith, Wilfred Cantwell. 1985. *Belief and History*. Charlottesville: University Press of Virginia.

———. 1998. *Faith and Belief: The Difference between Them*. Oxford, England: Oneworld.

Snell, Bruno. 1982. *The Discovery of the Mind in Greek Philosophy and Literature*. Translated by T. G. Rosenmeyer. New York: Dover.

Soll, Ivan. 1973. "Reflections on Recurrence." In *Nietzsche: A Collection of Critical Essays*, ed. Robert Solomon. Garden City, N.Y.: Anchor.

Sophocles. 1970. *Oedipus the King*. Translated by Thomas Gould. Englewood Cliffs: Prentice Hall.

Stambaugh, Joan. 1972. *Nietzsche's Thought of Eternal Return*. Baltimore: Johns Hopkins University Press.

Taylor, F. 1974. *The Alchemists*. New York: Arno.

Waite, A. E. 1970. *Alchemists through the Ages*. New York: Rudolf Steiner.

Wilde, Oscar. 1999. "The Decay of Lying." Pp. 1071–1092 in *Collins Complete Works of Oscar Wilde*. New York: HarperCollins.

INDEX